URBANDEVELOPMENT
IN
RENAISSANCE**ITALY**

URBAN DEVELOPMENT IN RENAISSANCE ITALY

Paul N Balchin

John Wiley & Sons, Ltd

Published in Great Britain in 2008 by John Wiley & Sons Ltd

Copyright © 2008   John Wiley & Sons Ltd, The Atrium, Southern Gate, Chichester,
West Sussex PO19 8SQ, England

Telephone   +44(0) 1243 779777

Email (for orders and customer service enquiries): cs-books@wiley.co.uk
Visit our Home Page on www.wiley.com

Other Wiley Editorial Offices

John Wiley & Sons Inc., 111 River Street, Hoboken, NJ 07030, USA

Jossey-Bass, 989 Market Street, San Francisco, CA 94103-1741, USA

Wiley-VCH Verlag GmbH, Boschstr. 12, D-69469 Weinheim, Germany

John Wiley & Sons Australia Ltd, 42 McDougall Street, Milton, Queensland 4064, Australia

John Wiley & Sons (Asia) Pte Ltd, 2 Clementi Loop #02-01, Jin Xing Distripark,
Singapore 129809

John Wiley & Sons Canada Ltd, 5353 Dundas Street West, Suite 400, Etobicoke,
Ontario M9B 6H8

Wiley also publishes its books in a variety of electronic formats. Some content that appears in print
may not be available in electronic books.

Executive Commissioning Editor: Helen Castle
Project Editor: Miriam Swift
Publishing Assistant: Calver Lezama

ISBN 978-0-470-03154-4 (hb)
ISBN 978-0-470-03155-1 (pb)

Cover design © Liz Sephton

Typeset in 10/13pt Sabon by Integra Software Services Pvt. Ltd, Pondicherry, India
Printed and bound by TJ International Ltd, Padstow, UK

To Julius, Tabatha and Arabella

CONTENTS

LIST OF FIGURES

LIST OF TABLES

PREFACE

Architecture may be described as history preserved in stone, and arguably expresses the political and economic attributes of bygone ages better than any other form of art. In Europe, nowhere is this more true than in Italy, particularly in respect of the history of the later Middle Ages (1250–1400) and the beginnings of the Early Modern Period (1400–1650), the period of its cultural renaissance. There has been a large number of books written on the architectural history of the Italian Renaissance, and on the political and economic history of the relevant centuries. However, although Mary Hollingsworth has written extensively about political patronage and property development in the 15th and 16th centuries (1994 and 1996) and Richard Goldthwaite has examined the relationship between economic factors and construction (1982 and 1996), particularly in Florence, very few books (if any) deal with the impact of both political context and economic growth on the development of Italian towns and cities over the full extent of the Renaissance in the Italian peninsula.

In consecutive chapters, therefore, this book sets out to explore the development of government in Renaissance Italy and how this affected the evolution of the built environment, and examines the relationship between economic development and the physical structure of Italian towns and cities. The author places patronage centre-stage, demonstrating how, in the public sector, the construction of both secular and ecclesiastical buildings was funded by republican, signorial and princely regimes at different times and in different urban areas throughout the Renaissance. In respect of the private sector, the book reveals how merchants, the *signori* and princes – both temporal and spiritual – individually funded the construction of churches, chapels, convents and family *palazzi*, while the mendicant orders channelled private donations into the construction of ecclesiastical buildings. Although public development was essentially the outcome of political aims and objectives and private building projects were determined largely by economic considerations, it must be recognised that the former was dependent upon the availability of economic resources (not least on tax revenue and 'invited' loans) while the latter normally only took place in periods of relative political stability.

In examining urban development in the Italian Renaissance, it is important first to explain how and why the term 'Renaissance' came into use, and over what period it applied. The word originates from the Italian *rinascita* – a term used by Giorgio Vasari in his *Lives of the Most Eminent Painters, Sculptors and Architects* (1550) to describe the revival of Classicism in the visual arts after a dormancy of over 1,000 years. However, it was not until the 19th century that the term took on a wider meaning: for example, in his *Civilization of the Renaissance in Italy* (1860) Jacob Burckhardt not only describes social and cultural development in Italy over the extent of the 15th and 16th centuries but argues that it was both markedly different from that which came before and from that which followed, and also substantially unlike human development in other countries in the same period of history.

It has become increasingly clear, however, that the Renaissance did not start or finish at specific moments in time; rather, it can be traced back to the 14th century or earlier and continued until the 17th century or beyond. Thus, although it might be argued that the Italian Renaissance *vis-à-vis* the revival of the classical style of architecture was confined to the years between 1420 and the Sack of Rome in 1527, the period popularly accepted more generally runs from around the early 14th century to the mid-16th century. Vasari even went so far as to state that there were three eras of creativity: the first beginning *c* 1300 with Giotto; the second occurring *c* 1410–20 with the architect Brunelleschi and the sculptor Donatello; and the third extending from the 1520s to the mid-16th century, the age of Michelangelo. Recently, however, it has been claimed that the Renaissance extends over an even longer period. In *The Renaissance in Europe* Margaret L King suggests that it began in 1300 and ended in 1700, although this demarcation applies to Europe as a whole rather than to Italy alone. In this book, the author similarly adopts a long period to define the Renaissance years in Italy, although here the boundaries are pushed back to *c* 1200 and forward to *c* 1680.

In discussing urban development in the 21st century, interest normally focuses on the many different land uses that constitute a city or town. High-, middle- and low-income housing inevitably receive some attention; industry and commerce are frequently considered; urban transportation is sometimes the subject of heated debate, with the provision of other infrastructural services often being a matter of some concern; and the development of recreational land is not immune from controversy. However, in examining the development of the cities and towns of Renaissance Italy, this book emphasises the evolution of grandiose *palazzi* and magnificent ecclesiastical buildings, and also refers to city walls, other defensive structures and the introduction of town planning schemes. Excluded from its scope is any consideration of housing for the poor and 'not so poor', partly because the book concentrates on the better designed, better constructed and higher-value buildings that still adorn the built environment of so many Italian cities rather than on the poor-quality housing and squalor of Renaissance urban areas long since extinct, and partly because the slums of Italy were broadly replicated across Europe (even as late as Dickensian times), whereas the fine Renaissance buildings and imaginative planning schemes of Florence, Venice, Rome and a host of other Italian cities were innovative – and unique. In examining urban development, further omissions are unavoidable, given the constraints of space. Many important towns and cities throughout Italy have not been considered (Turin, for example, only blossomed architecturally in the 18th century), descriptions of many interesting buildings even in the selected urban areas have had to be omitted and, since the book focuses on the urban arena, the development of villas in the countryside has been largely ignored. However, despite these necessary omissions, the author hopes that the book will shed some light not only on the causes of urban development in Renaissance Italy but also on the attributes of some of the more important secular and ecclesiastical buildings constructed in Italian towns and cities from the later Middle Ages to the second half of the 17th century.

In the preparation of this book, I owe a special debt of gratitude to Clive Davies for his tireless and good-humoured logistical support, Shean McConnell, and Chris and Valerie Wilcher for ensuring that my research – involving what seemed to be endless visits to Italy – was undertaken from a sound basis and in an efficient, reflective and pleasurable manner. I owe a debt of gratitude to the many academics across the disciplines who have inspired and assisted me in the preparation of this book. I am especially indebted to Helen Castle, Editor, Architectural Design, at John Wiley & Sons, for her encouragement during the earlier stages in the book's preparation and for her invaluable advice throughout its production; and so, too, I am grateful for the very considerable and patient help given me by Calver Lezama (Editorial Assistant on the Architectural List at John Wiley) and Amie Tibble and Miriam Swift (also at Wiley, as Executive

Project Editors). I would also very much like to thank Lucy Isenberg, freelance copy-editor, for the enormous and diligent efforts she made to ensure that the final typescript was in good order. My thanks too to Mario Bettella of Artmedia for achieving virtual miracles in processing the photographs. Last, I am considerably indebted to my wife Alicia for the incredible patience she has shown me throughout the preparation of this book.

Paul N Balchin
London

CHAPTER 1

INTRODUCTION

At the beginning of the later Middle Ages, Italy contained more large cities than any other country in Europe. This might not seem particularly remarkable since an increasing proportion of the peninsula's total population had begun to live in urban settlements as early as 1000 BC. As in the valleys of the Euphrates, Nile, Indus and Yangste millennia before, levels of agricultural production in Italy had started to yield an annual food surplus,[1] releasing part of the workforce to make a variety of goods ranging from textiles and pottery to metalware, bricks and wooden artefacts, and allowing some to engage in trade – activities that tend to cluster together in terms of location so as to benefit from economies of scale, including agglomeration economies. Viewed thus, urbanisation was the outcome of the spatial concentration of social surplus production.[2] It was a process that, throughout much of the 1st millennium BC, saw urban settlements of between 5,000 and 10,000 inhabitants founded by the Etruscans in northern and central Italy, while Italic tribes such as the Latini and Sabini created settlements throughout the rest of the peninsula, except in its heel and in Sicily where Greek colonisers established trading ports. By the late 4th century BC, the population of Italic Rome had probably reached 10,000 and was broadly similar in size to that of the largest of the Greek ports, Tarentum (present-day Taranto).

Urbanisation in Italy, to a large extent, was reflected in the size of Rome. Dependent on its imperial economy, the population of the city reached a peak of between 1 and 2 million around AD 100, but thereafter for a thousand years it declined as the result of invasion by hostile peoples and the lack of means to sustain its economy. By the time of Constantine (AD 306–37), numbers had dwindled to about 800,000; with the relocation of the imperial capital to Constantinople the population of Rome plummeted to 90,000 during the pontificate of Gregory the Great (c 600) and fell yet further, to only 35,000 in around AD 1100.[3] Elsewhere in the peninsula, urban populations were much smaller during most of the early Middle Ages than at the time of the empire, and many settlements simply disappeared.

A question must therefore be asked: how was it that the dormant urban areas of Italy came again to experience sufficient growth to enable the country to accommodate the greatest number of cities in Western Europe, and what were the factors that led to the increase in the degree of urbanisation in the peninsula? Like the question, the answer is in two parts. First, despite Italy being mainly mountainous – the Alps provide its northern border and the Apennines its north–south axis – the geomorphology of much of the peninsula is fundamentally favourable to human settlement (fig 1.1) and, once the political and economic instability of the Dark Ages receded towards the end of the 1st millennium, physical geography again exerted a positive influence over urban growth. In the majority of cases, cities were established on or near the coast, in river valleys,

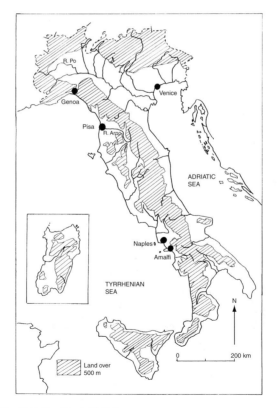

Figure 1.1   The physical structure of Italy

or in close proximity to mountain passes. With a lengthy coastline of some 3,500 kilometres protruding into the Mediterranean, population growth was particularly pronounced in the ports of Venice, Genoa, Pisa, Naples and Amalfi which, in establishing strong trading links with Byzantium and the Arab world, became major centres of population and European economic development as early as the 10th century. The three great riverine systems of the Po, Arno and Tiber were similarly conducive to urban growth, as were locations close to the 17 or more passes that traversed the Alps and the Apennines. Geomorphology, however, was not alone responsible for determining the location and growth of

Photo 1.1 Basilica of S Marco, Venice, *c* 830 (rebuilt 11th century). Reflecting Venetian trading importance, Europes most flamboyant cathedral combines Byzantine and western styles. With its Greek cross plan, large central dome and smaller domes over the aisles and transepts, the edifice is the focal point of the Piazza S Marco.

cities. Along the northern fringe of the Apennines a string of cities stretched along the important man-made route of the Roman Via Emilia, and it is along this route that urban growth was particularly spectacular in the central Middle Ages.

Second, there was an increased rate of migration from rural areas to the budding towns and older urban agglomerations, a result both of greater agricultural productivity throughout the peninsula and of greater employment opportunities in the cities, a process that, according to Lauro Martines, 'was well under way by the beginning of the eleventh century and would continue, on a massive scale, down to nearly 1300. The immigrants were the landless and the poor who worked with their hands, but also, and more visibly, the propertied: vassals and subvassals, knights, small landowners, random or itinerant country merchants.'[4] Urbanisation was particularly apparent in northern Italy in the 11th and 12th centuries. Minor settlements such as Prato and Macerata suddenly burgeoned into thriving towns; ancient cities such as Milan, Pavia, Cremona and Mantua, to quote Martines, 'were borne up once again in a rising flood of people, property transactions, commerce and feverish activity in the building trades'.[5] By the end of the central Middle Ages in *c* 1250, relatively minor river ports such as Florence together with the tiny cities of the northern plain – Piacenza, Cremona, Verona and Padua – also 'exhibited spectacular dynamism and . . . eagerly received foreign merchants or as eagerly dispatched their own'.[6]

Urban Development: the Political Dimension

Italian cities experienced substantial political upheaval during the early and central Middle Ages. Over a period of 500 years following the fall of the Western Roman Empire in the 5th century, the Italian peninsula was invaded by a succession of peoples – Ostrogoths, Byzantines, Lombards and Franks. Within the towns that survived both these traumas, 'real power ended by being local power in the hands of local magnates, usually bishops, though it was soon enough claimed or grabbed by cities'.[7] By the 12th century, most of northern and central Italy including Rome and the Papal State had been incorporated into the German-ruled Holy Roman Empire, Rome was capital of a small Papal State, Venice remained independent, and Naples and the foot of the peninsula were under Byzantine control. Sicily was subject to Arab rule from the 820s and Norman sovereignty from the 1070s until it was absorbed by the Holy Roman Empire in 1194.

However, in much of northern and central Italy in the 11th and early 12th centuries the Franconian rulers of the Holy Roman Empire were 'weak, absentee, or too pre-occupied with other concerns to devote time and energy to local issues',[8] and aided and abetted by the papacy in its struggle against the empire, ever more cities in northern and central Italy sought and gained independence from feudal suzerainty, though they remained under the overarching authority of the empire. Often in the wake of civic revolt in, for example, Pavia (1024), Cremona (1030–1), Parma (1037) and Milan (1036–7, 1040 and 1042–3), self-governing communes were established between the 1080s and 1138, as set out below:

Pisa	1080s	Piacenza	1090	Pistoia	1105
Lucca	1080s	Asti	1095	Verona	1107
Milan	1081	Cremona	1098	Bologna	1123
Parma	1081	Arezzo	1099	Siena	1125
Rome	1083	Genoa	1099	Florence	1138
Pavia	1084	Como	1105		

(Sources: Martines, *Power and Imagination*, p 18; Waley, *The Italian City-Republic*, p 199.)

Once established, the communes set up regular assemblies of citizens (*arenghi*) to debate matters of common concern and to elect consuls who would take responsibility for internal law and order, external affairs and strengthening the city's political authority over its surrounding territory – the *contado*.[9] Communes were also responsible for funding major building projects such as the construction of cathedrals, town halls and law courts. However, independence, even within the empire, soon became illusory. Following the demise of the Franconian emperors in 1137, their Hohenstaufen successors attempted to reassert direct control over many of the cities of northern and central Italy. To this end, Frederick I (Barbarossa) presided over the creation of *podestà* to assume responsibility for the administration of justice, finance and defence and to remove it from the hands of the consular authorities, for it was becoming clear that under their rule the cities were growing increasingly ungovernable due to civil strife and intra-communal power struggles among the ruling elites. To preserve neutrality, it became common practice to select the *podestà* from a city other than the one which required his services and, to prevent the holder of the office becoming too powerful, he was appointed for no longer than six months or a year.

At a time when the papacy was striving to gain temporal influence throughout the peninsula, greater imperial involvement in the affairs of the north, particularly in curbing consular power and responsibility, was ultimately a recipe for military conflict, notwithstanding any benefits that accrued. Aided and abetted by the papacy, in 1167–75 as many as 28 northern cities formed the Lombard

League and later defeated Frederick Barbarossa at the battle of Legnano in 1176. Although at the Peace of Constance (1183) Frederick I subsequently conferred constitutional autonomy on all communes, a further attempt to re-establish full imperial suzerainty was successful when Frederick II defeated a resurrected League at Cortenuova in 1237; but the price was continuing political instability for at least a further century. As a defence against imperial power, many Italian cities allied themselves with the papacy, while others, even more wary of papal intentions, supported the empire. During the early 13th century, the Guelph cities of Milan, Bologna, Florence, Lucca, Montepulciano and Orvieto gave their allegiance to the papacy, while the Ghibelline cities of Pisa, Pistoia, Arezzo and Siena demonstrated strong pro-imperialist sympathies. (Guelfs and Ghibellines are Italian political terms based respectively on the family name of the dukes of Bavaria 'Welf' and a castle of the Hohenstaufen dukes 'Waiblingen'. In the Italian-ised version, the terms entered common usage at the time of the Hohenstaufen Emperor Frederick's conflict with the papacy, 1235–50.) Within and between cities, tensions were often exacerbated by a similar but more complex division of loyalty, a recipe for internal insecurity in the centuries ahead.

It was during this period of papal–imperial conflict, and particularly in the second half of the 12th century, that many cities such as Pisa (1162), Cremona (1169–87), Milan (1170s), Brescia (1174–86), Bologna (1176–7), Bergamo (1190), Como (1190s) and Reggio (1199) built walls around their suburbs in an attempt to safeguard their autonomy.[10] Although such defences were constructed principally to repel invaders, over time they would come to serve an altogether different purpose. In a period when the urban population of Italy was increasing at a phenomenal rate (by over 50 per cent between 1150 and 1300), city walls provided the physical boundaries within which urban growth could occur and, in demarcating a finite urban space in which construction could take place, often encouraged programmes of planned development to combat squalor and ensure the most efficient use of land.

Urban Development: the Economic Dimension

Although geomorphology largely determines the location of towns and cities, the physical configuration of land *per se* does not provide a reliable indication of the extent to which, in terms of economic development, urban areas will expand, stay the same, or contract, nor does it suggest whether or not economic growth in one town or city will be at the expense of growth elsewhere. Urban growth in

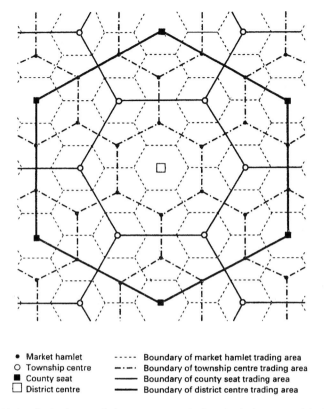

● Market hamlet ----- Boundary of market hamlet trading area
○ Township centre —·—· Boundary of township centre trading area
■ County seat ——— Boundary of county seat trading area
□ District centre ━━━ Boundary of district centre trading area

Figure 1.2 Christaller's theory of the arrangement of central places, used to illustrate the relationship between different-sized urban settlements and their market areas
Source: W Christaller, 1933.

economic terms is largely demand-led. A city is more likely to grow if the demand for its goods and services increases than if autonomously it increases the supply of products. The economic growth of cities in any country or region can be examined in relation to a number of interrelated theories such as Christaller's central place theory (fig 1.2), the urban base and cumulative causation explanations of urban growth, and the Keynesian macroeconomic income-generation approach.

Although it might seem somewhat bizarre to compare the spatial pattern and magnitude of urban growth in southern Germany with those of parts of northern and central Italy (particularly since many of the cities of Italy were developed by Rome as military settlements), there are a number of fundamental similarities that are worthy of consideration. In examining the distribution of urban settlements in the former region in the 1930s, Walter Christaller hypothesised that the distribution of localised services (retailing, wholesaling, banking and public services) accounts for the spacing, size and functional pattern of urban centres.[11] Assuming that urban settlements locate on a more or less even plain, service centres would be distributed regularly within a systematic pattern. Market areas or spheres of influence would take the form of a hexagonal mesh which would avoid either certain areas not being served, or other areas being served by overlapping hinterlands – consequences of a pattern of circular market areas.

The main function of each town would be to supply goods and services to the surrounding countryside – town and country being economically interdependent, but with larger towns also performing the role of centres of government. A hierarchy of centres would thus evolve. Towns with the lowest level of specialisation would be evenly distributed and surrounded by their hexagonally shaped market areas. For each rank of settlement, there would be a larger settlement with more specialised functions located at an equal distance from other centres with the same degree of specialisation. Such cities would have larger hexagonal hinterlands for their own specialised services. Even larger and more specialised settlements would have more extensive market areas (and areas of political control) and be situated broadly equidistant from one another.

Christaller believed that the lowest-ranked centres were likely to be located 7 kilometres from each other, while the highest ranked would be 186 kilometres apart; 'urban' populations would range in size from 800 to 300,000; market areas would contain between 45,000 and 32,000 square kilometres, and market area populations would range from 2,700 to 2,025,000. Since the number of settlements of successively lower rank follows a geometric progression $(1, 3, 9, 27 . . .)$, the pattern is referred to as a $k = 3$ hierarchy. Towns within the hierarchy would expand as a result of increased production of goods and services to satisfy an increase in demand from a growing population within their market areas, but generally they would remain within their rank and the rule of three would persist.

Christaller recognised that the hierarchy would be modified by long-distance trade, by transport routes and by administrative functions. Towns influenced by these factors would have larger populations than their local market would imply, and would be part of a $k = 4$ or even $k = 7$ hierarchy. Settlement would generally tend to be clustered along main routes such as river valleys and be larger at road junctions and river confluences, and as such their market areas were unlikely to be hexagonal. Manufacturing would also have an agglomerating influence, increasing population out of proportion to the size of the immediate market area. Taking these factors into account, and also acknowledging that urban population in Italy during the later Middle Ages and Early Modern Period was considerably less than that in southern Germany in the early 20th century, one can hypothesise

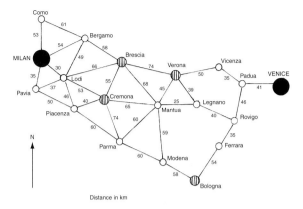

Figure 1.3 Central places on the North Italian Plain

that in general terms central place theory could explain the distribution of urban settlements particularly in the middle of the North Italian Plain (fig 1.3). Taking population data for around 1300,[12] Venice and Milan (both with around 100,000 inhabitants and about 310 kilometres apart) would qualify as regional capital cities, and settlements such as Bologna, Brescia, Cremona and Verona (each with more than 40,000 inhabitants and up to 85 kilometres from their nearest medium-size neighbour) would rank as second-tier cities, while settlements with yet smaller populations such as Pavia, Lodi, Piacenza, Bergamo, Brescia, Parma, Modena and Bologna would fall into a lower rank and be closer in proximity to each other. It is interesting to note that at each level of the hierarchy, the *contado* – the dependent area encircling or adjacent to a main city or town – very largely coincides with the market area concept of Christaller. On the eastern edge of the North Italian Plain, a relatively even distribution of settlements is less apparent, partly because urban development took place in a different political context than in the west (the region had not attracted the same degree of Roman occupation and it was relatively devoid of communal development in the central and later Middle Ages), and partly because the topography was less favourable to settlement (much of the region was marshland).

Examination of the urban base theory provides a further explanation for the variable growth of cities within a given geographical area. As devised by RW Pfouts,[13] the theory involves a consideration of the demand for the city's surplus output of goods and services from anywhere outside the settlement's boundaries. The more a city specialises, the more it undermines its self-sufficiency. Urban growth will thus depend upon the urban area's ability to export products (such as manufactured goods and banking services) to pay for its imported goods (for example, food and raw materials). The production of goods and services for export is known as a 'basic' activity and the output of products for distribution solely to the urban area itself is referred to as a 'non-basic' activity (for example, municipal services, building activity, local retailing). According to the theory, the growth of an urban area depends upon the ratio of basic to non-basic activities (as measured by the proportion of the working population involved in the production of each): the higher the ratio, the greater the rate of growth. Non-basic industries will be dependent upon the basic sector, the working population involved with the former providing much of the demand for the products of the latter. On the assumption that underlying economic, social and technological factors remain broadly constant, and that there is an absence of war, famine and plague, the development of basic employment in the town or city will stimulate a marked growth of non-basic employment to meet the higher local demand for goods and services. Thus any temporary instability resulting from an initial increase in basic employment (for example, the introduction of the silk textile industry in Florence in the 15th century) will be eliminated through an upward adjustment in non-basic employment (such as in local retailing). Dependent populations will similarly increase. The extent of the change in both the employed population and the total population will be a multiple of the initial increase in basic employment. If, for example, the basic to non-basic ratio is 1:3, then 2,000 more jobs in textile manufacture for export might increase total employment by 6,000 – or the dependent population from say 4,000 to 12,000.

The urban base theory also suggests that if an urban area loses some basic employment, less non-basic employment will be required and the settlement's population will decline at a multiple of the initial withdrawal of basic employment. Clearly, a decrease in total employment and population could equally be triggered by war, famine and disease.

The theory, however, has its weaknesses. For example, non-basic activity (rather than basic activity) could be the driving force in urban growth. From the later Middle Ages onwards, this might increasingly have been the case in cities accommodating the administrative apparatus of urban government, and in Rome *vis-à-vis* management of the Papal State.

However, would the growth of individual cities in medieval and Early Modern Italy (due to an initial increase in basic activity) have been at the expense of other settlements in the peninsula, and would the decline of particular cities (due to their loss of basic employment) have been the outcome of urban growth elsewhere? An answer is provided by Hoselitz, who in the 1950s argued that urban growth could be 'parasitic' as well as 'generative'.[14] He suggests that in the developed countries of the 20th century, urban growth was probably generative in that it stimulated economic growth and produced a 'surplus' in the wider urban region, whereas in developing countries – and by implication in Europe before modern times – growth was parasitic (ie, surpluses were extracted from surrounding regions and their settlements). The dependency theory, introduced by Myrdal in 1957, reinforced this approach.[15] Under laissez faire, according to this theory, cities grow parasitically by exploiting and holding back their surrounding regions. Myrdal suggests that economic growth follows the principle of 'cumulative causation', whereby once established in a city economic development promotes further local development – the 'spread effect', but this is only at the expense of surrounding areas or other areas elsewhere – the 'backwash effect'. The same was true of service activity, including administration. The implication is that, in relative and possibly in absolute terms, rich cities and regions get richer and richer, and poor areas, poorer and poorer. This might possibly explain why Florence, Venice, Milan, Genoa, Rome and Naples – for much of the time operating as independent entities – have remained the dominant economic powers in their regions and in the peninsula from the later Middle Ages to the present.

However, there is some evidence to suggest that there is an alternative explanation for the pattern of urban growth that developed in the later Middle Ages and beyond. In the 1960s, Boudeville posited that as a consequence of laissez-faire conditions growth trickles spontaneously down from larger to smaller cities.[16] Larger cities would thus perform a generative role in economic development across their regions: for example, during the 16th century Venice generated activity across its *terraferma* while Florence and Milan helped to stimulate urban growth elsewhere in their respective Tuscan and Lombard market areas.

Urban growth, however, can also be explained in macroeconomic terms by the Keynesian model of economic growth, a model which involves an assessment of the effect upon total income of the circular flow of money between producers and consumers, investment and savings, export earnings and import expenditure, and public spending and taxation (fig 1.4). This approach, developed with regard to a national economy by John Maynard Keynes in the early 20th century,[17] identifies money flows as export earnings, the earnings of externally employed factors, and government expenditure; money inflows are identified as import expenditure, payment for externally owned factors (used by producers in the urban area) and government taxes. Investment and savings may or may not be retained for use within the city, but net investment is an injection into the money flow, while net savings represents withdrawal.

Overall or aggregate demand for goods and services in an urban area rises if there is any initial increase in the circular flow of money between

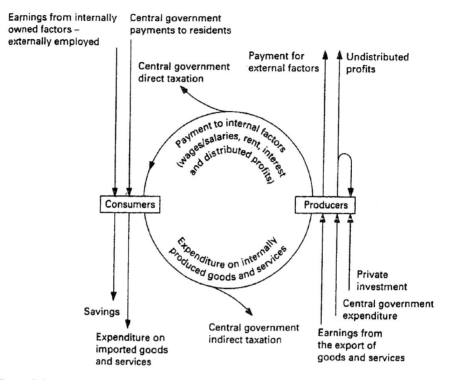

Figure 1.4   Money flows circulating around, injected into and withdrawn from an urban area

producers and consumers, and – if in aggregate – money injections (ie, invest-ment + government expenditure + export earnings) exceed money withdrawals (ie, savings + taxation + import expenditure). If the opposite trends occur, aggregate demand in the urban area declines. Normally, with an increase in aggregate demand, there is a corresponding increase in the demand for build-ings for both productive and non-productive purposes and for the general enhancement of the built environment; when aggregate demand decreases, the reverse is the case. Therefore, any initial increase (or decrease) in aggregate demand has a disproportionate effect on the eventual income of the town or city. The greater the marginal propensity to consume (MPC) or the smaller the marginal propensity to save (MPS), the larger the eventual increase in aggregate demand. The extent of this increase – the multiplier (K) – is measured accordingly:

$$K = \frac{1}{1 - MPC} \quad \text{or} \quad K = \frac{1}{MPS}$$

Since the Keynesian model suggests that there is a causal relationship between net injections into urban area monetary flow and the rate of urban economic growth, one may conclude – all things being equal – that not only did the export and re-export of manufactured goods and the provision of financial services contribute to the wealth of many of the Italian city-states during the central Middle Ages, but that given balance of payments surpluses the multiplier ensured that aggregate demand within these states increased at a disproportionately high rate, so heralding an economic and building boom in the 13th and early 14th centuries.

Urban Development: the Built Environment

Following the demise of the Western Roman Empire in the 5th century and its aftermath, urban development in Italy went into reverse. Although a plethora of churches was built in Italy between the 4th and 6th centuries, from Constantine's basilicas of S Giovanni in Laterano (*c* 313–20) and Old St Peter's (320) in Rome to the centrally planned church of S Vitale (547) in Ravenna, thereafter in the wake of successive barbarian invasions from the north architecture in Italy's crumbling, overgrown, squalid and depopulated cities went into decline for almost 500 years, except for the emergence of Byzantine architecture which came to maturity in the 9th century as exemplified by Venice's basilica of S Marco (*c* 830).

By the late 11th and early 12th centuries Romanesque architecture with its origins in France and Germany began to stamp its mark on the built environment throughout the length and breadth of Italy, but with a difference. In contrast to the development of the style elsewhere in western Europe, and alluding to its Early Christian and Byzantine origins, church architecture in Italy continued to make use of the basilica plan, cupolas and marble facing, while for the first time arches were employed for ornamental purposes rather than for entirely structural ones, and large detached campaniles and baptisteries became commonplace. Many Romanesque churches in Italy (as elsewhere) were also markedly different in scale from those that preceded them. To quote Bill Riseborough, 'new buildings were appearing for the first time in eight or more centuries whose size and height ... rivalled those of ancient Rome',[18] surely an indication of the Renaissance that was to come.

Yet, despite these common features, there are marked regional variations in style. In many cities of the Lombard Plain, Romanesque cathedrals and churches

Photo 1.2   Maestro Niccolò and others, church of S Zeno, Verona, begun 1120. One of the most distinctive Romanesque churches in Italy, with its large rose window and magnificent portal.

are broadly similar to those of northern Europe, except that in Lombardy they often have tall and stately campanile towers and large octagonal baptisteries not integrated with the main body of the building. Facades are often adorned by a projecting vaulted porch on a base of sculpted lions and a centrally placed wheel-window that allows daylight to penetrate the nave. There is relatively little additional external decoration aside from the open dwarf galleries that sometimes embellish an otherwise plain facade or apse. Examples of this form of architecture are found in the cathedrals of Modena (1099), Cremona (1107) and Parma (1117), the church of S Zeno Maggiore and cathedral of Verona (1120 and 1138), and the cathedrals of Piacenza (1120) and Ferrara (1135). In Milan, however, S Ambrogio (1080) does not quite fit this pattern. As an ancient building, founded by St Ambrose in the 4th century, it retains many Early Christian features such as a spacious entrance atrium and eastern apse and, together with its solemn two-storey gabled brick facade pierced by round-headed arches, presents an image quite unlike any other Lombard building of the period.

In Pisa, a very distinctive variant of Romanesque architecture emerged in the 11th and 12th centuries. Concentrated in the Piazza del Duomo, away from the densely built-up core of the city, the cathedral (1063) with its prominent transept, the round baptistery (1153) and the campanile (1173) display a unique sense of unity. All have marble facing, are adorned by open-arcaded galleries that rise all the way to the facade gable and around the building, and all are capped by terracotta roof tiles. The style was soon replicated, with modification, in Lucca both in the case of the cathedral of S Martino (1070) and in the church of S Michele in Foro (11th–12th centuries).

Romanesque architecture differs yet again in Florence, the city's baptistery and the church of S Miniato exhibiting an elegance of form that owes more to classical Roman models than to northern Renaissance church architecture, and the style is often referred to as 'Proto-Renaissance'.

In the south of the peninsula, in Apulia and Campania, Romanesque architecture is derived in part from Normandy following the conquest of these provinces

Photo 1.3 Niccolò and others, *duomo*, Ferrara, begun 1135. Exhibiting a mixture of Romanesque and Gothic Lombard styles, the building is noted for its monumental triple facade that focuses on a carved central portal.

Photo 1.4   Church of S Ambrogio, Milan, founded in the 4th century and reconstructed *c* 1150. The church, possibly the most interesting in Milan, is the progenitor of many of Lombardy's Romanesque basilicas.

by Norman crusaders in the 11th century. The most notable example of Apulian churches of this type is S Nicola (1039) at Bari, but others of similar design were begun at Bitonto, Barletta and Ruvo by the end of the 12th century. In Campania, Salerno cathedral (1076–85) is the most prominent building of Romanesque design. The Normans, in extending their conquests to Sicily (1061–91), inherited the strong Byzantine and Islamic culture on the island that soon manifested itself in a form of architecture that blended motifs of the three traditions, most prominently in the cathedrals of Cefalù (1131), Monreale (1174) and Palermo (1185), and the church of La Martorana (1146) also in Palermo.

In the 12th century, the proliferation of distinctive Romanesque secular buildings is no less impressive than is the distribution of ecclesiastical buildings of the genre. Notable examples include civic buildings such as the Palazzo del Popolo in Orvieto (1157), the *broletto* in Brescia (1187–1200) and the Palazzo della Ragione in Bergamo (1199); privately funded edifices such as the Torre degli Asinelli and the Torre Garisenda in Bologna, 70 or more towers at San Gimignano and numerous similar structures in Florence of which the Torre della Pagliazza and Torre della Castagna are but two examples; and the only Romanesque royal palace in Italy – the Palazzo dei Normanni (or Palazzo Reale) in Palermo, although the building also embraces Islamic and Byzantine features.

Despite its ubiquity elsewhere in the peninsula, Romanesque ecclesiastical architecture was markedly underrepresented in Venice and on its islands. Here, Byzantine influences were dominant well into the central Middle Ages, as is exemplified not only by the massive basilica of St Mark's but also by the 11th-century church of S Fosca and cathedral of S Maria Assunta on Torcello. There was also an absence of Romanesque influence over the design of secular buildings in the serene republic, Byzantine architecture being much in evidence well beyond the 12th century.

By about 1200, the stage was set for a massive building boom throughout much of urban Italy. Politically, cities were more representative than hitherto and provided a relatively secure arena in which the burgeoning demand for both secular and ecclesiastical buildings could be met. By the 13th century, urban areas

Photo 1.5 Buscheto and others, baptistery, *duomo* and campanile, Pisa, 1063–1173. Inspired by Moorish designs of Andulusia, and a legacy of Pisa's Golden Age, this ensemble of Pisan Romanesque buildings with its black and white marble facades is one of the most dazzling sights in Italy.

Photo 1.6 Guido Bigarelli da Como and others, Cathedral of S Martino, Lucca, begun 1070. Built in the Pisan-Romanesque style, its asymmetrical facade does not detract from the overall grandeur of the building, its frontage distinguished by the repetition of loggias and tiny columns, and a magnificent atrium.

were experiencing both population and economic growth, while wealth increased dramatically with the expansion of trade, banking and industrial production. That Italy had a very long tradition of applying innovative architectural styles to a wide range of new buildings augured well for a continuing supply of buildings to meet future demand.

However, although the Romanesque style prevalent during the 13th century was superseded by the Gothic paradigm, it is indisputable that in Italy the Romanesque not only exerted a moderating influence on the manner in which fully fledged Gothic architecture was adopted, but also inspired the re-emergence of classical design in the Early Renaissance of the 15th century.

The Political and Economic Rationale of Property Development

Throughout history there is ample evidence to suggest that a proportion of prestigious property development is driven by altruism or religious devotion. It is

Photo 1.7   Church of S Miniato, Florence, begun 1018. Located on a steep hillside in the Oltrarno, the building – with its stunning marble facade – is the finest Romanesque church in Tuscany and one of Italy's most beautiful buildings.

also manifestly true that, as Deyan Sudjic argues, 'architecture is used by political leaders to seduce, impress and intimidate'.[19] In Italy, this was certainly the case in the days of imperial Rome and again during the Renaissance. In the intervening period – except under republican rule in Venice – feudalism tended to tie people to the land and urbanisation went into reverse but, with the breakdown of feudal control and the development of quasi-independent city-states across much of northern and central Italy during the 12th and 13th centuries, urbanisation gathered pace and '[a]lmost all political leaders [began] using architects for political purposes. It [was] a relationship that [occurred] in almost every kind of regime and [appealed] to egotists of every description.'[20] At best, and as Sir Christopher Wren posited late in the English Renaissance, 'Architecture has its political Use; public building being an ornament of a Country; it establishes a Nation, draws People and Commerce; [and] makes the People love their native Country'.[21] In modern parlance, this might suggest that civic architecture could be used as a means of reducing social exclusion. At worst, and as Sudjic argued, 'when the line between political calculation and psychopathology breaks down, architecture becomes not just a matter of practical politics, but a fantasy, even a sickness that [in various ways] consumes its victims'.[22]

Within the private sector, economic growth enabled 'architecture [to become] the principal means by which Italians staked their claims to grandeur and magnificence; it was certainly the chief luxury they spent their money on; and it was the one art form the upper classes were interested in reading about and showed a passionate intellectual interest in'.[23] Clearly, the propensity to indulge in conspicuous consumption was greater among the rich than among the poor, and normally greater during periods of economic prosperity than at times of economic recession.

Although the architects of the Italian Renaissance might be criticised for not directly serving the needs of the community by pandering to the requirements of the state or the demands of the wealthy elite, there was nobody else who could fund the development of the built environment. Thus, it could be argued that

Photo 1.8 Cattedrale, Palermo, 1183. Despite the addition of a 15th-century Catalan-Gothic porch and an 18th-century Baroque dome, the golden-coloured stone building is essentially Sicilian-Norman in its attributes, exemplified by its triple-apsed eastern end and matching towers.

Photo 1.9   Palazzo del Popolo, Orvieto, 1157. Built of volcanic rock, this impressive *palazzo* displays its relatively few Romanesque-Gothic attributes to full effect, its majestic balcony, elegant windows and fluted battlements adorning an otherwise plain exterior.

whereas the powerful and the rich shaped the buildings of the Italian Renaissance, afterwards the buildings shaped the whole community by giving it a sense of civic pride and local loyalty – attitudes not normally found in cities without a rich architectural heritage.

The Beginnings of Town Planning in Medieval Italy

For the first time in over 500 years, town planning was gradually being redeployed as a means of ensuring that the built environment developed in a technically rational, aesthetically pleasing and symbolic manner. One of the first and most spectacular examples of Romanesque planning is the Piazza del Duomo in Pisa (fig 1.5). Here, the baptistery, cathedral and campanile are clearly visible both individually and as a unified group since the composition is situated on the axis of an exceedingly spacious grassy site that is surrounded by low walls as if to emphasise the scale of development.[24] On entering the *piazza* through the Porta Nuova, the visitor notices that the three buildings are both simple and contrasting in geometric form and share the same architectural style. They are arranged in a line: first the baptistery, then the cathedral and lastly the campanile slightly off centre. In their turn they are intended to symbolise entry into the church community, the celebration of mass and communion and, finally, the ascent to heaven.

Such an example of town planning serves to illustrate that in the 11th and 12th centuries, given a greenfield site on the edge of town, buildings could not only be constructed in relation to each other while being different in design, but could conform to an overarching scheme. However, in the ensuing centuries and notwithstanding the further development of greenfield sites, the more substantial examples of town planning are to be found in the central areas of cities, often associated with redevelopment, renovation or conservation, and often executed to accommodate previous or current laws relating to public health, access and circulation.

Photo 1.10   Piazza della Cisterna, S Gimignano, 12th century. Still partly paved by medieval bricks and containing a well dating from 1267, this triangular square is overlooked by some of the town's many towers.

This Book

In this introductory chapter, some of the political and economic factors that influenced the growth of cities in the early and central Middle Ages have been examined as a prelude to an analysis, in Part 1, of the impact of political change and economic cycles on the built environment in the later Middle Ages. Part 2 then describes the emergence of the Early Renaissance in the cities of the 15th century, and Part 3 explores urban development in the 16th century, the period of the High Renaissance and Mannerism. Part 4 concludes by setting out the principal aspects of urban development in the first half of the 17th century, focusing on the emergence of the Baroque. Each part covers a specific period, ranging from around 150 years (in the case of Part 1) to about 50 years (in Part 4). By using discrete time periods of relatively short duration, relevant comparisons can be made between the different factors determining or influencing urban development, a task that would be difficult or meaningless if one attempted to analyse the *raison d'être* of urban growth over the whole period from about 1200 to 1650.

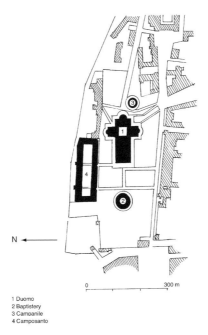

N ←

0   300 m

1 Duomo
2 Baptistery
3 Campanile
4 Camposanto

Figure 1.5   The Piazza del Duomo, Pisa

In each part of the book different chapters examine in turn: urban government and the degree of external stability; public patronage and the development of the built environment; the attributes of urban economic growth and decline; and private patronage and property development.

Notes

1 VG Childe, 'The urban revolution', *Town Planning Review* 21 (1950), pp 3–17.
2 D Harvey, *Social Justice and the City* (London: Edward Arnold, 1973).
3 RB Potter, *Urbanisation and Planning in the Third World: Spatial Perceptions and Public Participation* (Beckenham: Croom Helm; New York: St Martins Press, 1985).
4 L Martines, *Power and Imagination. City-States in Renaissance Italy* (London: Pimlico, 2002), p 9.
5 Ibid, p 10.
6 Ibid.
7 Ibid, p 7.
8 E Coleman, 'Cities and communes', in D Abulafia (ed), *Italy in the Central Middle Ages* (Oxford: Oxford University Press, 2004), p 29.
9 Ibid, p 35.
10 Ibid, p 51.
11 W Christaller, *Die Zentralen Orte in Suddeutschland* (Jena: Fischer, 1933).
12 Ibid; P Balchin, GH Bull and JF Kieve, *Urban Land and Economics and Public Policy*, 5th edn (Basingstoke: Palgrave, 1995), pp 27–31.
13 RW Pfouts, 'Reply to Harris on testing – the Base Theory', *Journal of American Institute of Planners* 24 (1958), pp 238–43; Balchin, *Urban Renaissance*.
14 BF Hoselitz, 'Generative and parasitic cities', *Economic Development and Cultural Change* 3 (1955).
15 G Myrdal, *Economic Theory and Undeveloped Areas* (London: Duckworth, 1957); P Balchin, D Isaac and J Chen, *Urban Economics: A Global Perspective* (Basingstoke: Palgrave, 2000), p 58.
16 JR Boudeville, *Problems of Regional Economic Planning* (Edinburgh: Edinburgh University Press, 1966); RB Potter, *Urbanisation in the Third World* (Oxford: Oxford University Press, 1992); RB Potter and S Lloyd Evans, *The City in the Developing World* (Harlow: Longman, 1998); Balchin et al, *Urban Economics*, p 60.
17 JM Keynes, *The General Theory of Employment, Interest and Money* (London: Macmillan, 1936); Balchin et al, *Urban Economics*, pp 55–6.
18 B Riseborough, *The Story of Western Architecture* (London: Herbert Press, 2001), p 58.
19 D Sudjic, *The Edifice Complex. How the Rich and Powerful Shape the World* (London: Allen Lane, 2005), p 2.
20 Ibid, p 8.

21 LM Soo, *Wren's Tracts on Architecture and Other Writings* (Cambridge: Cambridge University Press, 1998), p 153.
22 Sudjic, *Edifice Complex*, p 10.
23 R Goldthwaite, *Wealth and Demand for Wealth in Italy, 1300–1600* (Baltimore and London: Johns Hopkins University Press, 1995), p 222.
24 C Moughtin, *Urban Design. Street and Square*, 3rd edn (Oxford and Burlington, MA: Oxford University Press, 2003), pp 70–3.

PART 1

THE LATER MIDDLE AGES

CHAPTER 2

THE DEVELOPMENT OF URBAN GOVERNMENT AND PUBLIC PATRONAGE IN THE LATER MIDDLE AGES

Introduction

In the second half of the 13th century, nearly all the land in the upper part of the Italian peninsula was owned *de jure* by the Hohenstaufen emperors, whose domains stretched from the Alps to central Italy but excluded Venice, then an independent republic. In reality, many of the cities of northern and central Italy such as Milan, Parma, Pavia, Genoa, Verona, Bologna, Pisa, Florence and Siena enjoyed a substantial degree of autonomy and were free, within limits, to exercise *de facto* powers in economic as well as political matters. Further to the south, papal territories comprised not only the region around Rome but a swathe of land stretching from Perugia in the north to Terracina in the south. Even further south, Angevin territory included Naples and most of present-day Campania, Apulia (or Puglia), Calabria and Basilicata. Sicily, under Arab rule from the 820s to around 1040 and thereafter under Norman sovereignty, succumbed to Hohenstaufen rule from 1194 to 1275. The island then became an Angevin possession like its mainland neighbour, but only during a brief interlude before transferring to Aragonese rule in 1282. It is within this context that public buildings, both secular and ecclesiastical, were erected in profusion in the later Middle Ages.

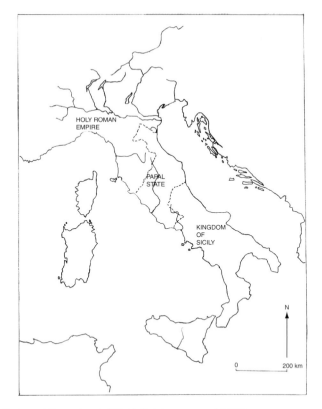

Figure 2.1   Italy and its major political divisions around 1250

Venice: The Serene Republic

Throughout the later Middle Ages and beyond, the government in Venice was renowned for its balance and stability, almost certainly an outcome of the city's constitution that reflected the highly stratified structure of society. The Venetian Republic combined attributes of monarchy, aristocracy and democracy. The head of state was the doge, a quasi-monarch elected for life by a special government committee. He was regarded as the symbolic heir to Emperor Constantine and, as such, expected to display temporal and spiritual leadership. However, the doge was not a prince. Although he was crowned in the Palazzo Ducale by his peers and not by priests, it was imperative that there should be a clear distinction between his office and his person.

Below the doge were the patricians – merchant 'aristocrats' who dominated the economic, political and cultural life of the city. They comprised around 4 per cent of the population and consisted of 200 families who, in exercising control over government between 1297 and 1323, published a 'Golden Book' restricting 'eligibility for political office to themselves and their descendants'.[1] In this respect, since the much-debated 'closure' (*Serrata*) defined and fixed membership of the ruling class and ring-fenced democracy through exclusion, constitutional developments in Venice coincided with political machinations in Florence where a small group of nobles seized ascendancy. Very few more Venetians gained patrician status until the 17th century. Patricians were expected to demonstrate their devotion to public duty and to extol the benefits of the city's political system in terms of its social order, justice and stability. To avoid creating a division of loyalties, or having to forfeit their political rights at home, patricians were obliged to marry only Venetian nobles, and could not 'serve a foreign state or even receive distinctions from other princes'.[2] By these means, patricians maintained tight control of their state and justified 'their position at the top of a clearly defined social structure that they had enshrined in law'.[3]

The Great Council, the Maggior Consiglio, was at the heart of patrician government. Since it was open to all male patricians over 25 years of age it boasted some 2,500 members by the early 16th century and was thus too cumbersome for effective decision-making. Real power was therefore delegated to small committees – to the Senate, the College and the Council of Ten – each chaired by the doge. The latter committee was particularly important since it had responsibility for state security. Patricians also performed an important role in strengthening ties between Church and state, largely to ensure that ecclesiastical power was in their hands rather than exercised by the papacy. The Senate, for example, 'selected the head of the Venetian Church, the Patriarch, and lay patricians drew up a list of nominations for cardinal that it submitted to the pope'.[4] The substantial wealth of S Marco, moreover, was administered by leading patrician laymen, the Procurators of St Mark.[5]

At a lower stratum of government were the *cittadini* or citizens, who comprised some 11 per cent of the population. *Cittadino* status was conditional upon applicants verifying long-term residence and the employment of at least two generations of their heads of family in non-manual trades – as merchants, industrialists, doctors, lawyers, sculptors and painters, for example. Foreigners could acquire citizenship only after 25 years' residence in the city. The *cittadini* were barred from political office and could only participate in government by staffing the civil service.

Altogether, a total of no more than 15 per cent of the population of Venice were involved in government in the 14th century, but this was sufficient – despite the Querini–Tiepolo conspiracy of 1310 and an attempted coup by a recalcitrant doge Marino Falier in 1355 – to maintain very stable government and to advance spectacularly the economic wellbeing of the city. Over the course of a century or more, the *Serenissima* (the serene republic) therefore celebrated the fruits of its strong and stable constitution by funding on a major scale the construction of the Palazzo Ducale, work on which started in 1340 and continued until 1442. The building acted not only as a city hall to accommodate the republic's Maggior Consiglio, but also as a courthouse and the doge's residence. The republic's concern for stable government was matched by its desire to strengthen its external security. To this end, the Venetian government substantially expanded the city's Arsenale in the mid-14th century to allow construction of state-funded galleys on an enormous scale. The Arsenale that had for long been an important warehouse and repair workshop was thus transformed 'into a massive industrial enterprise, probably the largest in the world' (see chapter 3).[6]

Aristocratic Communes and the Emergence of the *Popolo*

By the beginning of the 13th century there were probably 200 or 300 quasi-independent urban settlements or communes in northern and central Italy.[7] Imbued with a strong sense of clan loyalty, there was a tendency for clusters of noblemen to form tightly knit associations (*consorterie*) that exercised considerable economic and judicial powers over the activities of individual members. Corporate ownership of property meant that the relevant *consorterie* 'could impose harsh economic penalties on any member who broke the rules or acted against the interests of the association [while] in some cities *consorterie* had significant powers of justice, including even capital punishment, over their members'.[8] The formation of family militias exacerbated the struggle for communal power and often turned neighbourhoods into hostile zones where civil war was frequently waged between competing clans.[9]

Within this volatile socio-political environment, guilds of merchants emerged in city after city in the late 12th century, for example in Piacenza in 1154, in Milan in 1159 and in Florence before 1182. The expansion of international trade and the importance to the urban economy of bankers and merchants, particularly drapers, generated the establishment of organisations and pressure groups to control mercantile activity within the commune. Merchant guilds were thus set up in most of the larger inland cities of northern Italy by 1180 (well ahead of other cities in Europe), and as representatives of their city's commercial interests their elected heads began to stamp their mark on communal government as advisers and diplomatic agents. 'They [thus] aimed to influence communal policy in the field of large scale trade and sought to fix the norms that governed commercial practices.'[10]

Tradesmen and merchants not only established guilds for economic and judicial purposes, but also to defend themselves against powerful local *consorterie* whose members were reluctant to permit any challenge to control of their neighbourhoods by the 'posting [of] catapults, archers and crossbowmen on rooftops and towers [to] dominate the vicinage'.[11] Not only did this, in effect, create no-go areas over much of the city, it also laid down the conditions for communal violence.[12] However, across northern Italy in Florence, Siena, Lucca, Milan, Cremona, Bergamo, Brescia, Piacenza and Bologna ennobled entrepreneurs and bankers as well as *consorterie* 'fought for control of the supreme political office'.[13] Eventually, a long and bitter struggle broke out between the *popolo* (the people) and the nobility, with the former drawing 'its force and numbers from the middle classes, not from the poor, the day labourers, or the unskilled'.[14]

The struggle between the *popolo* and the nobility erupted in the 1190s, a decade in which a plethora of trade and crafts guilds were springing up all over northern Italy. Major confrontations between guilds and *consorterie*, or their equivalent, occurred in Brescia in 1196, in Piacenza in 1198, and in Milan between 1198 and 1201. Conflict also occurred in Padua in 1200, Cremona in 1201, Lucca in 1203, Siena in 1212, Montepulciano in 1229 and Pistoia in 1234.

Between 1190 and 1225, communal government was transformed by the emergence of a new executive, the *podestà* in what was a constitutional development 'connected, in most of the principal cities, with the advent of the *popolo*'.[15] Until around the mid-13th century, the *podestà* was normally elected for a one- or two-year term (this was limited to one year or less by 1400), and to ensure impartiality the office was usually filled by a 'nobleman from another province practised in arms or in law, and experienced in public life'.[16] The *podestà* not only wielded extensive executive and administrative powers, but also presided at communal councils and represented the commune in foreign relations. He was expected to keep civil unrest at bay, and at times of war it was likely that he would lead the communal army. Only in Mantua, around 1200, were the powers of the *podestà* mainly judicial.

Possibly because of political instability within the cities of northern and central Italy, aristocratically led communal governments (often with the support of the *popolo*) funded the construction of many municipal buildings, both secular and ecclesiastical, with the aim of promulgating civic pride and loyalty. Thus across these areas, virtually every city, large and small, built a Palazzo Comunale and a Palazzo del Podestà or the like, with many commissioning the construction of cathedrals (see chapter 4). Even the emperor Frederick II founded the University of Bologna in 1238 in an attempt, within a Ghibelline city, to engender a wider sense of loyalty to the imperial cause; while within the Papal State supporters of the pope constructed papal palaces as reminders of the temporal authority of the papacy.

Popular Government

The emergence of government by the *popolo* was, in large part, attributable to 'the demographic and economic expansion of the Italian cities from the twelfth to the mid-fourteenth century, which produced a rapid rise of new families and the movements that resulted in popular government'.[17] The increase in urban population in this period intensified and broadened the struggle for power, and produced a new political force within the commune – the *popolo*, an organisation founded by the guilds or *arti* and established to represent the various economic interests within each city. 'In Florence, there were (eventually) twenty-one of these organisations: seven "major" and fourteen "minor"'.[18] In a number of northern and central Italian cities, the interests of the *popolo* were often protected by companies of armed guildsmen under a *capitano del popolo* who, like the *podestà*, was normally appointed from outside.

In 1212 and after a period of civil strife in Milan, there was a breakthrough in the development of government by the *popolo*. The emperor Otto IV (1198–1214) intervened and a major settlement was agreed between the warring parties (*popolo* and *consorterie*) to the effect that henceforth half of all the offices of the commune were to go to the *popolo*, the other half to the *consorterie*. As Martines notes, comparable gains had already been made or were to be made by the *popolo* in 15 city-states, among them Lucca (1197–1203), Mantua (1204), Vicenza (1215–52), Bologna (1228–31), Florence (1244) and Genoa (1257). Government by the *popolo*, however, was entirely absent in Venice and never really developed in Genoa. In these coastal cities, 'the richer part of the middle classes were heavily engaged in shipping and maritime trade in the thirteenth century, and families from this stratum were drawn into government and into the patriciate' rather than into a strong popular movement.[19]

Within this political context, the urban economy and population of north and central Italy grew 'at a rate and in ways never to be repeated'.[20] Despite civil wars, the *popolo* was not only concerned with the promotion of trade and industry, to the considerable benefit of the urban economy, but was also committed to the enhancement of the built environment. Whereas aristocratic communes had been and continued to be responsible for much municipal architecture, popular communes 'promoted [not only] town planning and great construction projects, including city walls, public *palazzi*, cathedrals, but also new streets, paving of existing streets and sewerage systems' (see chapter 4).[21] The *popolo* was perhaps even more eager than the aristocratic commune to promote civic pride since government now reflected the interests of a larger proportion of a city's population. The *popolo* must also have found it easier than their predecessors to raise tax revenue, guild subscriptions and loans for building projects if an enhanced built environment was seen to benefit a wide cross-section of society.

However, because of political instability in northern and central Italy in the late 13th century, there was an incentive to strengthen communal government. Guilds thus 'came together in sworn confederations with elected leaders known variously as *anziani* or *priori*. By the mid-century, the *popolo* . . . were demanding a [much larger] share of communal office, fairer taxation, and an end to the ruinous feuding of nobles'.[22] In Florence, for example, a new government by 'Priors of the Guilds' was instituted in 1282, which was to become the 'pivotal magistracy for 200 years',[23] and was a victory for what JM Najemy has called 'corporatism', that is control of membership of executive committees by the professional and commercial corporations.[24] This was reinforced in 1293 when the *Ordinamenti di giustizia* (Ordinances of Justice) declared that in the interest of equality magnates would be excluded from the priorate and eligibility would be restricted to 'non-knights and guildsmen who "continuously exercised a craft"'.[25]

Since the Florentine *priori* were forever vigilant in ensuring that their city was both protected from invasion and, at the same time, had space to grow, they funded the construction of an outer set of walls (1284–1333) to enclose an area five times as large as that contained by the inner walls built between 1173 and 1175. The *priori* also supplied funds for the provision of fortified gateways within the outer wall, notably the Gate of S Gallo (1289) and the Gate of Prato (1284). However, in an attempt to promote civic pride and patriotism to the maximum, the Florentine government facilitated the construction of the city's massive cathedral, S Maria del Fiore (started 1296) and the enormous city hall, the Palazzo dei Priori (begun 1299).

The Emergence of Oligarchic and Signorial Power

By the trecento, political power in the city-republics had become concentrated in fewer and fewer hands. This was undoubtedly true of Venice (see pp 32–34), while in Genoa consuls were replaced by a *podestà* in 1191 who was in turn superseded by a *capitano del popolo* from 1257 to 1340. Civic pride in Genoa was probably at its greatest when the republic was at its most secure. In terms of the built environment this coincided with the publicly funded development of the Palazzo S Giorgio (1260), the Macello Nuovo (1291–2) and the Palazzo Lamba Doria (1298) (see chapter 4).

In Florence, the increasingly oligarchic nature of government went hand-in-glove with the public provision of funds for the construction of important construction projects that augmented the built environment of the city. The Gate of S Niccolò, the Porta Romana and the Gate of S Frediano were built into the city wall respectively in 1324; 1326 and 1332; the bell tower of the *duomo* was started in 1334; the Orsanmichele grain-store was begun in 1337; and work commenced on the Ponte Vecchio in 1345. Later in the century (starting in 1376), the imposing Loggia dei Lanzi was constructed in the Piazza della Signoria adjacent to the Palazzo dei Priori.

Signorial Government and the Built Environment

Signorial (or tyrannical) regimes, like their communal predecessors, recognised the importance of governmentally funded building projects, both secular and ecclesiastical. However, in addition to promoting civic pride and patriotism, new buildings were now also built to reflect the power and glory of the ruling family, with the aim not only of impressing the tyrant's subjects but also of intimidating external rivals. Despite somewhat different motives for promoting such development, there was little cessation in building work following the transition from communal to signorial rule. New regimes soon picked up where former governments left off, and very often building projects were on a grander scale and greater in number.

The larger cities of northern Italy

In 1260, the commune of Milan succumbed to signorial rule when the Torriani family took control of the city, predecessors of the Visconti who would rule Milan for 170 years from 1277. It is remarkable that whereas only one of the city's notable publicly funded buildings was constructed during the years of the republic, the Palazzo della Ragione (1228), the rest were built under the *signoria*: the Loggia degli Osii was started in 1316, the Campanile of S Gottardo in 1336, the massive *castello* in 1368, and the enormous *duomo* in 1386.

Following a lengthy period of republican governance, the commune of Bologna became a *signoria* in 1337 under Taddeo Pepoli with power subsequently being held in turn by the Visconti (1350–5), Giovanni Visconti di Oleggio (1355–60), and a papal legate (1360–76) before reversion to a short period of republican rule at the end of the Trecento. Unlike Milan, most secular public buildings in Bologna of the late medieval period were attributable to republican initiative. Work on the Palazzo del Podestà was started at the beginning of the 13th century, on the Palazzo Re Enzo in 1246, on the Palazzo d'Accursio in 1287, while work progressed on the Palazzo Comunale throughout most of the century. Under signorial rule, buildings on the site of the Palazzo d'Accursio were unified in 1336 to create a new town hall, and the subsequent return of a republican government augured the start of work on the massive church of S Petronio in 1390.

Broadly comparable to the other *signorie* of northern Italy, Ezzelino da Romano and subsequently the Della Scala (or Scaligeri) family governed Verona despotically during the 13th and 14th centuries but, in contrast to some of their signorial contemporaries elsewhere, notably enhanced the built environment of their domain by funding a wide range of public development projects. In the 13th century, work started on the Palazzo della Ragione, and in the following century the Palazzo Forli, the Torre del Gardello, the Palazzo degli Scaligeri, the Palazzo del Capitano, the Palazzo della Prefettura and the Castelvecchio and its Ponte Scaligero were all completed.

Previously, in 1237, the commune of Padua had been transformed into a *signoria* by Ezzelino da Romano and later it become a suzerainty of the Carraresi dynasty (1318–1405) before being absorbed by the Venetian Republic in 1405. With Padua losing its republican status, new construction work on publicly funded buildings all but ceased. Work had previously been undertaken on the Palazzo della Ragione from 1210 and on the Palazzo del Bò (the university) from 1222, but after an interlude of 30 years resumed with the return of republican rule (1254–1318) when a new town hall, the Palazzo del Consiglio, was built.

The smaller cities of northern Italy

Many of the smaller cities of northern Italy were satellites of Visconti's Milan. One of the earliest, Cremona, was annexed in 1334, but here the more important public buildings were constructed before it was taken over. The city's Palazzo del Comune was built between 1206 and 1245, its Torazzo – one of the higher bell towers in Europe – was completed by 1267, the *duomo* was started in 1274 and the Loggia dei Militi in 1292. Como became a satellite of Milan in 1335 after many years of inter-dynastic feuding with the Torriani. Although the city's *broletto* (started 1215) had been constructed during an earlier period of republican government, building work on Como's *duomo* started in 1370 many years after the city had become part of a regional Milanese state.

To the south, Pavia was annexed by Milan in 1359 (after an interlude of rule by the counts of Montefeltro who had earlier extinguished its republic). Although the city's *broletto* dates from the republican period of government, the Visconti funded construction of the family's Castello Visconteo (1360–5). In Brescia, although publicly funded construction work took place under a republican government until the second half of the 13th century, with the *broletto* (1187–1230) being the most notable project, the city was subsequently annexed by Milan under the Torriani and Visconti. The Visconti funded reconstruction of the huge *castello* from 1360 until its completion under the city's new rulers later in the century, the Veronese Scaligeri and Pandolfo Malatesta of Rimini. Bergamo, remaining a republic until the 14th century, afterwards became subject to Milanese rule under the Torriani and Visconti before succumbing to the rule of Pandolfo Malatesta of Rimini in the early 15th century. In contrast to some notable publicly funded construction work during the late 12th century, such as the Torre Civica, Torre di Gombito and the Palazzo della Ragione, nothing of importance was built in Bergamo under Milanese rule except the repressive *rocca* (fortress) erected by the Visconti in 1331. Piacenza, also tied to Milan, witnessed relatively little public building in the 14th century, most publicly funded construction work being carried out in the trecento under a republican regime: witness the city's *duomo* completed in 1233 and the Palazzo del Comune (started 1280).

In Ferrara comparisons cannot be made between the respective influences of republican and signorial government on the built environment. Not only was the city not a part of the Milanese domain, its long-serving local *signori*, the D'Este, rather than an external overlord commissioned both its Palazzo Comunale (started 1243) and the Castello Estense (begun 1385). Mantua, likewise not a Milanese satellite, remained a republic until the mid-13th century when it fell into the hands of signorial government. During its republican period, Mantua witnessed the construction of the *broletto*, the *Arengario*, the Palazzo della Ragione, and the beginning of construction work on the *duomo*. Thenceforth, first under the Bonacolsi family and from 1328 under the Gonzaga, the type of construction work changed. Instead of buildings that would satisfy the needs of the *popolo*, the signorial administrations funded construction of the Bonacolsi palaces and Torre della Gabbia, and the Castello di San Giorgio.

The Cities of Central Italy

As a maritime power, Pisa was possibly at its peak economically and politically after it had absorbed Corsica, Sardinia and the Balearic Islands between 1050 and 1100. However, as a Ghibelline supporter, Pisa was vulnerable to the strategic considerations of its landward neighbours, the Guelf republics of Genoa, Florence and Lucca. In 1284 Pisa was resoundingly defeated by Genoa at the naval battle of Meloria, and effectively forfeited its maritime interests in the Mediterranean. Although Pisa had become an independent commune in the 1080s, the shock of defeat and the loss of its overseas interests led to the demise of republican government and in due course to a succession of lordships, notably by the Gherardesca family (1316–41) and Gian Galeazzo Visconti (1396–1405). With its economic base reduced after 1284, new publicly backed development projects became a rarity. Whereas work continued on construction of the Baptistery (1270–84), and commenced on the Camposanto (cemetery) in 1278, only the final stages of the leaning tower, the campanile, took place in the closing years of the 13th century and were completed in 1301. Because of the enormous scale and cost of the construction projects that had been undertaken over the previous 200 years (*viz* the *duomo*, as well as those projects referred to above), no further public buildings of any note were constructed until the 16th century.

Pisa's neighbour and inland rival, Lucca, had become a self-governing commune in the 1080s, with its *popolo* granted a role in government from 1197–1203, and experienced the demise of its republican status in the aftermath of war with its neighbours Pisa and Florence in the 12th and 13th centuries. The city fell under the Ghibelline Uguccione della Faggiuola in 1314 and subsequently to Castruccio Castracani (1316–28), a Guelf. The city became the dominant power in western Tuscany particularly after defeating Florence at the battle of Altoascio in 1325, but under the rule of both della Faggiuola and Castracani,

Lucca witnessed the construction of very few public buildings, save for completion of the Duomo di S Martino and the church of S Michele in Foro (see chapter 4).

Across a swathe of central Italy, the Papal State was administered in broadly the same way as its northern counterparts. Taking advantage of the weakened power of the empire after the death of Frederick II in 1250, the papacy increasingly enforced its temporal authority over a number of secular rulers, both republican and signorial, in central and eastern Italy and thus consolidated the boundaries of the Papal State. In the 13th century, Viterbo was brought firmly into the papacy's orbit when the city's *capitano del popolo*, Raniero Gatti, presented as a gift a building that subsequently became known as the Palazzo dei Papi (and its loggia) to Clement IV in 1266–7. Even when in exile in Avignon (1309–77), the papacy was able to strengthen its hold on its territorial possessions in the peninsula through the sturdy efforts of the Spanish cardinal Gil d'Albornoz, and the so-called Egidian Constitution that divided the Papal State into seven provinces each ruled by a papal governor – a situation that prevailed for centuries. As part of this process, a *rocca* was built in Viterbo by Cardinal Albornoz in 1354 to secure the interests of the pope when the papacy eventually returned from Avignon; while in Spoleto, Orvieto and Assisi *rocce Albornoziana* were constructed in 1359, 1364 and 1367 respectively (see chapter 4).

Vestiges of republican rule

In central Italy in the 14th century a small number of cities retained their independence from external rule. Cortona, for example, was a flourishing Tuscan republican commune until 1325, during which time the commune funded construction of the Palazzo Comunale and Palazzo Pretoria before being taken over by a local family, the Casali, in 1325 after which relatively little further development took place for the rest of the century. In Umbria, Gubbio similarly retained its independence throughout most of the later Middle Ages despite being frequently at war with Perugia. Its republican government facilitated construction of the city's Palazzo del Bargello in 1302, the Palazzo dei Consoli in 1322 and the Palazzo Pretorio in 1349, and of the *duomo* throughout the earlier part of the Trecento. When the city came under the peaceful suzerainty of the Montefeltro counts of Urbino in 1387 (a rule that lasted until 1508), there was little need for the development of further public buildings. Orvieto was another Umbrian city that retained its independence throughout the later Middle Ages, notwithstanding competition for power between rival Guelf and Ghibelline factions. Civic pride was reflected in construction of the Palazzo Comunale in 1216 and the Palazzo Papale also of the 13th century. Above all, the *duomo* (started 1290) epitomised the commune's commitment to public expenditure on outstanding buildings (see chapter 4).

The Monarchial South

In the south of the peninsula, Naples was governed in the Middle Ages in turn by Byzantines, Lombards, Normans and German (Hohenstaufen) emperors. However, because of its power, and its proximity to Rome, Naples was seen as a threat to papal independence. Thus, with the death of Frederick II in 1250 and the disintegration of imperial authority in southern Italy, under the French pope Clement IV the papacy (as a temporal suzerain) played a key role in ensuring that Charles I of Anjou (1266–85) succeeded to the throne of Naples. After the death of Charles, the Angevins continued to rule the kingdom, impressively under Robert I (1309–43) but inefficiently in the latter years of the Trecento, with corruption and civic unrest endemic.

In Sicily, in the wake of Hohenstaufen rule, the island was similarly put under Angevin control but, following a popular uprising known as the Sicilian Vespers (1282), the island's nobles offered the crown to King Peter of Aragon, Sicily remaining an Aragonese possession until being subsumed under the Spanish Empire in the late 15th century.

In contrast to the rest of the peninsula, major state-funded construction projects were few and far between in the south. To be sure, successive Angevin kings in Naples facilitated construction of the massive Castel Nuovo in the late 13th century and the cathedral of S Gennaro between 1294 and 1332, but very little other development was directly promoted by the monarchy. In Sicily, although both Angevins and Aragonese rulers funded continuing work on Palermo's 12th-century cathedral over the following two centuries, there was very little other monarchial involvement in the development of the island's built environment during the later Middle Ages.

Conclusion

Within the cities of late medieval Italy, republican, signorial and monarchial governments recognised that, for their survival, there was a need to maintain internal stability and to defend their domains from external aggression. To these ends a spate of imposing public buildings were constructed throughout the peninsula in an attempt to engender civic pride and territorial loyalty. In the Republic of Venice, soon after the ruling class was closed to new members, the Senate commissioned construction of the magnificent Palazzo Ducale in 1324 as the seat of administrative and judicial power. Elsewhere throughout northern and central Italy, aristocratic government gradually evolved into popular communes, the first *popolo* being established in Lucca *c* 1197 and one of the last in Genoa in 1257. During this time, and over the following 80 years, town halls, palaces of justice and other buildings of civic government were built in profusion, from the Palazzo dei Priori in Volterra in 1208 to the Palazzo d'Accursio in Bologna in 1287. With the development of signorial government in cities such as Siena and Florence, there was no let-up in the development of imposing public buildings; quite the reverse: witness the Palazzo Pubblico in Siena (1297) and the Palazzo dei Priori in Florence (1299). In the turbulent 14th century, signorial governments seemed to place less emphasis on promulgating civic pride *per se* and more on defence or territorial aggrandisement. Visconti regimes thus built massive fortresses in Milan and Brescia, the Gonzaga of Mantua commissioned the construction of its gigantic Castello di S Giorgio, and the papacy funded the construction of a chain of fortresses from Volterra to Assisi. In monarchial Naples, the construction of defensive buildings took place earlier than in the north, the Angevins commissioning the Castel Nuovo in 1279.

There can be little doubt that a magnificent church can do as much for civic pride as an imposing town hall and, in addition, can engender loyalty to the city as effectively as a menacing *castello*. It is therefore understandable that throughout Italy in the later Middle Ages governments or their agents commissioned the cathedrals of Siena (1215), Orvieto (1290) and Florence (1294), and built such substantial churches as S Petronio in Bologna (1390) among a plethora of ecclesiastical buildings.

Chronology

1152–1250   Most cities in northern and central Italy lie within the domain of the Hohenstaufen Empire under, consecutively, Frederick I (Barbarossa)(1152–90), Henry VI (1190–7), Otto IV (1198–1214) and Frederick II (1215–50), but there is a high degree of local autonomy.
             In Genoa, unlike other cities in the north, the *popolo* never rose to prominence.

1172	In Verona, work begins on construction of the Torre dei Lamberti (completed 1464).
1187–1230	At Brescia, commune funds construction of city's *broletto*.
1187	In Verona, work starts on the *duomo*.
1190s–1250	Struggle between the *popolo* and the nobility (the *consorterie*) in cities across northern and central Italy. Emergence of a new urban executive, the *podestà*, to keep civil unrest at bay.
	Power sharing between *popolo* and *consorterie* adopted in ever more northern cities after intervention of Hohenstaufen emperor Otto IV in 1212.
	In Venice, in contrast to other cities in the north, the *popolo* never emerged as a political force.
1191	In Genoa, power is concentrated in fewer and fewer hands. Its consuls are replaced by a *podestà*.
1193	In Verona, work begins on Palazzo della Ragione.
1200	In Bologna, republic commissions construction of Palazzo del Podestà.
1206–45	In Cremona, work commences on Palazzo del Comune.
1210	In Verona, work begins on Casa dei Mercanti.
	Commune of Padua commissions construction of its Palazzo della Ragione.
1215	In Monza, work begins on *broletto*.
1215	In Siena, work starts on construction of city's *duomo*, S Maria Assunta.
1216	In Orvieto, works starts on construction of Palazzo Comunale.
1222	In Padua, Palazzo del Bò (university) commissioned by Emperor Frederick II.
1227	In Mantua, work starts on *broletto*.
	Emperor Frederick II founds University of Bologna.
1228	In Milan, republic commissions construction of Palazzo della Ragione.
1233	In Siena, *popolo* gains a role in government.
1233	In Piacenza, work on the *duomo* is completed.
1237	Commune of Padua transformed into *signoria* by Ezzelino da Romano.
1243	In Ferrara, D'Este commission construction of Palazzo Comunale.
1246	In Siena, work begins on renovating Fonte Branda.
1246	In Bologna, republican government commissions Palazzo Re Enzo.
1250	Death of Emperor Frederick II and succession of Conrad IV (1250–4). Holy Roman Empire controls most of northern Italy, the Papal State is suzerain of much of central and eastern Italy, and Angevins rule Naples and Sicily.
1252–8	Commune of Rome appoints a *capitano* and board of 'good men' to introduce a series of anti-baronial measures.

1254–1318	In Padua, republican government commissions new town hall, the Palazzo del Consiglio.
1257	In Genoa, executive power handed from *podestà* to *capitano del popolo*.
1260	**In Genoa, republic commissions Palazzo S Giorgio as seat of popular government.**
1260	Commune of Milan succumbs to signorial rule when the Torriani family takes control of the city.
1266	Hohenstaufen suzerainty in Naples superseded by Angevin rule under Charles I (1266–85); Sicily also ceded to Angevins.
1266–7	**At Viterbo, work begins on Palazzo dei Papi (and its loggia). The palace is a gift from the city's *capitano del popolo* to Pope Clement IV.**
1266	With the death of Manfred at the battle of Benevento, the Hohenstaufen dynasty is extinguished and much of northern and central Italy becomes fragmented under rival Guelf and Ghibelline factions, the former being supporters of the papacy and the latter supporting the emperor.
1267	**In Cremona work on Torazzo, funded by the commune, completed.**
1270–84	**At Pisa, work undertaken on Baptistery.**
1274	**Commune of Cremona commissions construction of city's *duomo*.**
1277	Visconti dynasty begins their 170-year rule in Milan.
1278	**At Pisa work commences on Camposanto (cemetery).**
1279	**At Naples, Angevin king Charles I commissions construction of Castel Nuovo.**
1280	**In Piacenza, work starts on construction of Palazzo del Comune.**
1282	In Sicily, following the Sicilian Vespers, Angevin overlordship replaced by Spanish rule under King Peter of Aragon.
	A new government by 'Priors of the Guild' established in Florence and becomes the pivotal magistracy of the city for the next 200 years.
1284	Genoa vanquishes Pisa at naval battle of Meloria. Genoa becomes dominant power in the Ligurian and Tyrrhenian Seas. Defeat leads to demise of Pisa's republican government.
1284	**Florentine *priori* fund construction of outer set of walls around city and numerous fortified gateways such as Gate of Prato and Gate of S Gallo (1289).**
1287	**In Bologna, republic commissions construction of Palazzo d'Accursio.**
1287	Middle-class oligarchy (*popolo grosso*) assumes power in Siena and establishes a Council of Nine whose members serve for two months at a time. This ensures stability for at least half a century.
1290	**At Orvieto, work begins on construction of *duomo*.**
1291–2	**In Genoa, republic commissions construction of Macello Nuovo.**

1292	**In Cremona, work starts on construction of Loggia dei Militi.**
1293	The '*Ordinamenti di giustizia*' (Ordinances of Justice) issued to exclude magnates from the priorate, and to confine membership of the body to 'non-knights' and guildsmen.
	In the 14th century, republican government in Florence is controlled by the guilds, with rotational membership of executive, the *signoria*, open to as many as 6,000 *priori*, each of whom is eligible to serve for no more than two months. Legislative power resides in even larger popular assemblies. The poor, however, are unrepresented.
1294	In an unsuccessful attempt to reduce the adverse effects of factional rivalry on urban governance, the political base of many cities is widened, for example around 10,000 of Bologna's population of 50,000 become eligible for office. But the role of *podestà* remains because of continuing communal disorder in many cities of northern and central Italy.
1294	**At Naples, work begins on construction of cathedral of S Gennaro.**
1296	**Florentine *priori* facilitate construction of city's new *duomo* of S Maria del Fiore.**
1297	In Venice, the *Serrate* ('closure') restricts political office to 200 aristocratic families and their descendants.
1297	**In Siena, work begins on construction of Palazzo Pubblico.**
1298	**In Siena, work starts on construction of Fonte di Ovile.**
1298	**In Genoa, republic commissions Palazzo Lamba Doria.**
1299	**Florentine *priori* commission construction of their seat of government, Palazzo dei Priori (later known as Palazzo Vecchio).**
1300–99	**In Verona, work undertaken on Palazzo Scaligeri (now Palazzo della Prefettura) and Palazzo del Capitano.**
1301	**In Pisa, campanile (leaning tower) completed.**
1302	**In Gubbio, commune commissions construction of city's Palazzo del Bargello.**
1309–77	Papacy in exile at Avignon. Under Egidian Constitution, Papal State subsequently divided into seven provinces, each ruled by a papal governor.
1311–13	Genoa ruled by Emperor Henry VII.
1314	Lucca becomes a *signoria* under Uguccione della Faggiuola following demise of its republican government.
1315	Army of Ghibelline city of Pisa defeats forces of Guelf city of Florence at Montecatani.
1316–25	**In Siena, work undertaken on Battistero di S Giovanni.**
1316–28	Lucca ruled by Castruccio Castracani.
	At Lucca, completion of Duomo di S Martino and church of S Michele in Foro.
1316–41	Pisa ruled by Gherardesca family.

1316	**Milan's Loggia degli Osii commissioned by city's *signoria*.**
1318–35	Genoa under protection of Robert of Anjou, king of Naples.
1318–1405	Padua is suzerain of Carraresi dynasty.
1322	**In Gubbio, commune commissions construction of city's Palazzo dei Consoli.**
	Commune of Cortona taken over by Casali *signori*.
1324	**In Florence, Gate of S Niccolò built into city wall.**
1325	Florentine army defeated by army of city of Lucca at Altoascio; Lucca subsequently recovers most of Tuscany for the imperial (Ghibelline) cause. Florence therefore temporarily suspends its constitution and grants executive power to a *podestà* Charles, duke of Calabria.
1326	**In Florence, Porta Romana built into city wall.**
1329	Formation of regional states begins with Florence absorbing Fiesole.
1331	**In Bergamo, Visconti fund construction of city's *rocca*.**
1332	**In Florence, Gate of S Frediano built into city wall.**
1334	**In Florence, work starts on bell tower of *duomo*.**
1335	Milan absorbs Como.
1336	**In Milan, *signoria* commissions Campanile of S Gottardo.**
	In Siena, Palazzo d'Accursio joined to Palazzo Comunale.
1337	**In Florence, work commences on Orsanmichele grain store.**
	Bologna becomes *signoria* under Taddeo Pepoli.
1339	In Genoa, a popular faction elects Simone Boccanegra as doge, but in response the oligarchic nobility puts city under wing of Archbishop Giovanni Visconti, lord of Milan.
	Venice starts to become a regional state by taking control of Treviso.
1340	**In Venice, work starts on construction of the Palazzo Ducale.**
1342–3	Because of economic crisis in Florence, brought on by collapse of Bardi and Peruzzi banks, city's constitution again suspended and a *podestà*, Walter of Brienne, granted executive power.
1345	**In Florence, work commences on new Ponte Vecchio, the previous bridge having been destroyed by floods.**
1347–98	A series of popular governments holds power in Rome, the first and best known being tribunate of Cola di Rienzo.
1348	Florence absorbs S Gimignano.
1348–9	Black Death reduces population of Italy by over a third.
1349	**In Gubbio, commune commissions construction of city's Palazzo Pretorio.**
1350–5	Bologna ruled by *signoria* under Visconti of Milan.
1350	In Siena, after the Black Death, the Council of Nine is dissolved by Emperor Charles IV. After 50 years of instability, Siena falls under the power of Gian Galeazzo Visconti of Milan in an alliance against Florence.

1351	Florence annexes Prato.
1354	**In Verona, Castlevecchio commissioned by Cangrande II Della Scala.**
1354	**At Viterbo, to secure interests of papacy, Cardinal Albornoz organises construction of *rocca*.**
1355	**In Verona, Cangrande II funds construction of Ponte Scaligero.** Bologna ruled by a *signoria* under Oleggio.
1358–90s	Popular government in Rome strengthened by election of seven 'governors', appointment of a Senator (equivalent to a *podestà*), and formation of a militia.
1359	Milan annexes Pavia. **At Spoleto, Cardinal Albornoz builds a *rocca*.**
1360–76	Bologna ruled by papal legate.
1360	**At Pavia, Visconti fund construction of Castello Visconteo.** **In Brescia, Visconti finance reconstruction of city's *castello*.**
1364	**At Orvieto, Cardinal Albornoz constructs *rocca*.**
1367	**At Assisi, Cardinal Albornoz builds his last *rocca*.**
1368	**In Milan, *signoria* under Galeazzo II Visconti commissions construction of city's *castello*.**
1376	**In Florence, work commences on Loggia dei Lanzi in Piazza della Signoria.**
1384	Florence absorbs city of Arezzo.
1385	**At Ferrara, D'Este commission Castello Estense.**
1386	**In Milan, the *signoria* under Gian Galeazzo Visconti commissions city's enormous *duomo*.**
1387	Communal government in Gubbio replaced by signorial rule under Montefeltro counts of Urbino.
1388–1407	**At Mantua, Francesco I Gonzaga commissions construction of Castello di S Giorgio.**
1390	**In Bologna, republican government commissions construction of massive church of S Petronio.**
1396	**At Como, work starts on *duomo* many years after the city's incorporation into the Milanese state.**
1396–1405	Pisa ruled by Gian Galeazzo Visconti.
1396–1409	After violent disturbances, Genoa accedes to French rule.

Notes

1 M Hollingsworth, *Patronage in Renaissance Italy* (London: John Murray, 1994), p 101.

2 P Burke, *The Italian Renaissance. Culture and Society in Italy*, 2nd edn (Oxford: Polity, 1986), p 47.

3 Hollingsworth, *Patronage*, p 101.

4 G Hanlon, *Early Modern Italy, 1550–1800* (Basingstoke: Macmillan, 2000), p 102.

5 Hollingsworth, *Patronage*, p 102.

6 D Mentzel, *A Traveller's History of Venice* (Gloucs: Chastleton Travel, 2006), p 88.

7 Duggan, *A Concise History of Italy* (Cambridge: Cambridge University Press, 1994), pp 42–3.

8 L Martines, *Power and Imagination. City-States in Renaissance Italy* (London: Pimlico, 2002), p 37.

9 Ibid, pp 37–8.

10 Ibid, p 38.

11 Ibid, p 40.

12 Ibid, pp 37–8.

13 Ibid, p 40.

14 Ibid.

15 Ibid, pp 41–2.

16 Ibid, p 42.

17 A Zorzi, 'The South', in JM Najemy (ed), *Italy in the Age of the Renaissance* (Oxford: Oxford University Press, 2004), p 149.

18 Duggan, *Concise History*, pp 43–4.

19 Martines, *Power and Imagination*, pp 48 and 138.

20 Ibid, p 63.

21 Zorzi, 'The South', p 149.

22 Duggan, *Concise History*, pp 43–4.

23 JM Najemy, *Corporation and Consensus in Florentine Electoral Politics, 1280–1400* (Chapel Hill, NC: University of North Carolina Press, 1982), p 17.

24 Ibid.

25 T Dean, *The Towns of Italy in the Later Middle Ages* (Manchester: Manchester University Press, 2000), p 214, n 4.

CHAPTER 3

PUBLIC PATRONAGE AND URBAN DEVELOPMENT

Introduction

In the cities of late medieval Italy, governments funded the development of magnificent and imposing secular and ecclesiastical buildings. Throughout much of Western Europe in the 13th and 14th centuries, the Gothic style of architecture was being adopted and it dictated the appearance of churches and urban palaces alike. However, as had been the case with Romanesque architecture hitherto, Gothic architecture was imported into Italy from across the Alps, but assumed a very different form throughout the length of the peninsula. Whereas in France, Germany and England, Gothic churches were characterised by their soaring verticality, flying buttresses, huge areas of glazed window, pointed arches, rib-vaulting and use of stone as the principal building material, in Italy these attributes were largely absent, and there was a much greater use of brick in construction often faced with marble. Italian patrons were still very much wedded to Romanesque influences, and there thus emerged a church architecture unique in Europe: Italian Gothic. It could be argued, however, that Gothic architecture found its full expression not in churches but in civic buildings, many of which were the finest in Europe.[1] Italian town halls in particular were notable for their distinctive design: 'Usually, they were entirely parallelepiped with arcades on the ground floor, while the upper floor contained a single great hall.'[2] Thus, it was in the secular sector that the greatest advances in architecture occurred during the later Middle Ages, developments which, in the course of time and particularly in Tuscany, would evolve into the distinctive architecture of the Early Renaissance.

The Larger Cities of Northern and Central Italy

Venice

The principal civic building of Venice is the magnificent Palazzo Ducale. Established by Doge Francesco Foscari in 1324, and initially under the direction of the stone craftsman Filippo Calendario, the *palazzo* not only became the seat of the city's government in all its manifestations, but also the sumptuous residence of the doge and the focus of imperial power (Venice being the only Italian state in the later Middle Ages to rule over an extensive empire).

The original government *palazzo*, which dated back to the early days of the republic, was superseded by the late medieval Palazzo Ducale, its pre-Renaissance phase of development extending over the period 1340 to 1442. Following the *Serrata* of 1297, the number of male members of the 200 families permitted to serve on the Maggior Consiglio (the Great Council) increased substantially, necessitating the provision of much larger premises. Notwithstanding the cessation of building work during the Black Death in 1348, the whole of the new Sala del Maggior Consiglio, built alongside the Molo (waterfront), was completed by 1365. Work already in progress literally around the corner, adjacent to the Piazzetta, was completed in 1442 with the construction of the Porta della Carta.

With loggias on the first two floors, the design of the Palazzo Ducale 'has ample Venetian precedents going back beyond such twelfth- and thirteenth-century palazzi as the Loredan and Farsetti to the . . . Fondaci Turchi'.[3] It has a heavy superstructure above, accommodating most notably the Sala del Maggior Consiglio, yet there is no sense of top-heaviness, while the openness of the building at its lower levels 'sets the Palazzo Ducale apart from other Italian communal places. There is no suggestion of impregnability.'[4] That the *palazzo* is completely unfortified, and that 'the public could wander freely in the lower portico and into the courtyard',[5] is in stark contrast to the security of civic buildings of the period in, for example, Siena and Florence.

Built mainly of Istrian stone and red Verona marble, the facade of the *palazzo* exhibits a blend of Islamic and Gothic elements. Delicate traceries were carved in a distinctly Moorish style, crenellations are akin to those crowning an Egyptian mosque rather than an Italian centre of secular power, and the inlaid tiles of the upper facade are distinctly Persian in design. The lower portico of the building, however, with its stocky columns and plain arches, is fundamentally Gothic.

Photo 3.1 Filippo Calendario, Palazzo Ducale, Venice, begun 1324. After being rebuilt several times since its foundation in the 9th century, as a symbol of Venetian power the *palazzo* gained a remarkable Gothic exterior in the 14th century, influenced substantially by Islamic motifs.

The creation, commercial exploitation and governance of the Venetian Empire, as well as the economic and political viability of the republic itself, were highly dependent on the establishment and maintenance of a naval dockyard and a sizeable fleet. While a large number of private shipyards had existed in Venice and on the islands of its lagoon for generations, and continued to account for most of the shipbuilding in the region well into the late Middle Ages, the republic constructed its Arsenale in the early 12th century to ensure that its shipping needs would be met. Initially the Arsenale provided only warehousing and repair facilities, embarking on shipbuilding in the early 14th century. Although in previous times the republic had relied on the services of smaller independent shipbuilders to supply its needs, the Arsenale had now quadrupled in size and was 'large enough to construct and maintain the Republic's entire fleet of merchant galleys';[6] at the time, it was quite probably the largest industrial enterprise in the world.

Largely because Venice was amply blessed with the mighty Byzantine cathedral of S Marco and the two enormous Gothic mendicant churches of S Zanipolo and S Maria Gloriosa dei Frari, the republic eschewed the widespread practice of commissioning a further major church as a symbol of civic identity and pride, especially as the Palazzo Ducale was undoubtedly absorbing a large proportion of the state's financial resources. However, work continued on S Marco's cathedral which, matched by the Palazzo Ducale, was the greatest of all symbols of Venetian identity. Founded in the 9th century, the basilica was rebuilt in the 11th century and its frontage and sides were constantly developed between the 12th and 15th centuries.

Genoa

Several decades before its maritime rival Venice had erected its principal civic building, the Palazzo Ducale, the Commune of Genoa facilitated construction of a spate of smaller but less impressive buildings, the most notable among which were the Palazzo San Giorgio, the Macello Nuovo and the Palazzo Lamba Doria. Located between the port and the Palazzo della Ripa (see p 131), and sited in what was then the centre of the city, the three-storey Palazzo San Giorgio was founded in 1260 as the seat of government headed by the *capitano del popolo*, Guglielmo Boccanegra. Gothic in detail, the three-storey *palazzo*, with its wide-arched single loggia providing access to its upper floors by means of steps from street level, was eminently suitable as a government building, but with the fall of Boccanegra it became a customs house before being assigned to the Banco di San Giorgio at the beginning of the 15th century.[7]

Founded by the Commune in 1291–2, and located on the edge of the principal commercial area of medieval Genoa, the Soziglia market, the four-storey Macello Nuovo (or new market) was a shopping development with retail premises at ground-floor level financed from the sale and rent of dwellings above. Overall, the Macello Nuovo assumed the appearance of a *palazzo* and, together with the privately developed Ripa, provided a model for future development across much of Genoa throughout the remainder of the Middle Ages.[8]

At the end of the 13th century, a medieval palace was donated by the Genoese commune to Admiral Lamba Doria as a reward for leading the Genoese fleet to victory against the Venetians at the battle of Curzola (1298). Henceforth known as the Palazzo Lamba Doria, the four-storey palace was soon reconstructed to produce a building with a ground-floor loggia supported by fine polygonal columns, and a facade and side walls built from striped black stone

Photo 3.2 Palazzo S Giorgio, Genoa, begun 1260. Built from the stones of a captured Venetian fortress, this fortified building was developed in the Gothic style as the seat of the city's government, but was overshadowed in the 13th century by the magnificence of Venice's Palazzo Ducale.

and white marble 'clearly defined by intervening cornices and ... enlived by ... pointed *quadrifore* which repeat the shapes and rhythms of the arcade below'.[9] Shorn of the defensive character that normally marked medieval *palazzi*, the new building recreated its predecessor's disciplined symmetry and repetitive rhythm. Thus, the Palazzo Lamba Doria 'is, of all the Early Gothic private palaces of Italy, among the earliest and farthest on the road towards a truly civil architecture'. [10]

Despite its great wealth, like Venice, the Commune of Genoa failed to commission the construction of major new churches in the later Middle Ages preferring, also like Venice, to fund further work on its principal church, the cathedral of S Lorenzo. However, although work started on the cathedral in 1099, over a century later it remained far from finished, partly because of a major earthquake in 1222. By the late 13th century, the two bell towers and lower facade had been completed and, following damage caused by a fire in 1299, the lower order of the nave, the apse and the wooden roof had been rebuilt by 1307–12.

Photo 3.3   Palazzo Lamba Doria, Genoa, soon after 1298. A fine example of a 13th-century Gothic *palazzo*, the four storeys of its facade are adorned with black and white stone and marble stripes while on the ground floor a portico is supported by robust polygonal columns.

Milan

Because the economy of Milan was less developed than that of Venice and Genoa, the city's government had fewer resources with which to fund major secular building projects than its maritime neighbours. This fact, coupled with the demise of republican government and the establishment of a *signoria* in 1311, resulted in relatively few notable publicly funded buildings being constructed in the city during the later Middle Ages despite Milan being by far the largest urban area in Lombardy during the 13th and 14th centuries. However, within the secular arena, there are three interesting exceptions: the Palazzo della Ragione, the Loggia degli Osii and the Castello Sforzesco.

The Palazzo della Ragione, begun in 1228, was commissioned by the *podestà* Oldrado da Tresseno after Milan had succeeded in gaining autonomy from

Photo 3.4 Palazzo della Ragione, Milan, 1228–33. Built to celebrate Milan's gaining autonomy within the Holy Roman Empire, the *palazzo* is one of the oldest town halls in Italy. Its upper floor was added in the 18th century.

the Holy Roman Empire. At ground-floor level, and indicative of its mixed Romanesque-Gothic origins, the building has seven arches in three rows along its length – the end arches being pointed and the others rounded – and two rounded arches along its sides. Above, the middle floor has a row of three-light windows above the arches but is otherwise walled up except for a small arched niche on the facade containing an equestrian statue of the building's founder.[11] The upper floor, of no particular architectural merit, was added in 1771.

More Gothic in style, although not entirely free of Romanesque elements, the Loggia degli Osii is situated behind the Palazzo della Ragione on the edge of the Piazza Mercanti. Funded by the *capitano del popolo*, Matteo Visconti, and possibly designed by Scoto da S Gimignano, work started on the three-storey building in 1316. With a rounded Tuscan-arched loggia at ground-floor level, and a pointed Lombard-arched loggia and *parlera* (central balcony) on the middle floor, the building is both airy and graceful, with its facade reduced 'to a mere framework'.[12] However, this effect is somewhat diminished since, on its upper floor, Romanesque blind-arcading is not only incongruously developed into *trifore* and statuary niches but sits uncomfortably on top of the loggia.

Built mainly for defence rather than to provide premises for civic government, the *castello* was situated just outside the city walls and was continuously expanded and strengthened throughout much of the later Middle Ages and Early Modern period. Founded by Galeazzo Visconti in 1368, its nucleus was substantially enlarged by the military architect Giovanni Magetti towards the end of the century for Galeazzo's successor Gian Galeazzo (1378–1402), when the building also assumed residential functions.

There were also comparatively few ecclesiastical buildings commissioned by the state, the church of S Gottardo and the *duomo* being notable exceptions. Funded by Azzone Visconti, work began on the former building in 1336. Designed by Francesco de'Pegorari, its most notable feature is its octagonal campanile. Above its square base, its brick shaft is surmounted at its peak by 'small, angular stone columns and four superimposed orders of cornices of small interlaced hanging arches',[13] which in turn lead upwards to 'a band of framed two-light openings, a loggia of columns and [a] belfry that terminates in a spire'.[14]

The latter building, the *duomo*, is not only one of the largest churches in the world – second only to St Peter's in Italy, but is also the only late-Gothic

Photo 3.5   Simone da Orsenigo and others, *duomo*, Milan, begun 1387. The largest late-Gothic cathedral in the world, not completed until 1813. An extraordinary building, it displays a unique mixture of Gothic and Baroque motifs – a result of its lengthy period of construction.

edifice of any note in the whole of northern and central Italy. Work on the *duomo* began in 1387 when Milan, having partly escaped the Black Death of 1348, was becoming increasingly prosperous as the administrative capital of a political hegemony that extended over much of the plain of Lombardy and beyond. The building was funded by Gian Galeazzo Visconti who sought to model it on the great cathedrals of Le Mans and Bourges rather than on earlier Italian structures. Work proceeded very slowly under the direction and consultancy of a succession of architects such as Simone da Orsenigo and Giovanni Grassi from Lombardy, Nicolas de Bonaventure and Jean Mignot from Paris; Johann von Freiburg and Hans Parler from Germany; and a mathematician, Gabriele Stornaloco, from Piacenza. Although the *duomo* is undoubtedly late Gothic, as exemplified by its vaulted structure, numerous flying buttresses and its 'forest of pinnacles and statues culminating in an octagonal cupola over the crossing',[15] its plan is not overtly 'un-Italian'. Like many other churches in the peninsula, it has a nave with double aisles, is almost as wide as it is long, has transepts with aisles and a polygonal apse and, even more pertinently, its nave and inner aisles have clerestories that are so small that they admit very little light, in stark contrast to equivalent northern European cathedrals of the 13th and 14th centuries. However, the building material throughout is white marble derived from Visconti quarries, an attribute that markedly distinguishes the *duomo* from many of the other great churches of northern Italy. The main building work, apart from its facade, was completed under Ludovico Sforza (1494–9), but after the addition of many classical and Baroque features it was eventually finished in 1805.

Florence

As mentioned in chapter 2, prior to its rapid development in the 13th and early 14th centuries, the Republic of Florence directly funded and executed the construction of city walls around its periphery since this was essential for the safety of the city. Although the walls of 1173–5 were still very much in evidence a hundred years later (and still are), a further ring of walls – considerably further out – was constructed between 1284 and 1333, increasing the area five fold. Numerous gates were built into the outer wall, of which the most notable are the Gate of S Niccolò (1324), the Porta Romana (1326) and the Gate of S Frediano (1332). Each is a substantial building in its own right, the Gate of S Frediano, designed by Andrea Pisano, being the largest of its kind.

Within its clearly defined boundaries, and possibly as an outcome of political instability, the physical development of Florence initially occurred in a largely *ad hoc* manner – with new secular buildings here, and new churches there – although there was a tendency to situate the more important edifices in central locations within the urban fabric. Prime examples of this trend include the Castagna Tower and the Bargello. Built with imperial funds in the early years of the 13th century, the Castagna Tower was donated to the Benedictine Order to guard the Badia but was subsequently granted to the commune which assigned it to the *Priori dell' Arte* (guild-leaders) as a base for political activity. In 1256, shortly after the city's *popolo* bounded into power, the commune commissioned construction of the Palazzo del Popolo as the seat of government, but within four years because of a shift of power the building became the Palazzo del Podestà. Known from the 16th century as the Bargello (the headquarters of the chief of police), the palace is an uncompromising mass built from regular blocks of stone, its solid walls pierced by small doors and windows and, with its tall corner tower, crowned by crenellations. Like merchants' palaces of the period, the Bargello contains a

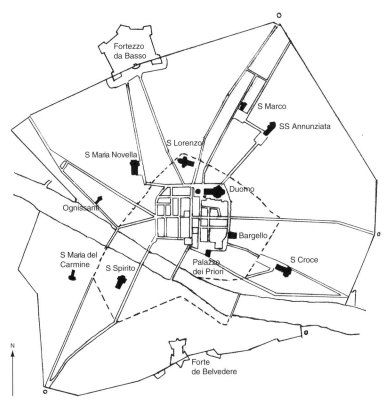

Figure 3.1　Florence within its city walls of 1173–5 and 1284–1333

central pentagonal courtyard from which an exterior staircase leads to the upper floors. Despite its grim and daunting aspect, the building is often considered one of the greatest achievements of 13th-century civic architecture.

By the 1290s, the Florentines had begun to set enormous store by the appearance of their city, and embarked upon a step-by-step plan of development. Florence now had a new representative government as an outcome of institutional reforms enacted by the *Ordinamenti di giustizia* of 1298 and, under its terms, the patronage of major building projects, both secular and ecclesiastical, was delegated to the guilds, the institutions at the centre of political power. 'This solution to the problem of exercising state authority was uniquely Florentine and contrasted with the solutions developed in Venice or the Italian courts. It also established guild rivalry as a powerful competitive spur to public patronage, a motive that can be seen behind many of the works of the early Florentine Renaissance' (see Chapter 7).[16] In 1299, the *Priori della' Arte* funded construction of the Palazzo dei Priori, a building designed to accommodate all the city's *priori* (guild leaders and senior judges) and its *Gonfalonier della Giustizia* (head of state). Designed by Arnolfo di Cambio, and sited at the eastern end of the newly created Piazza della Signoria, the *palazzo* arguably 'constitutes the greatest piece of civil architecture in Florence during the rule of the Comune [and] over time . . . rose to become a symbol of the city itself'.[17] A bulky block of a building, the *palazzo* is uniformly rusticated on its outer walls, its lower floor is almost devoid of windows and initially contained only two small doors, its middle and upper floors are pierced by regularly spaced two-light mullioned windows and crowning crenellations add to its fortress-like appearance. The building is surmounted by a tall crenellated campanile, which like the main building below is surrounded by a jutting walkway.[18] As at the Bargello, the core of the building is represented by a pentagonal courtyard. However, despite its magnificence and its nomenclature, the Palazzo dei Priori, like the Bargello before it, had 'not yet made the leap forward from fortress to palace' and, in terms of design, was rooted very much in the 13th century.[19]

Soon after completion of the Palazzo dei Priori, further development of the Piazza della Signoria was delayed because, in its vicinity, severe flooding of the Arno in 1333 damaged the Ponte Vecchio and necessitated its reconstruction, probably under the direction of Taddeo Gaddi and Neri di Fioravante. Whereas the earlier bridge had formed part of Florence's fortifications, the new three-arched structure (begun 1345) was no longer primarily defensive but has continued to this day to incorporate a street and double row of shops.

Many decades later, the *Arte della Lana* (wool guild) funded construction of the Loggia della Signoria (or dei Lanzi). Begun in 1376, the building is sited on

Photo 3.6 Bargello, Florence, 1256. A massive and daunting battlemented building constructed in *pietra forte*, and initially the seat of the city's government.

the southern edge of the Piazza della Signoria at 90 degrees to the Palazzo dei Priori. It was constructed to shelter both Florentine and visiting dignitaries from the rain, and provided a setting for political debate and the conduct of affairs of state. Constructed under the direction of Benci di Cione and Simone Talenti, the loggia with its narrow columns, tall and wide arches and horizontal skyline undoubtedly anticipates the early Florentine Renaissance.

Also in a central location, but 400 metres north of the Piazza della Signoria, work started in 1294 on replacing the old cathedral of S Reparata with a much larger and more impressive structure, the *duomo* of S Maria del Fiore. Financed mainly by the republican government from the proceeds of a poll tax and a subsidy from the city's treasury, responsibility for the building work was assigned to the *Arte della Lana* in 1332. The guild accordingly elected four of its members to constitute the *Opera*, a body charged with the day-to-day surveillance of construction activity, notwithstanding the often-acrimonious differences of approach pursued by the *Opera* and the mastermasons. Initially it was thought that work could continue simultaneously on the Palazzo dei Priori and S Maria del Fiore, particularly as Arnolfo di Cambio was the initial architect of the *duomo* as well as having responsibility for the *palazzo*. However, whereas the latter

Photo 3.7 Arnolfo di Cambio, Palazzo dei Priori, Florence, 1299. With fortress-like Gothic attributes, including a minimum of ground-floor entrances, the rusticated *palazzo* with its 94-metre-high bell tower looms over the Piazza della Signoria.

building was completed within a few decades (except for an extension in the 16th century), the cathedral was not finished until the mid-15th century. Part of the reason for the slow pace of work was that plans were continually amended by a succession of architects, among them Giotto di Bondone, Andrea Pisano and Francesco Talenti (father of Simone). During the latter's commission, the on-going plan for the cathedral 'was modified in 1357–68 by an astonishing number of committees of painters, sculptors and goldsmiths, including Taddeo Gaddi and Andrea Orcagna'.[20]

Of Gothic design, the plan of the cathedral integrates a longitudinal nave and two aisles with three circular apses at the eastern end of the cathedral each of which contains five side chapels. At the crossing of this configuration a large empty space awaited the construction of a dome, a wait that continued until 1418–36 when a novel approach to building a dome was applied by Filippo Brunelleschi (see p 182). While most of the cathedral is clad with rectilinear green and white marble panels, and incorporates such features as rounded blind arches, tall two-light windows in the main body of the church and large roundels in the clerestory and drum, the facade remained unfinished until the 19th century. To

Photo 3.8 Benci di Cione and Simone Talenti, Loggia dei Lanzi, Florence, 1376. Built as an assembly hall to accommodate government officials during public ceremonies, the building with its beautiful lofty arches became a guardroom of the Lanzi (footsoldiers) during the rule of Cosimo I.

avoid the cathedral appearing somewhat squat, particularly when compared to its counterparts in Siena and Orvieto (see pp 77 and 98), an ordinance of 1339 lowered the levels of the surrounding streets 'to allow the height of the rising new building to have the full visual impact'.[21]

In 1334 work began on the cathedral's campanile. Designed initially by the then *capo mastro* (head of works), Giotto di Bondone, the bell tower diverted resources from the cathedral and for a number of years put a virtual brake on development. Rising to a height of 85 metres, it stands on a base 15 metres square. Over a period of 30 years, its construction was directed in turn by Giotto, who built the lowest enclosed section; by Andrea Pisano, who was responsible for the middle section that contains windows, loopholes and statues; and by Francesco Talenti, who constructed the top section incorporating two- and three-light mullioned windows to lessen its weight. In contrast to the *duomo*, the surface of the campanile is tricoloured, being composed of red, green and white marble.

Photo 3.9   Arnolfo di Cambio, *duomo* of S Maria del Fiore, 1296. Compressed within a comparatively small *piazza*, the massive grandeur of one of the largest cathedrals in the Christian world symbolised the power and wealth of Florence throughout the Renaissance. Although its facade was not completed until the 19th century, it broadly conformed with the Florentine-Gothic style of the main body of the cathedral.

Between 1337 and 1404, work progressed on the construction and adaptation of the Orsanmichele. Built initially by Francesco Talenti, Neri di Fioravante and Benci di Cione as a loggia to house a grain market, it was converted into a church in 1367. Under the direction of Simone Talenti, in 1380 its arcades were enclosed by huge three-light windows but these were soon bricked up and replaced by tabernacles displaying the patron saints of the guilds. From 1404, the upper two storeys of the building accommodated a granary, but after 1569 they were used to house notarial archives.

Bologna

Concentrated around the centrally located Piazza Maggiore, during the later Middle Ages several notable civic buildings were constructed almost entirely from brick. Sited on the western edge of the *piazza*, the Palazzo Comunale with its tall

Photo 3.10 Giotto di Bondone and others, campanile of the *duomo* of S Maria del Fiore, Florence, begun 1334. This tall and slender Gothic bell tower (82 m in height) is Italy's most elegant campanile and a perfect complement to the (later) dome of the cathedral.

tower was founded in the early 13th century under a republican regime but saw further development over a long period of political flux until the late 16th century when its facade was adorned by a statue of Pope Gregory XIII, confirming the city's status as a Papal State. The Palazzo Comunale was gradually integrated with its neighbouring building, the Palazzo d'Accursio, as the result of the commune acquiring the latter building from Francesco d'Accursio on his return from the court of Edward I of England in 1287. Under the lordship of Taddeo Pepoli, the two palaces were joined together in 1336 to form an extended seat of government, and under Fieravante Fieravanti the building to the right of the main entrance was reconstructed in 1425–8 to facilitate its greater use. In the 16th century, when the palace acted as a residence for papal legates, battlements were built along the front and two sides of the building giving it a fortress-like appearance.

On the southern edge of the *piazza*, the Palazzo del Podestà dates from the beginning of the 13th century (a centrally placed tower, the Arengo, being added in 1212), and to its west the Palazzo Re Enzo was constructed in 1246, the palace taking its name from Enzo, king of Sardinia (a Ghibelline supporter) who was imprisoned in the building by a Guelph administration between 1249 and 1272

Photo 3.11   Palazzo Comunale and Palazzo d'Accursio, Bologna, 1336. Built of red brick, the conjoined edifice imposingly occupies the whole of the western side of the Piazza Maggiore and Piazza Nettuno, and exhibits a 13th-century facade to the left and a 14th-century facade to the right of its central portico.

following the battle of Fossalta (1249). Opposite, along part of the northern edge of the *piazza* and built initially in the 13th century, the Palazzo dei Notai was substantially modified and enlarged in 1381 under the direction of Antonio di Vincenzo, Giovanni Dionigi, Lorenzo da Bagnomarino and Berto Cavaletto. The palace was intended as an appropriate base for the city's lawyers who were instrumental in laying the foundations of European law in the Middle Ages. The eastern side of the *piazza* was not developed into a form that we can now recognise until the late 16th century (see p 327).

Beyond the Piazza Maggiore, two further secular civic buildings warrant consideration: the Collegio di Spagna and the Palazzo della Mercanzia. Founded by Cardinal Albornoz in 1365 for Spanish students and designed principally by Matteo Gattapone, the Collegio di Spagna is all that remains of the original medieval university prior to its reconstruction in the late 16th century (see p 329). The main building is both severe and sophisticated. The octagonal columns and two-tiered arches of its loggia are more substantial and taller at ground-floor level than on its upper storey, an effect that is visually emphasised by a parapet that reaches halfway up the columns of the upper storey. Surrounding a *cortile*, the loggia is capped by a virtually flat roof whose horizontality is interrupted on one side by the centrally sited facade and bell-screen of the chapel of S Clemente.[22] Very different in style from the *collegio*, the Palazzo della Mercanzia, begun in 1382–4, was not only commissioned by the communal council (in Florence the earlier *palazzo* was guild-funded) but physically had little in common with its Tuscan counterpart. Built to the plans of Antonio di Vincenzo and Lorenzo da Bagnomarino, the Palazzo della Mercanzia of Bologna features a tall loggia that supports a vaulted hall, and the building is crowned by a crenellated cornice.[23] It is rich in architectural detail and exhibits 'an elaborate marble balcony and baldachin, and a sculptural programme that wraps around three facades [to] distinguish the loggia from adjacent buildings'.[24]

Although Bologna can boast only one important ecclesiastical building commissioned by the commune – the church of S Petronio – the edifice is one of

Photo 3.12   Antonio di Vincenzo, church of S Petronio, Bologna, begun 1390. Gothic in style and one of Italy's finest brick buildings, the church was intended to be larger than St Peter's in Rome until funds ran out. While the lower part of the facade is adorned by an attractive doorway, the upper part is still devoid of marble cladding.

the finest examples of Italian Gothic and one of the largest mainly brick buildings in existence. Designed by the architect Antonio di Vicenzo and inspired by the airiness and light of S Maria Novella and the piers, columns and pilaster forms of the Duomo of Florence, the church is sited on the southern edge of the Piazza Maggiore, dwarfing the Palazzo dei Notai to its right. Intended to be around twice its present size to rival St Peter's, work on the building continued intermittently until the mid-17th century. The lower storey of the incomplete brick facade is constructed of pink and white marble, an imposing carving of the Madonna and Child is inset above the middle and largest of the three canopied portals. The sides of the building feature large Gothic traceried windows that rest on a high marble basement, but the western side is very clearly unfinished (it should have included a side aisle), money and land required for completion having been redirected by the city's suzerain (the papacy) towards construction of the new university.

Siena

Siena has a particularly fine late medieval Gothic town hall. Its Palazzo Pubblico was built between 1297 and 1310 to accommodate the city's Council of Nine, council chambers and administrative offices. The front elevation of the building is slightly concave since it wraps itself tightly around most of the southern edge of the city's central *piazza*, the Campo. The four-storey and crenellated central block of the *palazzo* was the first part of the building to be constructed. Its facade features travertine arches at ground level and a brick facade above, an arrangement that extends along most of the length of the building. The two crenellated wings of the edifice were initially two storeys in height, but a third storey of Gothic design was added to each wing in 1681. The facade is punctuated by regularly spaced three-light windows on its first and second storeys, and by two-light windows on the top storey of the central block. The eastern edge of the building is marked at ground level by an open loggia, the Capella di Piazza, built between 1352 and 1376 to celebrate the end of the Black Death, and by the Torre del Mangia above. Rising to a height of 102 metres, the tower, designed by Lippo Memmi and constructed by Agostino di Giovanni, comprises a tall brown brick shaft and a stone bell tower above.

In a city where rainfall is very unpredictable, it became a fundamental duty of medieval government to ensure an adequate water supply, not only to sustain the physical needs of the population but to maintain civic pride and patriotism. The commune thus allocated funds to construct as many as five major public

Photo 3.13 Palazzo Pubblico, Siena, 1297–1310. A very elegant Gothic town hall that, with the 102-metre-high Torre del Mangia, occupies the entire southern side of the Campo. The edifice is notable for its curved facade with its numerous triple bays and supporting arches.

fountains across the city, most notably the Fonte Branda in 1246 and the Fonte Nuova di Ovile in 1298. The former, anticipating the design of the town hall, displays three large Gothic arches set within a crenellated brick frontage, and the latter, constructed at the same time as the town hall and built to the same principles, features two fine pointed arches.

Siena, of course, is noted not only for its magnificent town hall and its sprinkling fountains but also for the magnificence of its *duomo*, S Maria Assunta. Built between 1215 and 1382, work on the massive edifice was commissioned by the commune and funded by tax revenue and loans derived from the wealth generated by the phenomenal rate of economic growth which the city enjoyed throughout much of the later Middle Ages.[25] Sited on the highest point in Siena, the front and much of the sides of the *duomo* stand on a plinth of white marble inlaid with black, reached by marble steps. The facade, of polychrome marble and adorned with ample statuary, features three enormous, richly decorated portals of equal height and size, triangular pediments above each portal (designed by Giovanni Pisano in 1284–5 and 1296–7), and a large rose window above. The sides of

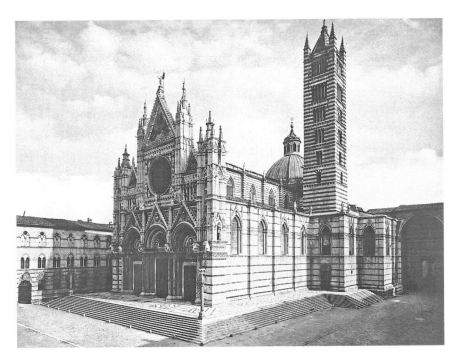

Photo 3.14 Giovanni Pisano and others, *duomo*, Siena, begun 1215. A conglomeration of Romanesque and Gothic motifs, the building is notable for its richly decorative facade (partly based on that of Orvieto cathedral), its horizontal bands of black and white marble and its tall if undistinguished Romanesque campanile.

the *duomo* exhibit white and green banding and contain two-light windows, but the similarly banded campanile, which stems from the eastern transept of the building, is pierced by windows that progress from a single opening on the lowest floor to a sixfold opening on its sixth.

However, although the *duomo* has many Gothic attributes, among which are its richly decorated facade and the artistry of Pisano, these 'are cancelled out by Romanesque features such as the domed crossing tower and, above all, by the insistent horizontal banding in polychrome marble which, according to one art historian, makes one feel "as if one were in the belly of a gigantic zebra" '.[26] A scheme to build an even larger edifice, the Duomo Nuovo, at 90 degrees to the present cathedral, was abandoned in 1348 as an outcome of the Black Death. Had it been constructed, its enormous nave would have been incorporated into the southern flank of the older cathedral turning it into a transept, and the resulting building in its entirety would undoubtedly have rivalled any large church in Italy.

As in many other cities of northern and central Italy, it was customary to build a baptistery close to the cathedral. In Siena, therefore, work began on the Battistero di S Giovanni in 1316 and was completed by 1325, in advance of work finishing on the *duomo*. Commissioned by the commune, the baptistery was built below the apse of the cathedral and was reached by a marble staircase from above. Its late-Gothic facade, added to the building in 1382, was left unfinished, albeit not in a crude form. The lower part of the marble facade, featuring three well-proportioned portals, is richly decorated with niches, crockets, pediments and elegant pillars. Above, the facade's upper storey is relatively free of ornamentation, its solid surface being relieved by three tall and narrow biforate windows.[27]

Verona

Under the Della Scala (or Scaligeri) dynasty, large numbers of civic buildings were constructed during its period in power (1260–1387). As heads of

Photo 3.15 Palazzo della Ragione, Verona, 1200s–1300s. Joined to the 84-metre-high Torre Lamberti (1172 to mid-1400s) the Romanesque *palazzo* has a courtyard surrounded by a portico on piers while its portal is reached by a fine external staircase.

communal government, the Scaligeri commissioned construction of the Palazzo della Ragione, the Palazzo del Capitano and the Palazzo della Prefettura. The Palazzo della Ragione contains a magnificent Romanesque courtyard surrounded by a portico on piers reached by an external Gothic staircase and is attached to the 12th-century Torre dei Lamberti which rises to a height of 84 metres. The Palazzo del Capitano is noted principally for its crenellated tower, while the Palazzo della Prefettura (formerly the Palazzo degli Scaligeri) is sited imposingly at one end of the Piazza dei Signori. Behind the *palazzo*, the Arche Scaligeri leads to an equestrian statute of Cangrande I ('Big Dog') and a remarkable Gothic cemetery containing the remains of the dynasty.

However, to enhance the family's security and that of Verona as a whole, Cangrande II Della Scala ('Top Dog') commissioned construction of the Castelvecchio as his home and fortress. Built between 1354 and 1375, the castle is an imposing brick fortress consisting of two main blocks and a keep, though for its defence it relied on its curtain-walling rather than on its more solid structures, all of which are crenellated. The two blocks of the building are divided

Photo 3.16 Palazzo della Prefettura, Verona, 1200s–1300s. With its machicolations, the *palazzo* was once the residence of the Scaligeri, but it subsequently housed the Venetian governors (the Palazzo del Governo) during which time (1533) Sanmicheli designed the fine classical doorway. Since the unification of Italy it has been known by its present name.

by the Ponte Scaligero which connects the Castelvecchio to the northern bank of the Adige. The bridge is also crenellated and is protected on the south bank by a drawbridge and the castle's keep, and by two successive drawbridges dividing its three unequal spans.

Photo 3.17 Castelvecchio and Ponte Scaligeri, Verona, 1354–75. Stemming from the stronghold of the Scaligeri and future rulers, the towered and battlemented Ponte Scaligeri connects the north and south banks of the River Adige.

Since Verona already boasted a large number of very fine churches, mainly Romanesque in design, the Scaligeri saw no need to increase their number, although work on the 12th-century Cathedral of S Maria Matricolare, sited in the secluded Piazza del Duomo, continued intermittently until the 20th century.

Padua

The only late medieval civic building in Padua of any note, one commissioned during its republican phase of development, is the Palazzo della Ragione. Begun in 1210, but rebuilt in 1306, the *palazzo*, located between the Piazza della Frutta and Piazza della Erbe, is a very substantial structure on two floors connected by a broad flight of stairs. Whereas the lower floor is used for commercial purposes, the upper floor or *salone* was the largest single-span room ever to have been constructed above another storey, and was used for centuries as the city's council chamber and law court. Adjacent to this building, the Municipio (constructed 1931–2) incorporates the 13th-century tower of the demolished Palazzo del Consiglio, also commissioned by the commune. Though founded by the Hohenstaufen emperor Frederick II in 1222, the Palazzo de Bò – no less a civic building than the Palazzo della Ragione – is the second oldest university in Italy after Bologna but was substantially rebuilt in the 16th century, embellished by a new facade in the 18th century and extended in 1938–9. Like Verona, the commune was disinclined to commission any further major churches in the city, Padua already being well endowed with ecclesiastical buildings, largely Romanesque in style (see pp 143–4).

The Smaller Cities of Northern and Central Italy

The development of secular buildings

The development of the built environment within the smaller cities of northern and central Italy, like that of the larger urban areas north of Rome, almost always included the construction of a town hall located on the edge of a central *piazza* with a court of law and the seat of the principal official of the city (the *podestà* and/or the *capitano del popolo*) normally in very close proximity. In addition, the city's *popolo* often commissioned its own building – the Palazzo del Popolo – while the pope sometimes resided in his own palaces in at least two cities outside of Rome. In addition there were other secular structures such as palaces, castles and *rocche* (fortresses) of the ruling *signori*.

The first small city to have its own town hall in the 13th century was Volterra with its massive stone-built Palazzo dei Priori, the oldest seat of local government in Tuscany. The palace served as a model for several town halls that followed within the region such as at S Gimignano and, more spectacularly, at Florence. Under the direction of Riccardo da Como, the four-storey crenellated town hall at Volterra was begun in 1208 and completed in 1257. It was built in the city's central square which later also accommodated the towered Palazzo Pretoria

Photo 3.18 Riccardo da Como, Palazzo dei Priori, Volterra, 1208–57. The austere *palazzo* with its battlemented tower is the oldest town hall in Italy and may have provided the model for the Palazzo Vecchio in Florence.

(1208) and the Palazzo del Podestà (1224). Unlike Volterra's town hall, the less lofty *broletto* at Mantua (1227) and Palazzo Comunale at Ferrara (1243) are brick-built, less austere and pointed the way to the development of the Palazzo del Comune in Piacenza (1280) which in representing 'the final flowering of the Lombard Arengario or Broletto' and being built of marble, red brick and terracotta and crowned by fishtail battlements, compares favourably with the all-brick Arengario at Monza built between 1250 and 1293.[28]

Whereas most of the town halls mentioned above are relatively small buildings, the Palazzo dei Priori at Perugia is probably the largest and most magnificent town hall among the smaller cities of Italy. Started in 1293 and completed in 1443, its long curving facade stretches along the Corso Vannucci to the Piazza IV Novembre. Designed by Giacomo di Servadio and Giovannello di Benvenuto, at street level the *palazzo* is punctuated by a series of arches interrupted by an elaborately decorated main portal, and an arch linking the Corso to the Via dei Priori. At first- and second-floor levels the facade is pierced by tightly spaced three-light Gothic windows and its northern end, which houses the huge Sala dei Notari, features a semi-pyramidal flight of steps leading from the Piazza

Photo 3.19 Palazzo del Comune, Piacenza, *c* 1280. One of the finest town halls in northern Italy. Built in the Lombard-Gothic style, it displays both a severe and harmonious aspect as demonstrated by its crenellation and the exclusive use of marble on the ground floor and brick on its upper storey.

IV Novembre to a Gothic portal set into the facade. The *piazza* provides an attractive stage for the proceedings of urban government. Its centre is blessed by the Fontana Maggiore, which is fed by a 5-kilometre-long aqueduct from Monte Pacciano. Built before the *palazzo* and the *sala* in 1278, as much to engender civic pride as to deter disobedience among the citizenry, the carved fountain with its two polygonal marble basins is arguably one of Italy's most attractive Romanesque monuments.

In the 14th century, two further town halls of note were constructed in the smaller cities of central Italy. Superseding Gubbio's first town hall, the 12th-century Palazzo del Bargello, the Palazzo dei Consoli (begun 1322), credited to a local architect Matteo Gattapone, is a very fine late medieval Italian civic building. The immense bulk of its three storeys required the levelling of much of the central area of the city to form the Piazza Grande and the adjoining site of the *palazzo*. Partly supported by arches and the slope of its site at

Photo 3.20   Giacomo di Servadio and Giovannello di Benvenuto, Palazzo dei Priori, Perugia, begun 1293. One of the largest and most imposing Gothic town halls in Italy, it forms with the Sala dei Notari, the Collegio di Cambio and the Collegio della Mercanzia an ensemble of considerable grandeur.

ground level, access to the building is by means of an external staircase from the *piazza* to a Gothic portal set into the facade at first-floor level and flanked on either side by two Gothic windows. Like so many other secular buildings of the period, the whole edifice, including its tower that rises to 98 metres above ground level, is crowned by crenellations. Opposite, the broadly contemporary Palazzo Pretorio (dating from 1349) was built according to the same plan as the town hall, and was similarly intended as an expression of civic power and authority.

With its origins in the late 14th century, the Palazzo Comunale in Montepulciano was among the last town halls to be built in late medieval Italy. Located in the Piazza Grande, the travertine *palazzo* was further developed in the 15th century under the direction of Michelozzo Michelotti and exhibits an unusual blend of Gothic and Early Renaissance attributes (see chapter 7). Also located in the Piazza Grande, the contemporary but less impressive Palazzo del Capitano del Popolo has been extensively rebuilt but still exhibits fine Gothic arches at street level and a bellcote on its roof.

In late medieval Italy and north of Rome the *popolo* became increasingly important as an integral part of government (see chapter 2), so that the Palazzo del Popolo, like the town hall, normally occupied a prominent site in a city's main or only *piazza*. One of the first examples of this genre in the 13th century is the Palazzo del Popolo in Todi (1213). The building features a loggia at its base, while a monumental flight of steps (built in 1267) connects the *piazza* at its base to its first-floor meeting rooms. On an adjoining site, and with part of its ground-floor loggia incongruously obscured by the steps of its neighbour, the Palazzo del Capitano was constructed in the 1290s to help maintain the integrity of the *popolo*. Further buildings of the same genre include the Palazzo del Popolo at Cremona (1256), the Palazzo del Popolo at Prato incorporated into the earlier Palazzo Pretorio (1284), the Palazzo del Popolo at S Gimignano (1288) and the massive Palazzo del Capitano at Mantua (*c* 1300).

Although they were used for ecclesiastical rather than secular occupants, papal palaces had many of the attributes of their civic counterparts. The Palazzo dei

Photo 3.21 Matteo Gattapone, Palazzo dei Consoli, Gubbio, begun 1322. Overlooking the Piazza Grande, this immense and austere Gothic town hall with its crenellations and 98-metre-high campanile is one of the most impressive medieval civic buildings in Italy.

Photo 3.22 Palazzo Comunale, Montepulciano, late 1300s. A battlemented Gothic town hall with a majestic rusticated facade and tower added in the 15th century by Michelozzo to imitate the Palazzo Vecchio in Florence.

Papi in Viterbo, begun in 1266 and subsequently donated to the pope by the city's *capitano del popolo*, is a rectangular two-storey crenellated building, akin to a medieval town hall. Sited next to the city's cathedral, it is constructed mainly from dressed stone, has a wide flight of steps at one end that provides access to the main portal set into the facade, and adjoins an open loggia on its right flank – a fine and decorative Gothic building that is arguably the best element of the combined structure. In Orvieto, the contemporary Palazzo Papale – also sited next to a cathedral – is constructed of yellow tufa, and having three-storeys is a more bulky building than its counterpart in Viterbo. It features large Gothic arches at ground level and three-light windows around its first floor where its main portal is connected to the cathedral's forecourt by a solid brick balcony and an external stone staircase. As in Viterbo, the pope's residence in Orvieto is crowned with crenellations.

Since in the 14th century signorial rule increasingly usurped power from the *popolo*, and political unrest threatened civil stability, new town halls and their like were superseded by castles and sumptuous palaces as centres of urban power. Begun in 1360, and largely completed by 1365, the Castello Visconteo in Pavia

Photo 3.23 Palazzo del Popolo, Todi, begun 1213. The crenellated *palazzo* is one of the country's oldest town halls and is loosely linked to the adjoining Palazzo del Capitano at ground level by an arcade with round-headed arches and massive piers. Access to its first-floor entrance is by means of a monumental staircase from the Piazza del Popolo.

was the first major example of this trend. Built for Galeazzo II and his heir Gian Galeazzo, the building was a rectangular structure with towers at each of its four corners and a massive courtyard within. While the towers contain four storeys, the wings have only two floors. Externally, the walls and towers are plain and are pierced by regularly spaced two-light windows, but surrounding the courtyard at ground-floor level a Gothic-arched portico supports an upper storey containing a row of four-light windows along its entire length that correspond to the arches below. The northern wing of the castle and two of the corner towers were destroyed by the French in 1527 in the aftermath of the battle of Pavia two years earlier.

Begun in 1385 and funded by Nicolò II, the Castello Estense in Ferrara was a further example of this trend. Designed by the military architect Bartolino da Novara, the *castello* is a compact symmetrical block surrounded by a moat and, with extensive machicolation and crenellation, its curtain walls enclose a rectangular courtyard while towers strengthen the main part of the building at

Photo 3.24 Palazzo dei Papi, Viterbo, begun 1266. Constructed on an impressive site overlooking a green gorge, the *palazzo* is notable for its open Gothic loggia.

its corners. Other towers, at the cost of symmetry, perform defensive functions elsewhere on the site.[29]

In Mantua during the later Middle Ages it was similarly considered necessary by the ruling *signori*, the Gonzaga, to conduct the business of urban government from within the safety of their battlemented palaces: the Palazzo del Capitano from 1328 and the Castello di S Giorgio from 1395. Under the direction of the architect Bartolino, the *castello* assumed a broadly similar configuration to that of its counterpart in Ferrara, and comprised a moat, a large single block, four corner towers, a number of secondary towers and a proliferation of machicolation and crenellation.

Defensive *rocche* were a further feature of late medieval Italy's built environment. In an attempt to maintain authority in the cities of the Papal States at a time when the papacy was ensconced in Avignon, and in an endeavour to extend its authority when it eventually returned to Rome, Cardinal Albornoz was instructed in turn by Innocent VI and Urban V to order construction of *rocche* throughout much of the length of the peninsula north of Rome. In 1354, the

Photo 3.25   Castello Visconteo, Pavia, 1360–5. Only three sides of the Gothic *castello* remain after the French destruction of its northern wing in 1527, but the brick building still retains much of its machicolated grandeur.

Rocca Albornoz was consequently constructed in Viterbo, further citadels with the same name were built in Spoleto in 1359 and at Orvieto in 1364 and, further north, Albornoz oversaw construction of the Rocca Maggiore in Assisi in 1367. These and other citadels provided the bases from which the papacy sought to extend its hold over the Papal States when it returned to Rome in the early 15th century.

The development of ecclesiastical buildings

While the larger cities of northern and central Italy invariably contained major ecclesiastical buildings of Gothic design, albeit with Romanesque traces, communal and signorial governments in the smaller cities north of Rome continued to commission churches that exhibited substantial Romanesque

Photo 3.26 Bartolino da Novara, Castello Estense, Ferrara, begun 1385. Dominating the centre of Ferrara, the bulky *castello* is protected by moats, a drawbridge and four fortified gateways and, at the time of its construction, was considered a major feat of advanced military engineering.

features. Although begun as early as 1135, the cathedral at Ferrara was not completed until the 14th century and displayed a mixture of Romanesque and Gothic styles on its three-tiered marble facade above and beside its 12th-century carved central portal. In Cremona, the *duomo*, originating in 1107 as a splendid Romanesque basilica, was not completed until the mid-14th century, by which time it was exhibiting many Gothic features. The fine west front incorporates a 13th-century Gothic tabernacle above the main door and a rose window of 1274, and further Gothic features evident in the north transept (1288) and south transept (1342) convert the basilican plan of the *duomo* into a Latin cross. The *duomo* is also blessed with one of the tallest medieval towers in Europe, the 112 metre (350 ft) tall Torrazzo, and stands adjacent to an octagonal baptistery dating from 1167.

At Parma, situated next to the 11th-century *duomo*, the baptistery successfully bridges the gap between Romanesque and Gothic design. Started in 1197, and

Photo 3.27 Castello di S Giorgio, Mantua, begun 1395. An austere brick edifice, machicolated and crenellated, its quadrangle is reinforced by massive defensive towers in each of its corners.

inspired by its counterpart in Cremona, this magnificent five-storey octagonal building designed by Benedetto Antelami is mainly of red Verona marble, its ground floor containing three doorways surrounded by carvings of biblical scenes, with five delicate galleries with short columns above.

Further south, the *duomo* of Spoleto is a much restored Romanesque church with a 12th-century campanile. Consecrated in 1198, its elegant facade is embellished by eight rose windows installed in 1207 and by a Renaissance portico dating from 1491. Relatively nearby, Orvieto cathedral is one of the most impressive buildings to have been constructed anywhere in Italy during the Middle Ages, but its initial architect – reputed to have been Arnolfo di Cambio – failed to design anything other than a Romanesque building. Funded mainly by the commune, work on the cathedral started in 1290 and Romanesque features gave way to Gothic elements with the appointment of a succession of new architects from 1310 to 1359, namely Lorenzo and Vitale Maitani, Niccolò and Meo Nuti, Andrea and Nino Pisano, Andrea di Cecco da Siena and Andrea Orcagna. Rising above a plinth of seven red and white steps, the enormous facade of the

Photo 3.28 *Duomo*, Cremona, completed mainly in the mid-1300s. Notable for its magnificent west facade, a mixture of Romanesque, Gothic and classical styles.

cathedral covers the west end of the building and incorporates a great rounded central portal flanked by smaller rounded portals to left and right. The decorative richness of the facade is displayed within its three sections, demarcated by four enormous fluted and pinnacled piers that stem from richly decorated pilasters. Sculptures, bas-reliefs and an almost excessive use of colour highlight the Gothic detail. The two side walls of the building exhibit alternate bands of grey basalt and white travertine and are pierced by ornate Gothic windows. Not finished until the end of the 16th century, work on the cathedral might not even have begun had not Pope Urban VI specifically ordered that it be built. The cathedral was intended to commemorate the 'Miracle of Bolsena' which the papacy believed had taken place in 1263 and confirmed the fact of transubstantiation.

In Tuscany, by contrast, the *duomo* of S Zeno and S Jacopo at Pistoia exhibits an imposing blend of Pisan Romanesque and Florentine Proto-Renaissance architecture. Dating from the late 12th century, the upper section of the cathedral is composed of dwarf galleries capped by striped marble decor in the Pisan tradition while, on the lower part of the facade, a colonnaded porch (added in 1311) is distinctly Florentine.

Photo 3.29 Benedetto Antelami, baptistery, Parma, 1197. Antelami's finest work, the edifice is arguably Italy's most harmonious monument.

In 1396, and using money raised by public subscription rather than from tax revenue and loans, work was commissioned by the Visconti on the construction of the Cathedral of S Maria Maggiore at Como. Anticipating architectural developments of the 15th century and designed initially by Lorenzo degli Spazzi, the cathedral was built mainly of marble and is arguably the first major example of Gothic–Renaissance fusion in Italy. While its rose windows, pinnacles and gargoyles are unmistakably Gothic, its delicately rounded arches are Early Renaissance in style.

Southern Italy and Sicily

Unlike architecture in northern and central Italy, the design of the more notable buildings of southern Italy – and particularly of those in Naples, its largest city – was largely influenced by the taste of the Angevin monarchs. Constructed between 1279 and 1292, the royal residence of the massive Castel Nuovo in Naples was built for Charles I by Pierre de Chaulnes,

Photo 3.30 Arnolfo di Cambio and others, Orvieto Cathedral, begun 1290. With its rich polychrome facade, the *duomo* is arguably the greatest and richest medieval monument in Italy.

Photo 3.31 *Duomo*, Pistoia, completed soon after 1311. The facade displays a pleasing mixture of Pisan and Florentine Romanesque motifs.

Photo 3.32 Lorenzo degli Spazzi, cathedral of S Maria Maggiore, Como, begun 1396. With rounded Renaissance portal and Gothic motifs harmoniously adorning its facade, the cathedral provides ample demonstration of how two consecutive styles of architecture can be successfully merged.

with Charles subsequently commissioning work on the city's new Gothic cathedral, S Gennaro (begun in 1294 and completed under Robert the Wise in 1323). Under the patronage of successive monarchs, a host of other Gothic churches were erected in Naples in the late 13th and early 14th centuries, among them S Lorenzo Maggiore and S Chiari (both Franciscan foundations), S Domenico Maggiore (a Dominican church) and S Maria Donnaregina.

In Sicily most medieval buildings of architectural and historical interest predate the later Middle Ages, but even in the 13th and 14th centuries they were essentially Romanesque in character rather than Gothic. This was certainly the case with the Palazzo Steri in Palermo, the second largest of the city's palaces after the Palazzo dei Normanni. Begun in 1307, the Norman building was commissioned by the Chiaramonte family, and from the late 13th century served as the palace of the Spanish viceroys. The late-13th- to early-14th-century church of S Agostino in Palermo has a spectacular facade, a latticework rose window and an unusually tall side portal adorned with lava mosaic designed by Domenico Gagini.

Town Planning

Following the construction of city walls in the late 12th and early 13th centuries, and during the subsequent hundred years preceding the advent of the Black Death when urban populations and urban densities were spiralling, communal government increasingly introduced measures to mitigate the problems associated with deficiencies in hygiene, security and circulation. In his vivid description of the physical environment of the cities of late medival Italy, Trevor Dean examines how in order to enhance public health governments secured an adequate water supply for domestic use and drain-cleaning, issued laws against water-, air- and noise pollution, and restricted the location of noxious industries such as butchering and tanning. To increase public safety, governments set the minimum width for streets, prohibited structures that obliterated light and forbade the

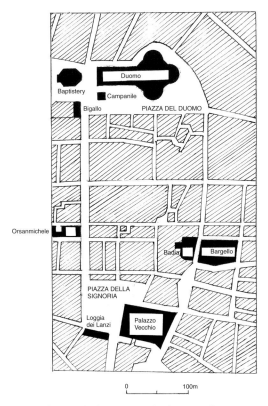

Figure 3.2 The planning of central Florence in the fourteenth century

obstruction of public roadways; and to aid circulation – and often using powers of compulsory purchase – carried out works to straighten, widen and pave streets to facilitate access to markets, fountains and key secular and ecclesiastical buildings, as well as enacting legislation to control horse-drawn traffic.[30] Town planning, dormant since the 5th century, thus re-emerged in central and northern Italy in the later Middle Ages and many of the attributes of urbanism not witnessed since the end of Roman civilisation – such as grid-iron street patterns, squares and prominent civic buildings – were superimposed on many of the haphazardly developed and run-down cities of the early and central Middle Ages. The transition of power from feudal to communal government in the 12th and 13th centuries was thus increasingly marked by the introduction of programmes of coordinated urban improvement.

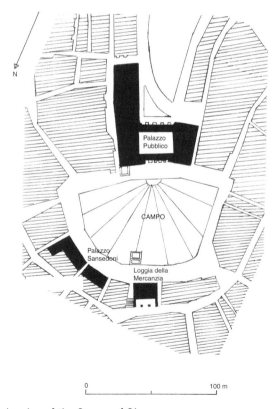

Figure 3.3 The planning of the Campo of Siena

In Florence, the cathedral and baptistery were linked to the grain market (the Orsanmichele) and town hall (the Palazzo dei Priori) by a new street, the Via dei Calzaioli, driven through an area of high-density commercial and residential development in 1294 (fig 3.2), and soon after (*c* 1298) the celebrated fan-shaped Campo of Siena was laid out as a forecourt on a slope facing the city's Palazzo Pubblico and its Torre del Mangia, still incomplete at the end of the 13th century (fig 3.3).

Where practicable, town planning made use of earlier Roman layouts, for example the oval form of the Roman amphitheatre in Lucca became elegantly preserved as the Piazza dell' Antifeatro, while in Verona not only is the Roman amphitheatre still the largest building in the city, but the Roman grid-iron pattern of the city's streets is still apparent and the main marketplace, the medieval Piazza delle Erbe, occupies the site of the Forum.

Conclusion

Throughout the 13th and 14th centuries, French Gothic architecture fused with the Italian Romanesque tradition to produce a plethora of prominent churches and secular buildings throughout much of northern and central Italy. During this period, a spate of publicly commissioned building projects was undertaken, aimed primarily at consolidating the power of communal government. However, during the first half of the 14th century, attempts were made for the first time since antiquity to improve the appearance of the city as a whole, not only through the construction of higher-quality buildings but also through the implementation of town planning schemes whereby a certain visual order would be imposed on development after many centuries of unregulated growth. But by the beginning of the 15th century, Gothic architecture had run its course in most of Italy and the stage was being set for the re-introduction of Roman Classicism, a style that in its purest form had been dormant for a thousand years.

Notes

1   P Nuttgens with R Weston, *The Complete Handbook of Architecture, From the First Civilizations to the Present Day* (London: Mitchell Beazley, 2006), p 97.
2   C Perogalli, 'The rise of the Milanese tradition: architectural culture and technical culture in the early medieval and Romanesque periods', in *Milano. Architectural Guide* (Turin: Umberto Allemandi, 1999), p 37.

3   J White, *Art and Architecture in Italy, 1250–1400* (New Haven and London: Yale University Press, 1993), p 539.

4   D Howard, *The Architectural History of Venice* (New Haven and London: Yale University Press, 2002), pp 95–6.

5   Ibid.

6   D Mentzel, *A Traveller's History of Venice* (Gloucester: Chastleston Travel, 2006), p 89.

7   E Poleggi, 'The medieval walled city', in *Genoa. Architectural Guide* (Turin: Umberto Allemandi, 1998), p 26.

8   Ibid, p 28.

9   White, *Art and Architecture in Italy*, p 69.

10 Ibid.

11 Perogalli, 'Rise of the Milanese Tradition', p 37.

12 White, *Art and Architecture in Italy*, p 259.

13 A Castellano, 'The development of civic building and the new image of the city in a European context', in *Milan. Architectural Guide* (Turin: Umberto Allemandi, 1999), p 43.

14 Ibid.

15 Ibid.

16 M Hollingsworth, *Patronage in Renaissance Italy* (London: John Murray, 1994), p 17.

17 G Zucconi, *Florence. An architectural guide* (Venice: Arsenale Editrice, 1995), p 42.

18 Ibid.

19 D Watkin, *A History of Western Architecture* (London: Laurence King, 3rd edn 2000), p 199.

20 Ibid, pp 106–7.

21 Ibid.

22 White, *Art and Architecture in Italy*, p 534.

23 D Friedman, 'Monumental urban form in the late medieval Italian commune: loggias and the Mercanzie of Bologna and Siena', *Renaissance Studies* 12 (3) (1998), p 328.

24 Ibid.

25 White, *Art and Architecture in Italy*, p 45.

26 Watkin, *History of Western Architecture*, p 196.

27 AM Von der Haegen and R Strasser, *Tuscany* (Cologne: Könemann, 2001), p 376.

28 White, *Art and Architecture in Italy*, p 63.

29 Ibid.

30 Ibid, p 513.

CHAPTER 4

ECONOMIC DEVELOPMENT IN THE LATER MIDDLE AGES

Introduction

The unprecedented growth in the urban population of northern and central Italy during the 13th and early 14th centuries not only increased the dependence of towns and cities on the rural economy but was also associated with the substantial development of long-distance trade which benefited the many urban areas located along the main trading routes between the Mediterranean and northern Europe. However, population and economic growth in Italy (as elsewhere in much of Europe) came to a halt between 1348 and 1349 when the Black Death not only decimated the total population of the peninsula by a third but also substantially reduced the urban workforce, markets, money supply and – in aggregate – the ability to generate wealth. However, the downturn in economic activity was short-lived. Many cities that may previously have been overpopulated now had populations closer to the optimum, whereby per capita output, income and expenditure rose to higher levels than before the plague. It is within this unstable economic context that, from time to time, private patrons commissioned a wide range of prominent secular and ecclesiastical buildings across much of northern and central Italy in this period.

Demographic Determinants of Economic Development

The population of Italy and her larger cities during the later Middle Ages can only be approximated. Quite possibly, the population of the peninsula increased from 7,300,000 in 1150 to about 11,000,000 in 1300,[1] a result of increased fertility due to the earlier age at which women married, rather than to a decline in mortality.[2] However, in the early 14th century, mortality rates increased as a consequence of poor harvests and famine, and at mid-century mortality peaked during the Black Death. As Denis Hay and John Law suggest, 'this trend is, as far as one can judge, parallel to similar movements in Europe at large and the sharp decline in the fourteenth century begins, in Italy as everywhere else, before the Black Death of 1348'.[3] During the latter half of the century, mortality rates remained high because of recurrent plague epidemics, and as an outcome of a hundred years of demographic disaster the population of Italy fell to about 8,000,000 in 1400.

Around 1340 the largest cities in Italy, with populations of some 100,000, were Venice, Milan and Florence; together with Paris, these constituted the four greatest cities of late medieval Europe. At the next level, with more than 50,000 inhabitants, were Genoa, Bologna, Siena, Naples and Palermo – cities of approximately the same size as Ghent, Bruges and Cologne. At the level of between 20,000 and 50,000 were Verona, Padua and Pisa and a large number of secondary cities in the peninsula, all of them about the same size as London, Bordeaux, Toulouse, Montpellier, Marseilles, Lyons, Barcelona, Seville, Toledo and the Hanseatic trading cities of the empire.[4] As with most of the other large urban areas of Europe at the beginning of the 21st century, the major Italian cities of today were already important settlements in the late Middle Ages.[5] Research by Daniel Waley suggests that in northern and central Italy, the most densely populated part of the peninsula, as many as 23 cities had each attained a population of over 20,000 by the end of the 13th century, and that this distribution remained broadly unchanged throughout the Renaissance and its aftermath.[6] In most of these cities, population growth did not recommence until the 19th century. However, if a city is defined as a settlement of at least 10,000, the number of such cities would be around 50, and even settlements with populations of as few as 5,000 to 10,000, of which there were many, enjoyed municipal independence.[7]

Clearly, population growth and economic development are inextricably linked, both in respect of the expansion of local trade and the exploitation of more distant import and export markets. An increase in urban population will normally add to its workforce, while a larger population will represent a larger local market. If the basic/non-basic theory and Keynesian macroeconomics (as outlined in chapter 1) are valid, it can be expected that both an initial increase in population and a hike in monetary injections into the local economy will raise both the population and the income of the urban area at a multiple rate. Also, one may assume that in the later Middle Ages, the Boudeville filtering-down theory (or even the 'no impact' hypothesis) helped ensure that a large number of cities in north and central Italy simultaneously enjoyed a high rate of economic growth, regardless of size (see chapter 1).

Urban–Rural Interdependency

In the later Middle Ages, the majority of cities in Italy were primarily market centres for locally produced commodities. To a very great extent, cities were dependent on their *contadi* for their basic food supply and raw materials, while the *contadi* relied upon the cities for the provision of manufactured goods and services such as banking. Larger cities such as Venice, Milan and Florence were exceptional in having to look further afield for their basic commodities, and it was essential for their economic prosperity that they were located favourably in relation to roads and waterways. The central place theory (see chapter 1) offers an explanation for the spatial distribution of cities across parts of northern and central Italy, not only in relation to local trade, but also in connection with long-distance trade which was superimposed on trade in locally produced commodities, not least in connection with the growth of the textile and metal industries, and the provision of commercial banking services in the 13th century.[8] However, Waley cautiously suggests that it is very difficult to generalise about the relationship between economic growth and population growth during the 12th and 13th centuries, since most cities – at least in northern and central Italy – experienced considerable political and economic change in the later Middle Ages.[9]

By 1250, or even earlier, labour, capital and enterprise (ie the mobile factors of production) were concentrated in the cities of Italy to an unprecedented degree in both the ancient or medieval world.[10] However, although urban economic growth was exponential, it was feared that it would not keep pace with the increase in the urban population and therefore by the end of the 13th century several cities sought to limit immigration from the countryside in an intuitive attempt to establish an 'optimum population' – that is, one in which output per head would be at its greatest.[11]

City governments, however, did not share a common approach towards immigration from the *contadi*, normally basing policy on what was perceived to be in the interest of the governing class. Moreover, policy was often changed over time according to short-term economic considerations: for example, in Bologna rural workers were attracted into the city in the 1230s to work in the textile industry, but – like present-day 'guest workers' – were encouraged to return to their *contadi* at times of economic downturn and famine in 1246 and 1259 when, in the latter year, as Waley describes, 'an attempt was made to expel all the city's poor as "unproductive"'.[12] Yet within a few years (ie by 1274) large-scale political expulsions from Bologna (numbering around 12,000) almost certainly reduced the city's population below its optimal level, and soon prompted measures to reverse this flow to remedy the shortage of labour in the city's industries[13] – a policy that undoubtedly drove up total output and probably also drove up output per capita.

Waley explains how the government of Bologna again involved itself in matters of migration by attempting, for strategic and agricultural reasons, to concentrate some of the city's 'surplus' population in new *borghi* being established within its region (an early example of a new town solution to urban congestion). Initially, grants of fiscal exemption were awarded to encourage employment within these new settlements, but when financial inducements were superseded by taxation (for example in Castelfranco in 1295) their population migrated away to neighbouring Modena. Elsewhere, cities either transferred some of their population to important fortified settlements *castre* or encouraged a flow of migrants back from vulnerable or abandoned *castre*, for example from Castel Imolese to Imola in 1210. Similarly, for both economic and strategic reasons, Parma destroyed 42 *castre* within its region in the late 13th century and prohibited their further occupation.[14]

Waley proposes that quite a high proportion of the population of most cities in Italy in the late 13th century would have been immigrants or descendants of recent immigrants. It has been estimated that in Pisa at this time, over half of the city's population were immigrants from its *contado*, many of whom would have been relatively wealthy – raising the level of demand for the city's goods and services.[15] As Christopher Duggan suggests, the influx of peasants also benefited the urban economy since it not only increased the size of the workforce but led specifically to the growth of artisanal industries, trade and money-changing.[16]

Long-distance Trade and Urban Development

From the beginning of the 2nd millennium, a 'commercial revolution' had been underway whereby merchants from Venice, Genoa, Milan and Florence and a host of other cities exploited opportunities for trade between 'northern Europe, where markets for luxury goods opened up . . . and the older markets in the Levant, where many of those goods were to be found'.[17] As Richard Goldthwaite points out, many north Italian cities were ideally situated midway between these market areas, and therefore their merchants developed trading links, gained expertise and generated profits in their role as traders and shippers.[18] Throughout the urban areas of northern Italy, entrepreneurs thus tapped sources of capital and set off across extensive trading hinterlands to develop and exploit markets, and by 1300 had firmly established capitalism in northern and central Italy and laid the foundations of an interdependent economy stretching from England and northern Germany to Byzantium and Egypt.

Venice and Genoa as trading rivals

The origins of Venetian trade with the Dalmatian coast date back to the 10th century or earlier; indeed, such trade was well established by the time the basilica of St Mark's was consecrated in 1094 and Venice adopted the symbolic ceremony of marriage with the sea.[19] In the 12th century, as Waley points out, there were possibly as many as 10,000 Venetian merchants and representatives in the trading colony at Constantinople. However, as a result of its involvement in the Fourth Crusade (1202–3), under the leadership of doge Enrico Dandolo and in the wake of seizing the ports of Zara and Durazzo and the island of Corfu, Venetian forces sacked and occupied the whole of Constantinople. The Serene Republic consequently annexed a 'Quarter and half Quarter' of the Byzantine Empire, including the coastline of the Peloponnese, numerous small islands in the Aegean, and Crete. The Venetians were eventually driven out of the region when a new emperor, Michael VIII Paleologos, re-established Byzantine rule in 1261, but not before they had enjoyed half a century or more as the pre-eminent Italian maritime power, whose trading expeditions left 'every year for Constantinople, Beirut and Alexandria . . . organised by the state, which also supervised the depositing of goods in the warehouses and the distribution of imported goods'.[20]

Although Genoa, Venice's principal maritime rival, reluctantly relinquished its power in the eastern Mediterranean during the early 13th century in the face of Venetian hegemony in the area, in the latter part of the century Genoa made increasingly forceful attempts to regain its former trading connections in the east. Thus, the first of a succession of wars between Venice and Genoa broke out in 1257 in which, as a result of a naval battle, the victorious Venetians expelled the Genoese from their colony in Acre. Naval engagements between the two belligerents continued until 1270 when the parties signed what was an inconclusive peace treaty.

The Development of Banking in Late Medieval Italy

Industrial activity, involving the import of raw materials and semi-finished goods on the one hand and the export of manufactured goods on the other, stimulated the commercial sector by injecting into the economy capital derived from international trade. Florentine merchants and bankers, like their counterparts in other Italian cities such as Venice and Genoa, set up businesses in market centres across Europe. Since the Florentines were often the most important group of merchants in the leading market centres of the continent, '[t]heir gold florin, first issued in 1252, became a standard international currency for all of Europe'.[21] Family businesses such as those of the Bardi, Peruzzi and Frescobaldi became pre-eminent in international banking in the Middle Ages by dint of their ability to foster commercial networks for the execution of foreign exchange and the international transfer of credit. As a consequence of highly integrated industrial and banking activity, Florence undoubtedly became one of medieval Europe's most prosperous cities.

The papacy was also a major player in the the international finance market. Without its credit transfer requirements that ranged across the breadth of Christendom it is unlikely that Tuscan banking would have developed at the pace it had achieved by the 14th century. More so than any others, Florentine bankers profited from the accumulating wealth of the papacy in its temporal role in the later Middle Ages. In the 14th century they benefited substantially from their financial involvement in the papacy's efforts to retain a hold on its international network of ecclesiastical finances while at Avignon. The strongest Florentine bank operating from Avignon, that of the Alberti, not only established control over papal finances throughout Europe, but also secured its position in the papal network so firmly that 'it was able to survive the break in diplomatic relations between the papacy and Florence occasioned by the War of the Eight Saints (1375–8)'.[22] Florentine banks were also involved in the financial activities of the papacy's sumptuous court, set up after it returned to Rome in 1417, and in the subsequent consolidation of the Papal States in central Italy.

It is thus remarkable that, despite its great wealth, the papacy played only a very minor role in commissioning buildings in Rome during the later Middle Ages, even though its interests were wholly confined to the ecclesiastical sector. Perhaps the papacy believed that its existing stock of early Christian and Romanesque churches was sufficient to meet its spiritual role, but it is likely that it preferred to prioritise its temporal aims, by indulging in a costly conflict with the empire that lasted until the 1260s. To fill the architectural vacuum in the papal capital, the Franciscans rebuilt the early medieval church of S Maria in Aracoeli (beginning in 1250), while the Dominicans commissioned the church of S Maria Sopra Minerva (in 1280). Not until the 15th century and its re-establishment in the Eternal City did the papacy begin to leave its mark on the built environment of Rome and the Papal State.

In contrast to Rome, and on a scale unprecedented elsewhere in Europe, the economic development of Florence throughout the later Middle ages generated the construction of a vast number of secular and ecclesiastical buildings, initially in the Romanesque style and later Gothic in design. Until around the mid-13th century, and motivated by a desire to display their wealth, newly enriched merchants tended to commission tower houses in the fashion adopted by the *consorterie* of an earlier age. Examples of this form of development include the Romanesque tower houses of the Vendove (or the Giberti), of the Corbizi (or Donati), the Marsili, the Amidei and the Alberti. However, by the late 13th century the merchant class could afford to commission palaces rather than tower houses, and this resulted in the construction of such Romanesque buildings as the Palazzo de'Mozzi (1260–73), Palazzo Ferroni (1289) and Palazzo Gianfigliazzi (1290).

Although the Badia Fiorentina (the Abbey of Florence) dates from the early Romanesque period (it was founded by the Benedictines in the 10th century), it was substantially renovated in the late 13th century in the Cistercian Gothic style. While the Benedictines could draw on funds derived from their rural estates across Europe, the Dominicans and Franciscans could draw upon alms collected from an increasingly prosperous Florentine merchant class for the construction of such buildings as the Dominican church of S Maria Novella (started 1246) and the Franciscan church of S Croce (begun 1294).

As a centre of banking, Venice attempted to catch up. Although the republic's silver *grosso*, introduced around 1200, was soon in circulation around the eastern Mediterranean in the wake of the Fourth Crusade, Doge Giovanni Dandolo (1280–9) subsequently introduced the gold Venetian ducat in 1284 to compete with the Florentine florin. After its value, in relation to silver, was fixed in the mid-14th century, the ducat became the most trusted gold coin in the eastern Mediterranean, remaining in use until the demise of the republic in 1797. A larger banking sector became associated with the further development of private palaces, the residences of a growing class of financiers and merchants. To satisfy the demand for more sumptuous buildings, a further generation of palaces was constructed along the Grand Canal and elsewhere, such as the Byzantine *palazzi* Vitturi and Moro, and the Gothic *palazzi* Soranzo at San Polo, Sagredo at Santa Sofia and the Arian Cicogna, although the latter style only achieved its most splendid manifestation in the 15th century (see chapter 7).

Elsewhere, in northern and central Italy there was a large number of other cities whose economic growth during the later Middle Ages facilitated construction of secular and ecclesiastical buildings. In Bologna, notwithstanding the large amount of fairly uniform private secular development that occurred in the 13th and 14th centuries, a great deal of newly accumulated wealth found its way, via the Franciscan and Dominican Orders, into the construction of the churches of S Francesco (started 1236) and Domenico (begun 1251). As in Bologna, privately funded building work in Verona was confined largely to the ecclesiastical sector. The Benedictines commissioned the churches of S Fermo Maggiore (part of which was built in the 14th century) and S Zeno Maggiore (started in the 12th century, but completed in the 13th and 14th centuries), and the Dominicans funded construction of the church of S Anastasia between 1291 and 1323. In contrast to both Bologna and Verona, in Siena private funds were injected into the development of a large number of secular palaces such as the Palazzo Tolomei (started 1208), the Palazzo Salimbeni (begun in the late 13th century), the Palazzo Sansedoni (1339) and the 14th-century Palazzo Buonsignori and Palazzo Chigi Saracini. However, Siena also witnessed the construction of the churches of S Domenico (1226) and S Francesco (1326), funded mainly from alms.

In the smaller cities of northern and central Italy, very few secular buildings of any architectural or historical interest were funded from private capital, the Torre and Case Guinigi (1300–50) in Lucca being a notable exception. Instead, private funds found their way overwhelmingly into ecclesiastical buildings commissioned mainly, but not exclusively, by the Franciscans and Dominicans. With money derived mainly from alms, the Franciscans built churches in Assisi, Padua, Cortona, Modena, Gubbio, Piacenza and Todi, while the Dominicans added to their stock by building churches in Orvieto and Perugia. As if to compete geographically, they each funded church-building in Vicenza, Pisa and Arezzo. Other religious orders such as the Augustinians also commisioned new churches, for example the Eremitani in Padua, while in the same city Enrico Scrovegni financed construction of the Scrovegni Chapel as the final resting place for his father.

The Black Death and its Demographic and Economic Consequences

Italy and much of the rest of Europe suffered a succession of severe epidemics throughout the 14th century, of which the Black Death was one of a series that recurred from time to time across the continent. Research by David Hackett

Fischer shows that, for example, in the Tuscan city of Pistoia the first plague broke out in 1339, and although it was not the Black Death but another pestilence, it 'probably killed a quarter of Pistoia's population in the city itself and the surrounding countryside'.[23] The city experienced further epidemics in mid-century, most notably the Black Death of 1347–9, 'the most devastating [outbreak] reducing the population by about a third'.[24]

The Black Death probably originated in Central Asia. From the Genoese trading colony of Caffa (now Feodosiÿa) in the Crimea, the plague was brought to Italy by the infected crews of Genoese trading ships that arrived in the port of Messina in Sicily in October 1347. By January 1348, the Black Death had reached Sardinia, Genoa and Venice. Although a few cities such as Milan escaped the epidemic, most were seriously affected, the plague killing anywhere between one- and two-thirds of their inhabitants. Italy, then with a total population of between 10 and 11 million, probably suffered the heaviest toll in Europe, Hackett Fischer commenting that the plague had 'found a vulnerable population [in the peninsula] that had outstripped the means of its subsistence and was already beginning to decline'.[25] It has been estimated by many historians that Europe lost up to 40 per cent of its total inhabitants. Taking into account births as well as deaths, it is probable that the total population plummeted 'from approximately 80 million at its peak in the early fourteenth century to 60 million or less after the Black Death, the largest decline in the cruel history of that continent'.[26]

Barbara Tuchman provides dramatic illustration from contemporary documentary evidence of how the Black Death impacted on day-to-day life in Italy; for example, a Franciscan friar of Piazza in Sicily reported that 'Magistrates and notaries refused to come and make wills of the dying [and what was worse] even the priests did not come to hear their confessions'.[27] She also notes that Boccaccio, in referring to the plague in Florence, vividly remarks in his introduction to the *Decameron* that 'One man shunned another ... kinsfolk held aloof, brother was forsaken by brother, oftentimes husbands by wifes; nay, what is more, and scarcely to be believed, fathers and mothers were found to abandon their own children to their fate, untended, unvisited as if they had been strangers'.[28] Tuchman describes how even prominent figures of the Early Renaissance fell victim to the Black Death, among them the brothers Ambrogio and Pietro Lorenzetti, master painters of Siena; Andrea Pisano, architect and sculptor of Florence; and the Florentine Giovanni Villani, the foremost historian of the day.[29] Once the Black Death had subsided, other epidemics recurred intermittently; as Hackett Fischer notes, in long-suffering Pistoia disease was endemic in 1357 and 1389, when 'bubonic plague came back and destroyed half the city's inhabitants in one final visitation'.[30]

The Crisis of the Late 14th Century

In true cyclical fashion, by the mid-14th century and like that of the rest of western Europe, the economy of Italy was in deep disorder.[31] Successive bouts of cold and wet weather had not only raised food prices dramatically but had brought in train famine and epidemics on a major scale across much of the continent. While some of the rich tended to grow richer, including the French popes who lived in luxury in Avignon, a large proportion of the population 'was so debilitated by hunger, disease, exploitation, war and disorder that a few years later it succumbed to a still greater catastrophe [the Black Death] that decimated up to 40 per cent of the population of Europe between 1348 and the early 1350s'.[32]

The price of food soared during the epidemic years of the 1350s but, with the decrease in the number of mouths to feed, fell rapidly thereafter. The decline in population also meant that 'houses and estates fell empty; and rents and land values declined roughly in proportion to the loss of population'.[33] Building activity came to a virtual halt, particularly in Siena where, because of the city's catastrophic population loss, work on its enormous cathedral was suspended, the building remaining unfinished to the present day.

Historians recognise that the full impact of the plague upon the Italian economy is difficult to assess. It is possible that with 11 million inhabitants in the early 14th century, Italy might have been overpopulated (ie given that its resources, output of goods and services per capita might have been comparatively modest), but when the number of inhabitants had fallen to around 8 million at the close of the century, the country's population might have approached its optimum level for the later Middle Ages (ie where, all things being equal, output per head is at its highest). Similarly, the population of many cities might have exceeded optimum levels before the Black Death, but became optimal after the plague had subsided. For families surviving the Black Death there were, according to Christopher Black, clearly more 'opportunities for land ownership or control, for job opportunities and prosperity'.[34]

Florence, in particular, proved very resilient. Although its population plummeted from a peak of around 100,000 in 1340 to about 30,000 during the Black Death, it then rose steadily to between 40,000 and 50,000 by the 15th century. And whereas death rates were high and birth rates low because of later marriages after the Black Death, Florence nevertheless remained one of the most dynamic cities in Europe; for generations it had attracted 'young, able and ambitious people from the surrounding countryside' a factor that in large measure kept population levels intact.[35] Construction activity, too, soon recovered. In 1350, the Davizzi family commissioned the Palazzo Davanzati, in 1352 the Confraternità della Misericordia (a charitable order) funded construction of the Loggia Bigallo, and in 1359 the Florentine Mercanzia resourced the building of the Palazzo della Mercanzia – all indications that the economy of Florence had quickly recovered from the ravages of the Black Death. Possibly, if to a lesser extent, this was also true of many other cities in Italy towards the close of the later Middle Ages.

It was, perhaps, the revival of economic activity across late-14th-century Europe that guaranteed the renewed success of the Florentine economy. The city's industrial and commercial sectors benefited from an increase in the demand for banking services and luxury goods of all kinds, particularly cloth. The luxury goods market expanded since wealth was more concentrated among those who had survived the demographic disaster and who, arguably, increased their propensity to consume as a reaction to the psychological shock they had suffered. Similarly, demand 'was generated by new needs and taste arising out of the consolidation of power by a number of princes all across Europe that resulted in the elaboration of bureaucratic government, the building-up of the military complement of power, and the growth of the sedentary court with its highly ceremonial lifestyle'.[36] Demand of this sort was particularly evident in Italy, where the precarious political situation of an earlier era evolved 'into a more stable multi-state system, for the most part in the hands of princes of one kind or another... [who] sought to consolidate their position and establish their legitimacy by engaging in the kind of consumption we associate with the splendor of the Italian Renaissance'.[37]

Urban courts in Italy and elsewhere in Europe fuelled demand both for banking services and luxury goods, and thus encouraged cities such as Florence to re-equip their industries for the production of such goods as could be conspicuously consumed, and to improve their banking services to facilitate investment in government projects. 'The zeal with which they went about this is evidenced by their appearance whenever business opportunities opened up – and by their success in dominating whatever market they operated in'.[38]

Throughout much of the 14th century, the Florentine economy also benefited from improvements in transportation, essential for the expansion of trade. Unlike its major competitors, Genoa and Venice, inland Florence – without a port and without a fleet – had little choice but to develop its commerce and industries. It could not depend on Pisa, its old adversary, and thus had to rely on Genoese shipping using other Tuscan ports, while eastwards trade often depended on Venetian shipping using Ancona.

Conclusion

The dramatic increase in urban population in Italy throughout the later Middle Ages was accompanied by unprecedented economic growth and wealth-generation. Apart from directly fuelling the development of private *palazzi*, the profits derived from long-distance trade and the development of industry and banking were often injected indirectly into the construction of ecclesiastical buildings by means of donations to the mendicant orders. While the Black Death of 1347–9 brought about a cessation in construction, soon after economic recovery brought with it yet again a spate of building activity – both in the secular and ecclesiastical sectors – to the benefit of the built environment.

Chronology

1100–1300	In Genoa, the Palazzata della Ripa, Palazzo Maruffi and Embriaci Tower funded by proceeds of long-distance trade.
1125	In Genoa, Martino Doria commissions church of S Matteo.
1150–1200	In Venice, Ca' Loredan and Ca' Farsetti constructed along Grand Canal.
1150	Population of Italy numbers some 7.3 million.
1154	Guilds of merchants established in Piacenza.
1159	Guilds of merchants formed in Milan.
1182	Guilds of merchants formed in Florence.
1200–1400	Despite intermittent wars, Venice and Genoa benefit substantially from expansion of trade, industrial development and banking.
1200–50	In Venice, the Ca' Pesaro (known as the Fondaco dei Turchi since the 17th century), the Ca' Donà della Madonnetta, the Ca' da Mosto and many other *palazzi* funded from proceeds of long-distance trade. Venetian Republic introduces silver *grosso*; it soon circulates around the eastern Mediterranean.
1202–3	Fourth Crusade brings sack and occupation of Constantinople. Venetian involvement enables Serene Republic to annex a 'Quarter and half Quarter' of Byzantine Empire.
1208	In Siena, work starts on Palazzo Tolomei.
1221	In Milan, Cistercian Abbey of Chiaravalle is considered.
1226	In Siena, Dominicans commission church of S Domenico.
1228–1350	Franciscans commission churches in Assisi, Padua, Cortona, Modena, Gubbio, Piacenza and Todi. Dominicans commission churches in Orvieto and Perugia. Both orders commission churches in Vicenza, Pisa and Arezzo.
1230s	Rural workers attracted into Bologna to work in the textile industry.

1234	In Venice, Franciscans commission church of SS Giovanni e Paolo.
1236	In Bologna, Franciscans commission church of S Francesco.
1246	In Florence, Dominicans commission church of S Maria Novella.
	Labour, capital and enterprise concentrated in Italian cities to an unprecedented degree in the ancient or medieval world.
1250	In Rome, Franciscans commission church of S Maria in Aracoeli.
1251	In Bologna, Dominicans commission church of S Domenico.
1252	Florence introduces gold florin. It soon becomes a standard currency throughout Europe.
	The Bardi, Peruzzi and Frescobaldi families of Florence rise to pre-eminence in international banking.
1257	Venetians expel Genoese from their trading colony in Acre, which Genoa subsequently loses.
1260	In Genoa, Augustinians commission church of S Agostino.
	In Florence, work commences on Palazzo de'Mozzi.
1261	A new Byzantine emperor, Michael VIII Paleologos, drives Venice out of the many areas of Byzantium it seized in 1202–3.
	Total annual value of goods passing through Genoa doubled since 1214.
1280s–1290s	High proportion of population of most Italian cities now immigrants or descendants of immigrants from their *contadi*.
1280	In Rome, Dominicans commission church of S Maria Sopra Minerva.
1284	Genoa defeats Pisa at naval battle of La Torre della Meloria.
1289	In Florence, work starts on Palazzo Feroni.
1290s	In Siena, work starts on Palazzo Salimbeni.
1290	In Florence, work begins on Palazzo Gianfigliazzi.
1291	In Verona, Dominicans commission church of S Anastasia.
1292	Total value of Genoese import and export trade amounts to 3.8 million lire, compared with only 936,000 lire in 1264.
	Republic of Venice introduces gold Venetian ducat to compete with Florentine florin.
1294	In Venice, Eremitani commission church of S Stefano.
	War breaks out between Venice and Genoa.
	In Florence, Franciscans commission church of S Croce.
1298	Genoese fleet under Lamba Doria defeats Venetian navy at the battle of Curzola.
1300	In Lucca, Guinigi family commissions the Torre and the Case Guinigi.
1300	The population of Italy rises to about 11 million. In northern and central Italy there are 23 cities with populations in excess of 20,000. Entrepreneurs have established capitalism in northern and central Italy and laid foundations of an interdependent economy stretching from England or northern Germany to Byzantium and Egypt. Manufacturing industry now well established in northern Italy: shipbuilding in Venice and Genoa, textiles in Florence (but also in

	Genoa, Cremona and Lucca), and textiles and armour manufacture in Milan, although in Milan manufacturing is small-scale.
	Construction industry busily employed responding to demand for privately commissioned secular and ecclesiastical buildings.
1309	Pope Clement V moves papal court to Avignon. Alberti bank of Florence, subsequently operating from Avignon, establishes control over papal finances throughout Europe.
1313	**In Verona, Benedictines and then Franciscans commission church of S Fermo Maggiore.**
1326	**In Siena, Franciscans commission church of S Francesco.**
1330	**In Venice, Franciscans commission church of S Mariagloriosa dei Frari.**
1339	**In Siena, work starts on Palazzo Sansedoni.**
1340	Woollen textile industry recently transformed, and there have been marked improvements in how merchants and bankers conduct business. Giant international banking families, particularly the Bardi and Peruzzi of Florence, have been spectacularly successful. Venice, Milan and Florence each have about 100,000 inhabitants. With Paris, these are the largest cities in Europe.
	Genoa, Bologna, Siena, Naples and Palermo each have population in excess of 50,000.
Mid-1340s	Economy of Italy, like that of rest of Europe, in deep disorder. Famine and epidemics rampant across much of continent. Large proportion of population debilitated by hunger, disease, exploitation, war and disorder: fertile ground for what is about to happen.
	Crash of the Bardi and Peruzzi banks, following an over-extension of credit to King Edward III of England. Incalculable effects on Florentine and international economy.
1348	**In Siena, extension to _duomo_ abandoned due to impact of Black Death on Sienese population and economy.**
1347–9	Black Death spreads throughout most of Italy. From 11 million, population of Italy plummets by over a third.
	Black Death strikes Florence where population falls to about 30,000 (compared to around 100,000 in 1340). With decrease in population, demand for food and buildings also decreases and food prices and rents plummet.
	Construction activity in Italy virtually comes to a halt.
1350–99	Because of their scarcity, artisans and craftsmen demand higher wages. Prices consequently increase and demand contracts causing deep depression particularly in manufacturing and construction sectors.
1350	**In Milan, Cistercians fund construction of tower of the Abbey of Chiaravalle.**

	In Florence, despite overall decrease in construction, Davizzi family commissions Palazzo Davanzati; other commissions follow.
1352	In Florence, Confraternità della Misericordia funds construction of Loggia del Bigallo.
1359	In Florence, merchants commission Palazzo della Mercanzia.
1377	In Venice, the recently completed Umiliati church of S Cristofaro Martire is renamed Madonna dell'Orto.
1378	Venetian fleet wins resounding victory over Genoese fleet off Salerno.
1378	Ciampo rebellion aims to encourage wool entrepreneurs to increase output and employment. Intermittent naval warfare between Genoa and Venice.
1379	After regrouping, Genoese fleet defeats Venetians at Polo.
1380	Venetian fleet defeats Genoese at battle of Chioggia.
1381	Treaty of Turin establishes peace between Venice and Genoa.
1390	Devastation of Black Death exacerbated by money famine.
1392–1402	Because of reduced demand, minting of silver coins ceases.
1400	Florence now has only 40,000 to 50,000 inhabitants. Population of Italy reduced to around 8 million, only 40 per cent of what it was in 1300.

Notes

1 D Hay and J Law, *Italy in the Age of the Renaissance* (Harlow: Longman, 1989), p 14.

2 D Hackett Fischer, *The Great Wave. Price Revolutions and the Rhythmn of History* (Oxford: Oxford University Press, 1996), p 20; C Duggan, *A Concise History of Italy* (Cambridge: Cambridge University Press, 1984), p 43.

3 Hay and Law, *Italy in the Age of the Renaissance*, p 14.

4 Various estimates based on data derived from B Tuchman, *A Distant Mirror. The Calamitous Fourteenth Century* (London: Papermac, 1989), p 96 and L Martines, *Power and Imagination. City-States in Renaissance Italy* (London: Pimlico, 2002), p 18.

5 RB Potter and S Lloyd Evans, *The City in the Developing World* (Harlow: Longman, 1998), p 6.

6 D Waley, *The Italian City-Republics*, 3rd edn (New York: Longman, 1988), p 22.

7 Ibid.

8 Ibid, pp 20–1.

9 Ibid, p 21.

10 PJ Jones, *The Italian City-State: From Commune to Signoria* (Oxford: Oxford University Press, 1997), p 168.

11 Waley, *Italian City-Republics*, p 22.

12 Ibid.

13 Ibid.

14 Ibid.

15 Ibid, p 24.

16 Duggan, *Concise History of Italy*, p 43.

17 D Friedman, 'Monumental urban form in the late medieval Italian commune: loggias and the Mercanzie of Bologna and Siena', *Renaissance Studies* 12 (3) (1998), p 326.

18 R Goldthwaite, *The Building of Renaissance Florence. An Economic and Social History* (London and Baltimore, MD: Johns Hopkins University Press, 1982), p 31.

19 G Procacci, *History of the Italian People* (London: Penguin, 1991), p 19.

20 Ibid.

21 Waley, *Italian City Republics*.

22 Goldwaite, *Building of Renaissance Florence*, p 35.

23 Hackett Fischer, *The Great Wave*, p 46.

24 CF Black, *Early Modern Italy, A Social History* (London: Routledge, 2001), p 22.

25 Hackett Fischer, *The Great Wave*, p 46.

26 Ibid, pp 44–5.

27 B Tuchman, *A Distant Mirror. The Calamitous Fourteenth Century* (London: Papermac, 1989), p 96.

28 Ibid, p 97.

29 Ibid, p 99.

30 Hackett Fischer, *The Great Wave*, pp 40–1.

31 Ibid, p 32.

32 Ibid, pp 41, 44–5.

33 Ibid, p 48.

34 Black, *Early Modern Italy*, p 22.

35 Hall, *Cities in Civilization*, p 78; see also P Burke, *The Italian Renaissance. Culture and Society in Italy*, 2nd edn (Oxford: Polity, 1986), pp 220–1, 239; V Cronin, *The Florentine Renaissance* (London: Pimlico, 1992), p 29; RS Lopez, 'The Trade of Medieval Europe: the South', in M Postan and EE Rich (eds), *The Cambridge Economic History of Europe*, 2: *Trade and Industry in the Middle Ages* (Cambridge: Cambridge University Press, 1952), p 303; R Trexler, *Public Life in Renaissance Florence* (New York: Harcourt Brace, 1980), p 11.

36 Goldthwaite, *Building of Renaissance Florence*.

37 Ibid.

38 Ibid.

CHAPTER 5

ECONOMIC GROWTH AND THE PRIVATE DEVELOPMENT OF THE BUILT ENVIRONMENT

Introduction

Private funds were required to satisfy the demand among the merchant and banking classes for productive space and residential accommodation; they were needed too by mendicant orders such as the Dominicans and Franciscans to enable them to bear the costs of constructing ecclesiastical buildings to meet their liturgical, preaching and other spiritual needs. Private building projects sometimes also required a degree of financial backing or a grant of land from government, but overwhelmingly economic growth ensured that funds flooding into both secular and ecclesiastical development emanated from private individuals and corporate bodies. However, despite the availability of such funds, there was a reluctance among private patrons to adopt unreservedly the innovative Gothic style that had become so fashionable in France and Germany. As in the 'public sector', there was a preference for hybrid architecture, stylistically part-Gothic and part-Romanesque. In the case of ecclesiastical architecture, buildings lacked 'the aspiring verticality of northern cathedrals',[1] while secular buildings were often battlemented and reminiscent of an earlier age, except in Venice where, in the absence of a Romanesque heritage, they continued to be essentially Byzantine.

The Larger Cities of Northern and Central Italy

Venice

The Palazzo Pesaro (renamed the Fondaco dei Turchi in 1621) and the neighbouring palaces of Ca'Loredan and Ca'Farsetti, are the most impressive examples of early-13th-century Venetian-Byzantine construction still extant. With the ground floor in each case used for storing merchandise and household goods, and the upper floor – the *piano nobile* – set aside for residential and office purposes, the most notable architectural attributes of these early palaces were the two-storey arcades along the waterfront; slender columns, narrow bays and tall stilted arches; and a ground-floor portico. Since buildings were closely spaced along the Grand Canal and in close proximity to it, little light could enter from the sides or the rear, thus the openness of facades on the waterfront was often not only decorative but essential if light was to penetrate the buildings at all.[2] Where palaces were not situated along the main canals, such as the

Photo 5.1 Fondaco dei Turchi, Venice, *c* 1200–1300. Venice's most important Veneto-Byzantine civic structure, reconstructed in 1869.

Palazzetto S Lio, arcades were absent, shops tended to occupy the ground floor, doors were framed by great stone piers and carved lintels, and biforate windows often adorned the facade of the *piano nobile*.

By the mid-13th century, it became increasingly the practice to abandon the ground-floor portico and to replace it by a single large water gate in the centre leading directly into the *androne* (the internal area for loading and unloading goods). Above, the *piano nobile* arcade was now confined to the centre of the facade and aligned with the *portego* inside, the room requiring the most light. Both the Ca' Dona and Ca' Donà della Madonnetta illustrate the application of these features and mark the early transition away from the Veneto-Byzantine style of palace architecture. The transition continued apace and saw the introduction into Venice of what Ruskin called the 'second' and 'third' orders of arch. The former is a round arch with a small cusp on its outer rim. This can be found encasing the eight windows of the *piano nobile* on the facade of the Ca' da' Mosto, even though the ground floor of this building retains fragments of a Veneto-Byzantine arcade. The latter, the 'third' order, in which the inner rim becomes pointed to form a stilted ogee arch, also began to appear by the middle of the century. In the Ca' Lioni, an external staircase leads from a central courtyard to the *piano nobile*, built into which there is not only a wide Byzantine archway but, to either side of it, a pair of ogee arches. It is questionable, however, whether Ruskin's description of the development of the Gothic arch is entirely credible. The different 'orders' or stages in the development of the Venetian Gothic arch often occurred simultaneously, possibly reflecting the tastes of the patron; the orders did not appear widely across Europe or even elsewhere in Italy; and the stilted ogee arch is undoubtedly of Islamic rather than of French origin.

With the expansion of trade and economic development in the 14th century wealth became increasingly concentrated among the ranks of the patrician class and was in large part reflected in the construction of sumptuous palaces on a substantial scale. More modest dwellings were built by middle-income groups who were rich enough to own their own land, with artisan cottages being provided by landowners for low-income groups who could only afford to rent. While very few middle- and lower-income buildings of any architectural merit survive (if, indeed, they were ever built), there are some notable palaces of the period that incorporate more advanced Gothic design features than hitherto, for example the Gothic ogee arch was now the vogue, as exhibited in the facade windows of the newly built *palazzi* Priuli-Bon, San Stae and Zorzi and the church of S Severo.

The prosperity of the Venetian population, albeit unevenly distributed, was in part donated to the Church, facilitating the building of many fine new churches. The mendicant orders were particular beneficiaries and were responsible for

Photo 5.2 Church of SS Giovanni e Paolo, Venice, begun 1333. An enormous Gothic brick church but with its fine facade unfinished.

introducing the Gothic style of architecture into Venice from mainland Italy in the 13th century. The Dominicans thus built the huge basilica of SS Giovanni e Paolo (or S Zanipolo) on land originally donated in 1234 by Doge Jacopo Tiepolo in the Castello *sestiero* (administrative district) east of the Canal Grande and far enough away from the centre of the city's power, the Piazza S Marco. A church of simple Gothic design was begun in 1246, but was later replaced by the present building that was started in 1333 and completed in 1430. Unlike other Dominican churches, S Zanipolo was not built at the head of a spacious marketplace or *piazza* since the site was poorly drained, but instead is fronted by a small L-shaped *campo* that seems disproportionately small for such a large and imposing building. It has a Latin-cross plan, three aisles and a transept, with polygonal apses terminating the arms of the plan.[3] The most striking attribute of the church's brick exterior is its simplicity. The three-part composition of the facade is crowned by three dainty Istrian stone pinnacles; it contains a centrally placed rose window and deep recesses intended for tombs (a magnificent portal with six Greek marble columns was added in the late 15th century); and, relying instead upon tie beams across the nave, there are no flying buttresses, only buttresses that act as thick piers placed at regular intervals along the external walls in which there are tall and narrow two-light windows.

Like the Dominicans, the Franciscans built their basilica on land donated by the republic. The site in the *sestiero* of S Polo to the west of the Canal Grande was not only some distance from the Piazza S Marco but far enough away from S Zanipolo so as not to draw upon the same private donors and same congregation. The original Franciscan church on this site was begun in 1250, but with growing needs it was superseded by the present church, that of S Maria Gloriosa dei Frari, begun in 1330. Very similar in size to S Zanipolo, the plan of the Frari is broadly the same as its Dominican counterpart. Like S Zanipolo, the Frari is made almost entirely of brick, its three-part facade is similarly crowned by three Istrian pinnacles, it also contains a centrally placed rose window and the sides of the building are supported by simple buttressing piers, with pairs of lancet windows set into the walls. Again like S Zanipolo, it occupies a confined space for such a large building, limiting its contribution to urban design.[4]

Of the smaller mendicant churches, S Stefano and the Madonna dell'Orto are perhaps the most notable. Founded by the Eremitani (formerly Augustinian

Photo 5.3 Church of S Maria Gloriosa dei Frari, Venice, begun 1330. Rivals the church of SS Giovanni e Paolo in size, composition and appearance.

hermits) in 1294, the church of S Stefano was rebuilt in simple Gothic style in the late 14th century. Containing three aisles but no transept, the brick structure of the new church is almost unornamented, typical of mendicants' churches in Venice in the late Middle Ages, and because of the complexities of land-ownership its sides rather than its facade overlook the large square in which it is located. Only the 14th-century entry portal designed and built by Bartolomeo Bon adds merit to this rather featureless church. In contrast, the church of the Madonna dell'Orto, founded by the Umiliati shortly after 1355, can be described as a smaller version of the basilicas of S Zanipolo and the Frari as epitomised by its plan, a brick structure and the three-part composition of the facade. Roofline statues of the Twelve Apostles sheltering in little Gothic niches add distinction to the facade.[5]

Genoa

Although constructed in the early 10th century, the Palazzata della Ripa performed an important function in the development of late medieval Genoa since its design had a substantial influence on the future development of private build- ings along the harbourside of the city. The *palazzata* was the outcome of an agreement between the city's consuls and its merchants whereby the latter would build a commercial arcade 900 metres long and, in return, be permitted to build houses for themselves above. During the later Middle Ages the increased prosperity of the city, predicated on the expansion of maritime trade, was reflected in the development of a number of sumptuous palaces. Several of these were incorporated into the Ripa, for example the *palazzi* Cattaneo, Durazzo and De Marini-Croce in the Piazza Banchi and Piazza De Marini; the *palazzi* Pinelli, Passano, Serra Gerace and Grimaldi-Fabiani; and the *palazzi* Cybo-Cellario, Negrotto-Durazzo, Pallavicino and Remondini in the Via del Campo. To a signi- ficant extent these developments sealed Genoa's future for the next 1,000 years as the principal port and centre of population on the western coast of Italy north of Naples, notwithstanding competition from Pisa until the late 13th century. Set apart from the Ripa, the Palazzo dei Maruffi with its flanking tower is perhaps the finest example of a secular building funded largely from trading profits. As a single-family residence with three storeys, the building has a 'grand entrance with an archaic single archway and equally archaic ashlar facing on the tower which is well-preserved despite the lack of crenellations on the crown'.[6]

Of the many private towers in the city constructed in the later Middle Ages, the Embriaci Tower is one of the best-known and most spectacular. Of rusticated ashlar, it rises to a height of 41 metres, and although it dates from the 12th century, like the Ripa it exerted considerable influence over future development. By the 13th century there were at least 66 private towers in the city, useful for defence or attack (site permitting), but perhaps even more important as symbols of wealth and power.

As in many other Italian cities in the 13th century, new-found wealth in Genoa was to an extent channelled into church building, often by means of donations to mendicant friars. Thus, the church of S Agostino was founded by the Augustinians in 1260. Constructed mainly from basic materials, the appearance of the church was improved by the addition of marble and cut stone that was used to decorate the facade and enhance the tall columns and capitals. The facade was substantially altered in the 17th century by being divided into three by pilasters, and by the addition of black and white banding, a pointed arch portal and a lunette. Private wealth was also used directly to fund church-building in Genoa, for example the church of S Matteo was founded by Martino Doria as the Doria family church in 1125; although rebuilt in 1278 and again in the 16th century, the original facade remains unchanged. With a facing of alternating black stone and white marble bands, the rather severe facade is redeemed somewhat by a large centrally placed lunette.

Milan

It is surprising that very few buildings of architectural merit were constructed in Milan in the later Middle Ages directly as an outcome of economic development. Despite the increase in trade and the growth of its many industries, the accumulation of wealth in the city was constrained by the small scale and organisational inadequacies of its enterprises, a weakness reflected in the low level of private expenditure on new secular and ecclesiastical buildings.

However, where it was possible to attract funds from afar, economic growth did indeed facilitate construction projects, for example the abbey of Chiaravalle, on the outskirts of the city, was founded by the Cistercian abbot Bernard of Clairvaux in 1135 utilising funds from its landed interests across Europe, the abbey church being consecrated in 1221. With a nave, two aisles and a transept, the abbey was completed in the 14th century by the addition of a particularly tall and elaborate octagonal lantern over the crossing, the general form of the abbey being based on contemporary church design in the Maconnaise and Toulouse.

Florence

As in Genoa and a host of other cities throughout Italy, there was a plethora of tower-houses in Florence in the later Middle Ages, many of which were built in the 13th century. Sited on the edge of the built-up area of the city, often as part of a larger defensive structure, or spread out within the inner areas of Florence, tower-houses of merchant families such as the Vendove, Corbizi, Marsili, Amidei and Alberti are still extant. Rising as high as six storeys, such towers were not only defensive but often controlled their immediate surroundings where members of their respective families resided and were employed. Sometimes, towers were used for industrial as well as residential purposes, for example the activity of dyeing occupied part of the tower-house of the Amidei.

By the late 13th century, with the increase in wealth, the merchant and new industrial classes of Florence were able to fund the development of *palazzi* in preference to adding to the stock of tower-houses. This process occurred quite rapidly, for instance an outstanding example of a *palazzo*, the Palazzo de'Mozzi, on the south bank of the Arno, was built as early as 1260–73 and constituted an 'early form of Renaissance palazzo [offering] a nice demonstration of the transition from the tower-house to the fourteenth-century model of a house'.[7] In contrast, the Palazzo Feroni Spini (started 1289), on the north bank of the Arno, assumed more of the features of a castle-keep, its great bulk 'being crowned with a complete circuit of jutting battlements'.[8] Initially three storeys high, the *palazzo* was soon transformed into a four-storey structure under new building regulations introduced at the end of the 13th century. With portals but no windows at ground-floor level, its facade is inset with regularly spaced basket windows from the *piano nobile* upwards, setting the standard that prevailed well into the 15th century. A very similar building directly facing the Feroni Spini, the Palazzo Gianfigliazzi, was constructed in about 1290. Reflecting the new regulations, this *palazzo* was also developed as a four-storey building but was crowned by even more exaggerated crenellations than those gracing the Feroni Spini. The Palazzo Frescobaldi, on the other side of the Arno, continued this stylistic tradition, as did other palaces built during the period straddling the 13th and 14th centuries.

Palace-building in late medieval Florence possibly reached its peak with the construction of the Palazzo Davanzati c 1350. With four storeys (and a roof-top loggia added in the 15th century), the facade rises above windowless rustication at ground-floor level and, like earlier palaces, is pierced by regularly spaced basket-handle windows on its upper floors. With the ground floor dedicated to commerce, an external staircase leads from the courtyard to the floors above.

Photo 5.4 Palazzo Davanzati, Florence, 1350. The best extant example of a 14th-century Florentine merchant's house.

However, because of the risk of civil strife in the aftermath of the Black Death, the palace's original owners, the Davizzi family (who were wealthy wool merchants), thought it prudent to secure the building with siege-proof doors, incorporated into its courtyard its own water supply, and built into its structure a huge storeroom with enough space for a year's provisions. The building was undoubtedly a product of the 'mature fourteenth century' and provided a model for further palace development in the 15th.

The mid-14th century also witnessed construction of a spate of new non-residential secular buildings, financed by the wealth generated from economic growth. Two such are the Loggia del Bigallo (1352–8) and the Palazzo della Mercanzia (c 1359). The loggia was funded by the Confraternità della Misericordia from charitable donations and was dedicated to the care of the sick, the orphaned, the elderly and the very poor. The building, located in the *piazza* of the *duomo*, features three bays that are open on two sides, two-light mullioned windows and a jutting roof. The Palazzo della Mercanzia became, around 1360, the permanent seat of the Florentine Ufficio della Mercanzia, which had previously occupied temporary rented accommodation since its founding in 1308. While the site on the edge of the Piazza della Signoria was owned by the commune, the Ufficio della Mercanzie secured a loan from the city's treasury to fund the cost of construction. A solid but not particularly attractive edifice, the building was deliberately constructed to conform with the design of its neighbour, so that its 'original roof line, the stringcourse levels, and the forms of the piers and the arches were set by the adjacent building, the city's war office'.[9] As such, its design resembled that of many other relatively nondescript secular buildings in Florence constructed in the late 14th century.

Through the conduit of religious orders, funds flowed into the construction of a large number of ecclesiastical buildings in Florence in the later Middle Ages. Initially, some of the wealth of the rural estates of the Cistercian Order found its way into the reconstruction of the city's 10th-century abbey, the Badia Fiorentina. Under the direction of the architect Arnolfo di Cambio, work was started in 1282 and was eventually completed under new direction when an hexagonal bell tower (attributed to di Cambio) was added to the abbey's main structure. With its biforate windows and pointed spire the abbey has become a major landmark on the skyline of Florence.[10]

However, it was through the medium of the mendicant Dominican and Franciscan Orders, rather than the Cistercians, that a substantial amount of

Photo 5.5 Arnolfo di Cambio and others, church of S Croce, Florence, begun 1294. Dominating the Piazza S Croce, this Gothic edifice is second only to the city's *duomo* in magnificence.

private wealth (together with some subsidy from the Florentine state) funded the construction of major ecclesiastical buildings. Transformed from the modest 11th-century church of S Maria delle Vigne on the same site, the very large Gothic church of S Maria Novella was built for the Dominicans over the period 1246 to 1360 (although the facade was embellished in the late 15th century). Of modified Cistercian design, the church, with its green, white and pink marble facade and plan based on a Latin cross, is 'the supreme and earliest complete example of the adaptation of the vaulted, aisled basilican design to mendicant needs'.[11] The church is also notable for being located on the north side of a large public open space, the Piazza S Maria Novella, whose five sides give the impression of a regular square from whatever angle they are viewed (see fig 5.1).

Figure 5.1 The Piazza of S Maria Novella, Florence

The Franciscan church of S Croce (started 1294) is undoubtedly a rival to the Dominicans' S Maria Novella, and since both churches are flanked by private chapels both orders would appear to have been successful in attracting wealthy benefactors. While the Dominican church is located on the western edge of the city, S Croce was built on the eastern fringe. Possibly designed by Arnolfo di Cambio, 'S. Croce is one of the largest and most richly decorated mendicant churches in Italy'[12] but differs markedly from S Maria Novella in having a plan based on an Egyptian rather than Latin cross; in being darker, less airy and less aspiringly Gothic than its Dominican rival;[13] and in having a facade that remained unfinished until the 19th century. S Croce also differs from S Maria Novella by dominating a deep four-sided *piazza*, and is particularly imposing when viewed from the latter's western end (fig 5.2).

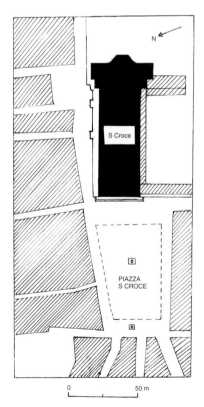

Figure 5.2 The Piazza of S Croce, Florence

Bologna

Economic growth in Emilia did little to generate private funds for the development of secular buildings in its largest city, Bologna. However, two of Bologna's largest churches, S Francesco and S Domenico, attracted a significant amount of private funding through donations to the relevant mendicant orders. Mainly French Gothic in style and built almost entirely of brick, the church of S Francesco was started in 1236 and completed in 1263. Its plan, with nine chapels radiating from an ambulatory, was based on sources in the Île de France. Externally, the chapels are supported by heavy flying buttresses interspersed by flat pilasters that define the angles of the faceted choir. 'The heavy forms pile up and they seem suddenly truncated since there is no visible pitched roof to give a final concentration to the vertical movement.'[14] Even so, S Francesco is possibly the most attractive church in Bologna. Of its two towers, the larger is finely surrounded by

Photo 5.6 Church of S Francesco, Bologna, begun 1236. One of the earliest examples of French-Gothic architecture in Italy, this enormous brick basilica overlooking the Piazza Malpighi is supported by flying buttresses.

decorative terracotta, and its massive screen facade is embellished with, among other adornments, two majolica plaques set in the pitch of the roof. By comparison, the church of S Domenico, begun in 1251, has few notable architectural features, but houses the relics of St Dominic and is thus one of the country's principal Dominican convents.

Siena

As a commercial rival of Florence throughout much of the later Middle Ages, Siena generated sufficient wealth to embark upon a wide range of building projects in both the secular and ecclesiastical sectors. The earliest secular building of note is the Palazzo Tolomei. Founded in 1208, and with a closed defensive aspect, the palace is slender and well proportioned consisting of a tall ground floor, central gateway and side portals; a *piano nobile* with five bays; and a shorter upper floor. While the ground floor is windowless, five regular biforate windows with finely structured tracery are set into the facade on each of the upper floors.[15]

Later in the 13th century, a Siennese credit bank commissioned construction of its headquarters, the Palazzo Salimbeni, a building that since 1472 has been the seat of the oldest bank in Europe, the Monte dei Paschi di Siena. Like the Palazzo Tolomei, the Salimbeni has a defensive appearance, with a Gothic gate encased in a 'Siennese arch' on the ground floor next to a row of slotted windows; six triforate windows adorned with tracery on the *piano nobile*; and plain rounded-arched windows on the upper floor.

The largest palace of the period, the Palazzo Sansedoni, extended along the north-eastern edge of the Campo. Beginning in 1339, three high residential towers dating from the early 13th century were conjoined and transformed into a single noble edifice. With its four-storey facade extending over 13 window bays, its architect Agostino di Giovanni ensured that the palace adhered to the prevailing building regulations which stipulated that design features and construction materials must conform with those of the Palazzo Pubblico (the town hall dominating the Campo). The palace's facade accordingly featured triforate windows and columns of pale travertine marble, and was crowned by crenellations over a frieze of round arches.[16]

Two further late medieval Siennese palaces are worthy of mention: the Palazzo Buonsignori and the Palazzo Chigi Saracini. The former is a late-Gothic building dating from the 14th century with a facade that features triforate windows and a battlemented crown (it is now the Pinacoteca Nazionale, a major art gallery). The latter palace, clinging closely to a curved street, has the lower two floors of its attractive facade constructed from pale travertine and the upper floor of red brick. The facade also features triforate windows under pointed arches and is crowned by large square crenellations.

As in many other Italian cities, church-building in Siena was substantially facilitated by the activities of the Dominican and Franciscan Orders. Their large churches in Siena, S Domenico and S Francesco, are 'two of the most important brick constructions in Central Italy'.[17] Situated on land that rises sharply above the Campo, building work on S Domenico started in 1226 and was carefully adjusted to the topography of its site by means of different floor levels. In 1340, the church was adorned by a campanile 14 years after the church of S Francesco was begun. The Franciscan church is both longer and wider than its Dominican counterpart, but lower and lighter, although its nave was raised in the late 15th century. As in Venice and Florence, the Dominican and Franciscan churches in Siena are at opposite sides of the city, on the periphery and close to its walls. By

Photo 5.7 Agostino di Giovanni, Palazzo Sansedoni, Siena, begun 1339. With three storeys of Gothic windows this conjoined brick building follows the north-east curve of the Campo.

imposing these locational constraints, the Siennese Republic not only attempted to limit the influence of the mendicant orders but ensured that central areas of the city would be preserved for administrative use and as the site of the city's *duomo* (see p 77).

Verona

Like the larger city of Bologna, Verona failed to attract funds from private individuals and commerce to facilitate the development of notable secular buildings in the city, and a similar deficiency limited construction of privately funded churches. However, an important exception to this lack of interest in church-building is the Dominican church of S Anastasia, the largest religious building in Verona. Built between 1291 and 1323, S Anastasia is of Gothic design and has a magnificent 14th-century doorway adorned with coloured marbles and carvings, polygonal apses, and a spired campanile.

Pisa

Although the city was not considered an attractive location for the injection of private funds into secular building projects, particularly after it ceased to be a maritime power following its defeat by Genoa in 1288, the Dominicans and Franciscans were nevertheless able to accumulate sufficient donations to fund respectively construction of the churches of S Caterina and S Francesco. While the facade of the large edifice of S Caterina was completed by 1310, S Francesco was blessed at an early stage in its development with an elegant Gothic campanile but had to wait until 1603 for its facade to be completed.

Padua

As in so many medium-sized cities in Italy, economic growth was more likely to be reflected in the construction of new churches than in the development of secular buildings. This phenomenon is dramatically demonstrated in Padua where the Franciscans used private funds for the construction of the massive

Basilica di S Antonio, one of the country's great pilgrim churches. Begun in 1232, and completed over a hundred years later, the church enshrined the body of St Antony (d 1231). The single gables of the building's facade incorporate both Romanesque and Gothic features, for example the round-arched doorway and general design are undoubtedly Romanesque but the central rose window and tall blind ogival arches are Gothic. The eight domes of the roof, however, are distinctly Byzantine and eastern – a style even more starkly illustrated by the small towers of the basilica akin to minarets, and by the basilica's two octagonal campanili.[18]

Photo 5.8 Basilica di S Antonio, Padua, begun 1232. Overlooking the Piazza del Santo, the edifice with its eight bulbous domes was built in the Romanesque-Gothic style reminiscent of S Marco in Venice.

The Franciscans were not the only mendicant order to fund the construction of a major church in Padua during the later Middle Ages. The Eremitani was built by its eponymous friars between 1276 and 1306, and later (in 1360) the order funded an addition to the lower part of the facade that involved provision of a broad doorway and tall deep arches that extended along the south flank of the building. A further ecclesiastical building of merit was constructed with funds from a lay patron. In 1303, Enrico Scrovegni commissioned what became known as the Scrovegni chapel, the final resting place of his father who had forfeited the right to a normal Christian burial on account of his unrepentant involvement in usury.

The Smaller Cities of Northern and Central Italy

In respect of the smaller cities of northern and central Italy, the Torre and Case Guinigi in Lucca are about the only extant secular buildings of any merit commissioned by private patrons. Built between 1300 and 1350, the buildings were commissioned by one of the city's richest families, the Guinigi, and whereas the Torre is a single redbrick structure 41 metres in height, the Case consisted of two large palaces facing each other, also built almost entirely of brick.

Photo 5.9 Attributed to Frate Elia or others, church of S Francesco, Assisi, begun 1228. The Gothic facade of the upper basilica of the famous two-storey church with its rose window.

Elsewhere, among the smaller cities, almost all privately funded buildings are ecclesiastical rather than secular. Using donations from the public and corporations, the Franciscans commissioned churches in Modena, Piacenza, Treviso, Vicenza, Cortona, Arezzo, Assisi, Gubbio, Todi, Orvieto, Rome (then a comparatively small city) and Palermo. The church of S Francesco in Assisi (1228) is a particularly notable example of the genre. It was one of the two 'first important Gothic buildings in Italy, after the French-inspired attempts of the Cistercians at Fossanova and Casamari [the other being S Francesco in Bologna]'.[19] S Francesco at Assisi was '[b]uilt on a sloping site with a substantial crypt forming a lower church'.[20] A staircase leading from the terrace of the lower church connects that part of the building to the transepts of the upper church. Its plan is 'a simple aisleless Latin cross with none of the complexity of detail or aspiring verticality of French Gothic',[21] and these attributes determined the basic shape of Franciscan churches throughout Italy. Likewise, its facade with a fine rose window and Gothic portal are replicated in many Franciscan churches throughout the length and breadth of the peninsula. In Rome, the church of S Maria in Aracoeli, begun in 1250, marks the early presence of the Franciscan Order in the city of the papacy, indeed it was Innocent IV who handed the original church over from the Benedictines to the Franciscans, who then reconstructed it in Romanesque rather than Gothic style.

The Dominicans, with similar financial resources, funded church-building in Treviso, Vicenza, Pistoia, Arezzo, Perugia, Orvieto, Spoleto and Rome. In Vicenza, the 13th-century Dominican church of S Corona is probably the most magnificent ecclesiastical building in the city, whereas in Perugia the church of S Domenico (begun 1305) is the largest. In Rome, the church of S Maria Sopra Minerva (started 1280) is the only Gothic church in the city and appears to be modelled on Florence's S Maria Novella, although its original frontage is entirely screened by a 15th-century facade.

Among the smaller cities under consideration, only San Gimignano had an Augustinian presence, members of that order commissioning a large Latin-cross church, S Agostino. Built between 1280 and 1298, the hall church contains three apsidal chapels, most notably the Capella di S Bartolo.

Conclusion

Cities in northern and central Italy were alone in the peninsula in experiencing the development of notable private buildings in the later Middle Ages. Derived from wealth accumulated from international trade, funds were injected into the development of private *palazzi* and ecclesiastical buildings throughout most of the 13th and 14th centuries, but in southern Italy and Sicily feudalism not only had an adverse effect on the prosperity of the whole region but also a lamentable effect on the development of urban areas, a situation reflected in the absence of extant buildings of the period in the cities of the south funded exclusively by private patrons or the mendicant orders.

Notes

1 D Watkin, *A History of Western Architecture*, 3rd edn (London: Laurence King, 2000), p 194.
2 D Howard, *The Architectural History of Venice* (New Haven and London: Yale University Press, 2002), pp 36–7.
3 G Zucconi, *Venice. An Architectural Guide* (Venice: Arsenale Editrice, 1995), p 38.
4 Howard, *Architectural History*, p 83.
5 Ibid, p 87.
6 E Poleggi, 'The medieval walled city', in *Genoa. Architectural Guide* (Turin: Allemandi, 1998), p 34.
7 G Zucconi, *Florence. An architectural guide* (Venice: Arsenale Editrice, 1995), p 38.
8 Ibid, p 39.
9 D Friedman, 'Monumental urban form in the late medieval Italian commune: loggias and the Mercanzie of Bologna and Siena', *Renaissance Studies* 12 (3) (1998), p 327.
10 Zucconi, *Florence*, p 28.
11 J White, *Art and Architecture in Italy, 1250–1400* (New Haven and London: Yale University Press, 1993), p 27.
12 Ibid, p 30.
13 Watkin, *History*, p 195.
14 White, *Art and Architecture*, p 25.
15 AM Von der Haegen and R Strasser, *Tuscany* (Cologne: Könemann, 2001), p 344.
16 Ibid, pp 352–3.
17 White, *Art and Architecture*, p 231.
18 P Blanchard, *Northern Italy from the Alps to Bologna* (London: A & C Black, 2001), p 430.
19 Watkin, *History*, p 194.
20 Ibid, p 195.
21 Ibid.

PART 2

THE 15TH CENTURY

CHAPTER 6

OLIGARCHIC AND SIGNORIAL GOVERNMENT IN THE 15TH CENTURY

Introduction

By 1400, the spatial configuration of the Italian states was markedly different from that it had taken in the later Middle Ages (see figs 2.1 and 6.1). In the north, overarching sovereignty was still the preserve of the Holy Roman Empire, but the area under imperial control was reduced to include 'only' what is now Lombardy and Tuscany. Venice – as before – remained autonomous. The Papal States in the centre and east not only included Rome and its hinterland but also former territories of the empire such as present-day Umbria, Marches and Emilia Romagna. The mainland part of the south was controlled by the French Angevins, while Sicily was under Aragonese rule.

Across this patchwork of states, inter-state rivalry provoked violent clashes throughout much of the quattrocento while, internally, power struggles were enacted to determine which form of civic government should prevail and who should rule. It is against this seemingly unpropitious backdrop that, throughout the 15th century, the built environment of many cities was transformed by public patrons.

External Security and Aggrandisement

In the early years of the 15th century, and after its defeat by Milan at the battle of Casalecchio, Florence was ruthlessly besieged by Gian Galeazzo Visconti

Figure 6.1 Italy in 1495

and his Milanese forces, until the two-year campaign was called off following Gian Galeazzo's death on 3 September 1402 as a consequence of plague. Ironically, only three years later, in an attempt to offset part of the cost of previous wars, Gian Galeazzo's heir Giovanni Maria Visconti relinquished Milan's hold over Pisa by selling the city to Florence for a sum of 200,000 florins. Unfortunately for Florence, Pisa resisted being sold to its Tuscan neighbour, and therefore Florence mounted a siege against Pisa to secure its surrender, and in the process gained a maritime outlet for its trade. A further Florentine–Milanese war took place between 1423 and 1428 when Giovanni Maria's successor, Filippo Maria Visconti, ordered the invasion of Florentine territory to recover his father's lost territories; but as on previous occasions, the war ended in stalemate. Thereafter, Florence enjoyed a comparatively long period of peace, sealed by the Treaty of Lodi (1454) which united Florence, Venice, Milan and the papacy in a defensive alliance against the Ottoman Turks who had seized Constantinople only a year earlier. In 1462, Florence faced a new threat. It came not from the Milanese to the north but from Siena, its long-standing enemy to the south. The Siennese invited Alfonso, duke of Calabria and son of King Ferrante of Naples, to lead its armies against Florence and, supported by Pope Sixtus IV, they prosecuted a war that was to last until 1479 when Ferrante and Sixtus, after lengthy negotiations, were forced to make peace with the Florentines. With only minor gains to its territory – Pisa in 1406, Cortona in 1411 and Leghorn ceded by the Genoese in 1421 – Florence was mainly the victim of the 15th-century impetus for territorial aggrandisement rather than a perpetrator. The same was not, however, true of the other major republic of the peninsula, Venice.

In the late 14th century, the Venetians expanded westwards by defeating the Scaligeri and incorporating Castelfranco, Conegliano, Sacile, Oderzo and Treviso into their domain; and in 1405 the *Serenissima* had eliminated its most powerful neighbour, the Carrara dynasty, and as a consequence gained Bassano, Belluno, Feltre, Vicenza and Carrara's capital itself, Padua. The republic's north-eastern territories were similarly expanded when, in 1420, Venice annexed Friuli and Udine, formerly possessions of the king of Hungary. Many Venetians, and particularly the aged doge, Tommaso Mocenigo (1414–23), were now becoming cautious about the risk of overextending their mainland possessions. However, Mocenigo's successor, Francesco Foscari (1423–57), was unconstrained in supporting a policy of territorial expansion. Thus, in his first year in office, he instigated a campaign to seize Bergamo and Brescia from their overlord Filippo Maria Visconti of Milan, a campaign that led only to a tenuous hold on these cities. Following intermittent warfare between Venice and Milan, under the Treaty of Cremona (1441), Venice eventually secured suzerainty over Bergamo and Brescia, as well as over Peschiera and part of the domain of Cremona. By the end of Foscari's period in office, the republic had pushed its mainland frontier virtually to the walls of Milan and had also incorporated Ravenna on the Adriatic coast.

Although the annexation of Constantinople by the Ottoman Turks in 1453 was a major cause of concern for Venice, not least for commercial reasons, ironically it helped to secure the republic's territorial integrity in northern Italy. At the Treaty of Lodi, an agreement between Venice, Milan, Naples, Florence and Rome not only created a united front against the Turks, but confirmed Venice's hold on Bergamo, Brescia, Padua and Treviso, although Venice was unable to retain Ravenna. As a consequence of Lodi, the mainland boundaries of the *Serenissima* remained intact for over 300 years, until Napoleon dissolved the republic in 1797. Venice also secured a long-term footing in the eastern Mediterranean when Cyprus was incorporated into its overseas empire – an eventual outcome of the marriage of the king of Cyprus to the Venetian Caterina Cornaro in 1468, of his subsequent death in 1473, and of his widow granting ownership of the island to the Venetian government in 1489. Elsewhere in its overseas empire, the number of its possessions diminished. Turkish incursions forced Venice to relinquish its hold on the important commercial port of Negroponte in 1479 and, following its defeat by Turkey at the sea battle of Sapienza in 1499, the republic forfeited its coastal fortresses in the Peloponnese leaving the Turks untrammelled access to the Adriatic.

Although Milan under the Visconti was a very considerable force in the 14th century, in the 15th century its power and influence were directed more at a vain attempt to maintain its position in the power-politics of Italy rather than at expanding its territorial interests. While Gian Galeazzo Visconti had seized control of Siena, Pisa, Perugia and Bologna, and defeated Florence at Casalecchio in 1402, his death in September of that year thwarted Milan's attempt to annex Florence. Subsequently, his heir Giovanni Maria (1402–12) sold Pisa to the Florentines in 1405, and his younger son Filippo Maria (1412–47) unsuccessfully waged war between 1423 and 1428 to regain territory previously lost to Florence, but – as if by way of compensation – secured suzerainty over Genoa (1422–35). With the demise of the Visconti dynasty in 1447, power shifted to the newly formed Ambrosian Republic in 1448 but, after two years of disarray within its ranks, the emperor bestowed the title of Duke of Milan upon the former condottiere, Francesco Sforza, who held the title from 1450–1466, founding a dynasty which was to rule Milan for almost 50 years.

While most of the second half of the quattrocento witnessed a period of relative peace following the Lodi settlement, the latter years of the century signalled the eventual downfall of Milan as an independent power. Although as a member of the Holy League together with Venice, Spain and the papacy, Milan participated in the defeat of a French army under the command of Charles VIII at Fornova in 1495, four years later Ludovico Sforza (1494–9) was forced to flee Milan as French forces under Louis XII (Charles's successor), aided and abetted by Venice, arrived at Milan's gates to stake Louis' claim to the duchy. Thereafter, the French would occupy Milan and its remaining possessions intermittently until 1525, when the city succumbed to imperial rule.

During the first half of the 15th century, Rome was still a relatively small and, in temporal terms, unimportant city. Even as the capital of Christendom, it was only just recovering from the long exile of the papacy in Avignon and the Great Schism. Rome, however, as the centre of power within the Papal States, was a major player in Italian politics and intent on territorial aggrandisement. During the first half of the quattrocento the papacy was content to go to the aid of others rather than to pursue its own territorial interests directly. For example, in return for armed assistance in the past Pope Eugenius IV (1431–47) eventually acknowledged Alfonso of Aragon and king of Sicily as the rightful king of Naples in 1442, rather than his fellow-countryman and previous incumbent the Angevin king René. In mid-century, the papacy was primarily concerned with the threat of further Ottoman incursion following the fall of Constantinople. Pope Nicholas V (1447–55) thus brought together at Lodi the former rivals of Florence, Milan and Venice to form a bulwark against the Turks and to cement broad acceptance of existing territorial boundaries in northern and central Italy in the hope of pre-empting further dispute.

In the late quattrocento, the papacy assumed an altogether more aggressive role. Pope Sixtus IV (1471–84) not only supported an ongoing war waged against Florence by the Siennese army under the command of Alfonso, duke of Calabria and son of King Ferrante of Naples, but also encouraged his nephew (some would say son) Girolamo Riario to seize the city of Imola from the Milanese as a base for further territorial expansion. Refused financial help for this venture by the Medici and displeased at Lorenzo de' Medici's rejection of the papal appointment of Francesco Salviati as archbishop of Pisa, Sixtus hatched the so-called Pazzi conspiracy in 1478 against the Medici. With encouragement from Sixtus, the Pazzi – commercial rivals of the Medici in Florence – hired two disaffected priests to murder Lorenzo and his brother Giuliano while the siblings attended mass in the *duomo*. Giuliano was brutally killed, but Lorenzo escaped and sought refuge in his *palazzo*. In the following year, Sixtus reluctantly ended his conflict with Florence after Lorenzo visited Naples and negotiated a peace treaty with Ferrante. Towards the century's close, other popes adopted a similarly proactive role in Italian affairs. Alexander VI (1492–1503) not only formed the Holy League (see above), but intervened directly in the affairs of Florence in 1497 when he excommunicated the priest Savonarola – *de facto* leader of the republic – for his refusal to join the League. When the entire city of Florence was subsequently threatened with excommunication, Florentines began to desert the priest and in 1498, charged with heresy, he was tortured, hanged and burnt at the stake.

After Angevin rule during the earlier part of the quattrocento, Naples and Sicily became conjoined during the reign of Alfonso of Aragon (1442–58). However, following Alfonso's death, the throne of Sicily was inherited by his brother John II, and Naples again became an independent state and passed to Alfonso's illegitimate son Ferrante I (1458–94). During the latter part of the century, the boundaries of Naples remained broadly unchanged despite the Neapolitan army – under the king's son, Alfonso, duke of Calabria – waging an inconclusive eight-year war in support of Siena against Florence, and the invasion and temporary occupation of Naples by King Charles VIII of France in 1495 to force the abdication of King Alfonso II (1494–5) in favour of his son, Ferrante II (1495–6).

Humanism and the Exercise of Civic Power

As in the later Middle Ages, in the 15th century the Italian states were either republican or signorial. Whereas popular and oligarchic republics enjoyed *de facto* independence since they were only very loosely attached to the Holy Roman Empire, the *signori* 'were [in theory] feudal lords, paying annual dues and owing military service to the Emperor in the case of Milan and Mantua or to the Pope in the case of Ferrara, Urbino and Naples. But in practice they [too] were independent and exercised absolute power over their dominions.'[1]

However, whether republican or signorial, most of the states of Italy were influenced by the emergence of civic humanism, an approach to government emanating from classical Roman and Greek literature concerning the role of man in society in general, and in politics in particular. Of Roman writers, Cicero specifically 'provided an idea of civic duty, of a moral citizen actively participating in government, whose decisions were guided by loyalty to his country rather than by self-interest',[2] while Greek political literature was represented principally by Aristotle who advocated that, in order to achieve political stability, power should be vested in a strong middle class as a means of achieving a balance between tyranny and democracy. Renewed interest in classical literature was facilitated by the establishment of new libraries for this purpose, such as that of S Marco in Florence (assembled by Niccolò Niccoli, 1364–1437), the Vatican library and the Biblioteca Marciana in Venice where original classical texts were diligently restored, copied and – thanks to the development of printing – rapidly disseminated. Important areas of interest included history, ethics and rhetoric. Because of their skill in these areas, leading humanists were appointed to important administrative and advisory posts in government, both republican and signorial, in most cities of the peninsula, many of them attaining positions of considerable power and influence in government.

Republican Government

The city-states of Florence, Venice, Siena and Lucca comprised the four major republics of the quattrocento, and each by then had become subject to oligarchic rule. Florence – despite its empathy for humanism – had gone one stage further and fell under veiled signorial government between 1434 and 1494 before re-adopting popular republican government (1494–1512), only to see this system replaced once more by undisguised signorial rule by the second decade of the 16th century.[3] Genoa, Bologna and Perugia oscillated between republican and signorial regimes. The foremost republics, Florence and Venice, had systems of government that had remained broadly intact since the 13th century, and in Venice, at least, its republican system survived until the late 18th century. It should not be assumed, however, that republican government was democratic in a modern sense, or that humanists ever advocated universal franchise.

In each of the Italian republics there was a very restricted class of politically enfranchised citizens and it was only this section of the urban population that was entitled to occupy the legislative, administrative and judicial offices of govern-ment. But while on average only about 2 to 3 per cent of a city's population were enfranchised, an even smaller proportion of the population – drawn from coteries of no more 200 to 600 men – held office.

In the quattrocento, Italian society became increasingly elitist, while 'regimes which had always been fundamentally oligarchic became increasingly aristo-cratic'.[4] This circumstance was exhibited in Florence, Venice, Milan and Rome, where power came to be vested in fewer and fewer hands, creating alarm and resentment not only 'among those who felt that their traditional decision-making powers had been extinguished',[5] but also among the populace in general since 'government was becoming more remote, more arbitrary [and] more unfathomable'.[6]

Although there were no popular uprisings as a result of resentment, the latter years of the century were marked by a series of conspiracies against those in power in places such as Milan, Florence and Naples. Italian regimes, moreover, could not be assured of the loyalty of cities under their suzerainty: for example, Florence could not necessarily rely on Pisa for support, Venice on Padua, or Milan on Parma.

By the beginning of the 15th century, most communes had lost their repub-lican status since hereditary principalities replaced the former free republican states. Simultaneously and with many communes weakened by instability, upheaval and the disruption of civil war, the more 'powerful cities flour-ished, gobbling up the less important and powerful cities and territories around them, and thus extending their influence over large geographical areas'.[7] Where power was transferred from the communes to heads of major aristo-cratic families, the *signori*, this often involved a power-struggle between the various factions over an extended period. Where from the outset power had been vested in a prince, the struggle to maintain power was invariably no less severe.

Within this context, it is not at all surprising that states strove to maintain control in their own way. Florence probably had the most centralised administration in Italy. A large number of officials were based in the city and there was a centralised system of taxation. Conversely, Naples and to a lesser extent Milan devolved control from the centre to local urban elites and the traditional nobility. Venice, however, practised a hybrid form of control. Edicts were issued from the centre, while a limited number of Venetian patricians supervised local institutions.[8] It was inevitable, therefore, that with elitism operating at the font of power, there was an absence of unity within the major Italian states of the 15th century. In contrast to Florence and Venice, the Renaissance courts were not concerned with conserving republican idealism but in promulgating the political power of their incumbent dynasties: 'In Milan [for example], the Sforza dukes were anxious to establish the legitimacy of their position as the rightful heirs of the Visconti, [while the] Gonzaga rulers in Mantua, the Este in Ferrara and the Montefeltro in Urbino were more concerned with promoting the prestige of their small courts as rivals to the more powerful states of Milan and Naples'.[9]

Against this background of power politics and continual jockeying for position, '[t]he culture of classical antiquity, above all the culture of imperial Rome provided new and potent imagery for the expression of absolute power'[10] throughout much of Italy. Signorial states, like their republican neighbours, not only adopted civic humanism as a template for good government but also undertook construction of magnificent secular and ecclesiatical buildings in the style of classical Rome in an attempt to engender civic pride and loyalty to the state. In the lesser principalities – overshadowed by larger and predatory neighbours – there was often an even greater need to construct imposing edifices as symbols of absolute power and authority.

Government in the Major Cities of 15th-century Italy

Florence

To a greater extent than any other Italian state during the quattrocento, Florence adopted humanist principles in both government and architecture. Influenced by

Dante (1265–1321) and Petrarch (1304–74), humanists such as Colucci Salutati (1331–1406) and Leonardo Bruni (1370–1444) held influential administrative positions in Florentine government between the late 14th and early 15th centuries. As chancellor of Florence from 1375 until his death over 30 years later, Salutati gained renown for his skill in drafting diplomatic communiqués to his city's external enemies during the War of the Eight Saints (1375–8) and the war with Milan (1402–5), when the Milanese *signore* Gian Galeazzo Visconti 'is reported to have said that a letter of Salutati was worth a troop of horse'.[11] However, although Salutati arguably did more than anyone to establish a humanist school of political thought in the early 15th century, his message was contradictory. On the one hand he performed a major role in protecting the 'liberty' of Florence against the invasion of a state under signorial rule (Milan), yet in his *De tyrannio* (1400) he wholeheartedly endorsed the institution of monarchy, suggesting perhaps that he valued the independence of the state above republican values *per se*.

Born in Arezzo, Leonardo Bruni 'was the central figure in Florentine humanism during the first half of the fifteenth century'.[12] Inspired by Salutati he became expert in Latin, while thanks to the influence of the Greek humanist Manuel Chrysoloras (1350–1415) he was also an authority on Greek. To praise Florentine republicanism, he published *Laudatio Florentinae urbis* (a panegyric on the city of Florence) in 1401, a literary contribution that played an important part in the development of civic humanism in that city. Like Salutati before him, he rose to the position of chancellor and exerted considerable influence over the politics and literary life of Florence. He is perhaps best known for his *History of the Florentine People*, 'the first major work of Renaissance historical writing'.[13] The work was particularly important in emphasising the ideological link between republican Florence of the quattrocento and republican Rome (509–31 BC), and for arguing that there was a relationship between republicanism, classicism and social well-being. One of Bruni's last publications, the *Commentary on the History of His Own Times*, focused on contemporary history until 1440 from a humanist perspective. Through writing a new kind of history by means of a continuous narrative of secular events and modelled on Roman historians, Bruni and other Florentine humanists replaced the centuries-old method of 'placing events within a providential Christian framework, running from the Creation through the Incarnation and the evolution of the Church'.[14]

Based on the evolution of republican government in Florence, the development of political theory and practice across much of Italy was greatly influenced by Bruni's histories. These broke with the medieval tradition of treating political thought as a quasi-theological discipline concerned mainly with the relationship between the *sacerdotium* and the *regnum* (Church and state).

Throughout most of the quattrocento the political status quo of Florence was maintained. Its richest families – the merchants, industrialists, bankers and lawyers – managed to keep humanism alive in the city at a time when rampant despotism was leaving its mark on the culture of Milan. It is not surprising, therefore, that through membership of the appropriate guilds, the richest mercantile elite exerted considerable influence over the built environment. Unlike the practice in other city-states, the government of Florence transferred responsibility for funding construction of major public buildings to the guilds. The wool merchants (the *Arte della Lana*) were given the responsibility for the paving and upkeep of the Piazza della Signoria, the construction of the dome of the cathedral, S Maria del Fiore, and completion of the Benedictine monastery of S Croce, while the silk merchants' guild (the *Arte della Seta*) was entrusted with the development of the Ospedale degli Innocenti, the foundling hospital, and Orsanmichele, the city's grain market.[15] It is notable that although bullion flowing into Florence as a result of favourable trade balances during the turbulent years of the early quattrocento was taxed to pay for military expenditure, it also helped indirectly to fund an extravagant public building programme focusing on the cathedral. Since the incidence of taxation fell on incomes rather than wealth, capital remained intact and much of it was duly invested into urban development.[16]

However, republican government and its activities were often diluted by the overarching power and influence of the Medici family. While never holding elected office, the Medici 'owed their prominence . . . to the astute and subtle manner in which they constructed a huge network of support [in the Signoria] among the upwardly mobile, whom they could assist with loans [and] also cultivated a large popular following in their quarter of the city, San Giovanni'.[17] Cosimo de'Medici (1389–1464), in particular, enhanced his family's role in banking by acquiring the papal account and their influence through patronage of the visual arts.

Cosimo's control over the Signoria inevitably produced hostility. This culminated in Cosimo's arrest in 1433 and detention in the Palazzo della Signoria by Rinaldo degli Albizzi and a small clique of fellow oligarchs. After the short period of exile that followed, Cosimo and his allies were swept back into power within a year, and without overturning the city's constitution the family remained in effective control of Florence until the end of the century, using 'subtle manipulation of the electoral process to maintain their supremacy'.[18]

Thus, although the Florentine constitution remained broadly intact throughout most of the quattrocento, it was subject to much adaptation to meet the political needs of the Medici, particularly of Cosimo and his supporters who were eager to increase their power and influence. Their machinations diminished the policy-making and judicial role of the legislative assembly and created a Council of Two Hundred in 1458 to allow themselves greater representation. Similarly in 1480, after the unsuccessful Pazzi conspiracy two years earlier against Lorenzo 'il Magnifico' (d 1492), and the war with the papacy that followed, the Medici faction replaced the Council of Two Hundred with a Council of Seventy selected from the old regime. This in turn elected a small number of ministers to advise Lorenzo directly, reducing still further the role of representative government. Clearly, a republican regime that had been fundamentally oligarchic for well over a century had now been supplanted by 'Florence's first real *signori*'[19] – the Medici elite – a development predicated on the belief that 'only those with experience of public affairs and a real commitment to the state could be trusted to lead it'.[20] The Medici, from Cosimo (1434–64) to Piero II (1492–4), therefore, not only resided in sumptuous surroundings, holding lavish court in the family's palace, the Palazzo Medici, but exercised real power from the city's seat of government, the Palazzo della Signoria (formerly the Palazzo dei Priori).

However, after years of mismanaging their financial empire, Medici power was on the wane during the final years of the quattrocento, and on Lorenzo's death in 1492 their demise seemed imminent. Lorenzo's heir, Piero de'Medici, was expelled by his signorial government on 9 November 1494 as a penalty for his complicity with French invasion plans (see chapter 10), and a new system of government was established in Florence by Christmas. The termination of Piero's authority and demands for a new constitution were also a consequence of the activities of the charismatic priest Girolamo Savonarola who acted as spokesman for a reforming faction within the old Medici party. Similar to the Venetian model, the new Florentine constitution was 'based on a Great Council, open to all male Florentines over 29 years old whose forefathers had held political office'[21] and a smaller executive Council of Eighty.

During the relatively brief period of republican control (1494–1512), Florence was governed entirely from the Palazzo del Popolo. During this time, the republic placed Michelangelo Buonarroti's newly completed statue of David – a symbol of independent Florence – outside the *palazzo*, and within its walls built the Salone dei Cinquecento, the meeting hall for the Consiglio Maggiore and a chamber that was subsequently adorned with two giant frescoes by Michelangelo and Leonardo da Vinci.[22] However, although a Medici no longer held the reins of government, power remained with the old ruling elite consisting largely of members of the Medici party or *Arrabbiati*. Of those elected to the Council of Eighty in 1495 'over three-quarters . . . had served on the Medici councils or were members of families represented'.[23] It was only a matter of time (1513) before the Medici again assumed overall power (see chapter 9).

Despite the long-term ascendancy of the Medici, the political stability of republican Florence was maintained throughout most of the quattrocento by the strength of its administration, arguably the most centralised in Italy. Large numbers of officials were based in the city to manage its day-to-day affairs and particularly its robust system of taxation. Civic humanism had clearly left its mark, and based on many of the same writings, but with greater use of Plato's advocacy of government by the elite, it was soon adopted in Venice, Milan, Rome, Naples and a host of smaller states to support both republican and despotic government.

Venice

Despite Venice having been a republic since the 11th century, humanism played a relatively minor role in the development of government in the city during the first half of the quattrocento. Unlike their fellow bureaucrats in Florence, the civil servants of Venice were not humanist. This was partly because their education in Latin and Greek suffered from the city's inability to attract humanist teachers, and partly because Venetian patricians – the political elite in charge of administering the republic and its overseas empire – showed remarkably little interest in humanism.

While Florence looked back to its classical roots, Venetians 'found their city's Christian traditions and Byzantine links far more enduring [and] fundamental to her culture'.[24] The emergence of humanism in the governance of the *Serenissima* in the early quattrocento was further constrained by the prevalence of traits similar to those exhibited in Medicean Florence, but whereas humanism was already planted in the collective psyche of the Florentine governing elite prior to the rise of the Medici, in Venice humanism had not yet arrived. In both states, age and experience were considered essential attributes for high office, there were growing divisions between rich and poor, with the reins of power being held mainly by the former, and as in Florence there was a 'drift towards decision-making in smaller councils in conditions of carefully preserved secrecy',[25] all at odds with the humanist tradition, even of the Venetian variety.

Similarities with Medicean Florence should not, however, be exaggerated. Arguably the principal difference between the governance of Venice and Florence was that throughout much of the quattrocento in the latter state real political power was exercised by one family – the Medici – whereas in Venice, as in previous centuries, power was normally wielded by patricians rather than the doge, who for much of the time was largely a figurehead. This did not provide an appropriate context for the emergence of humanism, since Venice possessed extensive external territories and needed to secure effective government in her possessions in the Adriatic and beyond. Ambassadors and the captains-general of the city's navy were therefore deemed to be of patrician status and, with the assistance of magistracies, assumed administrative powers and responsibilities in their postings, ranging from the maintenance of law and order to securing the export of grain to the *dominante*. In contrast, in the *terraferma*, local nobles were left in charge of urban affairs, 'such as the establishment of tax rolls, and each subject city was administered by two functionaries, a military governor with a small garrison, and a rector who coordinated local concerns with the overall policies of the republic, and arbitrated quarrels'.[26] The governance of Venetian possessions beyond the lagoon did not provide an appropriate context for the employment of administrators steeped in humanist values.

The introduction of civic humanism into Venice, however, received a somewhat unlikely boost in 1453 when Constantinople fell to the Ottoman Turks. Although Venice superseded the conquered city as the last surviving link with the Byzantine Empire, an empire that had replaced pagan Rome as the guardian of Christianity, this was insufficient compensation for the disruption of trade that resulted from Turkish territorial aggrandisement. Venice, therefore, widened the boundaries of its state in the *terraferma* in the mid-15th century, viewing itself as heir to Imperial Rome, and thus embracing Italian culture and with it humanism. However, in Venice civic humanism developed along very different lines from its Florentine counterpart, and with very different effects. Most notably, 'it was less concerned with reviving the classical past than with reinforcing its own heritage and its established links with the Byzantine East',[27] an emphasis that helped ensure the Venetian Republic's survival until the late 18th century, but that, with very few exceptions (such as the Porta Magna of the Arsenale (1460) and the East Wing of the Palazzo Ducale (1483–98)) delayed the adoption of the Renaissance style in the development of public buildings until the 16th century (see chapter 10).

Genoa

Once proud rival to Venice, Genoa found its republican status difficult to sustain after the loss of its Mediterranean trading outposts in the wake of the battle of

Chioggia (1378–81). The Genoese Republic functioned with varying degrees of efficiency and political consent between 1413 and 1422, 1435 and 1458, and 1478 and 1487 but during the late 14th and much of the 15th centuries the republic was ruled by France (1396–1409), Monferrato (1409–13), Milan under Filippo Maria Visconti (1422–35), France again (1458–61), and Milan under the Sforza (1464–78 and 1487–99). Under foreign rule for much of the quattrocento, very few public buildings were erected and none of any note, in sharp contrast to Venice's heritage of magnificent late medieval churches and imposing civic structures.

Milan

Although for more than 200 years Milan was governed by two successive tyrannical regimes, those of the Visconti (1277–1447) and the Sforza (1450–94), interrupted only by the short-lived Ambrosian Republic, both dynasties recognised the significance of humanism in governance and the arts. The Visconti owned an important library that housed valuable classical texts and humanist writings including works by Dante and Petrarch.[28] In an attempt to strengthen his widely unpopular regime, Filippo Maria (1412–47) employed humanists to extol the benefits of aristocratic rule in contrast to the relative instability of elected government in Florence; his successor the former condottiere Francesco Sforza, who had married Filippo Maria's illegitimate daughter Bianca Maria, found it politically expedient to appoint humanists such as Cicco Simonetta and Francesco Filelfo to posts in his administration to provide powerful propaganda for the new regime by stressing Sforza's military prowess and road to power.[29] As did their counterparts in Florence, Milanese humanists clearly made excellent civil servants and diplomats, and wrote important histories and biographies but, unlike their Florentine contemporaries, they eulogised the achievements of their ruling *signori* rather than the superiority of their city. Whereas the Milanese court eschewed Cicero's republican idealism, they readily accepted his writings when they 'provided a powerful new language to advertise status and prestige'.[30] Combined with the old medieval tradition of chivalry, the selective application of humanism to the maintenance of political power and influence in the state of Milan produced a culture very distinct from that of either Florence or Venice.

With his legitimacy as ruler assured, Francesco Sforza rapidly 'secured his new regime, consolidating power with concessions to the nobles who had supported his rise to power and by diplomatic alliances abroad',[31] so ensuring that he was able to retain the system of aristocratic government founded by the Visconti, blessed by Milanese humanists, and with his own men – rather than the old administration – in control. Similar to arrangements in Florence and the Venetian Republic, power was to rest with a small elite. A newly established Consiglio Segreto became the heart of the Sforza regime and consisted of a small number of appointed nobles, bankers, military captains and bureaucrats 'many of whom were enfeoffed with estates and aristocratic privileges'.[32] To further enhance his authority, Francesco Sforza replaced Visconti's 14th-century castle with his immense Castello Sforzesco (1451–66), funded construction of secular and eccelesiastical buildings in his capital – including the imposing Ospedale Maggiore (begun 1460), S Maria presso S Satiro (1482) and S Maria delle Grazie (1493) – and promoted church-building in Parma and Piacenza, then under the suzerainty of Milan (see chapter 7).

Rome

Far from enhancing security in the peninsula, the re-establishment of the papacy in Rome in 1415 generated yet more inter-territorial conflict in Italy than hitherto. Motivated by the need to replenish papal coffers, Pope Martin V embarked on a military campaign in the Papal States to 'oust those rulers who had taken advantage of the absence of the Papacy in Avignon and the political vacuum caused by the Schism'.[33] Henceforth, throughout the Renaissance and beyond, the papacy adopted a proactive policy in an attempt to bolster its power-base in Rome and secure its territorial possessions through processes little different from those employed by any other regime in the peninsula.

While the Great Schism (1378–1415) had reduced both the spiritual and temporal authority of the Church in Italy, it had also provided an opportunity for humanist scholarship to develop in a more secular environment than hitherto, most notably in Florence. However, after the return of the papacy to Rome it was the papal court – traditionally an important centre of patronage – that established a strong and important link between the humanists in Florence and Rome.[34] The papal court and its popes, such as Nicholas V (1447–55) in particular, recognised that despite the content of classical texts, humanism *per se* did not conflict with the authority of the Church. 'Even the writings of Lorenzo Valla (1407–55), a Roman by origin who used his linguistic skills to criticise the Latin

Vulgate translation of the Bible and the translation of Greek philosophers' words by several scholastics, did not upset the friendly alliance of classics and Christianity'.[35] But as it was considered inappropriate for Rome to focus on Cicero's belief in the virtues of republican rule (the basis of humanism in Florence), and since it was not in the interest of humanists in the Curia to challenge either the structure of authority within the Church or the pope's position as its head, Roman humanists disingenuously supported the papal claim to supremacy within the Church by regarding the papacy as the heir to ancient Rome.[36]

During the first half of the quattrocento, papal administration was also influenced by humanism within the field of architecture and town planning, particularly during the pontificate of Nicholas V. This was manifested very largely by Nicholas's extensive programme of urban renewal in the Eternal City, in which he repaired the Aqua Vergine (and therefore improved the city's water supply), widened streets, rebuilt bridges, restored the buildings of the Capitol, renovated major basilicas and many less prestigious churches, repaired St Peter's and enlarged the Vatican (see chapter 7).[37] In the second half of the 15th century the papal administration fell increasingly under the control of 'a sort of curia élite ... as politically-minded cardinals, pro-notaries, and senior papal officials fostered and extended their position through patronage and influence'.[38] However, although in Rome such patronage was exemplified by the construction of sumptuous palaces like the Palazzo Venezia (begun 1455) and the Palazzo della Cancelleria (begun 1474), these were essentially private residences rather than administrative buildings (see chapters 5 and 7), while during the quattrocento in the Papal States the Curia elite had both little influence and little real estate.

Naples

To the south of the Eternal City, and like Ferrara and Urbino to the north, Naples was a fief of the Church, but unlike these signorial cities, it was not a part of the Papal State. It was heavily taxed by Rome, and the Neapolitan Church and the pope nominated prelates to the kingdom's benefices. However, within this context Naples was riven by dynastic power struggles, perhaps more so than any other state in the peninsula. In an attempt to settle the Neapolitan succession, Joanna II (1414–35) barred her heir, Louis III of Anjou, from inheriting the throne, instead inviting Alfonso V, king of Aragon and Sicily (1435–58) to succeed her. However, the invitation was subsequently withdrawn, whereupon she offered the throne to Louis III's brother, René of Anjou. Following the death of Joanna II in 1435, war broke out between the competing Angevin and Aragon claimants (1435–42), with Alfonso of Aragon emerging victorious, proudly adding southern Italy to his many other Mediterranean possessions: Aragon, Catalonia, Valencia, Sardinia and Sicily.

Remarkably, in the quattrocento the kingdom of Naples became a centre of humanism as, like Francesco Sforza of Milan, Alfonso attempted to legitimise his regime. Disadvantaged as a political power in the peninsula (being just one of the many feudal possessions of the House of Aragon), Alfonso attempted to compensate for Naples' weakness by turning his court into one of the most magnificent in Europe, one noted for its lavish banquets and entertainments. Alfonso employed humanists such as Pontano and Leostello to provide propaganda for his rule and to promote him 'as heir to a long line of Neapolitan rulers which stretched back into Roman mythology, stressing the tradition of loyalty of the Neapolitan subjects to their leader and the loyalty of the city to Rome'.[39]

With its important positions filled by Spanish courtiers, the Aragonese government in Naples was soon installed in the Castel Nuovo, a building subsequently adorned with a specially commissioned gatehouse (1452) that reflected both the impact of humanism on design and the grandeur of Alfonso's reign (see chapter 7). His son, Ferrante I (1458–94), grandson Ferrante II (1495) and Ferrante's uncle, Federico (1496–1501), in addition to maintaining feudalism throughout their dominions, all developed symbols of tyrannical power and authority in Naples such as the massive Renaissance palace of Poggioreale (started 1487) and the Porta Capuana begun in 1485 as part of the systematic replanning of the city (see chapter 7).

Government in the Smaller Italian States

Siena and Lucca

The political development of the Tuscan republics of Siena and Lucca during the 15th century was far less notable than that of Florence or Venice. Siena never fully recovered from the Black Death, its population falling from around 100,000 to around 30,000 between 1348 and the early quattrocento. During most of this time – except for a brief period between 1399 and 1404 when the city-state became a domain of Giangaleazzo Visconti of Milan – the republican government was beset by factional infighting, intrigue and often real chaos. Throughout much of the quattrocento civil strife was institutionalised by a system of government in which each member of the ruling elite belonged to one of Siena's five *monti* or *ordini* that competed with each other for a monopoly of power.[40] To an extent, however, political instability was kept in check: first, in periods when government was conducted by a *balia* whereby a permanent magistracy effectively replaced traditional communal councils;[41] second, in periods of power-sharing when the city's *monti* agreed to work together for the common good; third, during the pontificate of Pius II (a Siennese) when the city-state 'effectively became a papal dependency'[42] (1458 and 1463); and, finally, when the *signoria* of the Petrucci (1487–1524) implemented, according to Hale, 'the most successful power-sharing exercise of the period, in which the Petrucci acted as particularly effective chairmen of the various coalitions by which Siena was governed'.[43]

It is noteworthy that in 1459, as well as imposing his authority over the city of Siena, Pius II enhanced his influence over a wider area by commissioning the redevelopment of his birthplace Corsignano in the Siennese *contado*. With the provision of a new cathedral, a bishop's palace, a town hall and a private palace for the pontiff, the settlement – renamed Pienza – exhibits one of the earliest examples of symmetrical Renaissance town planning, its form remaining intact to the present day (see chapter 7).

For a while Lucca too rejected republicanism, being governed by a *signoria* under the merchant Paolo Guinigi from 1400 to 1430 – an outcome of the disruption caused by war with Pisa and Lucca's subsequent annexation by Pisa during the 14th century. With Guinigi's fall from power in 1430, Lucca reverted to its former republican status, avoided being taken over by Florence and remained independent until it surrendered to Napoleon's army in 1799.

Mantua

Based in Mantua, the Gonzaga dynasty ruled the different cities within their domain as separate entities and were thus able to ensure that their state was not only politically stable but a centre of excellence. As Mary Hollingsworth explains: '[t]hrough judicious marriages, skilful diplomacy and, above all, through the creation of an illustrious court, the fifteenth-century Gonzaga rulers achieved a level of distinction for their city out of all proportion to its size'[44] – a situation made possible by innovations in secular and ecclesiastical architecture that produced such buildings as the Nova Domus of the Palazzo Ducale (1480) and the churches of S Sebastiano (begun 1460) and S Andrea (1470) (see chapter 7).

The Papal States

Unlike the comparatively compact territories of, for example, Florence, Milan or Venice, the Papal States stretched from 50 miles south of the mouth of the Tiber to the north-east across Italy as far as the mouth of the Po, and because of its extent and fragility few Italian states were so weakly organised. While Ferrarra, Rimini and Urbino were controlled by rulers whose subordination to the papacy was mere lip service, it was doubtful whether city states such as Bologna were under papal suzerainty at all.

Bologna

Throughout the 15th century, the papal city-state of Bologna was governed precariously by successive members of the Bentivoglio family supported either by Milan or the Empire. Thus, only when direct papal rule was restored in 1506 could the stage be set for the development of the built environment along Renaissance lines. It was essentially a north Italian city and tended to look to the Empire or Milan for support rather than southwards to Rome. On his succession, Giovanni II not only gained the reins of power but also married Sante's widow, Ginevra, niece of Francesco Sforza[45] thereby ensuring a continuing alliance with Milan. However, while Bologna attained great fame and prosperity under Giovanni, his increasingly despotic governance drove former allies, the Malvezzi, into opposition and exile from 'where they called upon Julius II to restore Bologna to direct rule',[46] a course of action he undertook in 1506 after an interlude from papal interference of more than a century. Only then, during a period of relative stability, did the city embark on constructing buildings in the Renaissance style (see chapter 10).

Ferrara

Ferrara, like Mantua, enjoyed political stability throughout most of the 15th century, and although the D'Este *signori* Niccolò III (1393–1441), Leonello (1441–50), Borso (1450–71) and Ercole (1471–1505) 'may have lacked the political influence of their powerful neighbours in Milan or Venice',[47] they were able to consolidate their power through incisive and efficient domestic and foreign policy, including the construction of *palazzi* such as the Palazzo Schifanoia (begun

1462) and the the promotion of a major town planning project that doubled the area of the city (see chapter 7). Consequently, as Ferrara, already an important centre in the 15th century, grew in size and prestige, the ruling D'Este dynasty followed the lead of the Visconti and Sforza in Milan and the Gonzaga in Mantua and increasingly exercised absolute power.

Rimini

On the Adriatic, the tiny state of Rimini had been ruled by the powerful Malatesta family for nearly 300 years since the dynasty was founded by Malatesta da Verucchio (1212–1312), but the excommunication of Sigismund (1417–68) – noted for his violent character as well as for his enthusiastic patronage of architecture, fine art and learning – brought about a temporary weakening of the city's ties with Rome, and under Pandolfo (d 1512) it surrendered to Venice. However, after the battle of Ravenna (1512) Rimini again became a despotic papal fief.

Urbino

Only nominally a papal state, Urbino had been acquired by the Montefeltro family '*in lieu* of debts owed to them by the papacy'.[48] The Montefeltro were famous as condottieri – the penultimate member of the dynasty, Count Federico da Montefeltro (1444–82) exercising power and influence both at home and considerably beyond his city's boundaries. Federico particularly enhanced his family's authority by developing the magnificent Palazzo Ducale (1468–72), giving Urbino a reputation for courtly splendour out of all proportion to its size. Under the rule of Federico's son Guidobaldo (1482–1508), Urbino suffered political turmoil following the French invasions of Italy and became 'the target of the ambitious Cesare Borgia, who occupied the city in 1502–3'.[49] Since Guidobaldo was without an heir, on his death Urbino was inherited by his nephew, Francesco Maria della Rovere who was kinsman to Pope Julius II, and thereafter the city never regained the same degree of independence and prestige it had experienced under Federico.

Inequalities of Wealth and the Promotion of Civic Pride

Governance whether by republican oligarchies or aristocratic *signoria* brought about a total reversion to rule of the rich, by the rich and for the rich. With an even greater concentration of wealth and power in the hands of the elite, the poor became poorer and their interests were ignored. Clearly, Italian states were becoming insecure, not because of external threats (although there were many) but because of wider dissension within. The ruling elite, however, sought to retain the reins of power by promoting a sense of civic pride among their subjects. Successful policies and efficient practices ensured that funds were available to facilitate construction of magnificent public buildings, both secular and ecclesiastical, which governments believed would enhance the power and prestige of their cities, and serve as an incentive for future generations to develop even more notable buildings, so generating yet further power and influence. The highly skewed distribution of wealth in the cities throughout much of Italy thus indirectly created the very conditions under which innovations in architecture could be promoted.

Conclusion

As in the later Middle Ages, the city-states and monarchial domains of 15th-century Italy protected themselves from external aggression by strengthening or expanding their boundaries and, in parallel, reduced the risk of civil unrest by seeking to promote a sense of loyalty and civic pride among their inhabitants. The quattrocento, like the trecento, was a period of turbulence. Florence was persistently at war with Milan during much of the first half of the century and then, after a short period of peace, in conflict with Siena and its allies. Venice, in its attempt to expand its empire westward, annexed – among other cities – Padua, Brescia and Bergamo, while Milan secured suzerainty over Genoa, albeit temporarily. Even Rome involved itself in territorial conflict, supporting the seizure of Imola by a cousin of the pope and, together with Naples, siding with Siena in its struggle with Florence. Domestically, most of the largest cities of Italy were on the brink of conflict – or in conflict – as their systems of government evolved. This was as true of republican Florence, Venice, Genoa, Siena and Lucca as it was of the signorial states of Milan and Mantua, or of Rome and the Papal States. In monarchial Naples, dynastic power-politics created at least as much insecurity as anywhere else in Italy. It is within this political context that governments throughout the peninsula commissioned both secular and ecclesiastical buildings – and introduced town planning schemes – not only to enhance their own political profiles but to engender a sense of local loyalty and civic pride among their inhabitants. In Florence, from the construction of the dome of S Maria del Fiore and the Ospedale degli Innocenti during the early decades of the quattrocento to the expansion of the Palazzo del Popolo in the final years of the same century, public patronage had a major impact on the built environment, and the same explosion of publicly funded development projects was repeated time and time again across Early Renaissance Italy. Public patronage, however, was not confined to Florence, Venice, Milan, Rome and Naples, although these cities boasted the greatest number of new buildings. Often, the smaller cities such as Siena, Lucca, Mantua, Bologna, Ferrara, Urbino and Rimini witnessed the construction of new public buildings whose architectural quality was comparable or superior to that of the major cities, even if the number of buildings constructed was fewer.

Chronology

1396–1409	Genoa ruled by France.
1399	Siena becomes domain of Gian Galeazzo Visconti, ruler of Milan.
1400–30	Lucca governed by a *signoria* under merchant Paolo Guinigi.
1402	Milanese siege of Florence called off on death of Gian Galeazzo Visconti.
1405	Giangaleazzo's hier Giovanni Maria Visconti relinquishes Milan's hold on Pisa by selling the city to Florence for 200,000 florins. Venice eliminates Carrara dynasty, and seizes its capital Padua together with Bassano, Belluno, Feltre and Vicenza.
1406	Florence mounts siege of Pisa to secure its suzerainty and a maritime outlet for its trade. Death of Florentine humanist Coluccio Salutati.
1409–13	Genoa ruled by Monferrato.
1411	Florence annexes Cortona.
1415	Return of papacy to Rome heralds succession of military campaigns to re-establish papal rule in its domains in central Italy.
1418–34	**In Florence, *Arte della Lana* (wool merchants) entrusted with funding and organising construction of dome of city's cathedral of S Maria del Fiore.**
1419–26	**In Florence, *Arte della Seta* (silk workers' guild) entrusted with development of Ospedale degli Innocenti, first major building of the Early Renaissance.**
1420	Venice annexes Friuli, formerly possession of king of Hungary.

1421	Genoa cedes Leghorn to Florence.
1422–35	Genoa ruled by Milan under Filippo Maria Visconti.
1423–8	War between Florence and Milan as latter city, under Filippo Maria Visconti, attempts to regain its lost territory.
1423–57	Francesco Foscari, doge of Venice, implements programme of territorial expansion.
1423	Venice instigates campaign to seize Bergamo and Brescia from Filippo Maria Visconti of Milan.
1430	With Guinigi's fall from power, Lucca reverts to republican status.
1433	Cosimo de'Medici arrested in Florence, but swept back into power after short exile.
1434	Florence ruled by signorial government.
1435	Alfonso V, king of Aragon and Sicily, crowned king of Naples.
1441	Treaty of Cremona confirms Venice's hold on Bergamo and Brescia, together with Peschiera and part of the domain of Cremona. Subsequently, Venice secures Ravenna.
1442	Pope Eugenius IV acknowledges Alfonso of Aragon as king of Naples. Naples and Sicily become conjoined.
1444	Death of humanist, Leonardo Bruni.
1447–55	**In Rome, under Pope Nicholas V, extensive programme of urban renewal undertaken.**
1448	Demise of Visconti dynasty: power in Milan shifts to Ambrosian Republic.
1450	Ambrosian Republic in disarray; emperor bestows title of Duke of Milan on Francesco Sforza. Sforza dynasty rules Milan for almost 50 years. Francesco Sforza establishes a Consiglio Segreto to enhance governance.
1451–66	**In Milan, Francesco Sforza replaces Visconti's 14th-century castle with his immense Castello Sforzesco.**
1452	**In Naples, Alfonso I commissions grandiose gatehouse to adorn his Castel Nuovo.**
1453	Constantinople annexed by Ottoman Turks.
1454	Treaty of Lodi unites Florence, Venice, Milan and papacy in defensive alliance against Ottoman Turks. Long period of peace between Florence, Milan and Venice follows. Venice's hold on Bergamo, Brescia, Padua and Treviso confirmed but its possession of Ravenna relinquished. Mainland boundaries of Venice remain intact until Napoleon dissolves the republic in 1797.
1455	**In Rome, work begins on construction of Palazzo Venezia.**
1458	Ferrante I becomes King of Naples (1458–94); Sicily becomes independent entity. In Florence, Cosimo de'Medici and his supporters create a Council of Two Hundred to gain greater representation.

1458–63	Under Pope Pius II (an adopted Siennese), Siena effectively a papal dependency.
1459	**Pius II commissions development of Pienza.**
1460	**In Venice, the Porta Magna of the Arsenale is completed.**
	In Milan, work begins on the Ospedale Maggiore.
	In Mantua, Ludovico Gonzaga commissions construction of church of S Sebastiano.
	In Bologna, until 1506, political instability militates against introduction of classical style of architecture.
1462	**In Ferrara, Borso D'Este commissions construction of Palazzo Schifanoia and promotes major town planning project to double size of city.**
1462	Siennese invite Alonso, son of King Ferrante of Naples, to lead Siennese army against Florence to secure territory in Tuscany. Siena supported by Pope Sixtus IV.
1464–78	Genoa ruled by Milan under the Sforza.
1468	**In Urbino, Count Federico da Montefeltro commissions development of magnificent Palazzo Ducale.**
1469	King Ferrante of Naples and Sixtus IV make peace with Florentines.
1470	**In Mantua, Ludovico Gonzaga commissions church of S Andrea.**
1474	**In Rome, work commences on Palazzo della Cancelleria.**
1478	Pope Sixtus IV implicated in the Pazzi conspiracy against Lorenzo de'Medici.
1479	Turkish incursions force Venice to abandon its commercial port of Negroponte.
1480	In reaction to Pazzi conspiracy, Medici faction in Florence replaces Council of Two Hundred with Council of Seventy.
	In Mantua, Federigo Gonzaga commissions construction of Nova Domus of Palazzo Ducale.
1482	**In Milan, Francesco Sforza commissions work on church of S Maria presso S Satiro.**
1483	**In Venice, work starts on construction of east wing of Palazzo Ducale.**
1485	**In Naples, Porte Capuana commissioned by Ferrante I.**
1487	**In Naples, Ferrante I commissions palace of Poggioreale.**
1487–1524	Siena ruled by *signoria* of the Petrucci.
1487–99	Genoa ruled by Milan under the Sforza.
1489	Cyprus incorporated into Venetian empire.
1493	**In Milan, Francesco Sforza commissions work on church of S Maria delle Grazie.**
1494	In Florence, Piero de'Medici expelled by his signorial government for compliance with French invasion plans. Signorial government then replaced by republic under control of all-male Grand Council of Florentines over 29 years old whose forefathers had held political office.

1495	Council of Eighty set up in Florence to exercise republican rule. King Charles VIII of France invades Naples to force abdication of King Alfonso II (1494–5) in favour of his son, Ferrante II (1495–6).
	Milan participates in defeat of French at Fornova.
1497	Pope Alexander VI excommunicates charismatic Florentine priest Savonarola.
1498	At instigation of Florentine Republic, Savonarola hanged and burned at the stake.
1499	Venice defeated by Turkey at battle of Sapienza and forfeits its coastal fortresses in the Peloponnese.
	Ludovico Sforza forced to flee from French under Louis XII as they arrive at the gates of Milan. French subsequently rule Milan until 1525.

Notes

1 M Hollingsworth, *Patronage in Renaissance Italy* (London: John Murray, 1994), p 158.
2 Ibid, p 15.
3 L Martines, *Power and Imagination. City-states in Renaissance Italy* (London: Pimlico, 2002), p 130.
4 M Mallett, 'Politics and Society', in G Holmes (ed), *The Illustrated History of Italy* (Oxford: Oxford University Press, 2001), p 74.
5 Ibid, p 76.
6 Ibid.
7 V Lintner, *A Traveller's History of Italy*, 3rd edn (Gloucester: Windrush Press, 1998), p 86.
8 Mallett, 'Politics and Society', p 76.
9 Hollingsworth, *Patronage in Renaissance Italy*, p 160.
10 Ibid, p 16.
11 JR Hale (ed), *The Concise Encyclopaedia of the Italian Renaissance* (London: Thames and Hudson, 1981), p 285.
12 Ibid, p 62.
13 Ibid, p 61.
14 G Holmes, 'Renaissance Culture', in G Holmes (ed), *The Oxford Illustrated History of Italy* (London: Oxford University Press, 2001), pp 93–4.
15 Hollingsworth, *Patronage in Renaissance Italy*, pp 17–20.
16 R Goldthwaite, *The Building of Renaissance Florence. An Economic and Social History* (Baltimore and London: Johns Hopkins University Press, 1982), p 59.
17 P Burke, *The Italian Renaissance. Culture and Society in Italy*, 2nd edn (Oxford: Polity, 1986), pp 215–16.
18 Ibid, pp 50–1.
19 D Waley, *The Italian City-Republic*, 3rd edn (New York: Longman, 1988), pp 171–2.
20 Mallett, 'Politics and Society', p 75.

21 Hollingsworth, *Patronage in Renaissance Italy*, p 8.

22 At the beginning of the 16th century, Leonardo da Vinci and Michelangelo were commissioned to paint enormous frescoes on opposite sides of the Salone dei Cinquecento, the recently constructed meeting hall of Florence's Consiglio Maggiore (Great Council) located within an extended Palazzo del Popolo (as the Palazzo Vecchio was called during republican periods of government). Leonardo's *Battle of Anghiari* was left unfinished or destroyed because he failed to master an experimental technique he was employing, while Michelangelo's *Battle of Cascina* was abandoned at the cartoon stage when he was summoned to Rome by Pope Julius II in 1505 to work on his tomb.

23 Hollingsworth, *Patronage in Renaissance Italy*, p 84.

24 Ibid, p 103.

25 Mallett, 'Politics and Society', p 75.

26 G Hanlon, *Early Modern Italy, 1550–1800* (Basingstoke: Macmillan, 2000), pp 49–50.

27 Hollingsworth, *Patronage in Renaissance Italy*, p 114.

28 Ibid, p 163.

29 Ibid, p 167.

30 Ibid, p 159.

31 Ibid, p 167.

32 Mallett, 'Politics and Society', p 75.

33 Hollingsworth, *Patronage in Renaissance Italy*, p 235.

34 G Holmes, 'Renaissance Culture', in G Holmes(ed), *The Oxford Illustrated History of Italy* (London: Oxford University Press, 2001), p 93.

35 Ibid, p 94.

36 Hollingsworth, *Patronage in Renaissance Italy*, pp 245–6.

37 Ibid, pp 240–1.

38 Mallett, 'Politics and Society', p 75.

39 Hollingsworth, *Patronage in Renaissance Italy*, p 188.

40 Hale, *Concise Encyclopaedia*, p 302.

41 Ibid, p 301.

42 Ibid.

43 Ibid.

44 Hollingsworth, *Patronage in Renaissance Italy*, p 16.

45 D Hay and J Law, *Italy in the Age of the Renaissance* (Harlow: Longman, 1989), p 217.

46 Ibid, p 219.

47 Hollingsworth, *Patronage in Renaissance Italy*, p 202.

48 Ibid, p 192.

49 Ibid, p 201.

CHAPTER 7

PUBLIC DEVELOPMENT AND THE RE-EMERGENCE OF CLASSICAL ARCHITECTURE AND TOWN PLANNING

Introduction

In rejecting the Gothic style of architecture during the quattrocento, northern and central Italy were the first regions in the world to re-adopt Classicism in building design. What, in particular, drove patrons and architects to seek an alternative to medieval taste? What signalled the Early Renaissance in architecture and planning? In answer, one need look no further than the emergence of humanism in late medieval Italy (see chapter 2). Although generations of scholars had studied classical texts to reinforce or determine their theological or philosophical beliefs, by the 14th century civil administrators were reading the classics more widely in the hope that the civilisation that had produced them, namely the Roman Republic, would provide a model for the development of forms of government worthy of the dignity of humankind. From this, it was but a short step to the rediscovery and careful study of the most important Roman treatise on architecture and town planning: Vitruvius's *De architectura*, written in about 27 BC and recovered from a monastery in St Gallen, Switzerland in 1416.

However, the Vitruvian impact on architecture in the quattrocento was not immediate. Although Filippo Brunelleschi (1377–1446) – the first and one of the greatest architects of the Early Renaissance – had visited Rome to gain an insight into classical design and structural technology, his earlier work in Florence was undoubtedly inspired more by the Tuscan Proto-Renaissance than by classical Rome. It was only after Leon Battista Alberti (1404–72) published *De re aedificatoria* in 1452 and Filarete (Antonio Alverino, c 1400–69) completed his *Trattato d'architettura* in the early 1460s that the full importance of Vitruvius's work was recognised, at least in much of Italy. Applying Vitruvian principles to contemporary requirements, both Alberti and Filarete focused on models of classical form, *viz* Doric, Ionic and Corinthian orders (fig 7.1), the Roman triumphal arch, the pedimented temple front and the dome and, in emphasising the importance of geometric harmony, demonstrated that in a harmonious building 'nothing could be added to or taken away except for the worse',[1] a concept neither desired nor understood during the Middle Ages.

By the mid-15th century, the design of important buildings, therefore, was no longer left to the practical master-builder but became the responsibility of a new professional, the architect who in measuring classical ruins and reading

Figure 7.1 The classical orders

Alberti and Filarete was obliged to become both archaeologist and scholar.[2] Architects, of course, did not operate in a vacuum. Their patrons were very often influential in matters of design, while architects were normally obliged to work closely with skilled craftsmen, building committees, material suppliers and corporate bodies such as guilds and confraternities (although the latter were more likely to be active in the private rather than public sector). It is in this context that civic governments commissioned a substantial number of prominent secular and ecclesiastical buildings of classical design throughout much of the quattrocento.

The Larger Cities of Central and Northern Italy

Florence

In the quattrocento, as in the later Middle Ages, the government of Florence was alone among the sovereign authorities of Italy in delegating responsibility for construction of major public buildings to the guilds, rather than assuming this role itself.[3] Begun in the trecento, the city's *duomo*, S Maria del Fiore, was still far from complete in the early years of the following century, essentially missing an enormous dome intended – according to a model of 1368 – to measure 45 metres in diameter and 100 metres in height from ground level. Because of its dimensions, by the second decade of the quattrocento no architect had yet found a solution to the problem of spanning the crossing where the dome was to be positioned. The cathedral's *Opera* (its works department), composed of members of the *Arte della Lana* (woolworkers' guild), therefore introduced a selection procedure in 1418 to appoint an architect capable of designing a suitable dome and of supervising work on the project. After much dispute, Filippo Brunelleschi was awarded the commission and began work on the dome in 1420. His winning design made it possible to construct the dome without the use of suspended scaffolding by 'building two shells of different strengths interconnected by carefully dimensioned stone ribs'.[4] Apart from producing an intricate design, Brunelleschi painstakingly selected the appropriate materials, produced new building tools and machinery where necessary, supervised construction and ensured that his enormous studio and workshop were appropriately coordinated and organised.[5] Completed in 1436, the dome become one of the most prominent features of the Early Renaissance, its size unsurpassed until the cupola of St Peter's in Rome was constructed a century and a half later.

Another Florentine guild, the *Arte della Seta* (silk weavers' guild) donated funds to erect Europe's first orphanage, the Ospedale degli Innocenti, and commissioned Brunelleschi to undertake its design and supervise construction. Built between 1419 and 1426, the facade of the building, constructed on a stepped plinth, is characterised by a lengthy arcaded portico facing out over a *piazza* (later known as the Piazza della SS Annunziata) and featuring the deployment of slender Corinthian columns, with an upper storey of simple pedimented windows resting on an entablature and aligned centrally with the arches below. Brunelleschi ensured that the overall design followed the architectural principles of Vitruvius: for example, the height of the pillars corresponds to the distance between the pillars; the same distance separates the base of the architrave and the beginning of the roof; and the distance between the top of the steps and the top of the cornice is twice the height of the pillars. In the interior of the portico, the height of the pillars equals the width of the arcade which, together with the pillars being spaced equidistant from one another, creates a series of modular

Photo 7.1 Filippo Brunelleschi, dome of the cathedral of S Maria del Fiore, Florence, begun 1420. An ingenious structure consisting of an inner and outer shell linked by props to counteract excessive thrust.

cubes along the length of the portico. Overall, the Ospedale degli Innocenti – Brunelleschi's first secular building – provided a model that was used throughout the quattrocento and beyond to determine the design of porticos, cloisters and courtyards throughout much of urban Italy.

Venice

In contrast to Florence, the Early Renaissance as witnessed in the development of Venetian public buildings did not manifest itself until the late quattrocento, an even longer delay than that experienced in the private sector. Public patrons employed the Late Gothic style well into the century, very often to spectacular effect. The Porta della Carta, for example, is a magnificent structure incorporated into a new entrance to the inner courtyard of the Palazzo Ducale. Funded by

Photo 7.2 Filippo Brunelleschi, Ospedale degli Innocenti, Florence, 1419–26. One of the earliest of Renaissance masterpieces notable for its arcade alongside the Piazza della SS Annunziata and its terracotta medallions by Andrea della Robbia.

Doge Francesco Foscari, designed by Bartolomeo Bon and begun in 1438, the gateway with its Gothic features is more reminiscent of the work of a jeweller than that of an architect, and was initially enhanced by the application of blue and gold paint, although this has long since been eroded.

A very different structure, the Porta Magna of the Arsenale, begun in 1460, marks the arrival of the Early Renaissance in the *Serenissima*. Financed by the republic under the dogeship of Pasquale Malipiero, designed by Antonio Gambello and inspired by the 1st-century Arch of the Sergii in Pola (present-day Pula), construction of the *porta* was motivated by the expansion of the Ottoman Empire and the eventual fall of Constantinople in 1457, and it was incorporated into major fortifications and a dock expansion scheme already underway. As a means of engendering patriotism, its classical facade was crowned by the winged lion of St Mark, a sculpture added in haste during construction.

By the 1480s, Early Renaissance style in Venice was well established. The east wing of the Palazzo Ducale was constructed between 1483 and 1498, a massive undertaking, and its impressive Scala dei Giganti was erected between 1484 and 1501. Under the patronage of a succession of doges, the east wing was largely designed by Antonio Rizzo and his successor Pietro Lombardo,

Photo 7.3 Attributed to Antonio Gambello, Porta Magna of the Arsenale, Venice, 1460. The first Renaissance structure in central Venice.

Photo 7.4 Antonio Rizzo and Pietro Lombardo, east wing of the Palazzo Ducale, Venice, 1483–98. Reconstructed after a fire, the edifice comprises four richly decorated storeys.

although the lavish ornamentation of its facade is attributable to Mauro Codussi.[6] The aesthetic quality of the wing is enhanced by the Scala dei Giganti connected to it from the courtyard below. The staircase, designed by Antonio Rizzo, is surmounted by collosal statues of Mercury and Neptune (symbolising the importance of trade and the sea to the wellbeing of Venice), and is overlooked by the Lion of St Mark placed above an arch on the first-floor loggia.

A final manifeston of Early Renaissance Venetian architecture is the Torre dell'Orologio (Clock Tower), commissioned by the republic and designed by Codussi and Lombardo. Built betwen 1496 and 1506, the tower was constructed above a large portal that leads to the Mercerie, the trading centre of Venice. While Codussi was responsible for incorporating its ornate mechanical clock, the lion of St Mark, a statue of the Virgin and the bell of the Moors, Lombardo designed the two side wings that were added subsequently.[7]

Photo 7.5 Mauro Codussi and Pietro Lombardo, Torre dell'Orologio, Venice, 1496–1506. Accommodates a remarkable clock showing the hours in Roman numerals and a movable inner ring displaying the signs of the zodiac.

Milan

Under Visconti and Sforza patronage a spate of building work was undertaken in Milan ranging from the city's *castello* to construction of a major hospital and the extension of ecclesiastical buildings. Founded in the 14th century by Galeazzo II Visconti (1355–78), the *castello* was subsequently enlarged by the military architect Giovanni Magatti on the instruction of Galeazzo's son, Giangaleazzo, and its residential quarters continued to be added to throughout the reign of the last of the Visconti rulers, Filippo Maria. The *castello* was largely destroyed by the Milanese when the Ambrosian Republic came to power, but when that was superseded by the rule of Francesco Sforza, as the new figurehead of Milan he immediately commissioned the architect 'il Filarete' (Antonio Averlino) and the military engineers Giovanni da Milano and Marcoleone da Nogarolo to design and build a new *castello* to replace the former structure.[8] Rather than acting as a bastion against external aggression, as the builders of the previous *castello* had set out to provide, the new edifice, the Castello Sforzesco, looked inwards towards the city centre. Under the direction of the Florentine architect Benedetto Ferrini,

Photo 7.6 Antonio Averlino (Filarete) and others, Castello Sforzesco, Milan, soon after 1450. A massive red-brick quadrilateral building with machicolated and crenellated walls. Overlooking the city, its facade is endowed with three defensive towers, the central one designed by Filarete.

the northern sections were developed for residential use while the southern facade of the *castello* facing the city centre was essentially defensive. Incorporating crenellations, machicolations, two sharply rusticated circular towers at each end and a three-tier central tower, the new *castello* was clearly intended to protect the ruling regime from opponents within Milan, rather than from those without.

In 1460, as a consequence of a series of plague epidemics, Filarete received a further commission from Francesco Sforza. This time he was asked to design a substantial hospital complex, the Ospedale Maggiore. While many of Filarete's proposals were implemented, some were later abandoned. As part of a symmetrical and geometric plan, he suggested the development of two square blocks, one each for men and women and each subdivided into two courtyards of equal size, together with systems for channelling water and providing ventilation. A centrally sited church would be provided within its own rectangular courtyard.

Some years later, Francesco's son Ludovico resumed the family's interest in commissioning major building schemes, and summoned an up-and-coming architect Donato Bramante to Milan from Urbino around the year 1480 to work on

Photo 7.7 Filarete, Ospedale Maggiore, Milan, begun 1460. Although intended to be classical in style, this hospital complex was completed with the use of Gothic motifs by local architects after Filarete returned to his birthplace in Florence.

various Sforza projects. His first commission, granted in 1482, was to contribute to the renovation of the pre-Romanesque centrally planned church of S Maria presso S Satiro. Work on the church had started in 1477, but an obstacle in the form of the via del Falcone prevented its full realisation. Bramante, therefore, by designing a classically inspired trompe l'oeil, convincingly gave the impression that the building's plan conformed to a Greek cross. Although he ensured that the inside of the church displayed a plethora of classical attributes such as Corinthian columns, corner pilasters, complete entablatures and semi-circular niches,[9] it is unfortunate that his design for the facade was never implemented and thus left no legacy upon the urban townscape.

Ludovico's contribution to the built environment of Milan began to increase substantially in 1493 when he entrusted Bramante with the rebuilding of much of the church of S Maria delle Grazie. Although the late Gothic Dominican church, designed by Guiniforte Solari, had been built as recently as 1463, Ludovico

Photo 7.8 Donato Bramante, church of S Maria delle Grazie, Milan, begun 1493. Bramante demolished Guiniforte Solari's chancel of 1465–90 and replaced it with a massive brick and terracotta Renaissance dome and drum, also adding a classical portal to the basilica's facade.

decided to demolish most of it in stages to allow a more modern structure to emerge. Bramante was thus able to provide a new chancel as a mausoleum for the Sforza family. Its large choir and dome, each with a profusion of classical features, intensify the experience of space and represent 'the last and most magnificent work that could be carried out with the technical and formal means of the Quattrocento'.[10] It might be thought that the plans for nave and facade were shelved following the fall of Ludovico and the Sforza dynasty in 1499, but it is possible that its current facade and porchway were designed by Bramante.[11]

Bologna

Like its prominent 15th-century ecclesiastical buildings, Bologna's newly constructed civic buildings of the quattrocento are overshadowed in scale and

Photo 7.9 Palazzo del Podestà, Bologna, remodelling begun 1484. The governor's palace is notable for its ground-floor arcade, its balustrade, rounded windows separated by pilasters on the upper storey, and an attic pierced by oculi.

number by their predecessors of the trecento, and there was relatively little new development. The Palazzo dei Notai (begun 1381) was further developed by Bartolomeo Fieravanti (1420–40), and between the 1440s and 1460s Aristotele Fioravanti was commissioned to extend the 13th century Palazzo d'Accursio to the right of the main portal (see Photo 3.11). Even the newly built Palazzo del Podestà, constructed between 1484 and the early seicento, was remodelled on an earlier building begun in the early 13th century, and incorporated the Arengo (a tall tower) that had been built in 1212.

The new *palazzo* was designed by an unknown architect but work on the building was executed by the stonemason Marsilio d'Antonio Infrangi-pane. The building incorporated many imposing and monumental features including sturdy half-columns set before the piers, unique four-leafed bosses on its pillars, impressive pilaster articulation, rusticated window surrounds and a projecting cornice with its balustrade.[12] As in late medieval Bologna, there was continued reliance on brick in the construction of public buildings throughout the quattrocento.

Rome

With a population reaching only 55,000 by 1500, and after the long absence of the pope, Rome was still a relatively small city when compared to Venice and Milan, both of which contained around twice that number of inhabitants by the turn of the century. Similarly, the number of new public buildings commissioned by the papacy was smaller than for other major cities in central and northern Italy. Although Nicholas V (1447–55) used papal funds to extend the original Vatican palace of the early 13th century by building the Cortile del Pappagallo, and Sixtus IV (1471–84) added the eponymous Sistine Chapel to the complex in 1473, both are relatively small-scale developments and architecturally of little significance, notwithstanding that the latter contains the Michelangelo frescoes executed in 1508–12 and 1535–41, some time after the building's completion.

Of the very few building projects financed by the papacy, the churches of S Maria del Popolo and S Maria delle Pace are the most prominent. The first, started in 1472, was funded by Sixtus IV and was the earliest domed

Photo 7.10 S Maria del Popolo, Rome, begun 1472. Founded 1099 but rebuilt in the late 15th century, the church is notable for its Early Renaissance facade.

church to be built in the Eternal City in the Early Renaissance style,[13] its basilican facade being the first example of this genre in Italy.[14] In 1505, a choir designed by Bramante was added to the structure in accordance with the spiritual needs of the Augustinian monks to whom the church was then donated. The second, S Maria delle Pace, also funded by Sixtus IV, was begun in 1482 and designed by Baccio Pontelli. It was built as a memorial church to commemorate a peace treaty concluded between Rome, Florence and other Italian states in 1478.[15]

The Smaller Cities of Northern and Central Italy

In the quattrocento, a large part of northern Italy was under the suzerainty of Venice and Milan and of those states that remained comparatively independent, Mantua and Ferrara were the most prominent – each containing a population of around 20,000. Under the Gonzaga, the largest building in Mantua, the Palazzo Ducale, was extended from its late medieval origins as the Palazzo del Capitano into an immense complex in the 15th century to include the massive Castello S Giorgio and the Nova Domus. Whereas the former building is of Gothic design and, being on a lakeside site, was constructed essentially for defensive purposes (see Photo 3.27), the latter building designed by Fancelli for Federico Gonzaga (1478–84) is classical in style and intended for residential use. It boasts a substantial 13-bay, two-storey facade, each storey with lower and upper windows, and an attic storey and loggia crowning a turret-shaped corner projection at each end, a configuration possibly inspired by palace design in Venice over the previous 200 years or more.[16] Although the Nova Domus is far from complete – it was intended to be part of a quadrangular block of similar buildings constructed around a spacious garden court – it nevertheless created a type that was to have many imitators over the following century and beyond.[17]

In the development of Mantua, the Gonzaga were equally notable in funding construction of churches. In 1460, work began on the church of S Sebastiano to replace a 10th-century oratory. Financed by Ludovico and designed by Alberti, the new church is a huge two-storey building conforming to a Greek-cross plan and comprising a large nave in its basement with a massive superstructure above. The facade of the basement originally had five arcades that led into the vestibule of the lower church, but rebuilding work in the early 20th century reduced this number to three, while the facade of the superstructure contains five openings, the outer two arched portals being reached by flights of steps similarly of recent origin. Four very plain pilasters support a deep entablature but this is broken in the middle by a window with an arch above which protrudes into the crowning pediment.

A decade after work commenced on S Sebastiano, Ludovico Gonzaga accepted an outstanding design from Alberti to replace a small church due to be demolished. After the death of Alberti in April 1472, Luca Fancelli – already commissioned to produce the design – faithfully followed Alberti's plans in their entirety. The facade of the resulting church of S Andrea is very largely determined by its main internal attribute – its dominating, aisleless and barrel-vaulted nave. The central feature of the facade is thus an enormous triumphal arch (possibly based on the Arch of Titus in Rome), a portal flanked either side by bays containing a door, niche and window in vertical sequence, with an entablature and cornice above supported by four giant pilasters on enormous plinths. Unusually, the facade is crowned by a pediment with an unusual *ombrellone* (canopy) above.

Photo 7.11 Fancelli, Nova Domus, Palazzo Ducale, Mantua, 1478–84. Classical in style, this two-storeyed residential villa was influential in the development of numerous urban and suburban villas in the cinquecento.

Photo 7.12 Leon Battista Alberti and Luca Fancelli, church of S Andrea, Mantua, 1470. Dominating the Piazza Mantegna, the basilica is an Italian Renaissance masterpiece noted for its classical facade, tympanum, triumphal arch and niches set between giant pilasters.

If one agrees with Heydenreich, S Andrea is architecturally the most important church built in the quattrocento;[18] undoubtedly it is the most original.

Whereas signorial patronage in Mantua continued apace throughout the quattrocento, in Ferrara this practice was far more subdued. Almost the only building of note to be constructed was the Palazzo Schifanoia. Commissioned by Borsa I in 1462 and designed by Benvenuto degli Ordini and Biagio Rossetti, the summer *palazzo* of the D'Este family has a brick facade pierced by windows and a portal which, in keeping with the style of the city, are encased within ornamented terracotta arches.

The principal cities of the Venetian inland empire, Verona, Brescia and Padua, each retained a high degree of civic responsibility throughout the quattrocento. In Verona, the Loggia del Consiglio was built between 1474 and 1493 as the seat of the city council, and with its elegant portico, pilasters, mullioned windows, polychromed marble facing and sculpted decoration represents the flowering of the Veronese Renaissance.[19] In Brescia, however, only the ground-floor loggia of the Palazzo Comunale was ready by the end of the 15th century; completion

Photo 7.13 Loggia del Consiglio, Verona, 1474–93. An outstanding Early Renaissance edifice in the Venetian-Renaissance style.

of the building had to await the mid-16th century. Nevertheless, with its sturdy columns partly encased within the arched wall of the loggia, the projections of the entablature above, and the roundels and busts that are placed in the spandrels, the loggia offers a foretaste of the grand style of classical architecture that was to emerge in the seicento.[20] Compared to its Veronese and Brescian counterparts, the Loggia del Consiglio at Padua, begun in 1501, is a much less decorative example of the genre.

Within the Milanese territories, the Visconti and Sforza dynasties arguably surpassed the Gonzagas of Mantua in funding the construction of buildings designed to reflect their power and influence over their domains. In addition to large-scale commissions in the city of Milan, the Visconti and Sforza contributed substantially to the development of major buildings in and near Pavia. However, the earliest of these, the Certosa (begun in 1396 and largely finished by 1473), while boasting some very fine Renaissance architectural elements especially on its west front, hardly contributes to urban development since it was erected in open

Photo 7.14 Filippino Grassi, Palazzo Comunale, Brescia, begun 1490. While the ground floor dates from the late quattrocento, the upper highly decorated floor was constructed in 1554–74, possibly under the direction of Jacopo Sansovino, Galeazzo Alessi or Andrea Palladio.

countryside and remains to this day in a rural setting. Ironically, the unfinished *duomo*, which is situated in the centre of Pavia, is a sad outcome of a not altogether successful collaboration between Cristoforo Rocchi, Giovanni Antonio Amadeo, Bramante, Francesco di Giorgio and possibly Leonardo da Vinci, who between them (and aided and abetted by Cardinal Ascanio Sforza) seemed intent on experimenting 'to achieve monumentality with all the means available at the time'.[21]

Despite self-glorification, like other *signori* the Sforza were willing to share government with the communes, and when new town halls or their like were required, communes often had a free hand in commissioning their design and construction. When Alessandro Sforza held court in the Adriatic city of Pesaro (1445–73), the commune commissioned construction of its Palazzo Comunale, the ground floor in 1450 and the rest of the building in 1470. Possibly designed by Giorgio da Sebenico, its modestly decorated facade overlooking the city's central *piazza* features an arched porticoed loggia on its ground floor supported by short rusticated columns, unaligned windows resting on a deep entablature

Photo 7.15   Cristoforo Rocchi and Giovanni Antonio Amadeo, *duomo*, Pavia, begun 1488.
An enormous cathedral with its initial designs modified by Bramante and Leonardo da Vinci.
Its dome – one of Italy's largest – was not added until 1884–5, and its facade not completed
until 1933, some would say unsuccessfully.

on the first floor, and a cornice and crenellation crown above. The building is
of note since it is a good example of a transitional design, midway between Late
Gothic and Early Renaissance.

Within the Papal States, two quasi-independent cities, Rimini and Urbino,
witnessed a remarkable flowering of Early Renaissance architecture. Throughout
much of the quattrocento, signorial authority in Rimini was exercised by Sigismondo Malatesta (1417–68), '[a] man of power and lust, ambitious and intel-
ligent'.[22] Sigismondo aimed to emulate the Medici and D'Este by making his
capital a centre of learning and humanistic culture, and as part of this process
sought to transform the modest friar church of S Francesco – in which many
of his ancestors were entombed – into 'a resplendent monument to his own
glory'.[23] With work commencing in 1450 under the direction of Alberti (his first
commission), the aisleless medieval church was clad in a shell of classical design:
its facade incorporating a triumphal arch (albeit unfinished) and large niches
intended for sarcophagi for himself and his mistress, and its sides containing deep

Photo 7.16 Attributed to Giorgio da Sebenico, Palazzo Comunale, Pesaro, 1450–70. Overlooking the Piazza del Popolo, the design of the *palazzo* is an interesting example of a building that incorporates both Late Gothic and Early Renaissance features.

arches planned to accommodate the tombs of notable poets and scholars. In part because Alberti was inspired by the design of antique Roman structures in Rimini, such as the Arch of Augustus, the reconstructed church of S Francesco became one of the most authentic representations of classical architecture yet achieved during the Renaissance, and was thus regarded with distaste particularly by Pius II who viewed it as a pagan temple.

Although Sigismondo stamped his mark on the city of Rimini, the scale of Federico da Montefeltro's influence on the built environment of Urbino was immeasurably greater. Instead of focusing his attention on the construction of a family pantheon, he oversaw the development of an enormous hill-top complex, the Palazzo Ducale (started 1450). Designed by Luciano Laurana in close collaboration with Federico, the *palazzo* arguably reflects the spirit of its patron more vividly than does any other building constructed in the quattrocento; remarkably, moreover, it could not have been inspired by models elsewhere in Italy since these had not fully emerged. On its western flank, and overlooking open countryside, the dominating feature of the Palazzo Ducale is a turreted facade incorporating a multi-storey loggia; the centre of the building is a spacious arcaded courtyard; and the eastern side of the *palazzo*

Photo 7.17 Leon Battista Alberti, church of S Francesco, Rimini, begun 1450. Dominated by a triumphal arch and displaying many other classical motifs, the unfinished edifice envelops an earlier Gothic church.

with its transverse wing overlooks the city's central square, the Piazza Duca Federico.

After Federico's death in 1482, the *piazza* was further adorned, this time by the church of S Bernardino. As one of the first square-shaped and domed memorial chapels of the Renaissance, and with a barely discernible nave, it was commissioned by his family, designed by Francesco di Giorgio Martini and completed by 1490.

The South

Naples had for long been the largest city in Italy, and its population increased to a staggering 150,000 by 1500 making it considerably larger than Venice and Milan. However, its size was not reflected in a proliferation of Early Renaissance architecture, despite the city being systematically replanned in the late quattro-cento. A major exception is the gatehouse of the Castel Nuovo. The edifice was commissioned by Alfonso I in 1452 and is the work of two Dalmatian architects,

Photo 7.18 Luciano Laurana, Palazzo Ducale, Urbino, begun 1450. The aesthetically pleasing courtyard of the palace, the Cortile d'Onore, became the prototype for a host of similar courtyards constructed in Italy throughout the Renaissance.

Pietro di Martino da Milano and Francesco Laurana, who set it between the two round towers of the late medieval castle. In contrast to the gloominess of the foreboding towers, the gateway is a cocktail of Roman classicism and ornate decoration, derived jointly from the architectural styles of Pola and the south. The gateway incorporates two triumphal arches set one above the other, the upper structure being attractively crowned with niches and a tympanum. In total, its features make the gateway 'the most outstanding example of the Aragonese *rinascità*' anywhere in the kingdom.[24] The only other prominent example of public development of the period is the Porta Capuana. With its design entrusted to the northern architect Giuliano da Maiano in 1485, and its execution undertaken by Neapolitan craftsmen, the attributes of this simple classical structure are in marked contrast to those of the gatehouse, and as an integral part of the city's development 'make it one of the most beautiful monuments of the period'.[25]

On the island of Sicily, its capital Palermo was virtually devoid of Early Renaissance building in the public sector. Rather than being influenced by the classical paradigm of northern and central Italy, it adhered to its Angevin and Catalan architectural legacy well into the quattrocento as exemplified by the great portico on the south side of its cathedral, designed by Antonio Gambara and begun in 1429 (see Photo 1.8).

Urban Planning during the Early Renaissance

Within the city-state of Siena, the hill settlement of Pienza was the scene of a remarkable transition. Its medieval core was transformed into an Early Renaissance urban centre that became the basis for urban planning in Italy throughout the following century and a half.

Between 1459 and 1462, Bernardo Rossellino was commissioned by Aeneas Silvio Piccolomini – formerly bishop of Siena and now Pope Pius II – to restructure

Photo 7.19   Pietro da Milano and Francesco Laurana, gateway of Castel Nuovo, Naples, begun 1452. A decorated triumphal arch commemorating the glory of the House of Aragon – a masterpiece of the Early Renaissance.

Photo 7.20 Bernardo Rossellino, *duomo*, Pienza, 1459–62. A classical facade masking a 'German-style' medieval hall church.

the village of the pontiff's birth, Corsignano, to enable it to become an epis-copal seat. In accordance with Pius II's commission, a new cathedral was built centre-place and while it incorporated a classical facade its interior was Neo-Gothic and reminiscent of a southern German hall church. On the edge of a newly laid-out trapezoid *piazza*, it was flanked to its right by the pontiff's palace (the Palazzo Piccolomini), built broadly in the style of the Rucellai Palace in Florence (also designed by Rossellino) and incorporating loggias at its rear overlooking the Val d'Orcia. To the left of the cathedral, Rossellino placed the far less imposing bishop's residence (the Palazzo Vescovile) and, opposite the cathedral, he sited a new Palazzo Comunale as the centre for civic administration (fig 7.2).

It is of note that while the facade of the cathedral was constructed mainly of white travertine, the remaining buildings were built from ochre sandstone,[26] and whereas fully rounded Ionic and Corinthian columns adorned the facade of the cathedral, Piccolomini's palace made do with shallow flat pilasters and the bishop's residence lacked orders of any sort. Overall, the centre of Pienza conveys an impression of restraint and a lack of flamboyance and the design of its cathedral – despite certain similarities in its facade with that of the church of S Francesco in Rimini – bears no comparison with the 'paganistic' style of Malatesta's church so abhorred by Pius II. Although Pienza saw no further development during the Renaissance after the death of Pius II in 1464, and still remains a small town, the planned core of the settlement could have formed the centre of a considerably larger planned city in the centuries ahead.

Remarkably, there were no other empirical examples of urban planning in 15th-century Italy, but planning theory – dormant since antiquity – saw a revival, exerting a gradual but definite influence on the configuration of urban development. Although the centre of Pienza was developed in a coordinated manner at broadly the same time, it differed very little from the urban core of countless medieval towns that had taken generations to evolve; had Pienza expanded into a town of some size, it almost certainly would have acquired the grid-iron street pattern that became the norm in much of Early Renaissance development, as it had been throughout much of the Roman Empire.

However, this traditional form of development did not find favour with Antonio Averlino – otherwise known as Filarete (c 1400–69) – who suggested an alternative approach to urban design. In the second of his 24 books, collectively entitled *Trattato d'architettura* and written c 1460, Filarete set out the attributes of what he called the 'ideal' inland city which he called Sforzinda (in tribute to his Milanese patron Francesco Sforza). In his 12th book he described the features of a coastal city, Plousiapolis, that were derived from an ancient classical settlement. In both cases, the cities would be based on an eight-point, star-shaped plan within a circle and contain: three central *piazzie* with a cathedral and ruler's palace around the main *piazza*; a town hall in the centre of the second *piazza* with a treasury and prison around its edges; and a marketplace and headquarters for the chief of police in the third *piazza*. However, Filarete's most innovative proposal was that, instead of a grid-iron pattern of squares and streets, there would be eight radial avenues connecting the *piazze* with the gateways of the outer walls of the city (fig 7.3). Among his other proposals, in recognising that there would be a locational segregation of public and private buildings (including churches and monasteries), Filarete argued that although residential use should not be separated from non-residential use, it should be segregated on the basis of class so that there would be separate housing, with different Greek orders, for gentlemen, common artisans and the poor.

Despite Giorgio Vasari's (1511–74) declaration that Filarete's treatise was the most ridiculous book ever written, by eschewing grid-iron street patterns in favour of radial planning Filarete had a substantial impact on High Renaissance planning in the cinquecento and over the ensuing centuries. In demonstrating his enthusiasm for the centrally planned form, Filarete also had a major impact

Photo 7.21 Bernardo Rossellino, Palazzo Piccolomini, Pienza, 1459–62. Very much influenced by Rossellino's Palazzo Rucellai in Florence.

Photo 7.22 Bernardo Rossellino, Palazzo Comunale, Pienza, 1459–62. An essential civic accompaniment to the bishop's palace and the *duomo*.

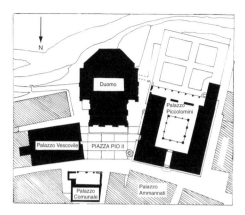

Figure 7.2 The Piazza Pio II, Pienza

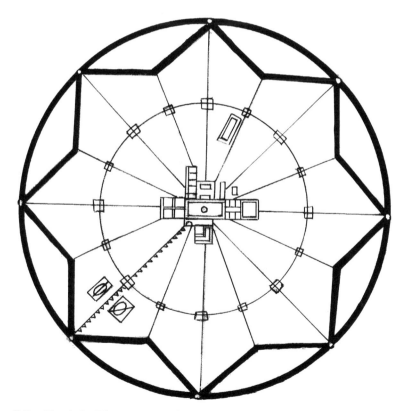

Figure 7.3 Sforzinda: Filarete's view of an 'ideal' inland city (1460)

on High Renaissance architecture, and without his influence Leonardo da Vinci, Donato Bramante and Antonio da Sangallo might not have advanced so enthusiastically the theory of centrally planned buildings in the 16th century.

Conclusion

Throughout Early Renaissance Italy, public patrons funded the development of new or reconstructed buildings for administrative, religious and other communal uses. In so doing, they collaborated with architects to ensure that the latest designs and concepts were employed since, in their view, this would add status to their buildings and serve to engender respect and civic pride. The re-emergence of both classical architecture and town planning in the 15th century not only helped governments achieve these ends but also provided a firm foundation for the further development of the genre in the cinquecento in which Classicism was transmogrified into Mannerism and, in turn, into Baroque by 1600.

Notes

1 I Sutton, *Western Architecture* (London: Thames and Hudson, 1999), p 130.
2 Ibid, p 126.
3 M Hollingsworth, *Patronage in Renaissance Italy* (London: John Murray, 1994), p 18.
4 RC Wirtz, *Florence* (Cologne: Könemann, 2000), p 56.
5 Ibid.
6 M Kaminski, *Venice* (Cologne: Könemann, 2000), p 137.
7 G Zucconi, *Venice. An Architectural Guide* (Venice: Arsenale Editrice, 1995), p 56.
8 L Patetta, 'Local Tradition and New Visions in Milan's Renaissance Architecture', in *Milan. Architectural Guide* (Turin: Umbirto Allemandi, 1999), p 66.
9 Ibid, p 47.
10 LH Heydenreich, *Architecture in Italy*, revd P Davies (New Haven and London: Yale University Press, 1996), p 113.
11 Patetta, 'Local Tradition', p 75.
12 Heydenreich, *Architecture in Italy*, p 120.
13 B Hintzen-Bohlen with J Sorges, *Rome and the Vatican City* (Cologne: Könemann, 2000), p 230.
14 Heydenreich, *Architecture in Italy*, p 63.
15 Hintzen-Bohlen with Sorges, *Rome*, p 168.
16 Heydenreich, *Architecture in Italy*, p 85.
17 Ibid, p 85.
18 Ibid, p 40.

19 P Blanchard, *Northern Italy from the Alps to Bologna* (London: A & C Black, 2001), p 116.

20 Heydenreich, *Architecture in Italy*, p 116.

21 Ibid, p 111.

22 Ibid, p 37.

23 Ibid.

24 Ibid, p 131.

25 Ibid, p 133.

26 D Mayernik, *Timeless Cities. An Architect's Reflections on Renaissance Italy* (Boulder, Col and Oxford: Westview Press, 2005), p 202.

CHAPTER 8

POPULATION TRENDS AND ECONOMIC EQUILIBRIUM IN THE 15TH CENTURY

Introduction

Although the repercussions of the Black Death of the mid-14th century were still evident in terms of population decline throughout much of Italy in the early quattrocento, there was a marked stabilisation of economic activity in the mid-15th century and a gradual increase in population. These circumstances were reflected in a surge of private property development as a means of showing off the new-found prosperity of the *nouveaux riches*, and in a spate of ecclesiastical projects funded by private donations.

Decrease in Population in the Aftermath of the Black Death

No late-14th- or 15th-century Italian city had a population as large as it had been shortly before the Black Death. In northern Italy, in particular, the population decline was dramatic: Venice lost 30 per cent of its inhabitants between 1338 and 1422, while over a comparable period the populations of Pisa and Siena plummeted by more than 70 per cent (table 8.1). Nevertheless, the region's largest

Table 8.1 Decrease in population of major northern Italian cities: 14th to 15th centuries

City	Date	Population	Date	Population	% decrease
Pisa	1293	38,000	1427	8,750*	77
Siena	1328	52,000	1460	15,000	71
Verona	1325	38,000	1425	14,225	63
Florence	1338	95,000	1427	40,000	58
Padua	1320	38,000	1411	18,000	53
Pavia	1320	28,000	1475	16,000	43
Milan	1300	150,000	1463	>90,000	40
Genoa	1290	60,000	1400	37,000*	38
Bologna	1320	54,000	1371	35,000	35
Venice	1338	120,000	1422	84,000	30

* Average of two estimated populations
Source: L Martines, *Power and Imagination. City-States in Renaissance Italy* (London: Pimlico, 2002).

cities – Milan, Venice, Florence, Genoa and Bologna – retained their pre-eminence as the largest urban areas in the peninsula.

The population of Italy, and that of individual towns and cities, would almost certainly have been higher in the quattrocento had there been an absence of high levels of localised morbidity and mortality. Plague, though less severe than the Black Death, was endemic over much of the peninsula. In Pistoia, for example, outbreaks of plague in 1410, 1418, 1432, 1436 and 1457, compounded by periods of famine, 'reduced the population from more than 40,000 souls in the late fourteenth century to less than 14,000 by the early fifteenth'.[1] Although few other communities were disadvantaged to the same extent as Pistoia, similar events occurred to a lesser degree in most Italian cities and extensively throughout Europe. Together with the scarcity of money (attributable to a shortage of precious metal), population decline had a deflating effect on prices throughout Europe.[2] Also, after about 1400, lower consumer demand enabled the agricultural economy to achieve a new equilibrium, generating a degree of prosperity. The stabilisation and then steady growth of the rural population calmed the chaotic conditions resulting from the Black Death and its aftermath and provided, through migration, a firm base for economic expansion, political regeneration and cultural development in the later 15th century.[3] Within this context, the Italian city-states went on to enjoy a lengthy period of 'economic recovery, stable growth and dynamic equilibrium in economic and demographic movements'.[4]

The Partial Recovery in Population by 1500

The populations of Florence and Venice increased gradually to 70,000 and 100,000 respectively by the end of the 15th century, and most other cities throughout the peninsula experienced similar growth, though the total urban population of Italy in 1500 was still smaller than before the Black Death.[5] Nevertheless, between 1440 and 1500 there was a remarkable economic and demographic upswing in particular in the cities of northern and central Italy.[6]

Table 8.2 shows that although by 1500 Italy had a population larger than those of Spain, England and Wales, and the Netherlands, it was nevertheless

Table 8.2 Population of major European countries and Italian cities, *c* 1500

	1500
France	15,000,000
Italy	10,000,000
Spain	6,500,000
England and Wales	3,750,000
N Netherlands	900,000
Paris	100,000
London	40,000
Amsterdam	14,000
Italian cities:	
Naples	150,000
Venice	100,000
Milan	100,000
Florence	70,000
Genoa	60,000
Brescia (1493)	56,060
Rome	55,000
Bologna	55,000
Mantua	28,000
Padua	27,000
Perugia	25,000
Parma	19,034
Modena	18,000
Bari	8,000
Total	771,094

Source: CF Black, *Early Modern Italy, A Social History* (London: Routledge, 2001).

substantially lower than that of France. However, since the area of Italy was also smaller than that of France (around 300,000 square kilometres compared to 540,000 square kilometres at present-day boundaries), and was more mountainous over most of its territory, the peninsula was 'one of the most densely populated and urbanized parts of Europe – especially in the north'.[7]

Also revealed by table 8.2 is the fact that the three largest Italian cities – Naples, Venice and Milan – were as large as or larger than Paris, and considerably more populous than London or Amsterdam. To an extent, this was an outcome of the political and economic factors in Italy that determined the population fortunes of individual cities, and the balance between a city and its *contado* (or dependent territory).

The increased concentration of economic power in Naples, Venice, Milan, Florence and Genoa – often at the expense of the peninsula's many medium-sized communities – was the result of political developments.[8] However, with many independent and quasi-independent cities run by communal oligarchies, dominant families or petty *signori*, political fragmentation restricted the development of a more integrated economy. Although the Peace of Lodi (1454) united Rome, Venice, Milan and Florence in a defensive alliance against the Ottoman Turks, and deterred the four larger powers of the peninsula from waging war upon one another, it did little to break down political fragmentation in the north or to stimulate economic growth.

Economic Stability in the 15th Century

Towards the end of the 14th century, economic conditions throughout most of Europe – which had been dire for nearly a hundred years – began to stabilise.[9] In addition to a gradual increase in population, '[p]rices ceased falling and began to fluctuate in a more regular way. A long period of comparative equilibrium followed in the fifteenth century'.[10] Within this context, trade, manufacturing and banking – all depressed throughout much of the 14th century – revived.

Trade

In Italy, trade was centred most notably on Florence and the ports of Venice and Genoa. The hinterlands of these cities were continental rather than local. Florence traded throughout most of Europe and, via Pisa, along the African and Asian coasts of the Mediterranean where the Turkish empire in the Levant provided a major outlet for Florentine cloth. Fortuitously, within that empire,

Florentine traders were able to take advantage of the collapse in the local market for craft goods resulting from the late-14th-century break up of the Mameluke Empire in Egypt and Syria, and of instability resulting from the Mongol and Turkoman invasions. Against this backdrop, Florentine luxury cloths faced little or no competition from indigenous sources.[11]

The successful economy of Florence, however, was to a large extent dependent upon its ability to develop complementary trade with the eastern Mediterranean. This region not only provided Florence with a substantial proportion of its raw materials, but contained major markets for the city's products. This ensured that the city, at the minimum, could realise balances or near-balances of payments. Concentrated within a relatively confined geographical area, trade with this region during the 16th century gave Florence 'a much sounder economic foundation than it had ever had before'.[12]

As in previous centuries, the hinterlands of Venice and Genoa served a much greater area than the Veneto or Liguria. In a sense, the economic hinterland of Venice 'was the whole of Europe because Venetian merchants were the principal middlemen in trade between Europe and the East [and] without serious competitors before the Portuguese began to use the Cape route at the end of the fifteenth century'.[13] Without doubt, Venice was the greatest merchant city in the world and owed its primacy to the massive scale of its importation of spices, silk and cotton and the export of woollen cloth, with trading deficits being settled in silver coins minted for the purpose. Although as a commercial power Genoa no longer enjoyed the same importance as it had in the 13th century, it nevertheless sought to compensate for the loss of its trading ports in the eastern Mediterranean and Black Sea by developing – through the export of grain and wool – economic relations with France, Spain and North America.[14]

Manufacturing industry

Although manufacturing activity was ubiquitous over much of northern and central Italy, Florence was undoubtedly the 'industrial town *par excellence*'.[15] Its leading industry, wool, organised by the merchants of the *Arte di Calimala*, processed and re-exported cloth from France and Flanders on a scale unequalled elsewhere. The textile industry of Florence in the quattrocento went from strength to strength. By the end of the century the supply of raw wool, at a reasonable cost, was secured by the increased importation of Castilian wool; at an even earlier date raw silk began to be imported on a significant scale from areas bordering the Caspian Sea, Spain and southern Italy. Textiles output was thus diversified by the dual production of woollen and silk products. Although the output of finished silk cannot be assessed with complete accuracy, it has been estimated that there were some 83 silk workshops in Florence *c* 1470 'compared to the 280 wool shops counted in the same survey',[16] and the scale of production was reflected in the *Arte della Seta*'s (silk guild) appropriation of some of the responsibilities of the *Arte della Lana* (wool guild) by the end of the century. Improvements in the quality of wool during the 14th century, and the adoption of silk as an important component of the textile industry in the 15th, were not only associated with the role of the guilds, but also geared to a parallel increase in labour skills – raising the quality of labour found in the textile sector as a whole.

During the quattrocento, the performance of the Florentine textile sector was impressive. Despite a dramatic decrease in the scale of the work in the aftermath of the Black Death, records indicate that there was no per capita decline in output in the woollen sector, while the output of a vigorous silk industry, chiefly targeted at foreign luxury markets, accelerated markedly, generating a secure inflow of income from abroad. In contrast to an earlier age, the textile industry of Florence was now not only using its own ships to import raw wool and silk, but the city's conquest of Pisa in 1406 and its purchase from Genoa of Livorno and Porto Pisano in 1421 gave the Florentine industry its own export outlets.

Elsewhere in Italy, woollen cloth was manufactured in Milan throughout the quattrocento,[17] while the manufacture of silk cloth – rooted in Lucca, Venice, Bologna and Genoa during the 13th and 14th centuries – spread to Milan, Ferrara, Modena, Pisa, Siena, Perugia, Rome, Naples, Palermo, Messina and Catania by the end of the 15th century.[18] Notwithstanding the importance of textiles to the urban economies of Italy, a range of other industries contributed to economic growth across the peninsula, particularly in its northern cities. The manufacture of armour and weapons was centred on Milan and Brescia; papermaking was widespread across the region, most notably in Verona; Venice dominated shipbuilding and was well known throughout Europe for its printing industry; and the construction industry expanded rapidly in the second half of the quattrocento in response to a building boom in major cities and provincial centres such as Cremona, Pavia, Bergamo, Brescia, Vicenza and cities across the length and breadth of the Papal States.[19]

Banking

Apart from its supremacy as a trading and manufacturing region, Italy retained its position – earned in the previous century – as the principal source of financial services in Europe. Profits generated in trade and manufacturing 'were transferred into banking, and Florentine financiers [notably the Medici, Pazzi, Rucellai and Strozzi] were among the biggest names in international banking'.[20] Florentine bankers '[w]ith big capital stocks and networks of subsidiaries that crossed Christendom... traded in Bruges, London, Paris, Barcelona, Marseilles and Tunis, and in the Levant'.[21]

After the return of the papacy to Rome under the pontificate of Martin V (1417–31) and later under Eugenius IV (1431–47), major Florentine bankers such as the Alberti, Spini, Ricci and Medici established close business ties with the papal capital and, through the provision of financial services to the Church, generated an enormous flow of income that benefited banking in general and the Medici in particular, 'who made their fortune in papal business'.[22] Since Rome was a major market for Florentine cloth, a steady supply of payments from the papal capital to Florence also added to the latter's wealth and enabled its elite to indulge in conspicuous consumption – a pattern of expenditure that 'dominat[ed] virtually every aspect of the rapidly expanding luxury trade'.[23] Clearly, Florence and Rome were symbiotically linked. The profits accumulated from commercial activity in the luxury sectors were often reinvested in the papacy, 'now more than ever in need of funds to pursue its policy of state-building in central Italy'.[24] Through this process Florentine bankers 'were able to dig deeper and deeper into papal finances as treasurers and tax collectors, at times virtually taking over the fiscal administration of the papal state and claiming possession of the papal tiara itself as security'.[25] Well into the 16th century, when two Medici – Leo X (1513–21) and Clement VII (1523–34) – headed the Church, papal Rome continued to be one of the most important centres for Florentine banking irrespective of whether individual banking families were out of favour with the pope.[26]

In addition to Rome, Naples provided a major market for Florentine merchants and bankers. Export earnings flowed into Florence from this connection, and accumulated fortunes enabled merchants such as Filippo di Matteo Strozzi and Giuliano Gondi – notable palace-builders of the Renaissance – to establish close business ties with King Alfonso. Both Rome and the eponymous capital of the kingdom of Naples were centres of wealth out of all proportion to the size of the territories they controlled in the peninsula. Aside from being the capital of Christendom, Rome tentatively ruled the Papal States, a responsibility it attempted to strengthen in the 15th century through the development of a solid bureaucratic structure, while as a Spanish possession Naples controlled an area that extended across the southern Italian peninsula to distant Catalonia, Valencia and Aragon. The population of both cities grew rapidly during the 15th century,

Rome from 17,000 to around 55,000, and Naples from 40,000 to about 150,000, making the latter urban area the largest city in Europe.[27]

Diffused across much of the western world were many other markets for Florentine merchants and bankers. Developing Europe's sole international banking system, Florentine bankers were not only 'linked through the technical facilities for dealing with one another [but] more than any other money their gold florin was the international standard of value'.[28] With considerably less expertise, would-be competitors were unable to counter the domination of Florentines in both their internal and external markets. Even in Geneva, and later in Lyons, Florentines were able to establish major centres for international clearance; with the opening up of Atlantic trade by Portugal and Spain Florentine merchants, already involved in the purchase of raw materials first from Aragon and then from Castile, gradually responded to business opportunities throughout Iberia.

North of the the Alps, markets were somewhat less assured. In northern Germany Florentine business incursions met with strong resistance from the Hanseatic cities and in England the Florentines were wary of repeating their mistake by once more over-extending credit to the monarch as they had done to Edward III in the 1340s to disastrous effect in the short-term. By contrast, in the Low Countries, Florentines were the principal bankers involved in international finance; in 'Poland Florentines were the leading Italian merchants, especially active in the commerce of luxury cloths';[29] and in Hungary – in contrast to England – Florentine bankers 'put their commercial wealth and financial skills at the disposal of the monarchy'.[30]

Because of their strong international profile, it was highly probable that the commercial and banking sectors in Florence were markedly more dynamic than before the Black Death. The range of goods and services traded was far greater than hitherto, and luxury markets everywhere grew dramatically. Florence's visible trade was based on 'a thriving home industry supplying a product that was a staple in virtually every luxury market'[31] and its invisible trade was rooted in financial services which were unmatched throughout much of the continent.

Administration

Florence was not alone in being host to a large service sector. As centres of administration, Rome and Naples were cities of officials and centres of power within their extensive domains. 'In the case of Rome, the hinterland was sometimes the Papal States, but for some functions it was the whole Catholic world'.[32]

These 'services' required management, and an important role was played by the pope's bankers, from the Medici to Agostino Chigi of Siena, best known for his patronage of Raphael. In the case of Naples, the hinterland for the services provided by judges, advocates, tax-collectors and their like was the kingdom of Naples or, in the reign of Alfonso of Aragon, his entire Mediterranean empire.[33]

Capitalism in the 15th Century

Was the economy of northern and central Italy in the 15th century capitalistic? The answer is undoubtedly yes. Economic forces had led to a 'concentration of capital in the hands of a few entrepreneurs and the institutionalisation of a rational, calculating approach to economic problems'[34] – two fundamental attributes of the capitalist mode of production. With regard to the emergence of industrial capitalism, it 'was possible for entrepreneurs to accumulate capital... because in some leading industries many of the workers were no longer independent craftsmen'.[35]

The division of labour was especially evident in the manufacture of cloth.[36] In the textile industry of Florence, in particular, 'it was no longer the master craftsman, but the capitalist entrepreneur [the *lanaiuolo*], who disposed of the wares to the customer... the entrepreneur merely directed the production process and marketed the finished product; he had no concern with manufacture, but controlled the whole process'.[37] The Florentine entrepreneur employed anything from a dozen to a few hundred craftsmen who in turn were organised by their *Arte della Lana*.[38] However, although several stages in the production of cloth took place in large workshops where male labour was paid on a daily basis, 'much of the spinning was done by women living at home... dependent on the entrepreneur who supplied them with the raw material'.[39] Although this system differed from 19th-century industrial capitalism in that large-scale production under the direct control of the manufacturer had not emerged, 'it is clear that the entrepreneur played a central role and that he exercised considerable control by indirect means'.[40]

Undoubtedly, aside from industrial capitalism 15th-century Italy also witnessed the emergence of commercial and financial capitalism. As great trading cities, Venice and Genoa were centres of commercial capitalism, while Florence and Genoa (in its dual role) presided over the birth of financial capitalism. The different forms of capitalism, moreover, were integrated and functioned as a major force for change. Arguably, the development of banking 'forged an economic revolution that caused it to lead Europe in the direction of full-blown capitalism. . . . The same Florentine citizens who [above all] were the world's greatest industrialists and merchants were at the same time banks of exchange. Production, trade and money-lending were all in the same hands.'[41] Banks were not only able to use their industrial and trading customers' deposits to extend credit for productive (and non-productive) purposes, but – in the case of Florentine banks – also collected papal taxes from the clergy and injected a large part of the revenue into the rising capitalist economy of Italy.

Undoubtedly, the attributes of each form of capitalism were broadly the same, in Italy as elsewhere. However, Robert Lopez suggests that although early capitalism was marked by the characteristic qualities of later capitalism[42] – *viz* the steady accumulation of capital in money and goods; the growing use of credit; the gradual separation of management from both ownership of capital and manual labour; the constant endeavour to improve methods of business and foster competition; the planning of large-scale operations to expand markets; and, above all, the desire for profit – he cautions that 'all this was on a far smaller scale, affected fewer people, and was much less pronounced than in the modern world'.[43]

Wealth and conspicuous consumption

Capitalist forms of organisation were unusually well developed in Italy by the 15th century, particularly in Florence, Milan and Venice, 'where so much of what we call the Renaissance was taking place'.[44] In examining the links between the development of the economy and the evolution of the visual arts – and specifically architecture and urban design – the most obvious question is: 'Was wealth a key factor? Did Italy have a renaissance because she could afford it?'[45] Some historians and planners claim that the 'dates do not fit' because the first buds in the flowering of the Renaissance in the 14th century appeared not at a time of economic boom, but during a recession in the earlier part of that century, a devastating plague in 1348–9 and, at best, a slow recovery towards the end of the 1300s.[46] Although there is an opposing view that, during this period, many merchants had a propensity to indulge in conspicuous consumption by spending on commissioned works of art (including new buildings) rather than investing in their businesses where profitability would be low or non-existant,[47] a more credible explanation of the relationship between the economic cycle and conspicuous consumption is that the development of the luxury market was attributable not only to the accumulation of wealth (over several generations) but also to its very narrow distribution among a small section of the population. Franco Franceschi reveals that in Florence in 1427 only about '1 per cent of households owned more than 25 per cent of the city's wealth . . . [a]nd in Bologna in 1509 less than 1 per cent of landowners owned more than a quarter of the land'.[48] Unequal distributions such as these were almost certainly common throughout much of Italy during the quattrocento, and suggest that as wealth increased in the economy as a whole most was creamed off by a small privileged elite to feed their insatiable desire to display visible symbols of their wealth, power and piety.

Clearly, the effective demand in 15th-century Italy for a product such as a new palace or a new church was determined by the level of wealth in the local economy, by how a city's political and social structures determined the way wealth was spent, and by how changes in the level and structure of wealth released sufficient sums of money to fund conspicious consumption. The decimation of population in cities throughout much of Italy during the second half of the 14th century (the population of Florence, for example, fell by two-thirds) often left extraordinary amounts of wealth in the hands of some of the survivors, while the accumulation of higher per capita wealth in state capitals such as Florence was sometimes substantially enhanced by wealth flowing into the centre as a consequence of territorial expansion over the hundred years following the Black Death. Even more importantly, during these years several cities successfully adjusted their economic performance to a changing situation in international markets in a way that stimulated growth. As we have seen, Florence transformed its textile industry and strengthened its commercial and financial operations abroad. As a result the city achieved a highly favourable balance of payments. Although much of its payments surplus 'was absorbed by the military costs of the city's territorial expansion and its emergence as a major Italian power . . . after the first third of the fifteenth century, with the stabilisation of political order abroad and the consequent lightening of the tax burden at home, the profits that were flowing into the city from international commercial and financial operations became available for conspicuous consumption'.[49] Clearly, increased demand for luxury goods such as palaces and villas in and around 15th-century Italian cities – and particularly Florence – occurred because more disposable money was available, and because urban populations – not least the Florentine elite – were more optimistic about the economic situation. Moreover, that spending, by calling into existence new forms of production, in itself brought about some major improvements in the performance of the economy during this period. More than any other, the construction sector best illustrates this proposition.

Economic theory and conspicuous consumption

The performance of the Florentine economy and its relationship with the built environment can, like that of other Italian city-states, be interpreted in macroeconomic terms by the Keynesian model of economic growth (see pp 12–14). Except for the supply of raw materials for its textile industry Florence was not dependent on imports from abroad, so the city enjoyed a favourable balance of payments, and – through the multiplier (see pp 13–14) – grew dramatically throughout much of the 15th century. Records show that large quantities of bullion flowed into the city as payments from importers in Flanders, Spain, Geneva, Naples and the Ottoman Empire.

Much of the bullion that entered the Florentine economy found its way into the conspicuous consumption of gold and silver products and other luxuries. The opening-up of new markets for Florentine goods in Naples, Rome, Constantinople, Lyons and elsewhere further added to this flow, creating an extraordinarily favourable balance of payments and facilitating a surge of private spending on building and the arts – following the lead of the Medici and other patrons (see chapter 11). There is little doubt that the considerable wealth accumulated by a relatively small merchant and banking elite during the early decades of the 15th century found its way into heavy expenditure on new buildings and their decoration.

However, in micro rather than macro terms, the economic growth of many cities in quattrocento Italy can be explained by the linkage model of urban development. Applying this model to the economy of Florence, one can assume that the quality of products had been continually improved during the 14th and 15th centuries, and that most of the production linkages around the industries under consideration were fully developed, while 'non-industrial' operations concerned specifically with finance and selling abroad forward linkages went beyond the scope of the industry and enabled Florentine enterprises to be leaders of Europe's commercial and banking systems. In general, backward linkages – mainly with northern Europe – were less evident, although from the 14th century such linkages were developed when supply channels from sources around the Mediterranean were opened up. With forward and backward linkages fully exploited, further urban development could only be achieved by using the profits of the industry to invest in improved technology to enhance productivity. However, while to an extent this took place, many merchants and bankers involved in the forward sectors of the economy also spent more and more of their wealth on the construction of buildings. With such an increase in demand, the construction industry developed its own linkages, 'backward towards the building-materials industries, and forward . . . to the craft industries producing those goods needed [in the] new and enlarged built environment'.[50] The construction industry and its related activities thus grew dramatically in the 15th century because 'much of the enormous wealth that had accumulated in Florence was invested in it'.[51] This became increasingly apparent from the 1430s onwards when the Italian political scene was relatively stable, taxation was low and business booming.[52]

Private Patronage and Property Development in the 15th Century

During the quattrocento, investment in buildings was not seen as an alternative to investment in industry or trade. While undoubtedly there was a tendency for the merchant classes to build up large rural estates or introduce new methods of estate management or farming technology (the Medici, for example, held vast estates in Tuscany early in the quattrocento, and Venetian patricians similarly accumulated and managed rural land in the Veneto), investment in urban property development took priority and occurred side-by-side with mercantile activity. The splitting of investment funds between these two sectors thus became the norm rather than the exception; for example the banker Giovanni Rucellai (whose investments were concentrated in Florence) and Giuliano Gondi (who made his fortune in Naples) commissioned, in turn, the construction of the Palazzo Rucellai in 1446 and the Palazzo Gondi in 1490 (both in Florence), while Filippo Strozzi (who had also enriched himself through Neapolitan investments) not only had enough disposable cash to cover the entire cost of his new Florentine palace (the Palazzo Strozzi, begun 1489), but sufficient to keep his business alive through further generations of his family. This was very much in line with the practice of rich Florentines, textile entrepreneurs and merchant bankers alike.

Merchants were not only patrons of secular property development, they also funded the construction of ecclesiastical buildings. Most notably, the Medici demonstrated that it was possible to expand their business interests across Europe while simultaneously funding heavily the development of both secular and ecclesiastical buildings. Although Giovanni di Bicci de' Medici (d 1429), using a substantial proportion of his banking wealth, confined his interests to commissioning the construction of the church of S Lorenzo (1418–28), his son Cosimo not only funded the Palazzo Medici (1444), the Villa Medici at Careggi (1457) and Villa Medici at Fiesole (1457) in the nearby Florentine *contado*, he also commissioned much of the convent of S Marco (1437). Later, in 1485, Cosimo's grandson, Lorenzo the Magnificent, commissioned the sumptuous Villa Medici at Poggio a Caiano, but did not continue the family tradition of financing development in Florence itself, largely because the profitability of his banking interests was now very much on the wane. The Pazzi family likewise split its building interests in Florence between the Capella Pazzi (begun 1429) and the Palazzo Pazzi (1462) (see chapter 6).

It is perhaps ironic that although newly created wealth in 15th-century Florence was heavily concentrated in just a few hands, 'there were few family companies with a life beyond two generations',[53] wealthy families such as the Strozzi, Gondi, Capponi and Guicciardini 'reveal[ing] little interest in the pooling of resources beyond the second generation'.[54] As a consequence, wealth became more widely distributed since the ownership of property and other assets became fragmented and shifted about with great frequency. Despite many *palazzi* in Florence retaining the name of their founder (Palazzo Medici, Palazzo Strozzi, Palazzo Gondi, Palazzo Pitti, etc), most major private buildings constructed in Florence in the quattrocento have changed hands time and time again over the past 500 years. A major exception, at least until well into the seicento, was capital held by the Medici, where wealth amassed by Giovanni di Bicci de'Medici was inherited by at least four or five generations of Medici – a result of the efforts of Cosimo, his son Piero and grandson Lorenzo 'to prevent the break up of the company's capital formation'.[55] The Palazzo Medici and many other buildings constructed by the family in the 15th century remained in their hands for 200 years or more. Aside from the Medici, mercantile families often experienced financial demise. Florentine palaces either had to be sold off because of bankruptcy, were never completed because of mounting debts, or were sold off by heirs since they had little collective interest in retaining ownership.[56] The accumulation of wealth and its distribution and fluidity clearly determined the history of architecture and *palazzo* development in Renaissance Florence. Undoubtedly, in the long run wealth circulated among an elite that remained fairly contained, albeit 'individuals within those ranks had diverse fortunes and new fortunes were not uncommon'.[57] It is remarkable that within this unstable financial environment a new and magnificent built environment emerged.

The processes under which property investment evolved in Florence were to a significant extent repeated elsewhere in northern and central Italy. In Venice, for example, successful merchants built up portfolios not just of mercantile activity but also of real estate investments. The Ca' d'Oro and the Palazzo Corner-Spinelli are but two of the many palaces built along the Grand Canal during the quattrocento as evidence of the wealth and social status of their owners.

However, major construction works in the non-governmental sector were not solely attributable to the financial proclivities of the wealthy. In Venice, possibly more than in any other major city, ecclesiastical buildings were commissioned by religious bodies other than the papacy, such as the Camaldolese monks who funded construction of the city's first Renaissance building, the church of S Michele in Isola (begun 1469). Church building in the *Serenissima* was also commissioned by patrician families such as the Capello who funded construction of the church of S Maria Formosa (1492), while confraternities – organisations based on a trade or region – commissioned sumptuous assembly halls where they met for prayer sessions, collected money for worthy causes and held masses for their members who were sick, dying or had recently died. Financed by voluntary contributions, the more notable confraternity buildings in Venice of 15th-century origin include the Scuola Grande di S Marco (begun 1437), the Scuola di S Giovanni Evangelista (1454) and the Scuola Grande di S Rocco (1489) (see chapter 9). Elsewhere in Italy there are numerous other examples of how private wealth – newly generated in the quattrocento from the profits of trade, banking and industry – facilitated construction of sumptuous palaces and magnificent churches in a largely unregulated domestic market.

Conclusion

Private patronage, both secular and ecclesiastical, led to the implementation of a large number of construction projects in Italy during the quattrocento that immeasurably enhanced the built environment. With wealth derived from the increase in both local and long-distance trade, the expansion of industry, the continued evolution of banking practice and the growth of public administration, the economy of much of Italy was not only able to support a higher level of private expenditure on buildings than hitherto but was destined to expand further in the cinquecento, so facilitating private patronage on an even grander scale.

Chronology

1390s	Economic conditions begin to stabilise following decades of uncertainty; instead of falling, prices begin to fluctuate in a more regular way.
1400	Population of Genoa about 38 per cent below that of 1290 but with about 38,000 inhabitants the city is fourth largest urban area in northern and central Italy. Throughout 15th century, Genoa develops trade with France and Spain to compensate for loss of trading ports in eastern Mediterranean and Black Sea, and becomes centre of commercial and financial capitalism.

1406	Florence annexes Pisa and secures an outlet for its exports.
1417–47	Under pontificacies of Martin V and Eugenius, Florentine bankers such as the Alberti, Spini, Ricci and Medici establish close business ties with the papal capital.
1418	**In Florence, Giovanni di Bicci de' Medici commissions construction of church of S Lorenzo.**
1421	**In Venice, Marino Contarini commissions Ca' d'Oro.**
	Florence purchases Livorno and Porto Pisano from Genoa and secures further outlets for its exports.
1422	Population of Venice 30 per cent below that of 1338 but with 84,000 inhabitants the city is second largest urban area in northern and central Italy. Venice develops as a major trading port throughout the century and becomes a centre of commercial capitalism.
1427	Population of Florence 58 per cent below that of 1338, but with 40,000 inhabitants city is third largest urban area in northern and central Italy. Florence develops as major trading, textile manufacturing and banking hub throughout the century, and becomes centre of financial capitalism, but 1 per cent of households own more than a quarter of the city's wealth in 1427.
1429	**In Florence, Pazzi family fund construction of Capella Pazzi.**
1437	**In Florence, remodelling of convent of S Marco funded by Cosimo de'Medici.**
1437	**In Venice, voluntary contributions fund construction of Scuola Grande di S Marco.**
1440–1500	Economic and demographic upswing in cities of northern and central Italy.
1444	**In Florence, work begins on church of S Spirito, funded by a commission involving wealthy Florentine families and monks.**
1444	**In Florence, Cosimo de'Medici commissions Palazzo Medici.**
1446	**In Florence, Palazzo Rucellai commissioned by Giovanni Rucellai.**
1454	**In Venice, voluntary contributions fund construction of Scuola grande di S Giovanni Evangelista.**
1457	**Cosimo de'Medici commissions Villa Medici at Careggi and Villa Medici at Fiesole.**
1463	Population of Milan 40 per cent below that of 1300 but with around 90,000 inhabitants city remains largest urban area in northern and central Italy. Develops as major industrial centre throughout the century concentrating on manufacture of armour and weapons.
1469	**In Isola, Camaldolese monks fund construction of church of S Michele.**
1470	In Florence, 280 workshops produce woollen cloth and 83 workshops silk.
1485	**At Poggio a Caiano, Lorenzo de'Medici commissions Villa Medici.**
1489	**In Florence, Palazzo Strozzi commissioned by Filippo Strozzi.**
	In Venice, voluntary contributions fund construction of Scuola Grande di S Rocco.

1490	In Florence, Giuliano Gondi commissions construction of Palazzo Gondi.
	In Venice, Corner family commissions Palazzo Corner-Spinelli.
1492	In Venice, Cappello family funds church of S Maria Formosa.
1500	Italy has population larger than that of Spain, England and Wales, and the Netherlands; Naples, Venice and Milan are as large as or larger than Paris. Italy is one of the most densely populated and urbanised parts of Europe.
	From lower levels earlier in 15th century, populations of both Venice and Milan have now grown to 100,000, population of Florence has increased to 70,000, and the inhabitants of Genoa number 60,000. Naples is the largest city in Italy with a population of 150,000, and the population of Rome has grown to 55,000 from, respectively, 40,000 and 17,000 in the early 15th century.

Notes

1 D Hackett Fischer, *The Great Wave. Price Revolutions and the Rhythm of History* (Oxford: Oxford University Press, 1996), p 48.

2 Ibid.

3 D Herlihy, *Medieval and Renaissance Pistoia* (New Haven: Yale University Press, 1981), pp 28–46.

4 Hackett Fischer, *The Great Wave*, pp 49–51.

5 Ibid.

6 L Martines, *Power and Imagination. City-States in Renaissance Italy* (London: Pimlico, 2002), p 169.

7 CF Black, *Early Modern Italy, A Social History* (London: Routledge, 2001), p 21.

8 Ibid.

9 F Franceschi, 'The economy: work and wealth', in JM Negemy (ed), *Italy in the Age of the Renaissance* (Oxford: Oxford University Press, 2004), p 125.

10 Hackett Fischer, *The Great Wave*, pp 49–51.

11 R Goldthwaite, *The Building of Renaissance Florence. An Economic and Social History* (Baltimore and London: Johns Hopkins University Press, 1982), p 37.

12 Ibid, p 41.

13 P Burke, *The Italian Renaissance. Culture and Society in Italy*, 2nd edn (Oxford: Polity, 1986), p 229.

14 Ibid.

15 Ibid.

16 Goldthwaite, *Building of Renaissance Florence*, p 43.

17 G Barbieri, *Economica e politica nel ducato di Milano* (Milan: n pub, 1938).

18 Franceschi, 'The economy', p 131.

19 Ibid, p 132.

20 Burke, *Italian Renaissance*, p 230.

21 C Duggan, *A Concise History of Italy* (Cambridge: Cambridge University Press, 1984), p 51.

22 P Hall, *Cities in Civilization* (London: Weidenfeld & Nicolson, 1998), p 84.

23 Goldthwaite, *Building of Renaissance Florence*, p 35.
24 Ibid.
25 Ibid.
26 Ibid.
27 Ibid.
28 Black, *Early Modern Italy*, p 219, table 2.2.
29 Goldthwaite, *Building of Renaissance Florence*, p 39.
30 Ibid.
31 Ibid, p 41.
32 Burke, *Italian Renaissance*, p 230.
33 Ibid.
34 Ibid, p 231.
35 Ibid.
36 Ibid.
37 Hall, *Cities in Civilization*, p 83.
38 Ibid.
39 Burke, *Italian Renaissance*, p 231.
40 Ibid, p 232.
41 Hall, *Cities in Civilization*, p 83.
42 Ibid, p 81; see also RS Lopez, 'The Trade of Medieval Europe: the South', in M Postan and EE Rich (eds), *The Cambridge Economic History of Europe 2: Trade and Industry in the Middle Ages* (Cambridge: Cambridge University Press, 1952), pp 320–1.
43 Lopez, 'The Trade of Medieval Europe', pp 320–1.
44 Burke, *Italian Renaissance*, p 232.
45 Ibid.
46 Ibid, p 233; Hall, *Cities in Civilization*, p 112.
47 Ibid, p 88.
48 Franceschi, 'The economy', p 141.
49 Goldthwaite, *Building of Renaissance Florence*, p 30.
50 Ibid, p 51.
51 Ibid.
52 Ibid, pp 59–60, 63.
53 Ibid, p 64.
54 Ibid.
55 Ibid.
56 Ibid, p 66.
57 Ibid.

CHAPTER 9

PRIVATE PATRONAGE AND THE RE-EMERGENCE OF CLASSICAL ARCHITECTURE IN THE 15TH CENTURY

Introduction

During the Early Renaissance, the underlying determinants of demand for major building projects in the private sector were population growth, economic stability, the emergence of capitalism, the increase in wealth and conspicuous consumption, and the inclination of private patrons to promote and fund the construction of imposing secular and ecclesiastical buildings. As in the public sector, patrons quickly opted for the classical style of architecture based, to a large extent, on the tenets of Vitruvius, and promulgated by generations of architects throughout the quattrocento and beyond.

The Major Cities of Central and Northern Italy

Florence

In response to the demand among Florence's wealthy bankers and traders for stately urban residences some 30 *palazzi* were built in the city between 1450 and 1478 alone.[1] Often of considerable size, these *palazzi* shared a number of design attributes. They usually contained three storeys, of which the most important floor was the middle storey, the *piano nobile*; each storey was clearly divided from that above and/or below by a string course cornice and each storey in succession diminished in height; voussoirs normally capped both portals and windows (the latter tending to be absent at ground-floor level); and facades were somewhat anachronistically rusticated, the degree of rustication usually decreasing with each successive storey, while upper storeys were faced with smooth ashlar. At the base of the Florentine palace, a stone bench ran around the exterior for the comfort of visitors waiting to be admitted. The top of the building was crowned by entablatures and projecting cornices, and the structure was usually cube-shaped with harmoniously arranged arcaded courtyards in the centre. As if to establish some continuity with the past, to display a degree of civic patriotism and confirm the standing of its owners in society, the Florentine *palazzo* of the quattrocento was much influenced by the design features of the city's *palazzi* of previous centuries, most notably the massive Palazzo dei Priori (1299–1314) and the even earlier Bargello, but also the Palazzo Canigiani of the late 14th century.

With his enormous banking wealth at his disposable, and with his role in the political life of Florence quickly evolving, though not assured, in 1444 Cosimo

Photo 9.1   Michelozzo Michelozzi, Palazzo Medici, Florence, begun 1444. The Medici family residence from 1444 to 1540. In its austerity and use of rustication it served as a prototype for other famous Florentine palaces.

de'Medici commissioned Michelozzo Michelozzi to design a *palazzo* on the Via Larga (now the Via Cavour) as a family residence and business headquarters. Not wishing to appear too ostentatious and risk the animosity of his political rivals, he eschewed Brunelleschi's plans for an enormous *palazzo* in favour of a more modest though still substantial building by Michelozzo. After its initial completion *c* 1450, the Palazzo Medici became the prototype for subsequent *palazzi* across quattrocento Florence and beyond. In addition to the features outlined above, the *palazzo* was distinctive in being an island block with no immediate neighbours and in having a hanging garden on its western side, but it was far from 'ideal'. Its ground floor, on the Via Larga front, originally contained three portals (until windows were placed in the outer two entrances in the 16th century) and five small openings, but none of these were aligned with the rows of arched biforate windows above, windows that were flanked by Doric columns on the *piano nobile* and Corinthian columns on the second floor. After its acquisition by the Riccardi family in 1659, the *palazzo* was extended along the Via Larga from 10 to 17 bays, so disrupting the original proportions of the building.

Photo 9.2 Bernardo Rossellino, Palazzo Rucellai, Florence, 1452. Lacking rustication and incorporating classical pilasters and capitals of the three orders, Rossellino's palace was the most dignified residence in Renaissance Florence.

Many other notable *palazzi* followed the Medici model; for example, the Palazzo dello Strozzino (started 1451) displays considerable similarity to the Michelozzo prototype (and was probably initiated by him, although its completion is attributed to Giuliano da Sangallo), but others exhibit marked design variations. The Palazzo Rucellai (begun 1452), commissioned by the enormously wealthy banker Giovanni Rucellai as his family residence, designed by Leon Battista Alberti and executed by Bernardo di Matteo Gambarelli Rossellino, was 'in stark contrast with Michelozzo's model of a Florentine palazzo'.[2] Not only is its three-storey facade clad with uniform flat ashlars of varying sizes and courses but, in accordance with the canons of Vitruvius,[3] its bays are bordered by stacked Ionic, Doric and Corinthian pilasters, as in the Coliseum in Rome. This differentiated the palace from others developed in Florence at around the same time that were predominantly astylar (lacking facade orders). On the horizontal plain, and as with other Florentine palaces, a stone bench is attached to a plinth at ground level; above, decorative entablatures separate the floors from each other while vertically two straight-lintelled portals and small oblong openings at ground-floor level are aligned with arched biforate windows in each of the bays on the *piano nobile* and upper storey. A roof cornice supported by an entablature completes the building at its highest elevation. Although the Palazzo Rucellai is arguably the most outstanding secular building in Florence,[4] it is marred by being restricted to seven bays, and is thus not in accordance with Alberti's idea of proportion which, in order to accommodate the two portals, would have required eight. Although the intention was to extend the building to the east to provide a further bay, this was not to be.

An even greater variation on a theme is provided by the massive Palazzo Pitti. Commissioned by the exceedingly wealthy Luca Pitti in 1457 in his desire to outdo in grandeur the Palazzo Medici, the initial design has often been attributed to Filippo Brunelleschi. It has even been suggested that it was the same design that Cosimo de'Medici had rejected for his palace a decade or so earlier. However, since Brunelleschi died in 1446, another architect or architects must have been responsible for at least the construction of the building, if not its design. The three-storey facade is uniformly and heavily rusticated, each storey is of equal height, and balustrades of the Ionic order separate each floor. Initially, the facade at ground-floor level was punctuated by a central round-arched portal flanked by two round-arched windows of similar size and interspersed with four smaller rectangular windows, while on the floors above there were seven round-arched windows as large as those on the ground floor – creating a total of seven vertical axes. During the 16th and 17th centuries, the palace was both extended to the rear to create a three-wing layout, and considerably lengthened, particularly

Photo 9.3 Palazzo Pitti, Florence, 1457. Controversially attributed to a design by Brunelleschi, the palace's entire massive facade is rusticated with rough-hewn gold-coloured blocks.

on the ground floor and *piano nobile*, adding substantially to the number of portals and windows on the facade. However, unlike Alberti's Palazzo Rucellai, there were few if any classical features, and in contrast to the Palazzo Medici the design of the *palazzo* remained unique. The Palazzo Pitti also differed from

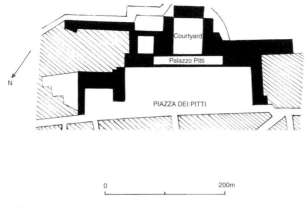

Figure 9.1 The Piazza dei Pitti, Florence

other Florentine *palazzi* in that it embraced an enormous dominating *piazza*, the Piazza de' Pitti, whose width is as extensive as the palace's facade (fig 9.1).

Like the Palazzo Pitti, the comparatively diminutive Palazzo Antinori lacks Roman-inspired ornamentation. Designed by Giuliano da Maiano in 1461, the plain facade of the building is embellished only by the use of regular ashlars of *pietra forte*. There are no columns, pilasters or pediments. The palace's simple elegance is enhanced by the location of its portico, which is off-centre in the third of six bays. The ground floor is largely windowless, except for three small rectangular openings, while there is a row of six windows on both the *piano nobile* and upper floor. In keeping with other Florentine *palazzi* of the period, the building is crowned by a large overhanging cornice.

The Palazzo Pazzi and Palazzo Gondi, commissioned respectively in 1462 and 1490, are two further palaces that differed significantly from the 'norm'. Financed by the Pazzi family and designed by Benedetto da Maiano, the former palace – while conventional in many respects – is distinguished by biforate windows with moulded arches and carved decorative motifs on the two floors above a rusticated base; the latter palace, financed by Leonardo Gondi and designed by Giuliano da Sangallo, although clearly based on the Medici prototype, displays the effect of grading blocks in relation to their size and position on the facade, which incorporates finely dressed cushion-shaped blocks and concealed joints in the lower storey, and ornamented cross-shaped features interspersed with the window arches above.[5]

Commissioned by Filippo Strozzi in 1489 on his return from exile in Mantua, the Palazzo Strozzi was the outcome of improved relations with the Medici with whom a family dispute had been festering for many years. Based on designs by Benedetto da Maiano and Simone del Pollaiuolo (*il Cronaca*) and on a model by Giuliano da Sangallo (probably at Lorenzo de'Medici's insistence), construction of the palace on an even larger scale than had first been proposed was not only approved by Lorenzo de'Medici but generously encouraged with the aim of enhancing the grandeur of the city. The enormous bulk of the magnificent and ambitious palace, the largest in quattrocento Florence, was exposed to adjacent streets on three of its four sides, while at its core the building contained an elegant courtyard. Its three-storey facades are rusticated but the coarseness of the rustication diminishes with each successive storey giving 'the surface an unobtrusive, but regular ornamented pattern'.[6] The facades are punctuated by massive central portals with close-set voussoirs, flanked on either side by four small rectangular windows, and above there are nine arched biforate windows – also with voussoirs – sitting astride the cornices at the base of each of the two upper storeys. The building is crowned by an entablature and a massively projecting roof cornice, partly unfinished.

While economic growth facilitated the development of urban *palazzi* in quattrocento Florence, it also stamped its mark on the construction of ecclesiastical buildings. Again, it was Cosimo de'Medici who took the lead. In 1418 he was one of several financiers to commission Brunelleschi to design the church of S Lorenzo and oversee its construction. Originally built in the 4th century and reconstructed during the Romanesque period, Brunelleschi completely reorganised the nave and two aisles along classical lines, and incorporated a sacristy (the Sagrestia Vecchia), 'one of the earliest and most important examples of architectural theory' ever realised.[7] However, although in accordance with contemporary architectural thinking he attempted to centralise the space by placing a dome over the crossing, this could not be achieved because of the Latin-cross plan of the church. Since S Lorenzo had become, in effect, the family temple of the Medici (and was later to become their pantheon), Cosimo continued to finance the development of the church long after money from the other contributors had run out,

Photo 9.4 Benedetto da Maiano and Simone del Pollaiuolo (*il Cronaca*), Palazzo Strozzi, Florence, begun 1489. Last but one of the finest Renaissance palaces in Florence, its three rusticated storeys are given equal prominence.

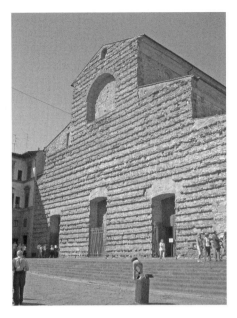

Photo 9.5 Filippo Brunelleschi, church of S Lorenzo, Florence, begun 1418. The Medici family church stylistically thoughtful and measured in terms of its use of classical motifs but with a bare, unfinished facade.

but like so many other Florentine churches its facade has remained stark and unfinished to the present day, 'a counterweight to the lushness of the interior'.[8]

Economic growth also enabled other patrons to commission prominent architects to undertake work in the ecclesiastical sector. One such patron – unusual even by the standards of the 15th century – was Ambrogio Traversari, a Camaldolese monk who became an accomplished and influential resident at the monastery of S Maria degli Angeli – the complex being a focus of a small-scale but lucrative trading enterprise in the heart of Florence. In 1434, he was able to persuade his order to entrust Brunelleschi with the construction of a new church for the monastery. The result was an octagonal building, and although Brunelleschi might have had a circular structure in mind since a circle might suggest that 'there is no beginning or no end' and thus to believers might symbolise God, or in a Platonic sense an 'Idea', such a shape was clearly unsuitable for liturgical purposes. Thus he opted for an octagon which would accommodate chapels on seven of its sides, and a square portico substituting for a chapel on its remaining side that would act as a truncated nave. The building is capped by a large cupola, also octagonal. With its design probably based on that of the

Temple of Minerva Mendica in Rome, the church of S Maria degli Angeli thus became the first centrally planned building of the Renaissance, a precursor to many more particularly in the 16th century.

However, most patrons of ecclesiastical work in quattrocento Florence were secular. When Brunelleschi was appointed by a specially convened commission to rebuild the 13th-century Augustinian church of S Spirito, the redevelopment was not funded predominantly by the Augustinians but by donations from wealthy Florentine families, particularly the Frescobaldi, although monks from the nearby monastery made minor contributions. The rebuilt S Spirito is generally regarded as the most perfect of Brunelleschi's designs. Construction commenced in 1444, and Antonio Manetti, Giovanni da Gaoile and Salvi d'Andrea became responsible for its completion after Brunelleschi's death in 1446. Like the church of S Lorenzo, the facade remains unfinished, though its unadorned surface is broken up by three portals, a central oculus and a gable with side volutes (the latter superstructure being added in 1758). As with the Medici church, the unadorned surface of the facade gives no clue to the magnificence of the interior which articulates to an

Photo 9.6 Filippo Brunelleschi, church of S Spirito, Florence, begun 1444. Overlooking the Piazza S Spirito, the facade of this magnificent Renaissance church remained unfinished until the 18th century, when it acquired an entirely unadorned covering.

even greater extent than demonstrated at S Lorenzo the geometrical rigour of classical architecture as set out by Vitruvius.[9]

Of all the secular patrons, Cosimo de'Medici remained paramount. He extended his influence on Via Larga and its periphery by financing the restoration and transformation of the church and convent of S Marco in 1437, over 500 metres north of the Palazzo Medici. It has also been suggested that by funding the construction of ecclesiastical buildings, and mindful of the heresy of usury, he atoned for some of his more dubious business activities. Belonging originally to the Silvestrini, the 13th- and 14th-century complex of S Marco was ceded to the Dominicans of the Osservanza by Pope Eugenius IV in 1434, and it was in 1437 that Cosimo commissioned Michelozzo to add tribuna and a polygonal apse to the original church and raise its presbytery. Subsequently, in 1444 Cosimo entrusted Michelozzo with the design of an elongated library on the first floor of the adjacent monastery, and in 1451 work was completed on a cloister – the cloister of S Antony – to the right of the church. Finally, behind the body of the church and incorporated in the convent, Michelozzo built the cloister of S Domenico. Possibly the most beautiful monastic building in Italy,[10] S Marco was also noted for containing the first ever public library, an initiative of Cosimo's in response to a bequest by Niccolò Niccoli. In the 16th, 17th and 18th centuries the church of S Marco underwent much modification, largely along Baroque lines, culminating in the construction of a new facade in 1780.

One of the most prominent quattrocento patrons of ecclesiastical buildings after Cosimo de'Medici was the wealthy Florentine banker Andrea Pazzi. In 1429 he commissioned Brunelleschi to design a building that would act both as a funeral chapel for the Pazzi family and as a chapterhouse for the Franciscans. Later known as the Pazzi Chapel, the building was constructed at the eastern end of the first cloister of the church of S Croce, and although completed two decades after Brunelleschi's death under one or more other architects, the finished chapel broadly followed Brunelleschi's original design. The elegant portico, possibly designed by Alberti and Rossellino, embraces the entirety of the facade and encloses a high central arcade which is supported externally by six delicate Corinthian pillars whose continuity is broken in the middle by a triumphal arch. Above, an attic provided with Corinthian double pilasters is crowned by a projecting roof cornice. Internally, the chapel is essentially square and capped by a central hemispherical cupola.

Cosimo de'Medici continued to finance the development of ecclesiastical buildings. In 1444, he commissioned Michelozzo once again, this time to modernise the 14th-century Servite church and monastery of the Santissima Annunziata. While there were few design problems associated with Michelozzo working initially on the atrium of the church and later on its large cloister, controversy raged when Michelozzo added a polygonal choir – built on a central plan – to a formerly Gothic nave, which he reconstructed according to the tenets of classical design. The choir was being financed by Ludovico Gonzaga, marquis of Mantua (a responsibility he sought following his recent command of the Florentine army), and Ludovico objected to Michelozzo's approach. In 1455, Michelozzo was thus dismissed and over the following 21 years was succeeded first by Manetti and then by Alberti. As a consequence, Michelozzo's polygonal choir was transformed into a rotunda, inspired – like Brunelleschi's church of S Maria degli Angeli – by the temple of Minerva Medica in Rome. The imposing portico that faces the Piazza SS Annunziata was not added until *c* 1559–61, and over the next two centuries much of the interior was overlaid with Baroque decoration.

The last major ecclesiastical project of the quattrocento saw the completion of the facade of the Dominican church of S Maria Novella. The Florentine banker Giovanni Rucellai commissioned Alberti to undertake the work around 1456. The lower zone of the facade was framed at its sides by pilasters, while two engaged Corinthian columns were placed either side of a large central portal defined by narrow pilasters and – in the fashion of Alberti – a triumphal arch. The lower zone is separated from the upper part of the facade by a wide rectangular strip with square inlays, the attic above incorporates a central circular window and side volutes with decorative circular motifs, and the entire facade is crowned by an extraordinarily ornate triangular pediment, also with a circular motif. The facade of S Maria Novella is thus one of the very few in Florence to be completed during the quattrocentro.

Milan

While Milan was the largest city in Italy in the quattrocento and its wealthiest, very few if any notable buildings were constructed at this time purely as an outcome of underlying economic factors. Unlike the Medici and their merchant compatriots in Florence, the Visconti and Sforza dynasties were not first and foremost private citizens, but heads of state. Consequently, the very substantial building work that they commissioned (see pp 188–92) was more likely to have been motivated by a desire to consolidate their role in government and enhance their political power than to display their wealth and gain influence, however substantial, over the body politic. As such, building work commissioned

Photo 9.7 Leon Battista Alberti, facade of S Maria Novella, Florence, begun 1456. Situated at one end of the Piazza S Maria Novella, the Tuscan-Romanesque church was completed in the mid-15th century when its facade was embellished with classical motifs to harmonise with existing decoration.

by the Visconti and Sforza can be regarded principally as public sector rather than private sector development and an outcome of largely political rather than economic factors.

Venice

As in Florence, urban development in Venice during the Early Renaissance was substantially determined by economic factors, but in marked contrast to the Tuscan city, here the Gothic style of architecture continued well into the quattrocento. As an outcome of the *Serenissima*'s attachment to maritime trade and colonisation in the Adriatic, Aegean and Levant, contact with mainland Italy and its revival of Classicism was delayed until at least the 1460s. It is of note that there was also a delay in the later Middle Ages, and for broadly the same reason, in the appearance of Gothic architecture within a city predominantly Byzantine.

Of the several late Gothic *palazzi* of Venice, the Ca' d'Oro and Ca' Foscari are arguably the most prominent and, not surprisingly, overlook the Grand Canal in the tradition of their Byzantine and early Gothic predecessors. The Ca' d'Oro is a spectacularly decorated example of the flamboyant Gothic style of architecture derived from the Palazzo Ducale. Commissioned by Marino Contarini in 1421, and designed and executed mainly by Matteo Raverti, the three-storey Ca' d'Oro exhibits the application of an exceedingly high degree of decorative imagination and technical skill in the design and construction of its facade, with its fine stone tracery, its inlaid polychrome marble and its gilt decorations.[11] The larger four-storey Ca' Foscari was commissioned in 1452 by the most famous – or infamous – doge of the quattrocento, Francesco Foscari. Although it is fundamentally Gothic – it is pierced by polyforate windows that on the first floor take the form of trilobed ogees, and on the second floor display tracery comparable to that found in the Ca' d'Oro and Palazzo Ducale – an ornamental marble band decorated *all'antica* and placed above the arcades signals the revival of Classicism.[12]

It was not until the latter years of the quattrocento, however, that there emerged a truly hybrid example of a *palazzo* – the Palazzo Corner-Spinelli. Designed by Mauro Codussi and built *c* 1490, the building boasts a facade that

Photo 9.8 Matteo Raverti, Ca' d'Oro, Venice, 1421. The most exquisite Gothic palace in Venice, alluding to its Veneto-Byzantine ancestry. Its elegant facade is notable for its tracery and bright polychrome and gilded decoration (carefully restored).

Photo 9.9 Ca' Foscari, Venice, 1452. Built as a residence for the doge, Francesco Foscari, this Gothic edifice is adorned by tracery, fine marble columns and a decorated frieze.

combines 'the clear forms of the Renaissance with the liveliness of the Gothic'.[13] The basement of the facade is rusticated and punctuated with small windows and a central arched portal. At the level of the *piano nobile* and the upper storey, enormous biforate windows beneath an oculus are encased within single common arches, while attractive balconies and coloured stone decorations further adorn the facade. The compact block of the facade is edged by classical pilasters, which together with its other features create a 'monumentality which no previous palazzo facade had to show'.[14]

As confraternities or religious associations of merchants – whose main function was to provide works of charity often in association with the clergy – some notable Venetian *scuola* were established in the late quattrocento. One of the most prominent, the Scuola Grande di S Giovanni Evangelista, was founded as early as 1261 but it was not until the mid-15th century that it was able to commission construction of a building of its own next to the church of S Giovanni Evangelista.[15] Like the Palazzo Corner-Spinelli, the new building provided a mix of late-Gothic opulence and fashionable classical style that would epitomise the institution's prosperity and culture.[16]

Built between 1454 and 1512 and designed by Pietro Lombardo and Mauro Codussi, work progressed in stages. Initially, the side facade with its ogee windows was constructed; later a distinctive marble frame took shape to create a homogeneous space; and further work included the portal and interior stairway.[17]

Also founded in the 13th century (in 1260), the Scuola Grande di S Marco likewise lacked an appropriate building of its own. This deficiency was eventually remedied by an agreement between the Scuola and the Dominican friars from SS Giovanni e Paolo in 1437 to make land available close to their church, and a new building for the Scuola was subsequently constructed under the direction of the eminent architects Bartolomeo Bon and Antonio Rizzo. In 1485, soon after it was completed, it was destroyed by fire and thereafter the Scuola commissioned in turn Lombardo and his sons, and Codussi, to reconstruct their building. Lombardo and his sons Tullio and Antonio designed the lower part of the elevation, including the fine portal, between 1485 and 1490, while Codussi was responsible for the upper part of the facade including the curvilinear crown built between 1490 and 1495.[18]

Photo 9.10 Mauro Codussi, Palazzo Corner-Spinelli, Venice, *c* 1490. The first palace built in classical style in Venice with rustication of the ground floor and balconies above.

Photo 9.11 Pietro, Tullio and Antonio Lombardo, and Mauro Codussi, Scuola Grande di S Marco, Venice, 1485–95. At 90 degrees to the church of SS Giovanni e Paolo, and overlooking the church's eponymous *piazza*, the facade of the *scuola* is both sumptuous and attractive.

Church design, like that of *palazzi* and *scuole*, increasingly eschewed neo-Gothic parameters and adopted Classicism as the quattrocento progressed. The reconstruction of the 9th-century convent church of S Zaccaria in 1444–1500 is a notable example of the transition from late-Gothic to Early Renaissance style. Although the earlier church had close links with the Venetian nobility since it acted as a sort of pantheon for the doges, and its convent accepted only the daughters of patrician families, the nuns rather than the doge or the Consiglio Maggiore commissioned rebuilding work. At first, Antonio Gambetto worked on the high basement of the facade, intricately Gothic in style and distinguished particularly for its verticality and narrow blind arches, but after Gambetto's death in 1481 Codussi designed and organised the construction of the upper part of the facade that, 'with its small number of large arched-windows and free-standing columns',[19] is undoubtedly classical. In contrast to S Zaccaria, the church of S Michele in Isola – designed by Codussi and built between 1469 and 1478 – is the first truly Renaissance

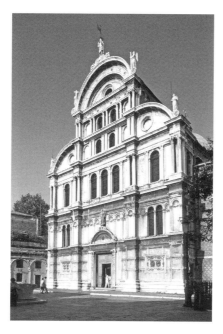

Photo 9.12 Antonio Gambetto and Mauro Codussi, church of S Zaccaria, Venice, 1444–1500. Looking down onto the Piazza S Zaccaria, the church's towering facade successfully combines Gothic and classical architectural attributes.

building in Venice. Commissioned by the Camaldolese monks, the simple facade of the church is constructed of Istrian limestone and its singular attributes include curvilinear buttresses, a semicircular pediment and central oculus.[20]

Belief in the miraculous powers of a painting of the Virgin Mary displayed in a house in the *sestiere* of Cannaregio throughout much of the quattrocento prompted the inhabitants of the district to funded construction of a church – S Maria dei Miracoli – to accommodate the devotional image more reverently. Funded by private donations and votive offerings, local residents duly commissioned Pietro Lombardo and his sons to design the church and execute its construction on the site of the now-extinct convent of S Chiara. From 1481 to 1494 they produced a building 'which looks more like a charming jewel case' than an evangelical edifice.[21] On all four external walls, the relatively featureless lower order is divided by regularly spaced Corinthian pilasters and capped by a horizontal entablature, while the upper order comprises arches, arched windows and Ionic pilasters. The facade contains a central portal with a curved pediment

Photo 9.13 Pietro Lombardo and sons, church of S Maria dei Miracoli, Venice, 1481–94. Like a bejewelled casket, one of the most attractive buildings in Europe.

above the entablature, and a semicircular pediment crowns the whole structure, while above the choir there is a dome and minaret-shaped turrets.[22] Virtually the whole building is clad with polychrome marble 'selected, cut, set and inlaid with a remarkable level of skill and imagination'.[23] While, in this way, work on the exterior was undoubtedly influenced by 13th-century Venetian marble encrustation, the building's ornamental reliefs are essentially classical.[24]

Although the design of S Maria dei Miracoli is an extreme example of Venetian individuality, albeit with Early Renaissance adornment, the design of the nearby church of S Maria Formosa reverts back to Byzantine fundamentals, and was undoubtedly influenced by the Basilica of S Marco. It was built on the site where it was believed that in the year 636 the Virgin Mary had appeared in the guise of a buxom matron (a *formosa*), and where two churches sharing the name S Maria Formosa had been constructed in the past. The first, founded in the 7th century, was superseded by a medieval church in the 11th century, but by the quattrocento this in turn needed to be replaced. Funded by local residents in general and the patrician Cappello family in particular, work on the new church was entrusted to Mauro Codussi and commenced in 1492. Codussi designed and executed a building with an abbreviated Greek-cross plan, capped by a dome above its crossing and three smaller domes above each of its two aisles, with three apsidal chapels at its eastern end. The building took many years to complete. Although its elevation facing a canal dates from 1542 and its design is probably attributable to Codussi, the Baroque facade that overlooks the *campo* was not completed until 1604, a hundred years after his death, and the campanile dates similarly from the seicento.[25]

Genoa

During the relative economic stagnation experienced by Genoa following what was effectively defeat by Venice in the War of Chioggia (1378–81), and prior to its recovery in the 16th century, very few private palaces were commissioned in the city in the cinquecento, and there was a complete dearth of new church building. Of the palaces erected in the quattrocento, only three were prominent: the Palazzo Spinola dei Marmi, the Palazzo Lamba Doria and the Palazzo Doria in Vico d'Oria. The first was commissioned by Giacomo Spinola and designed by Bissoni and Leonardo Riccomani. Built between 1445 and 1459, the *palazzo* was essentially late medieval in style, although the insertion of five niches with marble statues into the facade imparted a classical flavour.[26] The second, the Palazzo Lamba Doria, dating from 1486, is a cacophony of styles with its loggia arcades from Lombardy and Venice, window surrounds from Liguria and Piedmont, and encrustation from Tuscany, producing overall – as if by magic – a somewhat Moorish composition, especially in its use of colour.[27] The third, the Palazzo Doria in Vico d'Oria, also dating from the late quattrocento, is notable for demonstrating the functionality and aesthetic appeal of a monumental staircase set within a courtyard of Tuscan style – an arrangement inspired in part by the *scala apperta* of the Venetian *palazzo*, and an ornamental design feature that was to figure prominently in Genoese palaces in the cinquecento.[28]

Bologna

Among the major cities of northern and central Italy, Bologna is one of the most important centres of quattrocento palace development, noted particularly for its extensive use of brick (as in previous centuries) and for fusing late Gothic and Early Renaissance styles of architecture.[29] Mid-15th-century palaces of this sort include the Palazzo Bologna-Isolani, the Palazzo Bentivoglio (demolished 1507), the Palazzo Fava and the Palazzo Pallavicini. The first two of these were essentially late Gothic in design and incorporated street arcades, a very traditional feature of Bologna. The latter palaces were far more transitional. In addition to displaying finely pointed brickwork and elegant window arches, they both accommodated courtyards with open arcades on both lower and upper storeys, and compared very favourably with their Florentine counterparts in terms of spaciousness and elegance.[30] Only with the development of the Palazzo Senuti Bevilacqua did a truly Early Renaissance *palazzo* emerge. Begun in 1480 and designed by Marsilio Infrangipane and Tommaso Filippi, the building was broadly Florentine in style. Eschewing frontal arcading on the ground floor, the entire facade was rusticated, but in contrast to the Florentine manner, rustication took the form of facet-cut ashlar, first used in the Castello Sforzesco in Milan, and like other contemporary *palazzi* in Bologna it was graced with a spacious courtyard.[31]

With construction of most of Bologna's prominent ecclesiastical buildings occurring in the 13th and 14th centuries, church building in quattrocento Bologna is overshadowed by *palazzo* development, but nevertheless the city boasts a few churches of architectural interest, funded mainly from private donations. Influenced by the overwhelming presence of S Petronio (started 1390), church design throughout the quattrocento was based almost entirely on late Gothic parameters. For example, the facade of the church of Giovanni al Monte (designed 1474) 'shows Venetian influence in its segmental pediments',[32] the semicircular pediments of the facade of the little church of Corpus Domini (1478–80) are similarly Venetian Gothic, and the large aisleless church of S Giacomo Maggiore (started *c* 1458) exhibits both Venetian and Florentine Gothic attributes, although it incorporates a Bolognese feature, a loggia along its south front, constructed between 1477 and 1481.

Rome

As in Venice, Genoa and Bologna, the Early Renaissance emerged in Rome later than in Florence, but in contrast to architectural developments in northern Italy, the revival of Classicism in Rome emanated not from the patronage of merchants and bankers, nor even from donations from across the social classes, but from the papacy. The first manifestation in the Eternal City of a renaissance in architecture is the Palazzo Venezia. Commissioned by the Venetian cardinal Pietro Barbo in 1455, the three-storeyed palace was constructed in the grounds of the church of S Marco, and remained the Venetian's residence after he succeeded to the papacy as Paul II in 1464. It was then that the building was substantially enlarged, its facade being extended to embrace an additional four windows on each of its floors. The architect's identity remains uncertain, although it is possible that Leon Battista Alberti designed the outer walls of the *palazzo* and that Antonio da Sangallo was responsible for the half-finished arcaded courtyard. With its tower and castellated enclosing wall, the *palazzo* might seem to exemplify an intermediate stage between a fortified manor house and a 'typical' Renaissance palace of the Florentine or Venetian genres where there are normally few defensive attributes.[33] However, in true Renaissance style, the small top windows of the *palazzo* were centred above the larger windows of the *piano nobile*, and these in turn were centred above the smaller windows of the ground floor; and whereas the older facade to the left of the portico was pierced by irregularly spaced windows, there are regularly spaced windows to the right of the portico. The influence of the Renaissance was more marked in the courtyard. Here, the two completed arcades boast Doric half-columns at ground-floor level and Corinthian half-columns on the floors above, separated by a deep entablature, as inspired by the nearby Coliseum or Theatre of Marcellus.

Photo 9.14   Palazzo Venezia, Rome, 1455. The first large Renaissance building in Rome but still employing crenellations in the fashion of a medieval palace.

In addition to commissioning work on the *palazzo*, Paul II made even greater use of his site by funding both the construction of a *piazzetta* featuring two-storey arcades and octagonal columns and a large garden court, and a two-storey portico to provide a benediction loggia for the church of S Marco.[34]

Photo 9.15 Palazzo della Cancelleria, Rome, 1486–98. A masterpiece of the Renaissance with its graceful facade and double order of pilasters.

Over 30 years after the Palazzo Venezia was initially commissioned, Cardinal Raffaello Riario began funding construction of the Palazzo Riario, aided to an extent by rent income from ground-floor shops along one side of the building. In contrast to the Palazzo Venezia, the Palazzo Riario was entirely classical in style, the first building in Rome to be fully informed by the Renaissance.[35] It is not known who was responsible for the design of the building – Alberti, Donato Bramante and Andrea Bregno have all been suggested. However, work on the *palazzo* was undertaken between 1486 and 1498 – after the death of Alberti and before the arrival of Bramante from Milan. Flatly rusticated on each of its three storeys, its facade is pierced by regularly spaced windows, separated by pilasters in rhythmic sequence on the *piano nobile* and upper storey. Inside, the building contains the reconstructed 4th-century church of S Lorenzo and an impressive square courtyard, the latter possibly inspired by that of the Palazzo Ducale in Urbino of 1464–6 (see pp 202–4). With arcades around both its ground and first floors supported by Doric columns and matched immediately above by pilasters, the four courtyard walls are crowned by an overhanging cornice. The building is better known as the Palazzo della Cancelleria since it was confiscated by the papal Curia following Riario's alleged involvement in the Petrucci conspiracy against Pope Leo X in 1517 and used subsequently as its chancellery.

The Palazzo Castellesi Corneto is the third of the Early Renaissance palaces of Rome to have been funded from the private wealth of cardinals and their families. Commissioned by Cardinal Adriano Corneto, the design of the *palazzo* has been attributed to the same architects who were responsible for the construction of the Palazzo della Cancelleria, but more specifically it is very likely that Antonio Bregno played a significant part in its design, assisted in supervision of the work by Bramante or Antonio da Sangallo.[36] In general terms, the facade is very similar to that of the Cancelleria, although it boasts double pilasters on both its *piano nobile* and upper storey, arched openings on the former, and a double attic above.[37] Overall, the design might be considered to be more satisfactory than that of the Cancelleria since the facade has only seven bays approximating to a double square, whereas the elongated and irregularly shaped Cancelleria has 14 and thus is not as neat or as comprehensible.

The Smaller Cities of Northern and Central Italy

In the smaller cities of Italy north of Rome during the Early Renaissance very few of the privately funded buildings that were constructed were secular; most were ecclesiastical. The Palazzo dei Diamanti in Ferrara is one of the few exceptions. Commissioned by Sigismondo d'Este in 1493 and designed by Biagio Rossetti, the palace is perhaps the most decorated *palazzo* of the Early Renaissance. Although it was undoubtedly inspired by the Palazzo Senuti Bevilacqua in Bologna, its exterior is far more imaginative. The 8,500 masonry blocks that form its facade are faceted in such a way that their axes face upwards on the ground floor, are level on the *piano nobile*, and tilt downwards on the upper storey. The ground floor is separated from the *piano nobile* by an elaborate cornice and the top storey, the mezzanine, is pierced by oval lucarnes. The sides of the central portico

Photo 9.16   Biagio Rossetti, Palazzo dei Diamanti, Ferrara, begun 1493. Best viewed on the diagonal, this palace takes its name from the 8,500 diamond-shaped bosses that constitute its facade.

and the corners of the building are mounted on truncated pyramids, while the seven-bay facade is framed by ornately carved pilasters.[38]

Another exception is the Palazzo Raimondi in Cremona. Designed by the architect Eliseo Raimondi for his own use, the building (begun 1496) almost 'has an artistic character of its own',[39] although its facade of tile-like square bosses, coupled pilasters and moulded cornices and window surrounds is reminiscent of features previously developed in Bologna and Ferrara and applied later by Bramante in Rome. Even so, Raimondi's *palazzo* provided a model for numerous buildings of a similar sort that were developed across northern and central Italy during the early years of the cinquecento.

The first privately funded ecclesiastical building to be developed among the smaller cities during the Early Renaissance is the Capella Colleoni in Bergamo. Funded by the mercenary general Bartolomeo Colleoni, designed by Giovanni Antonio Amadeo and built between 1470 and 1473, the edifice is decorated in an extravagantly bizarre manner, and incorporates 'complex and excessively subdivided forms of windows and decoration [that] stand out from the chequered

Photo 9.17 Giovanni Antonio Amadeo, Capella Colleoni, Bergamo, 1470–3. Embedded in the northern side of the church of S Maria Maggiore, the chapel is an amazing confection of stunningly decorated multicoloured marble, and one of the more important Renaissance buildings in Lombardy.

surface of the facade'.[40] With an array of dwarf columns and pilasters piling up upon each other in tabernacles, the chapel presents an object lesson on how not to conform to Albertian criteria, a lesson quite probably heeded by Codussi when designing buildings in the *Serenissima*.

Other churches in these lesser cities were often the outcome of voluntary donations and votive contributions to commemorate the supposedly miraculous powers of the Virgin Mary. In Cortona, for example, the church of the Madonna del Calcinaio (begun 1484) was designed for this purpose by Francesco di Giorgio Martini. Subdivided into two storeys separated by a narrow string course, the long aisleless building conforms to a Latin-cross plan and incorporates a dome on a high drum above the crossing and large pedimented windows on its sides.[41] Its facade is marked by a large arched portal with a round window above and is crowned by a large triangular pediment. In 1485, a fairly similar building, the church of the Madonna delle Carceri, was started in the Florentine city of Prato. However its architect, Giuliano da Sangallo (appointed by Lorenzo de'Medici) based the church not on a Latin but on a

Greek cross in the manner of Brunelleschi, while its external walls are decorated with simple coloured encrustations set within a framework of coloured pilasters.[42]

Photo 9.18 Giuliano da Sangallo, Church of the Madonna delle Carceri, Prato, 1485. An early example of a Renaissance Greek-cross church derived from the style of Brunelleschi.

In the smaller cities of the north, monastic orders too financed church building from private donations, and also drew upon income from their rural holdings for this purpose. The Franciscans, for example, funded construction of the church of S Francesco in Ferrara and in 1494 entrusted Biagio Rossetti with the design of the building and execution of the work. The outcome was a multi-domed structure with a somewhat plain facade incorporating pilasters, volutes, a large portal with a pedimented arch and a round window and crowning pediment above.[43] In 1498, Rossetti was commissioned to design the Carthusian church of S Cristoforo, a very different structure from that of S Francesco. Although the Carthusian church was also multi-domed, the exterior of the brick church featured blank arcading and terracotta ornamentation 'characteristic of Rossetti's classicism'.[44]

The South

Naples

Of the many private *palazzi* of Naples, very few were constructed during the Early Renaissance. However, of those that remain, their design was clearly much influenced by Tuscan or north Italian models.[45] The Palazzo Cuomo, for example, was built between 1464 and 1490, probably to the design of the Florentine Giuliano da Maiano. The dominating attributes of its facade are seen, above a high plinth, in its heavily rusticated ground floor incorporating a large central arched portal set in voussoirs while, above, rustication is markedly smoother and the tall upper floor is virtually windowless.[46]

The smaller cities of the South

In the southern peninsula and in Sicily there is very little evidence of private patronage in the development of buildings during the quattrocento. Only in Palermo and Messina is there some evidence that the Renaissance influenced the proclivities of private patrons at all, albeit in a superficial and unusual form. In Palermo, and springing from their Angevin and Catalan roots, the Palazzo Abatellis and Palazzo Aiutamicristo are the only private secular buildings of any note to have been developed at the close of the 15th century. Although the former is characterised by an imposing rusticated facade in the Tuscan manner, it is bordered unconventionally by two corner towers; and while both *palazzi* contain courtyards at ground- and first-floor levels, the arcades of the Palazzo Aiutamicristo in particular are completely unrelated to one another.

Rustication is also in evidence in the church of S Maria della Scala in Messina. Funded by private donations, the church was built in the latter half of the quattrocento. Although its facade, in a conventional way, incorporates a central portal with a round arch at ground-floor level and a centrally positioned arched window above, it is unusual in that it is characterised by a rusticated and window-less basement and an upper floor edged by faceted pilasters and adorned by cushion-shaped window-sill blocks.[47]

Conclusion

Across the length and breadth of 15th-century Italy private patrons – both secular and ecclesiastical – commissioned the development of sumptuous *palazzi*, magnificent religious buildings and distinctive *scuole* in their quest to display their wealth and power or to confirm their spirituality and social responsibility. To protect or enhance their status in society, merchants, bankers, the papal aristocracy, religious orders and confraternities were all anxious to demonstrate that, in their adoption of the classical style of architecture and in their commissioning of grandiose buildings, they were in their private capacity as important and innovative as any government.

Notes

1   RC Wirtz, *Florence* (Cologne: Könemann, 2000), p 250.
2   G Zucconi, *Florence. An architectural guide* (Venice: Arsenale Editrice, 1995), p 70.
3   Vitruvius, *Ten Books of Architecture* (New York: Dover Publications, 1960).
4   Wirtz, *Florence*, p 248.
5   LH Heydenreich, *Architecture in Italy*, rev edn P Davies (New Haven and London: Yale University Press, 1996), pp 143–4.
6   Ibid, p 145.
7   Wirtz, *Florence*, p 272.
8   Zucconi, *Florence*, p 60.
9   See Vitruvius, *Ten Books*.
10 Heydenreich, *Architecture*, p 25.
11 G. Zucconi, Venice. *An architectural guide* (*Venice*: Arsenale Editrice, 1995) p 40.
12 M Kaminski, *Venice* (Cologne: Könemann, 2000), p 47.
13 Ibid, p 65.
14 Heydenreich, *Architecture*, p 98.
15 Kaminski, *Venice*, p 260.
16 Ibid.
17 Zucconi, *Venice*, p 52.
18 Ibid, 53; Kaminski, *Venice*, p 458.
19 Ibid, p 420.
20 Zucconi, *Venice*, p 49.
21 Kaminski, *Venice*, p 405.
22 Heydenreich, *Architecture*, p 92.
23 Zucconi, *Venice*, p 51.
24 Kaminski, *Venice*, p 405.
25 Ibid, p 447.
26 Heydenreich, *Architecture*, p 129.
27 Ibid.
28 Ibid.
29 Ibid, p 118.
30 Ibid, p 119.
31 Ibid, p 120.
32 Ibid, p 118.

33   C Woodward, *Rome* (Manchester: Manchester University Press, 1995), p 65.
34   B Hintzen-Bohlen with J Sorges, *Rome and the Vatican City* (Cologne: Könemann, 2001), p 43.
35   Woodward, *Rome*, p 67.
36   Ibid, p 68.
37   Hintzen-Bohlen with Sorges, *Rome*, p 69.
38   Heydenreich, *Architecture*, p 122.
39   Ibid, p 115.
40   Ibid, p 107.
41   Ibid, p 137.
42   Ibid, p 142.
43   Ibid, p 121.
44   Ibid.
45   Ibid, p 134.
46   Ibid.
47   Ibid, p 130.

PART 3

THE 16TH CENTURY

CHAPTER 10

THE ASCENDANCY OF PRINCIPALITIES AND SPANISH RULE IN 16TH-CENTURY ITALY

Introduction

In the cinquecento the boundaries of many of the Italian city-states were very broadly the same as those in the previous century (see figs 6.1 and 10.1). Although Rome was sacked by imperial forces in 1527, the Eternal City soon recovered and the Papal States remained as extensive as they had been in the quattrocento, if not more so, while to the north-east the boundaries of the Venetian Republic throughout most of the century continued to embrace Bergamo, Brescia, Verona, Vicenza and Padua. However, an expansionist Florence incorporated Pisa within its domain in 1509 and Siena in 1557, while major parts of the peninsula were occupied by foreign powers: for example, Milan fell to France in 1499, and to the Holy Roman Empire in 1535 after a period of home rule as a Sforza duchy (1521–35). In 1556, Milan became a Spanish dominion under a governor and, throughout most of the cinquecento, Naples and Sicily were ruled by a succession of Spanish viceroys.

Where there were boundary changes, these occurred mainly in the first half of the cinquecento when parts of the peninsula were plagued by persistent wars often on a much greater scale and conducted with greater ferocity than hitherto. In the second half of the century, however, relative peace brought about a

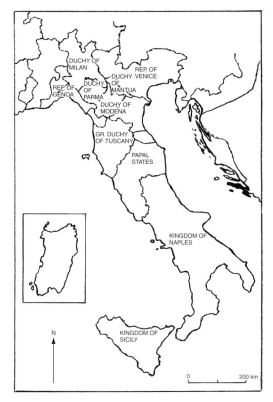

Figure 10.1 Italy in 1559

virtual cessation in attempts at territorial aggrandisement. The Treaty of Cateau-Cambrésis of 1559 had confirmed that, with only minor alterations to boundaries, the spatial integrity of the Spanish dominions of Sicily, Naples and Milan, the duchy of Tuscany, the Papal State and the Venetian and Genoese Republics would be maintained; and at the battle of Lepanto (1571) a massed navy of Venetian, Spanish and papal galleys not only defeated the naval forces of Sultan Selim II of Turkey but demonstrated that, when faced with an external threat, the territorial powers of Italy were capable of protecting their strategic interests in coalition, rather than in opposition. It is within this context of external stability that strong princely rule (both secular and ecclesiastic) emerged throughout much of northern and central Italy, the Venetian Republic – for the most part – maintained its integrity, and Spain was able to consolidate its hold over its Italian possessions. External and internal security thus provided the backdrop for a massive increase in urban development in Italy, both in the number of governmental and religious buildings constructed and in their size.

The Ascendancy of Princely Rule

Within the context of war and peace in cinquecento Italy princely government was on the ascendant and republicanism was on the wane. With Florence succumbing to princely rule in 1539 and Siena's incorporation into the duchy of Tuscany in 1554, only Venice, Genoa and Lucca retained their republican status throughout the rest of the century and beyond. Elsewhere in much of the peninsula signorial and monarchial rule came to dominate Italian politics as astute princes invariably attempted to legitimise their positions by producing new or amended constitutions (that often survived until the 19th century), while appeasing their subjects with financial reforms and political concessions. In the Papal States, Milan, Ferrara, Mantua, Florence and Naples (from the early 16th century), and lesser principalities in the peninsula throughout most of the quattrocento and cinquecento, 'the principle of monarchy was supreme, but councils [and] senates [often] enabled the nobility to feel closely involved in government'.[1] The pragmatism of this approach was such that it could be applied to virtually every city in Italy, but when less astute princes failed to adopt it, the consequences were often rebellion or civil war. Pragmatism was also extended to the development of the built environment. In the cinquecento, as Richard Goldthwaite suggests, 'it was second nature for the Italian ruling class to regard urban renewal of capital cities as an expression of power'.[2] While evidence of this extends from Milan in the north to Palermo in the south, 'urban renewal in Italy was not exclusively a princely activity. Oligarchs as well as princes viewed the city as a natural extension for the physical expression of their authority',[3] as is vividly demonstrated by Venice and Genoa.

The Larger States of Northern and Central Italy

Rome

Following the removal of the papacy to Avignon for much of the 14th century, Rome in the quattrocento struggled to reassert itself in Italian power-politics, but in the cinquecento it arguably became the leading power in the peninsula, since Milan and Naples – Rome's historic rivals – were now under foreign rule.[4] Owing to its location in the north-east, Venice could not be expected to be a dominant force in Italy, while the political influence of Florence – no longer an economic powerhouse – was in decline.

The built environment of Rome was transformed over a period of a hundred years from a run-down medieval city into a magnificent capital of Christendom. In their quest to reassert papal authority, a succession of popes commissioned a series of *grands projets* throughout much of the cinquecento, seeking to resurrect the ancient glories of Rome and to reinforce their spiritual and temporal authority. Julius II (1503–13) led the way. He became 'one of the great patrons of the sixteenth century. In scale and ambition, his projects rivalled those of his imperial predecessors'.[5] First and foremost, and using an ever-increasing volume of revenue collected from across Catholic Europe, he commissioned the rebuilding of St Peter's, a responsibility he bequeathed to his successors which they then assumed throughout the 16th and early 17th centuries. He was also responsible, among many other developments, for the construction of the massive Belvedere court that connected the old papal palace next to St Peter's with the 15th-century Belvedere Villa. Later in the century, Clement VII funded the construction of the Zecca or papal mint (1530), and Paul III (1534–49) not only continued to fund and oversee the construction of St Peter's but commissioned the development of the Piazza del Campidoglio and the reconstruction of the Palazzo Senatorio and the Palazzo dei Conservatori as the centre of civil government. Subsequently, Pius IV commissioned the Porta Pia (1561) and S Maria degli Angeli (1563), and Gregory XIII commissioned the Palazzo del Quirinale (1574). However, although in office for only five years (1585–90), '[i]n terms of quantity, Sixtus V was easily the greatest patron in sixteenth-century Rome'.[6] Although his first priority throughout his pontificate was St Peter's, and he commissioned the construction of the Palazzo del Laterano during his first year as pontiff, he is noted in particular for developing a network of wide, straight avenues across the city punctuated with obelisks, statues and fountains and linking its principal churches (see chapter 2). While building work on such a scale was dependent on 'the use of materials extracted from ancient fora and other sites of antiquity, Rome undoubtedly had recovered her ancient grandeur'.[7]

Venice

Since the Republic of Venice was a state with an exceedingly robust constitution, it witnessed very few changes in its system of government during the 16th century save for its consolidation of power throughout the cities of the *terraferma*. Nonetheless, it was recognised in the *Serenissima* that 'architecture played a crucial role in state propaganda, aimed at impressing foreigners with the might of the Republic and reinforcing the myth of harmony and stability at home'.[8] Its exceptional constitutional strength was reflected in the Senate's ability to fund, in their entirety, the reconstruction of the Fondaco dei Tedeschi during the early years of the cinquecento (the old German warehouse having been burnt down in 1505), and the development of a number of major public buildings in its core, for example the imposing Procuratie Vecchie (begun 1500), the Palazzo dei Camerlenghi (1525), the Zecca (1536), the Loggetta of the bell tower (1537), the magnificent Biblioteca Marciana (started 1537), and the Procuraie Nuove (begun 1586). In the words of Goldthwaite, these developments 'resulted in one of the most remarkable squares to evolve in any comune and one of the most notable exemplifications of the humanist ideal of a focussed plan in the history of urban development'.[9] Nor was the religiosity of the republic neglected during this period of development. To commemorate the city's deliverance from the plague in 1577 and to give thanks to the Almighty, the Senate commissioned construction of the church of Il Redentore on the island of Giudecca (see chapter 11).

Genoa

The Republic of Genoa, constitutionally fragile in the quattrocento and often under foreign suzerainty, evolved substantially in the 16th century. When Genoa switched its allegiance from France to Spain in 1528, its senate decided to rationalise and strengthen its constitution by allowing only those families serving before 1506 to hold senior office under the doge. The city was thus blessed with comparatively strong government for the years ahead, albeit in the form of a despotic aristocracy. However, the consolidation of power in the hands of 28 *alberghi* or associations of extended families created tension between the ' "old" noble families, with the greatest wealth and the longest political pedigrees, and the ambitious new families desiring access to civic office'.[10] Inter-family rivalry was in part reflected in the construction of magnificent palaces in the newly developed Strada Nuova (see chapter 10). With sites on the *strada* provided by the republic, development profits were used to finance other state projects throughout the city as part of a programme of urban renewal which included the fortification of the harbour and repairs to the city walls.[11]

In 1575–6 tensions in Genoa erupted in civil war between the 'old' and 'new' families that ended only when King Philip II of Spain brokered an agreement between the two adversaries. This allowed 300 new families to join the ruling oligarchy, and as many as 10 families to be admitted annually. Since new families joined the old in restricting access to office, the accord was never kept. However, the size of the governing patriciate remained remarkably constant – numbering 2,000 to 2,300 adult male nobles by the end of the century. The Genoese constitution thus became very resilient. It remained in place for over two centuries despite many challenges to its legitimacy, and in the late cinquecento, at least, provided a sound foundation for the continuation of a building boom that had got underway by mid-century.

Milan

In complete contrast to Venice, but somewhat like Genoa, Milan experienced the instability of war and occupation during the early decades of the 16th century, the city falling first to the French and then, in 1521, to imperial forces. However, the Holy Roman Emperor Charles V was cautious about adding Milan to his Habsburg domain, only doing so in 1535 after 14 years of rule by Duke Francesco II Sforza. Charles put in place a Senate or supreme court, based on a French-style *parlement*, that 'had wide discretion over the interpretation and application of laws, with the right to register royal decrees before they took effect'.[12]

Government was devolved to nine autonomous districts (Milan, Pavia, Cremona, Lodi, Como, Novara, Alessandria, Tortona and Vigevano), 'each with its own economic policies and tax lists'.[13] Citizens of the *dominante* were privileged at the expense of the rural population since they alone were exempt from the *corvée* (compulsory labour service) and a wide range of taxes; they were also not subject to feudal courts.

Below the Senate, the Milanese great council retained a great deal of its former autonomy and power, even though under the Habsburgs it 'shrank to an elite of two hundred noble families, in a tight assembly of just sixty members'.[14] Lawyers and physicians tended to close ranks to exclude non-Milanese – such as the Spanish – from encroaching upon their areas of expertise, and the craft guilds continued to exercise influence over economic policy.

Even the Church was insulated from imperial patronage due to 'the intransigence of Carlo Borromeo, archbishop and papal nephew',[15] and also protected by the ultimate court of appeal for Spanish Milan, Naples and Sicily (the Council of Italy) that cautioned governors not to adopt measures that would run counter to ecclesiastical interests. However, papal taxation was greater in the duchy 'than anywhere else in northern Italy, and . . . Milan also contained a patchwork of 1,600 feudal jurisdictions' that yielded feudal dues.[16]

The governor of Milan was Madrid's chief functionary in the duchy. His 'secret' council, which comprised political and military advisers, exercised jurisdiction over edicts, legislation, war and alliances, and oversaw criminal trials and tax cases before these were dealt with by magistrates. Around 60 per cent of the council's members were Spaniards and Italians not native to the duchy; the remainder were Milanese or Lombards. Governors could also use their authority to mediate border disputes between other Italian states, for example between Parma and Mantua, and further afield could help ensure that French designs on Naples were blocked and French communications with its ally, Venice, were impeded. However, the powers of the governor were not unlimited. They were counterbalanced by the authority of the emperor, the Senate and a professional civil service. Thus although Ferrante Gonzaga (in office 1546–55) was responsible for the construction of massive bastioned fortifications around Milan, he was removed from office 'as a result of protest and subsequent investigation'.[17]

Aside from the commune, which commissioned the Palazzo dei Giureconsulti in 1562, the other principal patron of building development was the Church, in the person of Cardinal Carlo Borromeo (1538–84). Using funds raised in his diocese, Borromeo commissioned a large number of ecclesiastical buildings in Milan including S. Angelo (1552), the Canonica degli Ordinari (1565), S. Lorenzo (1574) and S. Sebastiano (1582). He was also responsible jointly with the Jesuits for commissioning S Fidele (1569).

Florence

Like other Italian states, the once-proud Republic of Florence faced an uncertain future during the first two decades of the 16th century. This was not because of an external threat, but due to the Medici setting their sights on power after an 18-year absence from government. Following short periods of participation in the city's administration by Giovanni de'Medici in 1512–13, Giuliano II in 1513 and Lorenzo III in 1513–19, Giulio de'Medici became effective ruler of Florence in 1519 (before being elected Pope Clement VII in 1523). However, his successor, Ippolito de'Medici failed to gain the support of the Florentine population, and – possibly inspired by the Sack of Rome – the city rose up to depose him in 1527 and restored the republic. Despite the new regime proclaiming universal liberty – or because of it – infighting 'quickly alienated many of the most influential families, leading to plotting, banishments, confiscations and imprisonment'.[18]

In their efforts to regain power in Florence the Medici sought the support of the Habsburg emperor Charles V, whereas the republic turned to France in its attempt to secure its constitutional position. The emperor therefore layed siege to the city in 1529, and on its surrender imposed Alessandro de'Medici (1531–7) on Florence as duke. With the unconditional support of both Charles V and Pope Clement VII de'Medici, Alessandro assumed the role of a despotic monarch, only to be assassinated by a distant relative in the sixth year of his rule.

In 1537 Alessandro was swiftly succeeded by his cousin Cosimo de'Medici (Cosimo I, 1537–74) who, to shore up the regime, 'murdered opponents at home and replaced elected magistrates with appointees, legislated, named and revoked judges, and modified court sentences at will'.[19] In addition, he granted church benefices to loyal clients, and reinforced the security of the capital by erecting three stout citadels around its built-up area, each commanded by a non-Florentine in the hope of ensuring loyalty from the elites of the periphery.

Cosimo also strengthened his rule by setting up a sort of privy council, the *Practica Segreta*, to advise on policy, and he maintained favourable relations with the Habsburg Empire which, with its help and after a two-year siege, 'yielded him Siena in 1559 and the title of grand duke of Tuscany a decade later'.[20] The efficacy of public policy was also enhanced by the expansion and centralisation of the civil service in the newly constructed Palazzo Uffizi, which was soon connected by means of an overhead corridor to the Pitti Palace that had become the ducal residence in 1549. Built between 1560 and 1580, the Uffizi 'provided visible evidence of the reorganisation of the ducal administration, with each of its 13 new agencies separately housed in its own section of the building behind a uniform classical facade'.[21] Under the Medici, Tuscany benefited from peace and stability. From the Uffizi, the Medici grand dukes administered territories with a conscientious attention to detail that ensured their efficient rule until the dynasty's demise in 1737.

The Smaller Cities of Northern and Central Italy

The cities of the Papal State

North-east of Rome, the Papal State was a honeycomb of princely courts, chief among them the court of Urbino, the courts of the papal vicars such as the Bentivoglio of Bologna, the Sforza of Pesaro, the Malatesta of Rimini, and the

Colonna and Orsini clans of Rome, powerful by virtue 'of their vast feudal estates, where they administered justice, collected taxes, enacted local laws, and raised small armies'.[22] In legal terms, the duchy of Ferrara was also a papal state, 'but the Este lords of the city enjoyed such dynastic eminence and so complete an autonomy that they ranked as independent princes'.[23]

The Papal States in the cinquecento were to a great extent consolidated by military means as papal forces took several of them back into the fold once the papacy returned from Avignon and after the Great Schism that followed. In due course they were placed under the control of 'a network of urban governors to dispense justice and make provisioning'.[24] To compensate for the loss of revenue from areas that had embraced the Reformation and Protestantism (mainly in northern Europe), to tighten control over its still very extensive territories and to regenerate Rome as the papal capital, the papacy increased taxation in the Papal States and sought donations from elsewhere in Christendom to meet the costs of rebuilding the city. To secure yet more ground and to further bolster its authority (to the advantage of its finances), the papacy annexed fiefs when princes died hierless and 'in 1578 recovered some fifty castles in one swoop by "verifying" feudal titles'.[25]

The duchy of Urbino was one fief annexed in this way. It consisted of territories that had been conquered by the Montefeltro dynasty around the Marches town during the 13th and 14th centuries, but when Guidobaldo Montefeltro died without an heir in 1508 the duchy passed to Francesco Maria della Rovere who, like his predecessors, held it as a papal fief with the right to grant sub-fiefs. 'To the towns, his regime dispatched zealous functionaries to defend and extend the ducal prerogative',[26] and in 1573, towards the end of the century, state loyalty was severely tested because Guidobaldo II imposed new taxes on Urbino without consultation, thereby provoking a revolt that was brutally crushed despite mediation by the city's nobles. 'Typically, the revolt led to deep tax cuts under Guidobaldo's son, Francesco Maria II (1574–1631), who led the life of a private lord in Pesaro.'[27] Despite having purchased Pesaro from the Sforza in 1512, the Della Rovere dynasty ruled over a state that was not large enough to rank even as a secondary power. Thus 'with only about 150,000 inhabitants around 1600, the Della Rovere dukes submitted themselves first to Venetian dominance and then to Spain'. On the duke's death in 1631, and in the absence of a dynastic successor, 'the territory passed to Rome, although the papal league continued to administer it separately. The courts of Urbino and Pesaro simply vanished, and their courtiers removed to Rome and Florence'.[28] While very few buildings of any merit were constructed in 16th-century Urbino, in large measure due to political instability and the absence of a patron of the influence of Federico da Montefeltro

(1422–82), in Pesaro there was a public building boom on an impressive scale soon after the city had become state capital in 1536. In an attempt to enhance its prestige, Francesco Maria I (1490–1538) not only commissioned the enlargement of the Palazzo Ducale and the construction of a new villa, Il Barchetto, but also the restoration of the 15th-century Villa Imperiale.[29] In light of such major developments, it seems particularly ironic that the city ceased to have a long-term political identity of its own.

Bologna, the largest of the smaller cities of the north, also ceased to be of any real political importance in the cinquecento, though its decline was earlier than that of Urbino and Pesaro. After more than 60 years of Bentivoglio communal rule, it was incorporated into the Papal State in 1506 and was ruled directly by a papal governor. In contrast to the wide array of public buildings that was constructed in the later Middle Ages and the quattrocento, relatively little governmental commissioning was undertaken in the cinquecento – the Portico dei Banchi and Archiginnasio, both begun in 1561, and the vast Neptune statue completed in 1566 being notable exceptions – aside from the continued development of the arcaded streets that so characterise the city.

Ferrara

Ferrara remained autonomous throughout the 16th century and, like Milan under the Visconti and Mantua under the Gonzaga, the city had been ruled by one dynasty – the D'Este – for an inordinate period. The D'Este had controlled a state that had become a lively centre of culture in Italy, but after the death of Alfonso II (1559–97) – who died without an heir – his Palazzo Paradiso became the seat of the university at the turn of the century, a transformation that provided a fitting epitaph for the family. The future status of Ferrara, however, was uncertain. Although 30 years earlier Pope Pius V had proclaimed that the city would come under papal jurisdiction in the absence of heirs, Alfonso's illegitimate cousin Cesare d'Este (who had already inherited Modena and Reggio from his uncle) laid claim to Ferrara and raised troops to protect its territory from seizure. In response, the pope raised an army too, and war in northern Italy seemed imminent. When France declined to support Cesare, he withdrew and relocated his capital to Modena, and in 1598 Ferrara reverted to the papacy.

The cities of the Venetian terraferma

In contrast to Ferrara, the principal cities of the Venetian *terraferma* – Brescia, Padua, Verona and Vicenza – continued to be governed as in the quattrocento, ie by the local nobility, and were fertile ground for the development of new civic buildings throughout the following century. In Brescia, an upper storey was added to the magnificent 15th-century Palazzo Pubblico between 1554 and 1574; in Padua, the city authority commissioned the Porta S Giovanni in 1528, the Porta Savonarola in 1530 and the imposing Palazzo del Capitaniato in 1532, while the civic university commissioned the courtyard of the Palazzo del Bò in the 1540s; in Verona, the city's administration funded construction of the daunting Porta Nuova and Porta Palio in 1531 and 1547, and the enormous Palazzo della Gran Guardia in 1609; and in Vicenza, the government commissioned the magnificent Basilica (or Palazzo della Ragione) in 1549, and the Loggia del Capitano in 1571.

Mantua

As an imperial fiefdom, under the Gonzaga the duchy of Mantua flourished throughout most of the 16th century. In the 1530s, it gained the marquisate of Montferrat on the marriage of Federico II (1519–40) to a Palaeologus princess – heir to a defunct Byzantine throne. It was during Federico's reign that Mantua witnessed the expansion of the dynasty's centre of power, the massive Palazzo Ducale (see chapter 11). Federico Gonzaga's successor, Guglielmo (1560–87), a gifted but miserly administrator, 'pruned back the court, eliminated patrician tribunals, and centralised justice and finance for his personal advantage'.[30] Nevertheless, this did not stop him from using the recently constructed Cortile della Cavallerizza of the *palazzo* as a symbol of his power and prestige and, specifically, 'as a grandiose setting for courtly entertainment',[31] nor from demonstrating his piety by commissioning a new palace chapel, S Barbara, in 1562.

Parma and Piacenza

Formerly possessions of the duchy of Milan, Parma and Piacenza became a Farnese domain under joint papal and imperial tutelage in 1545 as a result of the marriage of Pier Luigi, illegitimate son of Cardinal Alessandro Farnese (later Pope Paul III) and Margarita of Austria, daughter of Charles V. However, even though Charles V advised Pier to rule Parma's urban and feudal aristocrats sensitively, 'his overt centralization, his dismantling of feudal castles, and his citadel in Piacenza kindled widespread dissent against him'.[32] Pier Luigi was consequently assassinated by the state's aristocrats in 1547 – aided and abetted by the duke of Mantua and possibly by his father-in-law, the emperor. Pier Luigi was succeeded by his son Ottavio who consolidated his power over the state in 1556 as a Spanish client. Ottavio adopted a more prudent approach to the rights of the nobility than had his father, pacifying Parma until after his death in 1587. However, his successor Alessandro Farnese (1587–93), who had risen to the rank of commander-in-chief of Europe's largest land force, the Spanish army in Flanders, 'mistrusted the aristocracy [and mindful of Pier Luigi's fate] paid for Parma's citadel out of his own revenue, drawn not just from the duchy, but also from estates held in Latium, in the Abruzzi and Lombardy' (see chapter 16).[33] Farnese rule henceforth became despotic, minimising the role of an aristocratic tier of government.

Lucca and Pisa

The smallest of the remaining republics, Lucca allied itself with Spain in the 1520s for an indefinite period, despite the city's strong political links with France and its profitable trading relations with Lyons. Despite or because of factional infighting in the quattrocento, a consensus emerged by the 1550s that ensured that power was exercised by an electorate and oligarchy composed of families of long residence, much akin to the Venetian model. Also like the Venetian Republic, Lucca remained independent until the end of the 18th century, in Lucca's case due in no small measure to the reconstruction of its defensive walls in the 16th century.

While nearby Pisa fell to Florentine rule in 1509, under the Medici the city's built environment was enhanced through a number of construction projects. The redevelopment of an existing square during the latter part of the century, known thenceforth as the Piazza dei Cavalieri, was flanked by such buildings as the Palazzo dell'Orologio, the Palazzo dei Cavalieri and the church of S Stefano commissioned by Cosimo I and his illegitimate son Giovanni de'Medici between 1562 and 1593. A later Medici patron, Ferdinando I, funded construction of the Loggia dei Banchi, the city's wool and silk market (1603–5).

Siena

While republican government was secure in Venice throughout the cinquecento, and consolidated in Genoa, in Siena it was extinguished. Between 1502 and 1525, the city was under the signorial rule of Pandolfo Petrucci but subsequently its governmental structures were reformed ten times between 1525 and 1552.[34] Fearing that the city would fall prey to French ambitions, Emperor Charles V ordered the construction of a citadel in the city to accommodate Spanish forces as a defensive measure, but the Siennese consequently rose up and sought help from French, Florentine and papal forces who were soon in control of the city. Since the Florentine contribution to the coalition was supplied by Filippo Strozzi, a sworn enemy of the Medici, Cosimo de'Medici, duke of Tuscany allied himself with imperial and Spanish interests and sent a Tuscan army to lay siege to Siena in 1554–5, a conflict that reduced the city's population from 40,000 to a mere 8,000 in just one year – proportionately a greater loss than that incurred during the Black Death. In return for war services, Emperor Charles's successor, Philip II, permitted Cosimo to annex Siena in 1557 and incorporate it into the duchy of Tuscany, so ending the city's status as an independent republic. As the city became little more than a provincial market centre there was little new building development, its medieval structures such as the Palazzo Pubblico, the Campo and the *duomo* remaining intact to this day and in a remarkable state of preservation (see chapter 3).

The South

Naples

South of Rome, the kingdom of Naples was partitioned as an outcome of a secret agreement concluded in November 1500 between France, Spain and Venice. Published in June 1501, the treaty – also signed by the pope – was intended as an offensive pact against the Turks; under its terms France was to govern Naples and the Abruzzi; Spain was to acquire the southern part of the kingdom, including Apulia and Calabria; and Venice was to retain the Apulian ports. Lacking the support of his baronage, Federico, the king of Naples, succumbed to the might of France as French forces occupied the capital in August 1501, so terminating a line of kings.[35] Naples at this time was coveted by Ferdinand of Spain, king of Sicily and Sardinia. Following military campaigns against the French between March 1502 and January 1504, France was 'compelled to acknowledge Spanish mastery in the south'.[36]

From 1504, Naples (as the major part of the Two Sicilies) was ruled by Ferdinand, King of all Spain (until 1516), subsequently by Charles I (Charles V, Holy Roman Emperor) until 1556, then by Philip II until 1598 – during each reign through a succession of viceroys, 23 in total throughout the century. Spanish rule continued until 1713 when the former kingdom of Naples (and Sicily) fell under Austrian rule, while Sicily became a Savoyard possession.

Due to Naples' extraordinary size in both spatial and demographic terms (the city accommodated 150,000 people in 1500 and 250,000 in 1600), it was deemed necessary for the civic government to comprise representatives from six electoral districts. Sitting permanently – unlike parliament which only met occassionally – its principal responsibilities were to raise local taxes and manage the city's tribunal, ensure adequate provision of grain and maintain or expand the 'physical plant' of the capital[37] – including works of urban renewal initiated by the viceroy. The latter function was a major priority since Naples was threatened externally by the Ottoman Turks and internally by continual unrest. The viceroys thus had very strong motives for commissioning visible statements of their authority in their capital. 'During his twenty-one years as Viceroy (1532–53), Pedro Alvarez de Toledo gave visual expression to the authority of the Spanish crown, and his own position, in a major scheme of urban renewal in Naples, designed to improve the city's defences and create a fitting arena for the display of Spanish power' (see chapter 11).[38] The city walls were duly strengthened, the hill-top fortress of Castel Sant'Elmo was rebuilt, the Castel Nuovo restored, the Castel Capuano transformed and the Via Toledo was 'planned as a grand residential street for palaces of the nobility'[39] – a street in which the nobles were required to live most of the year to reduce dissent in the provinces.

Palermo

While the city of Palermo has comparatively few public buildings dating from the cinquecento, the Sicilian capital is noted for its two main thoroughfares that run from the south-east to the north-west and intersect close to the highly ornamented Piazza Pretoria. Commissioned in 1574, they constitute the basic components of a town planning project implemented under Spanish rule (see chapter 11).

Conclusion

Although the Sack of Rome brought a temporary halt to urban development in the Eternal City, public patronage in Rome throughout the rest of the cinquecento resulted in the construction of grandiose edifices on a scale unseen since antiquity. To a lesser extent – though in their own way no less exuberantly – urban development projects were undertaken in other cities throughout the 16th century, particularly in the four decades of relative peace which followed the signing of the Treaty of Cateau-Cambrésis in 1559.

Chronology

1499	Milan falls to France.
1503	**In Rome, Pope Julius II commissions construction of Cortile del Belvedere and rebuilding of St Peter's.**
1504–5	Following joint French and Spanish rule post-1501, Naples becomes Spanish dominion and is ruled by viceroys until 1713. However, in *de jure* terms, Naples remains fief of the Roman Church while a substantial amount of power is devolved to the barons.
1505	**In Venice, after destruction by fire, Fondaco dei Tedeschi rebuilt with republican funds.**
1508	Julius II establishes League of Cambrai with France, Spain and Holy Roman Empire to confiscate Venetian territories on the mainland. Venice placed under blanket excommunication.
1509	Battle of Agnadello. French forces defeat Venetians and compel Venice to yield to the Papal State its conquests in the Romagna south of the Po.
1509	Florence incorporates Pisa within its domain.
1510	Julius revokes excommunication of Venice and forms an alliance with Florence, Naples and Spain against France. France defeated by papal forces at Novara.
1512	**Venetian Senate commissions construction of Procuratie Vecchie.**
1514	French armies invade Italy and defeat papal forces at Marignano.
1521	Under Charles V, imperial army seizes Milan from French; the city subsequently becomes a Sforza duchy for a period of 14 years.
1525	Imperial army resoundingly defeats French at Pavia. Pope Clement VII establishes Holy League comprising Rome, Venice and France to limit power of Charles V. **In Venice, Senate funds construction of the Palazzo dei Camerlenghi.**
1527	Rome sacked by imperial forces comprising 15,000 German mercenaries.

	Ippolito de'Medici fails to win support of the Florentine population; Florence once again establishes republican rule.
1528	Genoese senate strengthens republic's constitution by limiting number of families eligible for office under the doge to those in office before 1506; this creates rivalry between 'old' and 'new' families.
	In Genoa, inter-family rivalry reflected in construction of grandiose palaces in Strada Nuova.
1529	Charles V lays seige to Florence; on its surrender, Alessandro de' Medici imposed as duke of the republic.
1529	Charles V imposes Treaty of Cambrai on France whereby French renounce all claims on Italian peninsula.
1530	Imperial forces seize Florence and replace republic with Medici rule.
	Within three years of Sack of Rome, a succession of popes embarks upon further development of Eternal City.
	In Rome, Pope Clement VII funds construction of Zecca or papal mint.
1532–53	**In Naples, viceroy Pedro Alvarez de Toledo organises major programmes of urban renewal.**
1534–49	**In Rome, Pope Paul III commissions development of Piazza del Campidoglio and reconstruction of Palazzo Senatorio and Palazzo dei Conservatori.**
1535	Milan falls to Holy Roman Empire. Charles establishes a Senate or supreme court to govern the city.
1536	**In Venice, Senate commissions construction of republic's Zecca.**
	Pesaro becomes capital of papal state of Urbino.
	In Urbino, Francesco Maria I commissions enlargement of Palazzo Ducale, construction of a new villa and restoration of Villa Imperiale in new state capital.
1537	**In Venice, work commences on Loggetta of the bell tower and on the Biblioteca Marciana.**
	Alessandro de'Medici assassinated in Florence.
	Florence succumbs to princely rule under Cosimo I (1537–74).
1549	**In Florence, Cosimo I vacates Palazzo Vecchio in favour of Palazzo Pitti, which becomes his official residence.**
1552	**In Milan, Carlo Borromeo commissions the church of S Angelo.**
1554	Siena incorporated into duchy of Tuscany. To help govern the duchy, Cosimo establishes *Practica Segreta*.
	Parma and Pienza become Farnese domain under joint papal and imperial tutelage.
1556	Milan becomes Spanish dominion under a governor.
1557	Florence incorporates Siena within its domain.
	Little new building development occurs until 19th century, preserving medieval core of city.
1559	Treaty of Cateau-Cambrésis confirms spatial integrity of kingdoms of Sicily and Naples, duchy of Tuscany, Papal State and Venetian and Genoese Republics.

	In Florence, Cosimo I commissions construction of Palazzo Uffizi as his administrative headquarters.
1561	In Rome, Pope Pius IV commissions Porta Pia.
1562	In Milan, senate commissions Palazzo dei Giureconsulti.
	In Pisa, the Palazzo dell'Orologio, Palazzo Cavalieri and church of S Stefano commissioned by Cosimo I and Giovanni de' Medici.
1563	In Rome, Pius IV funds construction of S Maria degli Angeli.
1565	In Milan, Cardinal Carlo Borromeo commissions Canonica degli Ordinari.
1569	In Milaneo Carlo Borrom, helps fund Jesuit church of S Fidele.
	Cosimo I becomes Grand Duke of Tuscany.
1574	In Rome, Pope Gregory XIII commissions Palazzo del Quirinale.
	In Milan, Carlo Borromini commissions rebuilding of church of S Lorenzo.
1575–6	In Genoa, inter-family rivalry eased by decision to increase number of families eligible for senior office to 300.
	In Genoa, political stability consequently provides sound foundation for continuation of mid-century building boom.
1577	In Milan, Carlo Borromeo commissions church of S Sebastiano.
	In Venice, to commemorate deliverance from plague, senate commissions church of Il Redentore.
	In Palermo, major thoroughfares built through centre intersecting at Piazza Pretoria.
1585–90	In Rome, Pope Sixtus V funds continuing work on St Peter's, commissions construction of Palazzo del Laterano and develops network of wide, straight avenues across the city.
1586	In Venice, senate commissions Procuratie Nuove.
1598	Alfonso II dies without an heir and Ferrara reverts to papacy, so ending centuries of D'Este patronage.

Notes

1 C Duggan, *A Concise History of Italy* (Cambridge: Cambridge University Press, 1984), p 68.

2 R Goldthwaite, *Wealth and Demand for Wealth in Italy, 1300–1600* (Baltimore and London: Johns Hopkins University Press, 1995), p 189.

3 Ibid, p 188.

4 L Martines, *Power and Imagination. City-States in Renaissance Italy* (London: Pimlico, 2002), p 219.

5 M Hollingsworth, *Patronage in Sixteenth-Century Italy* (London: John Murray, 1996), p 10.

6 Ibid, p 91.

7 Ibid, p 97.

8 Ibid, p 153.

9   Goldthwaite, *Wealth*, p 183.
10 G Hanlon, *Early Modern Italy, 1550–1800* (Basingstoke: Macmillan, 2000), p 51.
11 Hollingsworth, *Patronage in Sixteenth-Century Italy*, p 236.
12 Hanlon, *Early Modern Italy*, p 72.
13 Ibid, p 22.
14 Ibid.
15 Ibid, p 72.
16 Ibid.
17 JR Hale, *A Concise Encyclopaedia of the Italian Renaissance* (London: Thames and Hudson, 1981), p 215.
18 Hanlon, *Early Modern Italy*, p 53.
19 Ibid.
20 Ibid, p 54.
21 Hollingsworth, *Patronage in Sixteenth-Century Italy*, p 266.
22 Martines, *Power and Imagination*, p 220.
23 Ibid.
24 Hanlon, *Early Modern Italy*, p 60.
25 Ibid.
26 Ibid, p 56.
27 Ibid, p 57.
28 Ibid.
29 Hollingsworth, *Patronage in Sixteenth-Century Italy*, p 219.
30 Hanlon, *Early Modern Italy*, p 56.
31 Hollingsworth, *Patronage in Sixteenth-Century Italy*, p 301.
32 Hanlon, *Early Modern Italy*, p 57.
33 Ibid, p 58.
34 Ibid.
35 Martines, *Power and Imagination*, p 281.
36 Ibid.
37 Hanlon, *Early Modern Italy*.
38 Hollingsworth, *Patronage in Sixteenth-Century Italy*, pp 224–5.
39 Ibid, p 225.

CHAPTER 11

PUBLIC PATRONAGE, ARCHITECTURE AND TOWN PLANNING: FROM CLASSICISM TO MANNERISM

Introduction

Whereas Florence was the seed-bed of the Early Renaissance, Rome was the epicentre of the High Renaissance during the early cinquecento, followed to a lesser extent by Venice in the 1530s and a host of other cities throughout the rest of the century. The classical style of architecture was gradually superseded by Mannerism, while new buildings were often not only larger than hitherto but also more ornamented. Town planning schemes on a scale not seen since antiquity now ensured that whole areas of cities could be developed in an integrated and grandiose manner. Politically motivated urban development in 16th-century Italy was unprecedented.

Although humanism provided the rationale for public-sector decision-making in the quattrocento, the works of Niccolò Machiavelli possibly explain why despotic and republican regimes were eager to be major patrons of new buildings and planning projects in the cinquecento and beyond. In *Il Principe* ('The Prince'; 1513), Machiavelli posited that because the world is corrupt a strong government – in other words, a dictatorship – is necessary to maintain authority, and any means can be used to further this end providing they are effective in securing the aims of government. Thus it could be construed by governments that the patronage of impressive and costly buildings was justified if, through promoting a sense of deference and awe, this helped to achieve their political objectives in respect of internal security and defence. In a later work, *Discourses on the First Ten Books of Titus Livy* (1516–19), Machiavelli, more moderately, suggested that the best form of government might be a democratic republic whose goals would be to create or maintain a state with attributes of independence, security and a well-ordered constitution. In this scenario, instead of stimulating deference and awe, the development of magnificent public buildings, both secular and ecclesiastical, would engender a sense of civic pride in the citizenry and make it easier for government to follow its political agenda. With only Venice remaining a republic in the cinquecento, it might be suggested that Machiavelli's *Prince* offers a more appropriate guide to the motivation of public patrons throughout most of Italy than do the *Discourses*.

The Major Cities of Central and Northern Italy

Rome

The emergence of the High Renaissance can be attributed respectively to two giants of their time, one political and one architectural: Giuliano della Rovere and Donato Bramante. Born in Albisola near Savona in 1443, and in due course accumulating eight bishoprics and one archbishopric, Giuliano was elected pontiff as Julius II (1503–13). Bramante, who was born in Urbino in 1444, practised his profession in Milan and later on a relatively small scale in Rome before becoming Julius's architect-in-chief in 1505, in which capacity he both designed the enormous Cortile del Belvedere and the reconstructed basilica of St Peter's and supervised the early stages of their construction. With the deaths of both Julius and Bramante respectively in 1513 and 1514 (ironically – like their births – only one year apart), the greatest epoch in architectural advance since antiquity came to an end. However, the scene had been set for lesser achievements in design and urban development in Renaissance architecture which would continue, albeit in a much modified form, for more than a century.

The Cortile del Belvedere was the first of Julius II's great projects. Extending northwards from St Peter's, the *cortile* connects the Vatican Palace to the originally separate Belvedere villa built for Innocent VIII (1485–7) on the summit of the Vatican Hill. About 100 metres (984 ft) long and 30 metres (328 ft) wide, the new structure was divided into three stepped terraces of different sizes. The western boundary of the lowest terrace was marked by the pope's private apartment, the Appartamento Borgia, while the northern and southern edges of the terrace – 17 bays in length – were defined by arcades and loggias three storeys in height with the ground floor of each supported by Doric half-columns, the middle floor by Ionic pilasters and the upper floor by Corinthian pilasters and Doric columns. This section of the *cortile* was laid out as an open-air theatre and was subsequently used for pageants and tournaments, the pope enjoying an unobstructed view from the top floor of his palace.

Photo 11.1 Donato Bramante, Cortile del Belvedere, Rome, begun 1505. The two-storey northern wall of the courtyard contains a central semi-domed exedra.

The middle terrace of the *cortile* originally had steps and areas for seating overlooking the lower section, but in 1580 Sixtus V abandoned this arrangement and built a connecting wing across the *cortile* to accommodate the Salone Sistino and Cortile della Biblioteca. The highest terrace contained a formal garden and was edged longitudinally by one-storey loggias, 14 bays in length. Initially, there was also a single-storey loggia across its northern end screening the facade of the Belvedere villa, but this was walled up in the late cinquecento and, as an outcome of plans by Pirro Ligorio, was topped by a second storey pierced by a large semidomed exedra containing successive flights of convex and concave semicircular steps.

The Cortile del Belvedere was a consummate exercise in perspective and one of Bramante's greatest achievements. It is testimony to his skill as an architect that when he began work on St Peter's, the *cortile* was completed by Baldassare Peruzzi and Antonio da Sangallo very much in accordance with his plans. However, much of the *cortile* has been subsequently altered, and in the lower terrace in particular the original Bramantian designs are barely discernible except for the Porta Julia. Despite such deviation, in the words of Wolfgang Lotz, 'no Roman building had a greater influence on the secular architecture which followed than the Belvedere Court. It largely determined the idea of the relationship between architecture and landscape which developed in the sixteenth century'.[1] Bramante's ideas and formal language left an indelible imprint on the work of all the leading architects of cinquecento Italy, from Raffaello Sanzio (Raphael; 1483–1520) to Domenico Fontana (1543–1607).[2]

Photo 11.2   Donato Bramante and others, Basilica of St Peter's, Rome, 1506–1626. Originally intended to conform to a Greek-cross plan, the basilica was extended by the addition of two bays and an enormous portico in the early 17th century, greatly impairing the view of its dome from the Piazza S Pietro.

The second of Julius's great commissions was the reconstruction of the basilica of St Peter's. The original edifice was built by Emperor Constantine in AD 318, supposedly over the tomb of St Peter, but by the quattrocento it was in a very poor condition and largely untouched except for the enlargement of its choir by Bernardo Rossellino during the pontificate of Nicholas V(1447–55) and the addition of a benediction loggia in the late 15th century. Therefore, in 1506, three years after his succession, Julius held a competition to design a new basilica,[3] a test not unsurprisingly won by Bramante despite his approach to renewal being at odds with that of the pontiff. Whereas Julius wanted to retain parts of the old St Peter's, notably the choir and the loggia, Bramante persuaded him to opt for complete reconstruction. Bramante even wanted to rebuild the Vatican Palace (including the Sistine Chapel), in addition to the Cortile del Belvedere on which work had already started, but funds were not available for comprehensive development despite tax revenue from the Papal States, donations from across the Catholic world, receipts from the sale of indulgences and assistance from Henry VIII of England during the early years of his reign. Moreover, Julius had a preference for a longitudinal basilica but Bramante suggested that a centrally planned building would be more appropriate to the needs of the Church and proposed that such a building should have a Greek-cross plan set in a square measuring about 182 metres (600 ft), four equally long arms, a central space surrounded by a broad ambulatory with smaller domes in each of its four corners, and a hemispherical dome 45 metres (150 ft) in diameter. In accepting a proposal on this scale, Julius was accused of wanting to build himself what was in effect an enormous tomb and to otherwise show off, but despite these allegations he remained loyal to Bramante.

When Julius II died in 1513, much of the western end of the Constantinian basilica had been demolished and only the four large piers needed to support the drum of the dome had been built. These were constructed of travertine as well as incorporating cheaper material; but this did not allow for the substructure. His piers were beginning to crack and Bramante was threatened with imprisonment. He died a year after Julius – some said fortuitously – leaving no more than inconsistent sketches of how the work should continue and including the possibility of a nave which he had eventually been coerced into providing.

Immediately after the death of Bramante in 1514, Leo X entrusted Raphael with rectifing the faults that had become apparent in the reconstruction of St Peter's. In his new role as director of works, Raphael produced a plan which included a substantial nave that would extend Bramante's Greek cross by a full five bays eastwards while retaining the basic elements of Bramante's design. Raphael also built a wooden model of his proposal, but little building work was done in the years leading to his untimely death in 1521. Baldassare Peruzzi (1481–1536) soon succeeded his master as architect of St Peter's, but fled to Siena – his birthplace – during the Sack of Rome in 1527.

During the years in which Bramante and Raphael presided over the reconstruction of St Peter's, a mutually influential relationship emerged between the development of the basilica and the centrally planned churches of S Maria della Consolazione in Todi (begun 1508) and the Madonna di S Biagio in Montepulciano (started 1518) (see Chapter 13). The latter church was designed by Antonio da Sangallo the Younger (1483–1546) who had worked under Bramante, Raphael and Peruzzi on St Peter's. However, despite Peruzzi's departure from Rome there was very little work for Sangallo to undertake on the basilica during the chaotic aftermath of the Sack of Rome, though resources were available for him to complete his commission on Bramante's S Maria di Loreto by 1534 (see p 387–388). In an attempt to get work resumed on St Peter's, Paul III (1534–49) appointed Sangallo as his chief architect in 1539, but the outcome was disappointing. Sangallo proposed a major alteration to Bramante's bi-axial plan, which, in keeping with the times, involved the provision of a large vestibule on the eastern arm of the Greek cross, but the plan was still rudimentary at the time of the architect's death. While it was not adopted, it did set in train a number of other proposals throughout the rest of the cinquecento, both sympathetic and inimical to Bramante's concept of centrality.

When Michelangelo Buonarroti (1475–1564) succeeded Sangallo as architect of St Peter's in 1546 the basilica remained as it had been at the time of Bramante's death more than 30 years earlier. During the intervening years, Raphael and Sangallo had eschewed the full rigour of a centralised plan, but Michelangelo adhered very much to Bramante's approach despite the tenets of the Counter-Reformation which emphasised the importance of the nave. However, Michelangelo's plan was no slavish copy of Bramante's proposal. It was considerably bolder. He produced 'a drastically simplified square plan in which the dome became the single overwhelming feature supported on massive piers',[4] and while Bramante had intended his dome to be hemispherical, Michelangelo's dome was to be pointed in the Florentine manner and set on a high drum. In addition, Michelangelo provided a high undulating wall above and around the apses and corners of the square-shaped plan, and proposed a single entrance within an enormous projecting portico to demarcate the eastern edge of the basilica.

Following Michelangelo's death in 1564, Giacomo Barozzi da Vignola (1507–73) and Pirro Ligorio (1510–83) immediately began supervising work on two of the four cupolas which Michelangelo had proposed for the corners of the ambulatory and, under Giacomo della Porta (1533–1602) and Domenico

Fontana, work continued on the dome and lantern until completion between 1590 and 1595, albeit in a markedly different form from that proposed by Michelangelo.

Appointed architect of St Peter's in 1603 by Clement VIII, Carlo Maderno (1556–1629) finally completed the basilica in 1612, over a century after the foundation stone had been laid. In compliance with the new liturgical requirements of the Council of Trent (1545–63), the papacy – no doubt influenced by the design of Il Gesù constructed in 1568–84 (see chapter 13) – considered it necessary to sacrifice centrality and to incorporate a substantial nave to accommodate a larger congregation than would otherwise have been possible. Maderno thus added three bays to the eastern side of the ambulatory and built a colossal eastern portico and long polychrome facade rising from a triple flight of steps. The facade is adorned with eight giant columns across its length and has two giant pilasters at each end, all supporting a centrally pedimented entablature. Above that, there is a largely unadorned attic, surmounted by a balustrade and statues. Above each end of the facade, the stumps of two demolished campanili – originally designed and built in their entirety by Bernini in the early 17th century – were reconstructed as clock towers by Giuseppe Valadier in 1788. In finer detail, the facade is pierced by three large rectangular doorways on its ground floor, interspersed by two smaller rounded entrances, while on the upper storey there are seven rectangular pedimented windows together with a central balcony from where newly elected popes are proclaimed and give their blessing.

Without belittling the work of later architects, Bramante and Michelangelo can be credited with the overall appearance of St Peter's as we see it today. However, it must not be forgotton that without the imagination and drive of a succession of popes, from Julius II to Clement VIII, and the enormous resources of the Vatican, the largest and most magnificent edifice erected during the Renaissance would not have been constructed.

In 1530, many years before the completion of St Peter's, a papal mint or Zecca was established to help the Vatican recover from the Sack of Rome and to channel financial resources towards the reconstruction of the basilica. Designed by Antonio da Sangello, the facade of the otherwise unadorned building was graced by a triumpal arch motif and framed tondi between coupled Corinthian pilasters, all resting on a heavily rusticated but low basement that acted as a plinth.

Although on a smaller scale than Vatican projects, the development of buildings tailored to the needs of secular government was only marginally less impressive than its ecclesiastical equivalent. During the second half of the 16th century and first half of the 17th, the Campidoglio (or Capitol) again

Photo 11.3 Michelangelo Buonarroti and others, Palazzo dei Conservatori, Rome, 1564–8. Situated on the south-western side of the Piazza del Campidoglio, the magnificent palace is notable for its use of Giant orders.

became an important focus of power in Rome following the reconstruction of the Palazzo dei Conservatori, the renewal of the Palazzo Senatorio and the construction of the Palazzo Nuovo. Although the Palazzo dei Conservatori had been rebuilt by Nicholas V in *c* 1450 to provide new accommodation for the administrative functions of the governing magistrates of the city, it was remodelled – with the use of further papal funds – by Della Porta and Guidetto Guidetti between 1564 and 1568 from a design previously produced by Michelangelo. The facade, the first during the Renaissance to incorporate giant pilasters of Corinthian design, contains a recessed ground-floor colonnade supported by subsidiary Ionic columns and surmounted by an interrupted entablature, a *piano nobile* pierced by seven rectangular windows, and is crowned by a high entablature, a balustrade and statues. The only major deviation from the plan of Michelangelo is that the central window of the *piano nobile* is larger than the others on the floor and has a broken-bed triangular pediment whereas the rest have broken-bed segmental pediments.

Photo 11.4 Michelangelo Buonarroti and others, Palazzo Senatorio, Rome, 1592. Spanning the Piazza del Campidoglio, the imposing palace – Rome's town hall – is notable for its double staircase with converging flights, and a campanile.

The second palace to be redeveloped, the Palazzo Senatorio, was originally an 11th-century fortress. It accommodated the Senate from *c* 1150 and was redeveloped in the 13th century. Again based on the designs of Michelangelo and their interpretation by Della Porta, but this time with the assistance of Girolamo Rainaldi, the three-storey facade of the *palazzo* was rebuilt after 1592 to stand on a new rusticated base which together with giant pilasters and coats of stucco screened the former building behind. The facade is further adorned by a double-ramped staircase that leads to the central portal on the *piano nobile*, and is crowned by a balustrade and clock tower that, having been constructed in 1582, predate the rest of the renovated facade.

The third palace, the Palazzo Nuovo – sited opposite its counterpart, the Palazzo dei Conservatori – was begun in 1603 under the patronage of Clement VIII, and like its two neighbours on the Campidoglio was based largely on a design by Michelangelo. It was not, however, completed until 1644–54, but during the course of construction its two architects Girolamo and Carlo Rainaldi, like Della Porta before them, departed slightly from Michelangelo's design by focusing attention on the centre of the upper facade.[5] Like the facade of the Palazzo dei Conservatori, that of the Palazzo Nuovo was constructed bay by bay over a lengthy period since only a limited amount of money was allocated to the projects and this only on a piecemeal basis.

Photo 11.5 Michelangelo Buonarroti, Porta Pia, Rome, 1561–5. In all its Mannerist glory, the south section of the gateway was Michelangelo's last new building.

During the latter years of his life, Michelangelo produced plans for a major gateway in the Aurelian Wall, the Porta Pia (implemented between 1561 and 1565), and the adaptation of the main hall of the ruined Baths of Diocletian into the Carthusian church of S Maria degli Angeli (commenced 1563). Facing inwards towards the city, the Porta Pia is dominated by a large gateway framed by fluted pilasters and an entablature, and crowned by a triangular pediment. This in turn is surmounted by a tall superstructure that supports a broken-apex pediment, while below the superstructure, the gateway is flanked by brickwork that incorporates blind windows and other detached motifs similar to those designed for the attic of St Peter's.[6] On the outer side of the gateway, by comparison, far less attention has been paid to architectural detail. While construction of the Porta Pia was financed directly by the civic authorities, work on the church of S Maria degli Angeli was subsidised by Pius IV, who granted the monks free use of the site. As with so many other church buildings of the cinquecento, S Maria degli Angeli was built in the shape of a Greek cross with side chapels, a plan that broadly coincided with the layout of the bath hall. With these two relatively minor projects, the direct involvement of Michelangelo in the development of the built environment of Rome came to an end but, as has been discussed above, his plans inspired others to continue his work well into the 17th century, often with only minor amendments.

Photo 11.6 Flaminio Ponzio, Ottaviano Masherino and Carlo Maderna, Palazzo del Quirinale, Rome, begun 1574. Overlooking the Piazza del Quirinale, the spacious and dignified palace, with an imposing portal and balustrade, was the official residence of the pope until the unification of Italy in 1861.

In the last quarter of the cinquecento, awash with wealth the papacy commissioned two enormous and sumptuous palaces to the east of the Tiber, some 3 to 5 kilometres from the confines of the Vatican. The first of these, the Palazzo del Quirinale, was begun in 1574 and designed by Flaminio Ponzio, Ottaviano Mascherino and Carlo Maderno. Built on a site near the summit of the Quirinale Hill, the palace was one of the summer residences of the pope before becoming, in turn, the official residence of the Italian monarchy (1870–1945) and of the President of the Republic (since 1947). Largely of two storeys, the core of the palace was constructed around a courtyard accessed from without through a ceremonial portal surmounted by a balcony: behind the core an extensive garden is framed by lengthy two-storey blocks, one of which runs alongside the Via del Quirinale.

The second of these palaces, the Palazzo del Laterano, was commissioned by Pope Sixtus V as part of his programme to redevelop Rome (1585–90). The palace, the design of which was entrusted to Domenico Fontana, was constructed on a site previously occupied by the 4th-century Patriarchium, a building that had fallen into long-term decay after the papacy had not only exiled itself to Avignon in 1309 but subsequently taken up residence in the Vatican Palace in 1377 on its return to Rome. After having the Patriarchium demolished, Fontana supervised the construction of a three-storey 'U'-shaped palace around a large courtyard, the outer walls of the palace being pierced by long rows of windows and its main facade containing a centrally placed portal surmounted by a balcony. Although intended as another summer residence for the popes, it soon fell out of favour

Photo 11.7 Domenico Fontana, Palazzo del Laterano, Rome, 1585–90. Rebuilt over 250 years after it was almost destroyed by fire, the palace was intended as the papal summer residence, but a succession of pontiffs showed a preference for the Palazzo del Quirinale. On the right is Fontana's porticoed Benediction Loggia (1586).

for this purpose and instead came to accommodate the administration of the Roman bishopric. Adjacent to the Palazzo del Laterano, the northern facade of the 4th-century church of S Giovanni in Laterano was enhanced by the addition of a two-storey benediction loggia in 1586–9, again commissioned by Pope Sixtus V and designed by Fontana.

Venice

Fires and other physical disasters in Venice were responsible for much rebuilding in the early 16th century. In 1505, the Fondaco dei Tedeschi, a canal-side warehouse used by German merchants, was burnt down, and because the Venetian Senate wished to maintain the city's trading importance, it quickly funded the building's reconstruction – a massive square edifice with a central courtyard.[7] The facade of the new warehouse differs from other contemporary buildings along

Photo 11.8   Fondaco dei Tedeschi, Venice, begun 1505. A bulky and, except for, its enormous portico an almost featureless edifice in keeping with its commercial function.

the Grand Canal thanks to its simplicity.[8] Because its frescoes by Giorgione have faded, its four storeys now lack ornamentation, except for a five-arch portico on the canal's edge, pairs of regularly spaced windows on its three upper floors, balconies on its western and eastern wings and decorative crenellations along its cornice. The building is now the city's central post office.

Apart from the reconstruction of the 12th-century Campanile in Piazza S Marco in 1511–14, as a result of damage caused by lightning in 1489, the next example of a physical disaster necessitating the redevelopment of a major building was a fire in 1512 that seriously damaged the Procuratie. Situated on the north side of the Piazza S Marco, since the 12th century the building had housed the administrative offices responsible for all government building work in the square. To maintain this function, the *proto* Scarpagnino (Antonio di Pietro Abbondi; d 1549) was commissioned in his capacity as a master builder to organise the reconstruction of the Procuratie,[9] later to be known as the Procuratie Vecchie. The building that resulted incorporated a motif of 100 narrow semicircular openings above a portico of 50 arches. Its two-storey facade – nearly 150 metres (500 ft) in length – anachronistically emphasised the city's Veneto-Byzantine heritage,[10]

Photo 11.9 Bartolomeo Bon the Younger, campanile S Marco, 1511–14. After damage by lightning in 1489, the 95-metre-high bell tower built to replace an earlier structure that had been damaged collapsed in 1902 but was faithfully reconstructed soon afterwards.

and continued to display its origins after Jacopo Sansovino (1486–1570) added an upper storey and new entablature in 1532. Today, the upper storey is still used for offices while the portico accommodates a row of shops (*botteghe*) and cafes.

In 1514 a further fire devastated most of the buildings in the marketplace of the Rialto. Within a year, Scarpagnino's plan for the renewal of the area was selected from a total of seven competing designs.[11] Although the plan respected the existing layout of the market, the new building is classical in terms of its homogeneous structure, uniform height and its full-length porticoes and cornices. As in the cinquecento, at street level today there are separate spaces for different trades, while 'on the upper floors [there] are administrative offices, and in particular the offices of the magistracy'.[12] Although not a direct outcome of a fire, the Palazzo dei Camerlenghi (begun 1525) was in effect built to commemorate the completion of the reconstruction of the Rialto. Funded by Doge Andrea

Photo 11.10   Antonio di Pietro Abbondi ('Scarpagnino') and Jacopo Sansovino, Procuratie Vecchie, Venice, 1512–32. A lengthy 160-metre structure originally built to accommodate the residences and offices of the procurators of S Marco. The edifice is supported by 50 arches at ground-floor level.

Gritti and designed by Guglielmo Bergamesco, the richly ornamented building is faced with white Istrian stone and performed three separate functions in its capacity as the central meeting point of the Rialto and its administrative core: it provided a loggia for merchants, accommodated three Lords of the Exchequer (the Camerlenghi), and served as a prison for tax evaders.[13]

In 1227, the risk of fire rather than its actuality had motivated the relocation of the Zecca (mint) from the densely built Rialto to the Molo on the edge of the Bacino di S Marco. Between 1536 and 1545, however, the Zecca was rebuilt both to meet the huge demand for new coins during a period of economic boom, and as part of a programme to renovate both the Piazzetta and Piazza of S Marco. Funded by Doge Andrea Gritti and designed by Jacopo Sansovino in his role as 'proto supra le fabbriche di S Marco', the building has a heavily rusticated exterior that extends over the half-columns – on the one hand giving it 'a severe, fortresslike character',[14] but on the other presenting 'an intriguing mixture of the sophisticated and the crude . . . a favourite Mannerist device'.[15] Although the

Photo 11.11 Guglielmo Bergamasco, Palazzo dei Camerlenghi, Venice, begun 1523. At the base of the Rialto Bridge, the curiously angled palace with its ornate classical facade initially provided offices for the Venetian exchequer.

new building was originally of two storeys, Sansovino added a third storey in 1558–66 where the rusticated motif is replicated. With the demise of the Venetian Republic in 1797, the Zecca became redundant and the building subsequently became part of the Biblioteca Marciana.[16]

Sansovino's second commission in the *sestiere* of S Marco was the Loggetta of the Campanile (1537–49). More a piece of decorative sculpture than a building, its three arcades of composite orders were initially used as a meeting place for the nobility, but from 1569 this function was superseded by its use as a guardhouse – the *loggetta* being conveniently situated immediately opposite the Porta della Carta of the Palazzo Ducale facilitating security particularly during sessions of the Maggior Consiglio.[17]

Located on the western side of the Piazzetta S Marco opposite the Palazzo Ducale, the Biblioteca Marciana is arguably the greatest secular building constructed in Venice – if not in Italy – during the High Renaissance. Designed by Sansovino and constructed between 1537 and 1554, the library was built to house the huge collection of volumes which the republic had accumulated over the centuries, together with works emanating from Constantinople during the final years of Byzantium. Completed by Vincenzo Scamozzi (1548–1616) in the late cinquecento, the ground floor of the two-storey building consists of a 21-arched tunnel-vaulted loggia that runs in front of *botteghe* while, externally, its piers are faced with Doric half-columns. The fenestrated upper floor also contains 21 openings, but these are narrower and the wall surfaces wider than their ground floor counterparts in order to accommodate supporting Ionic columns and inner Ionic half-columns that encase the round-headed windows. Whereas on the upper floor the positioning of columned plinths allows only the provision of window balustrades, above an ornately decorated frieze the projecting cornice is crowned by a continuous balustrade surmounted by statues and obelisks.[18] In terms of its correct application of classical orders and its use of bases, friezes and cornices in high relief, the library undoubtedly gave the Venetians 'exactly what they were seeking – a transposition of the ancient Roman style of building to Venetian soil'.[19]

On completion of his work on the Biblioteca Marciana, in 1555 Sansovino was commissioned by the Council of Ten to design the Fabbriche Nuove of the Rialto. With construction funded by a loan from the Zecca and from money raised by renting out shops, the elongated and narrow three-storey building follows the gentle curve of the Grand Canal. It consists of an arcade on its ground floor supported by rusticated orders, all in Istrian stone. Above its entablature there is a fenestrated first floor with each of its bays demarcated by Ionic pilasters, and a similarly designed upper floor but with bays demarcated by Corinthian pilasters. Built to house the magistracy that controlled the Rialto and to provide premises suitable for negotiating loans and trading in luxury goods, the building broadly retains its original use by currently accommodating government offices and various legal departments.[20]

By the 1560s, the republic recognised the need for a new prison and allocated a site for its construction adjacent to the Palazzo Ducale but separated from it by the mouth of the Riva degli Schiavoni.[21] Designed by the *proto* Antonio da Ponte and built over the period 1563 to 1614, the Palazzo delle Prigioni Nuove is classical in style and, like Sansovino's Zecca, has a roughly rusticated facade in keeping with its fortified function.[22] The structure was completed in the early 17th century by Antonio Contin.

Photo 11.12   Jacopo Sansovino, Zecca, 1536–45 and Biblioteca Marciana, 1537–54. The Zecca (left) displays a severe facade but is distinctly classical, albeit in an exaggerated form, while the *biblioteca* (right) – Sansovino's masterpiece – harmoniously uses Istrian stone to emphasise its Doric and Ionic orders, elaborate frieze and balustrade.

Nearby, and at around the same time, a new building – the Procuratie Nuove – was under construction on the southern side of the Piazza S Marco. Designed by Vincenzo Scamozzi in 1586 as a right-angled extension to the Biblioteca Marciana, the new procurator's office, located opposite its older counterpart, is a three-storey, elongated block of 35 bays. Like the library and the Procuratie Vecchie, its ground floor is an arcade lined on its inner side with *botteghe* and cafes but, above, similarities are less in evidence. Unlike the library there are two upper storeys rather than one, and unlike the older *procuratie* classical rather than Veneto-Byzantine features prevail. The facades of both upper storeys contain rows of pedimented rectangular windows aligned with, but narrower than, the arches of the arcade. Supporting columns grace the facade of the *piano nobile*, half-columns adorn the upper floor, and balustrades provide further ornamentation on both the middle and upper floors. In keeping with the classical design of the library, there is a strict adherence to the upward sequencing of orders – Doric, Ionic and Corinthian. During Scamozzi's involvement with the project only 10 bays were finished; the remainder were completed under Baldassare Longhena's supervision in the 17th century.

Photo 11.13   Jacopo Sansovino, Fabbriche Nuove, Venice, begun 1555. A 100-metre-long arcaded market building, with offices above, it clings elegantly to the curve of the Grand Canal.

After his work on the prison, in 1588 Antonio da Ponte was commissioned to design a new bridge over the Grand Canal at the Rialto. The Venetian Senate had been considering replacing the former wooden bridge since 1514 following the structure's collapse, yet could not decide between the plans produced by some of the greatest architects of the cinquecento, including Sansovino, Scamozzi, Palladio and, allegedly, Michelangelo. In the end Da Ponte's proposals were selected, possibly because they displayed his skills as a hydraulic engineer as well as his experience as a master builder.[23] The new Rialto Bridge was constructed between 1588 and 1591, and being of stone had to be of sufficient scale to permit large barges to pass beneath, while its high geometric arch had to be sturdy enough to support a shopping street bordered by pedestrian walkways. Soon after the completion of the Rialto Bridge, the senate funded construction of what became an equally famous bridge, the Ponte dei Sospiri (Bridge of Sighs). Built between 1595 and 1600 under the direction of the *proto* of the Doge's Palace, made of Istrian stone and highly ornamented, the bridge spanned the Riva degli Schiavoni linking the Palazzo Ducale to the Prigioni Nuove.

Photo 11.14   Vincenzo Scamozzi and Baldassare Longhena, Procuratie Nuove, begun 1586. At 90 degrees to the Biblioteca Marciana, the lengthy *procuratie* was built on the southern side of the Piazza S Marco in the same style as the library, except for the addition of a third storey.

In contrast to the papacy in Rome, the Venetian senate seemed reluctant to commission ecclesiastical buildings, leaving this task largely to the monastic orders. However, after a devastating plague in 1575–6 which killed between a half and a third of the population of Venice, the senate commissioned construction of the church of the Redentore in 1577 to thank the Redeemer (*Il Redentore*) for the salvation of the remaining populace. Located on the island *sestiere* of Giudecca, and designed by Andrea Palladio (1508–80), the church built from Istrian stone is both centrally planned and longitudinal. Whereas Palladio had a preference for centrality, he was mindful of the strictures of the Tridentine Council (Council of Trent) which had prescribed longitudinal places of worship.[24] Palladio therefore adopted an approach that would statisfy both his aesthetic predilections and the liturgical requirements of the Church: he based his plans for the new church on those that had already been applied in the construction of S Giorgio Maggiore (see Chapter 13). The outcome is a Latin-cross church centred on a massive hemispherical dome bordered by twin pinnacle towers and crowned by volutes and a lantern. Its facade is dominated by overlapping gables, each supported at their edges by Corinthian pilasters and aided by two more centrally placed Corinthian half-columns below the outer gable. Its large round-arched central

Photo 11.15   Antonio da Ponte, Rialto Bridge, Venice, 1588–91. Located in the topographical centre of Venice, the 16th-century stone bridge, like its wooden predecessors, links the two sides of the Grand Canal.

portal, clearly designed to attract worshippers, is set between half-columns and flanked by aedicules containing statues.[25] It is unfortunate that Il Redentore in all its glory is not visible from the Piazzetta S Marco or from anywhere else in Venice other than the outer shoreline of the Dorsoduro and from the Canale della Giudecca.

Genoa

In contrast to Venice, and with the major exception of the development of the Strada Nuova in the second half of the cinquecento (see Chapter 13), public patronage in Genoa was on an altogether smaller scale – possibly the legacy of political instability throughout the earlier part of the 16th century (see Chapter 10). The first of the few late-16th-century projects funded by the Senate of the Republic was the Porta del Molo, begun in 1550. Designed by Galeazzo Alessi (1512–72), the gateway was intended not only to be an integral part of the city's defensive wall but also to serve as a facility for

Photo 11.16 Andrea Palladio, church of Il Redentore, Venice, begun 1577. Possibly the most successful of Palladio's churches, the Redentore with its handsome facade was built to commemorate deliverance from the bubonic plague of 1575–6.

collecting duties. Facing the city, the *porta* is pierced by three arches divided by Doric pilasters; on its seaward side the gateway is set between two pincer arms designed to repel invaders, while its ornamentation – such as Doric half-columns, pilasters and niched exedra – was intended to impress foreign traders.[26]

The second notable public project undertaken in this period was the redevelopment of the Palazzo Ducale. Under the architectural direction of Andrea Ceresola (otherwise known as Vannone), work on the new palace began in 1591 and continued for about 30 years, during which time a spacious entrance hall was added to the original palace and courtyards were added at either end of the building. Today, little remains of the 16th-century palace and its predecessor, and much of the site has been occupied since the 1860s by a neoclassical building designed by Simone Cantoni.[27]

The last major secular building to be commissioned by the senate was the Loggia dei Mercanti. Designed by Vannone and Giovanni Ponzello in 1589 and completed in 1595, the loggia became a key building in the regenerated Piazza Banchi, the old commercial heart of the city. Its construction was largely self-financed from rents paid by multifarious stallholders trading in its large hall.[28] The Piazza Banchi was already the location of the church of S Pietro, designed by Bernardo Cantoni in 1572 and completed by Ceresola and Ponzello in 1585. Funded by the senate, like Il Redentore in Venice, the church was built to commemorate the end of a plague and, as in the case of the later Loggia dei Mercanti, shop rents enabled the project to be self-financing. It is of note that shops occupied the ground floor of the building while, above, a wide terrace and a balustrade separate sacred and commercial uses.[29]

Milan

Few public buildings of any importance were constructed in Milan during the first half of the cinquecento since, following its occupation by France from 1499 to 1521, the city became the focus of armed conflict between the armies of Francis I and the emperor Charles V. In 1535, under a victorious Charles, Milan became subject to direct rule by imperial governors backed by occupying Spanish troops, but on Charles's death in 1556 Milan became part of the Spanish Empire and remained a Spanish possession – under a succession of viceroys – until it was ceded to Austria in 1713. To add a further dimension to this political scenario, the municipal government of Milan was broadly in the hands of a quasi-independent senate but ecclesiastical jurisdiction in the city, after the deliberations of the Council of Trent, became increasingly the responsibility of the Church particularly under Cardinal Carlo Borromeo (Archbishop of Milan, 1560–84). There were thus three patrons of urban development in the Milanese public sector during the second half of the cinquecento: the Spanish Empire, the senate and the bishopric.

The empire was particularly concerned with defending Milan from invasion in view of the city's turbulent past. In 1549, Ferrante Gonzaga, imperial governor of Milan (1546–55), therefore commissioned a military engineer, Giovanni Maria Olgiati, to direct construction of a circuit of bastioned walls to enclose the defences of the 15th-century Castello Sforzesco which would contain within its bounds an extensive urban area.[30] The Spanish Walls, as these defences were called, were entirely functional and devoid of ornamentation. However, Ferrante did not confine his patronage solely to secular projects. In 1552 he seconded his personal architect Domenico Giunti to the service of the Minor Franciscan Observants to assist them in replacing their former 15th-century church that Ferrante had previously demolished for military reasons.[31] Although the resulting longitudinal church with its high barrel vault and little ornamentation was daunting in its austerity, by the end of the century it had at least gained a Mannerist exterior.

Civic government was somewhat more generous in enhancing the built environment, providing funds for the construction of two notable secular buildings in the centre of the city, the Palazzo dei Giureconsulti and the Palazzo dei Capitani di Giustizia. The first of these is situated on the north side of the Piazza dei Mercanti and was designed by Vincenzo Seregni in 1562. Apart from incorporating its 13th-century tower, the new palace replaced an earlier building that had accommodated the magistracy and offices of the commune since the late Middle Ages. The ground floor of the new palace is of particular merit since it incorporates Serlian arcading on coupled columns,[32] while the flat rusticated surface of the building is amply decorated with herms, mouldings and masks.[33] The latter building, the Palazzo dei Capitani di Giustizia, was begun in 1578 but only completed after 1605 when a military engineer Piero Antonio Barca assumed responsibility for supervising the work. It is not surprising, therefore, that the rectangular building, which encloses two courtyards, has a turret in each of its four corners.[34]

The Church was by far the greatest patron of architecture in late-16th-century Milan. On taking up residence in his diocese in 1565, Cardinal Borromeo immediately embarked upon a succession of building projects designed to enhance the functioning and influence of the Church in the viceroyalty. The first of his notable

Photo 11.17 Vicenzo Seregni, Palazzo dei Giureconsulti, Milan, begun 1562. Situated in the Piazza dei Mercanti, the commercial heart of cinquecento Milan, the palace was constructed to accommodate the city's law courts.

projects was the renovation of the Palazzo Arcivescovile (Archbishop's Palace) for which he entrusted Tibaldi Pellegrini in 1568 to construct new monumental courtyards adjacent to the Canonica degli Ordinari (House of the Franciscan Friars). The second of his projects saw his direct involvement in the reconstruction of the Jesuit church of S Fedele. Since the original church of that name had only recently been assigned to the order, in 1567 Borromeo was able to dissuade the Jesuits from employing a member of their own order – Giovanni Tristano – to design the new building, but rather to endorse his own choice, Pellegrini. Thus, from 1569, a new church emerged under Borromeo's architect that incorporated 'an aiseless two-bay nave succeeded by a domed sanctuary',[35] the like of which was never again adopted by the Jesuits, who henceforth based the design of all their new churches on their mother church in Rome, Il Gesù (see Chapter 13).[36] Borromeo's next project was the reconstruction of the dome of the 4th-century quatrefoiled church of S Lorenzo, badly damaged after its collapse in 1573. Work was entrusted to Martino Bassi who added eight large piers to the crossing to provide support for an octagonal entablature and, above it, an enormous dome over 20 metres (65 ft) in diameter.[37] During the latter stages of construction, a *tiburio* (artificial drum) pierced with window openings was erected around the dome, giving the impression from the ground that the building is top-heavy and the dome shallow rather than hemispherical.[38] Borromeo's last building of note, the church of S Sebastiano, was built in response to his vow to commemorate the end of the plague of 1576. Designed by Pellegrini in 1577, and with construction beginning immediately thereafter, the round centrally planned structure was in keeping with its votive dedication, but in contravention of the *Instructiones* of the Church in respect of layout.[39] However, the building was not completed until well into the 17th century, by which time, and under the direction of Fabio Mangone, a *tiburio* was erected over the original drum.[40]

Florence

At the close of the quattrocento, the Florentine Republic injected funds into the provision of a new hall on the eastern side of the Palazzo della Signoria to hold the assemblies of the Consiglio Maggiore. Known as the Salone dei Cinquecento, its design was entrusted to Simone del Pallaiolo Cronaca in 1495, and its internal decoration was, in part, undertaken by Leonardo da Vinci and Michelangelo.[41] However, like Milan, Florence suffered from the disruption of military conflict and political insecurity during the early years of the cinquecento. After the fall of the republic in 1512, it was ruled by successive members of the Medici family – including two future popes – before embarking upon a further period of republican government (1527–30). Her forces defeated by imperial troops in 1531, Florence succumbed to Medici rule once more.

It was thus not until the third decade of the 16th century that the Florentine state resumed its patronage of major building projects. The first of note was the Fortezza da Basso, an obvious response to the defensive needs of the city. Commissioned by Alessandro de'Medici in 1534, Antonio da Sangallo oversaw construction of a heavily rusticated fortress to the north of the city that was intended not only to act as a bulwark against aggression from without, but to protect Florence from internecine strife within. As a defence against iron cannonballs, the fortress's rustication was shaped into globes and diamond tips, while its pentagonal plan not only enhanced security but facilitated the provision of projecting gun platforms.[42] The security of Florence was further improved in 1552–4 when, in response to a commission from Cosimo I, Benvenuto Cellini and Giovanni Battista Belluzzi renewed the city walls and ensured their full integration with the defences of the Fortezza da Basso.[43]

Photo 11.18 Martino Bassi, church of S Lorenzo, Milan, soon after 1573. This ancient church was largely reconstructed in classical style, and in accordance with its original octagonal plan, during the late 16th century but its classical facade was not completed until 1894.

By the middle of the century, attention had shifted to commercial provision. On the orders of the recently appointed Grand Duke Cosimo I, the Loggia del Mercato Nuovo (Loggia of the New Market) was constructed in one of the city's traditional marketplaces. Designed by Giovanni Battista del Tasso in 1546 and completed in 1564, the rectangular building has respectively three and four arches on its shorter and longer sides, while its sturdy columns demarcate the trading areas.[44] The time was also ripe for the further improvement of the Palazzo della Signoria. Under a succession of architects – Baccio, Giovanni Battista del Tasso and Giorgio Vasari – elaborately decorated residences were created between 1532 and the 1560s for different members of Cosimo's family and, under Fernando I, Bernardo Buontalenti was commissioned in 1588 to give a unified appearance to the exterior of the palace.[45] However, by this time Cosimo I had relocated his residence from what henceforth became known as the Palazzo Vecchio to the Palazzo Pitti, a more recent building dating from 1457–70. Purchased by Cosimo in 1549, Bartolomeo Ammanati was commissioned in 1558 to extend and renovate the building so as to provide appropriate grand-ducal accommodation.

An ideal composition of palace, courtyard and garden emerged.[46] From the rear elevation of the original building a courtyard, open at its far end, was constructed towards the Boboli Gardens currently being laid out on a slope behind the palace. The two wings of the courtyard were rusticated in broadly the same manner as that adopted for the original building – an attribute also applicable to the Doric, Ionic and Corinthian semi-columns that ornamented the whole of the rear facade – and, from the courtyard, twin tunnel-like ramps connected the palace to the serenity of the gardens.[47]

Photo 11.19 Bartolomeo Ammanati, courtyard, Palazzo Pitti, Florence, begun 1558. Soon after becoming the residence of the Medici, the palace was extended by the addition of two wings and a courtyard in distinctive Mannerist style.

Soon after Ammanati was commissioned to work on the Palazzo Pitti, he was appointed to design a new bridge over the River Arno, the Ponte Santa Trinità. Begun in 1558 and completed 12 years later, the beautiful bridge was testimony to Ammanati's technical skills which he successfully deployed to span the gaps from pier to pier with eliptical arches, so creating the illusion that the parapet wall stretched virtually unsupported from one side of the Arno to the other.[48]

A later architect, Buontalenti – fresh from his work on the Palazzo Vecchio – was entrusted by Duke Ferdinand I with the design of a counterpart to the Fortezza da Basso to defend the southern edge of the city and, if need be, provide a refuge for the occupants of Palazzo Pitti. Started in 1590, the new bastion, the Forte Belvedere, was located on the eastern edge of the Boboli Gardens, was star-shaped in accordance with contemporary military models, and incorporated a captain's residence almost as grand as any Medici villa.[49]

The Smaller Cities of Northern and Central Italy

Padua

In the Venetian city of Padua, publicly commissioned architecture of the High Renaissance is represented by a small but very distinctive range of buildings. Among the most imposing edifices are the Porta S Giovanni and Porta Savonarola, both designed by Giovanni Maria Falconetto, and begun in 1528 and 1530 respectively. Located to the west of the city centre and set into the city walls that for 11 kilometres encircle much of the present core, both gateways are reminiscent of a Roman triumphal arch, contain dominical vaults, have high attics that served as platforms for cannon emplacements, and have lateral doors that are blind on their outer sides. However, there the similarities end. Whereas both sides of the Porta Savonarola are supported by Corinthian columns on high pedestals, only the city side of the Porta S Giovanni is so articulated.[50] There is consequently a curious conflict between the aesthetic qualities of the gateways and their defensive attributes. Except for its flat pilasters, the outer facade of the Porta S Giovanni is relatively unadorned and would almost certainly have been able to withstand bombardment more easily than the columned outer side of the Porta Savonarola; moreover, the former gateway is heavily rusticated in contrast to the smooth-faced ashlar of the latter, again rendering the Porta S Giovanni better equipped to defend the city from external foes.[51]

The further development of Padua's medieval university elicited no such conflict between military and aesthetic requirements. Aestheticism prevailed. In the 1540s, Andrea Moroni was commissioned to design a new *cortile* within the Palazzo del Bò, the university's headquarters. Although it might appear that its design was based on the conventional monastic model found widely across

Europe – and often adopted by universities, including Oxford and Cambridge – it could also be argued that with its double loggias and classical imagery, it is akin rather to the central courtyard of many a secular *palazzo* in Florence or Rome.

At the end of the cinquecento, there was a further addition to Padua's modest stock of contemporary public buildings, the Palazzo del Capitanio. Built between 1599 and 1605 on the site of the former castle of the Carrara dynasty, although substantial the new building has relatively few notable attributes except for its magnificent tower reconstructed by Falconetto in 1532 to house an astronomical clock that dates from 1344.

Vicenza

Even fewer public buildings of note were constructed in 16th-century Vicenza than in Padua. Of these, two stand out: the Basilica and the Loggia del Capitanito, both in the Piazza dei Signori. The former building, designed by Andrea Palladio in 1549, encases the medieval Palazzo della Ragione and is one of the finest Late Renaissance buildings in the Veneto, if not in Italy. Probably inspired by Sansovino's Biblioteca Marciana in Venice, the double-storey Basilica, of white Istrian stone, presents an image of classical regularity which belies its unevenly spaced openings at ground-floor level that were designed to conform with the irregularities of the earlier *palazzo*.[52] Set into the piers of its facade, Doric half-columns on the first floor and Ionic half-columns on the second support projecting entablatures and, within each opening, two pairs of smaller free-standing columns of the same consecutive order provide support for the round arches of the lower and upper arcades.[53] Further ornamentation on the upper floor is provided by discontinuous balustrades and on the cornice by a balustrade interrupted by plinthed statues above each half-column.

Whereas the Basilica is a building of considerable length, the Loggia del Capitaniato, which stands opposite, is incredibly short. Designed by Palladio in 1571, the three bays of the building are encased by four giant Composite half-columns mounted on substantial piers. The Loggia is sometimes criticised as coarse and looking 'like the remains of an antique building which has its arcades and upper storey forced into it',[54] but above the tall arches of its ground-floor portico the windows, discontinuous balustrades with supporting triglyphs, and stucco ornamentation elegantly make use of the available space and are not out of harmony with Palladio's later style of architecture.

Photo 11.20   Andrea Palladio, Basilica, Vicenza, begun 1549. The most awe-inspiring edifice of the Venetian Renaissance and one of Palladio's finest creations.

Verona

Influenced by Falconetto's city gates at Padua, Michele Sanmicheli incorporated classical motifs into his two gateways in Verona. Commissioned by the Venetian Republic, Sanmicheli began work on the Porta Nuova in 1531 and on the Porta Palio in 1547. The former gateway – whose outward-facing facade is mainly rusticated, flanked by artillery towers and utilises flat pilasters to encase its central portal – is unashamedly defensive, but the Porta Palio, without artillery emplacements and with four pairs of giant fluted Doric columns to the edge its central and lateral portals, is despite rustication more decorative than defensive.[55] Built shortly after Falconetto's counterparts in Padua, the Veronese gateways vary markedly from those of their nearby neighbours in terms of defensive attributes. Both the Porta Nuova and Porta Palio feature not only the particularly sturdy Doric column instead of the more slender Corinthian order, but unlike the Paduan gateways with their towering attics, the Veronese gateways hardly rise above the encircling walls.[56]

Photo 11.21 Andrea Palladio, Loggia del Capitianato, Vicenza, begun 1571. Built for the Venetian military commander, the unfinished loggia is notable for its giant Composite orders.

Bologna

Developing gradually from the later Middle Ages, by the 16th century the Piazza Nettuno and Piazza Maggiore were firmly established as the adjoining centres of Bologna's civic administration. To celebrate the importance of the city as a constituent part of the Papal State – the city had been taken by Rome in 1505 – Pope Pius IV commissioned the renovation of the Piazza Nettuno in the 1550s, and the provision of the Neptune Fountain, designed by Tommaso Laureti and executed by Giovanni da Bologna in 1565. Slightly earlier (*c* 1555), the entrance gateway to the Palazzo Comunale was constructed to the design of Galeazzo Alessi, and in 1580 a bronze statue of Pope Gregory XIII by Alessandro Menganti was mounted above it. The Piazza Maggiore was also updated in the same period. In 1561, Pius's favourite architect, Jacopo Barozz ('Il Vignola'), was commissioned to design a regular facade for the eastern side of the *piazza* to mask the many irregular medieval buildings and unevenly spaced side streets that stretched back from the *piazza*. The new structure, known as the Portico dei Banchi, has as many as four storeys, although it appears at first glace to be a two-floor building. Its ground-floor arcades are surmounted in sequence by a mezzanine floor, an entablature, a first storey with triple windows in each bay, a further mezzanine, and a crowning entablature. Giant Corinthian pilasters separate the ground-floor arcades and integrate street level with the lower of the two entablatures, while pilaster strips separate the bays above. With this degree of articulation, the Portico is arguably 'one of the great achievements of urban architecture in sixteenth-century [Italy]',[57] and in terms of enhancing the main *piazza* of a city is comparable to that of Sansovino's Biblioteca Marciana in Venice.

Photo 11.22   Michele Sanmicheli, Porta Nuova, Verona, begun 1531. One of the four sturdy city gates designed to protect entry into Verona from the south.

The 16th-century development of Bologna's core was not just confined to the Piazza Nettuno and Piazza Maggiore. To the south of the Piazza Maggiore a new university complex, subsequently known as the Palazzo dell'Archiginnasio, was constructed to house the city's legal and artistic schools. Commissioned by Pius IV in 1561 and designed by Antonio Morandi (known as Terribilia), the new

Photo 11.23 Giacomo Barozzi ('Il Vignola'), Portico dei Banchi, Bologna, begun 1561. Occupying the whole of the eastern side of the Piazza Maggiore, the handsome facade was built to mask a set of buildings of little architectural merit.

building accommodated an array of classrooms on its first floor, and rent-yielding shops on its ground floor that utilised space within an arcaded loggia.

Piacenza

As the capital of the newly established dukedom of Parma and Pienza throughout much of the second half of the 16th century, Piacenza was chosen as the location for the state's administrative palace, the Palazzo Farnese. However, although building work started in 1558, Giacomo Vignola's plans for a massive rectangular building incorporating a courtyard and open-air theatre were never completed. Although the Farnese dynasty was unable to continue to fund the project, and the court moved to Parma early in the seicento, the huge facade of the unfinished palace still flanks a major thoroughfare of the city and dominates the townscape.

Pisa

The Tuscan city of Pisa witnessed a similar spate of construction activity in the middle and late cinquecento, although the type of buildings erected was very different from those developed in Bologna. Commissioned by Cosimo de'Medici I in 1561 and designed mainly by Giorgio Vasari, an existing square close to the Piazza del Duomo was redeveloped to accommodate the reconstructed Palazzo Comunale, the new Palazzo dell'Orologio and the church of S Stefano. The first of these, renamed the Palazzo dei Cavalieri, was begun in 1561, the second was started in 1564, and the church of S Stefano was commenced in 1565 with its facade designed not by Vasari but by Cosimo I's illegitimate son, Giovanni de'Medici.

Photo 11.24 Giorgio Vasari, Palazzo dei Cavalieri, Pisa, begun 1561. Dominating the Piazza dei Cavalieri, the facade of the enormous palace is adorned with plaster graffiti and busts of the Medici.

The Palazzo dei Cavalieri is particularly notable. Constructed to accommodate the Cavalieri di Stefano – a military order founded by Cosimo – the palace's angled four-storey bulk is, like the Palazzo dei Senatori in Rome, notable for a double-ramped external staircase that rises up to its central portal, while its facade is decorated with distinctive graffiti patterns still very much in evidence.

Siena

Siena was well served by its stock of medieval civic buildings, so the High Renaissance has little impact in its built environment in the cinquecento other than in the reconstruction of its protective walls. With the invention of the iron cannonball at the end of the previous century, existing walls – with or without their customary round towers – became pregnable, a cause of concern particularly when a city was in conflict with a more powerful predator. With the walls of Rome breached by the army of Charles V in 1527, smaller cities became increasingly aware that capture was now more likely than in the past or, if they chose to hold out, that they might face destruction. Siena, in particular, was aware of its defensive shortcomings, and thus after fleeing from Rome in 1527 Baldassare Peruzzi was appointed by the republic as chief architect responsible for fortifications. Like Antonio da Sangallo the Younger and Michelangelo, Peruzzi also had skills in engineering and fortification and put these to good effect by adding triangular bastions to the city's fortifications, structures that would enable defensive artillery to fire parallel to the curtain walls and thus repel the enemy before they were able mount a final attack. However, despite a further strengthening of the walls in 1550, Siena was unable to prevent its conquest by Florence in 1557 after a lengthy siege.

The Cities of Southern Italy

A great deal of public development took place in 16th-century Naples and Palermo but most was undertaken within the context of town planning (see below). A major exception to plan-led development was the reconstruction of the fortress of Castel Sant'Elmo on a steep hillside in Naples, north-west of the port. The project was commissioned by the city's viceroy, Don Pedro de Toledo in 1537 and designed by Pedro Luis Scrivà. Replacing an earlier fortress built in 1329–43, the new star-shaped citadel conformed to the latest military designs that were being emulated by other cities throughout the peninsula in the cinquecento, such as Siena. However, unlike most new fortifications – with the possible exception of the Fortezza da Basso in Florence – it was intended to deter internal insurrection rather than provide protection from an external enemy.

Town Planning in 16th-Century Italy

Rome

In the context of the Counter-Reformation, and because of fragmentary urban development in preceding centuries, the papacy sought to make Rome the grandest city in Christendom in an attempt to strengthen its political and ecclesiastical hold over the Catholic world, and in an endeavour to impress and influence non-Catholics. Programmes of large-scale town planning were thus undertaken in Rome during the cinquecento more extensively than in any other city in Italy or, indeed, elsewhere.

The first important planning project involved the redevelopment of the Campidoglio (the Capitol), a site of political importance overlooking the Forum. Commissioned by Pope Paul III in 1538 to design an imposing *piazza* on the Campidoglio to mark an impending visit by Emperor Charles V, Michelangelo proposed a new square (the Piazza del Campidoglio) in front of the Palazzo dei Senatori facing St Peter's – a symbol of Christianity – to the north-west rather than pointing south-eastwards to the Forum with its pagan origins.[58] The 12th-century *palazzo* on the Campidoglio, the Palazzo dei Senatori, was provided with a new Mannerist facade that included the addition of a great double-ramped staircase,[59] and the structure was framed by two new buildings: the Palazzo dei Conservatori (that enveloped a mid-14th-century guildhall) to the south-west, and later the Palazzo Nuovo to the north-east. The Palazzo dei Conservatori and Palazzo Nuovo are at 80 degrees – rather than at right angles – to the Palazzo dei Senatori, so forming a trapezoid rather than a square or rectangle,[60] a device employed at Pienza by Rossellino in the mid-15th century to trick the eye into believing that the principal building in the *piazza* (in Pienza's case, a church) is more imposing than it might otherwise appear (fig 11.1).

The centrepiece of the Piazza del Campidoglio, and perhaps its dominant feature, is an antique bronze equestrian statue of Marcus Aurelius (not the first Christian emperor, Constantine, as was initially thought). Brought to the *piazza* in 1538, it stands on a plinth in the middle of an attractive oval pavement adorned by a stellar inlay,[61] a novel feature in Renaissance town planning.

From the north and west, access to the *piazza* is by means of a steep ramp known as the Cordonata. Designed by Michelangelo but modified by Giacomo della Porta in *c* 1578, the Cordonata leads into the *piazza* through a gap in a balustrade that is surmounted by a line of statues including the colossal antique sculptures, discovered in the 16th century, of the twin heroes Castor and Pollux with their horses.

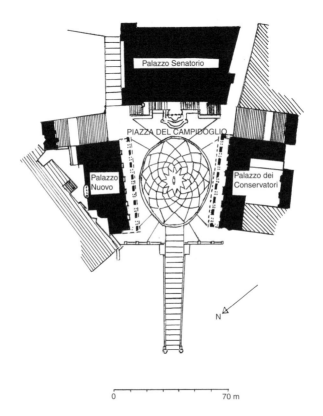

Figure 11.1 The Campidoglio, Rome

The whole project took over a hundred years to complete, but it is testimony to the perfection of Michelangelo's original designs that they were implemented almost without alteration by successive generations of architects. Not only was 'Michelangelo's transformation of the Campidoglio... the most brilliant of all

Renaissance town-planning schemes',[62] but '[i]t forms a link between the early Renaissance *piazza* such as the Piazza della Santissima Annunziata in Florence and the later Baroque developments in Rome'.[63]

Town planning in cinquecento Rome was not confined to *piazze* however grandiose the effect. As patrons, the papacy was also concerned with facilitating the development of grand vistas across the Eternal City. Under Popes Julius II (1503–13) and Leo X (1513–21), Rome matched or even surpassed Florence in the development of broad, straight streets leading between focal points within the urban core (fig 11.2). Already, during the pontificate of Alexander VI (1492–1503), the Borgo Alessandro had been constructed to connect the Vatican with the Castel S Angelo, and under Julius II two further streets were developed: the Via Lungara along the west side of the Tiber linking the Vatican with the Trastevere, and the Via Giulia along the east bank of the river and bordering the densely built-up area of the city. Later, under Leo X, the Via Leonina (now the Ripetta) was constructed to connect the Porta del Popolo with the Ponte S Angelo.[64] And these were just the beginnings. Under Pope Sixtus V (1585–90), Rome underwent a major programme of urban development within a very short period that in terms of town planning put the city years ahead of any rival. Under the direction of Domenico Fontana, the chaos of medieval Rome was transformed into an intelligently planned urban area that set the seal on the future development of cities across Europe. Wide streets were created to connect the major nodes across the city and in particular the seven main pilgrimage churches of Rome.[65] Offices and privileges were awarded to cardinals and other members of the Roman elite to encourage them to construct sumptuous *palazzi* and imposing churches along these thoroughfares and, with the consequential increase in property values, betterment taxation could be relied upon to offset the cost of construction.

To add ornamentation to highway engineering and to emphasise the importance of a location, Sixtus V funded the positioning or repositioning of obelisks in front of prominent buildings or at the end of a new street, for example in front of S Maria Maggiore, the new Palazzo del Laterano and St Peter's, and where the Via Ripetta, Via del Corso (Via Flaminia) and Via del Babuino (Via Paolina) converge at the Piazza del Popolo. In the Foro di Traiano and Piazza Colonna, Sixtus V crowned the antique columns of Trajan and Marcus Aurelius with the statues of St Peter and St Paul. Thus, in the words of Kenneth Clarke, the development of Rome in the second half of the cinquecento represented 'the most grandiose piece of town planning ever attempted'[66] and was all the more surprising since 'it was done only fifty years after Rome had been (as it seemed) completely humilitated – almost wiped off the map'.[67]

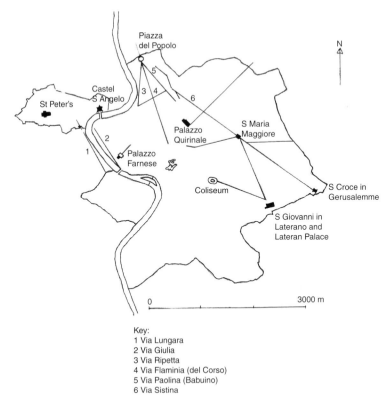

Figure 11.2 Street development in Rome in the sixteenth century

Key:
1 Via Lungara
2 Via Giulia
3 Via Ripetta
4 Via Flaminia (del Corso)
5 Via Paolina (Babuino)
6 Via Sistina

Venice

Funded from the enormous wealth of the procurators of S Marco, the Piazza S Marco is one of the most famous squares in the world, and because it was paved soon after it was completed, it is the only square in Venice to be called a *piazza*. All the other squares in the city except the Piazzetta S Marco are called *campi* because, for many years after their construction, they were often used for grazing and other agricultural pursuits. Reconstructed over the period from the late 15th century to the early 19th century, and situated opposite the western-facing facade of the Basilica of S Marco, the *piazza* is bordered on its long northern side by the 15th-century Procuratie Vecchie (which contains the Torre dell'Orologio at its eastern end), on its similarly lengthy southern side by the 16th-century Procuratie Nuove, and on its narrower western side by the early-19th-century Napoleonic Wing (which replaced Sansovino's 16th-century church of S Giminiano). All three blocks are colonnaded in broadly the same style and create an image of unity, Napoleon quipping that the *piazza* was the 'finest drawing room in Europe'. But the French emperor might not have had this impression had the building line of the Procuratie Nuove not been moved south of the alignment of the former building and its enclosed Campanile. With the Campanile standing alone as a consequence of the realignment, the Procuratie Nuove benefits from a unified design throughout its full length (fig 11.3).

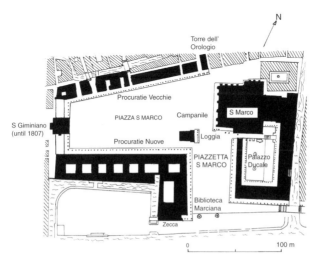

Figure 11.3 The Piazza and Piazzetta S Marco, Venice

In contrast to the Piazza S Marco, the Piazzetta with its Gothic Palazzo Ducale and Late Renaissance Biblioteca Marciana is an object lesson in creating harmony from disunity. In producing plans for the publicly funded library in 1537, Sansovino was very much aware of what, until then, had been the overwhelming presence of the doge's palace and the adjacent Basilica. However, in designing the long unbroken ornamented facade of the library, which runs parallel to the palace and at 90 degrees to its waterside facade which, like the palace, looks out over the Canale di S Marco, he was able to match the older building in grandeur. However, to avoid dominating the *piazzetta* and competing untactfully with the Doge's Palace, the Biblioteca Marciana was constructed as a two-storey building whereas the Palazzo Ducale is externally a three-storey edifice and, in consequence, the roof line of the library was kept below that of the palace.

Genoa

For centuries the patricians of Genoa had lived in densely populated areas adjacent to the harbour. However, with their extraordinary increase in wealth in the wake of Andrea Doria's seizure of power in 1528, they sought more congenial conditions away from the built-up areas. Thus, in 1550 and in response to a collective petition from the elite, Doge Lucca Spinola decreed that a new residential street would be constructed on vacant land to the north-east of the old city. It would provide revenue to fund the restoration of the Cathedral of S Lorenzo and the further development of the Molo while at the same time satisfying 'the demands of a social class at the height of its economic prestige derived from financial dealings with the greatest powers in Europe'.[68] A committee of seven patricians was subsequently appointed to organise the early stages of development – land expropriation, demolitions and site preparation – and then sold off building lots by auction in 1551, 1558–9 and 1561.[69]

After the elite had acquired land for development, Galeazzo Alessi and Bernardo da Cantone (the commune's official architect) became responsible for the design of individual properties and for the layout of the new street, the Strada Nuova. Because of Genoese involvement in the Corsican war of liberation (1551–8) construction was delayed until the late 1550s,[70] but from 1558 to 1584 work began on the first eight *palazzi*, namely the Palazzo Pallavicini-Cambiaso (1558), the Palazzo Spinola Gambaro (1558), the Palazzo Pallavicino Carrega (1558), the Palazzo Doria Spinola (1563), the Palazzo Lercari Parodi (1571) and the Palazzo Cattaneo Adorno (1584). Later, other palaces were built along the same street, most notably the Palazzo Grimaldi Doria Tursi (completed 1596) and the Palazzo Brignole (Bianco) (started 1580). The most recent addition was the Palazzo Brignole (Rosso), begun as late as 1671.

Throughout the construction stage, development had to comply with strict planning regulations, thus along the full 300 metre (330 yard) length of the Strada Nuova, all 'frontages are aligned... alleys 3.5m (12 feet) wide separated each palazzo from its neighbour... height as well as the width of the facades was prescribed, and the portals of opposite palazzi had to face each other'.[71]

It is often claimed that town planning was as important to the development of Genoa as it was to Rome and Venice, and it is also suggested that Genoese planning was superior to its Venetian counterpart because the city enabled the Strada Nuova with all its patrician *palazzi* to be largely developed within the space of 40 years, whereas equivalent development in Venice along the Grand Canal was spread over several centuries. However, both claims can be refuted. In comparison to Rome and Venice, town planning in Genoa took place on a very small scale and had little impact on the overall image of the city. Today, most visitors to Genoa are unlikely to head for the Strada Nuova (renamed the via Garabaldi in the 19th century) or are completely unaware of its existence, but in Rome and Venice very few tourists fail to visit the Campidoglio or the Piazza S Marco and one suspects that these differences might have been apparent already in the late cinquecento. But as an exercise in the use of planning regulations, and in terms of enhancing the built environment (albeit for a small social elite), the development of the Strada Nuova was 'one of the most important urban projects in Europe'.[72]

Florence

Developed almost 200 years after the construction of the late medieval Palazzo Vecchio and Loggia dei Lanzi, the Palazzo degli Uffizi is the third civic building of prominence in the Piazza della Signoria complex. However, instead of hugging the edges of the *piazza* like the older buildings, it projects southwards towards the River Arno and is broadly aligned with the statues of Michelangelo's *David* (1504) and Baccio Bandinelli's *Hercules and Cacus* (1534). Later, Ammanati's Neptune fountain (1560–75) and the equestrian statue of Cosimo I by Giambologna (1595) assume the same alignment, while in the middle distance the dome of the cathedral is clearly visible from the Uffizi over the rooftops on the north side of the *piazza*.

After Florence annexed Siena in 1557, the Uffizi was commissioned by Cosimo I to house the many offices necessary to govern his expanded domain. Following the demolition of existing property, or its retention for incorporation into the new development, work began on the construction of the Palazzo degli Uffizi in 1559, although the pace of construction was constrained by the poor load-bearing qualities of the sandy soil, a problem partly overcome by sophisticated engineering and the use of iron to reinforce the building. Designed by Vasari until his death in 1574, and completed by Bernardo Buontalenti and later by Alfonso Parigi the Elder, the Uffizi accommodated as many as 13 different government offices.[73] Built from *pietra serena*, a grey Italian sandstone, an elongated courtyard is lined with continuous buildings whose Doric-columned ground-floor arcades not only provide coherence and continuity, but support a mezzanine floor and two upper storeys pierced by numerous windows. On the ground floor, access to each magistrature was secured by a separate entrance under the arcades and, extending over three bays, each magistrature occupied space on the ground floor, the mezzanine and the first floor.[74] The top floor was used from the beginning as an art gallery. The Uffizi's sheer scale has made it not only the most important Florentine building of the cinquecento, but one of the most impressive urban projects of 16th-century Italy.

Whereas the Uffizi took at least 20 years to complete, the Corridoio Vasariano (Vasari's corridor) was reputedly built in only five months.[75] In 1549, when Cosimo I moved his official seat from the Palazzo Vecchio to the Palazzo Pitti, he ordered a corridor to be built to connect his administrative headquarters with his place of residence across the Arno. From the Uffizi, the corridor follows the line of the river north-westwards within a tall arcade and then traverses the Arno above the shops of the Ponte Vecchio before stretching south-westwards, past the church of S Felicità, to the Palazzo Pitti, a distance of some 350 metres (400 yd). In its unadorned and utilitarian way, '[the] corridor . . . is an outstanding feat in urban design'[76] which, aside from facilitating

Photo 11.25 Giorgio Vasari, Palazzo Uffizi, Florence, 1559. An enormous piece of 16th-century public sector redevelopment on a site previously occupied by housing and a church between the Piazza della Signoria and the Arno.

communication between two important nodes, 'served as a portico along the Arno, as a crowning course along the Pontevecchio, and as a loggia overlooking S Felicità'.[77]

There was, too, another significant example of town planning in cinquecento Florence. A kilometre to the north, with a loggia designed by Giovanni Caccini and attached to the quattrocento church of SS Annunziata in 1601–4, work on the Piazza della SS Annunziata was almost finished. It only required the positioning of Giambologna's equestrian statue of Ferdinando I close to the centre of the *piazza* in 1608 to complete the many architectural and planning initiatives of the previous two centuries to create one of the finest enclosed Renaissance squares in Italy. Designed in outline by Brunelleschi while he was engaged on the Ospedale degli Innocenti (1419–26), by the close of the cinquecento the *piazza* was demarcated on three

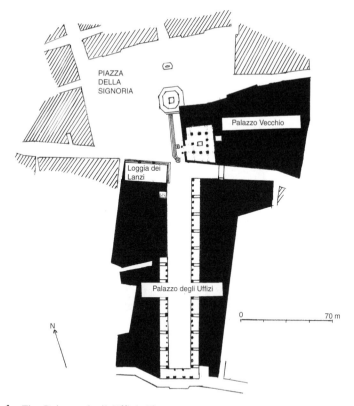

Figure 11.4 The Palazzo degli Uffizi, Florence

sides by arcades: those of the Ospedale on the south-east, those of Antonio da Sangallo's Confraternità dei Serviti opposite the Ospedale (1516–25), and those of the church of SS Annunziata across its north-eastern end. The south-western end of the *piazza* is devoid of Renaissance architecture and from it runs the Via dei Servi that connects the square with Brunelleschi's great dome.

The outcome of two centuries of development is thus a small and intimate *piazza* that appears rectangular since it is 75 metres (246 ft) long and 60 metres (197 ft) wide; however, if the arcades are discounted, then the Piazza della SS Annunziata is almost a perfect square.[78] Overall, and this is perhaps its finest attribute, 'the strong visual structure of the architectural composition holds the space together maintaining a tremendous sense of enclosure and completeness'.[79] Thus, the porticos with their sensitively designed columns and arches 'unify the composition and almost completely mask the function of the surrounding buildings',[80] an attribute shared by very few other *piazze* in Italy.

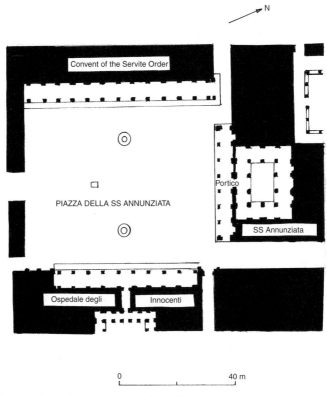

Figure 11.5 The Piazza della SS Annunziata, Florence

Photo 11.26 Giovanni Caccini and others, loggia, SS Annunziata, Florence, 1601–4. Situated at the northern end of the most beautiful square in Florence, the loggia provides a magnificent frontage to Michelozzo's Early Renaissance church.

Bologna

It is not only *piazze* where the use of arcades creates a sense of unity in the built environment. Arcaded streets produce a similar outcome. Although in the planning and development of a city a straight street often provides an aesthetically pleasing view, it is not essential that all buildings that line the street should be identical or even fairly similar. A strong motif, such as an arcade at ground-floor level, does much to create unity in street design, and at the same time provides shade from the sun's rays or shelter from the rain and snow.[81] This has been recognised in a host of Italian cities for centuries but particularly in Bologna where 32 kilometres (20 miles) of street arcades have enriched the townscape since at least the cinquecento. Interestingly, in the quattrocento development of arcades was restricted since the city's ruling Bentivoglio family believed that arcades would inhibit police control and the movement of troops, '[b]ut in the sixteenth century papal and municipal government legislation made clear that they [should be] developed with the twin motives of commercial-social utilitarianism and the beautification of a proud city'.[82]

Naples: new town — in town

Streets, of course, could be used for multifarious purposes. In the city of Naples, a major thoroughfare, the Via Toledo, was constructed in 1536 to provide passage for the troops of the Spanish viceroy, Don Pedro de Toledo, to move between the port, the projected residential area in the Spanish quarter and the citadel of Sant' Elmo.[83] In creating the route between two strategic nodes, the port and the citadel, it became logistically desirable in 1553 to develop the Spanish quarter in between and, like other new developments of a military nature, this adopted a classical Roman grid plan. Whereas Spanish patronage had a significant impact on the built environment of Naples from 1504 (when the kingdom of Naples became a viceroyalty of Spain) to the early 18th century when under the Treaty of Utrecht (1713) Naples was ceded to Austria, many of the buildings constructed in Naples in this period were designed by architects from central or northern Italy who had migrated south in search of commissions.[84]

Palermo

Densely packed with medieval buildings and with a chaotic infrastructure, Palermo in the cinquecento was ripe for redevelopment. Funded by the vice-royal administration and largely supervised by Giuseppe Spadafore (d 1572), two major thoroughfares were therefore constructed across the city: the Cassaro (or Via Toledo), begun in 1565, stretches in a straight line through the city from its south-western to its north-eastern periphery, and was extended further towards the sea in 1581; and the Via Maqueda (now the Corso Vittorio Emanuele), commenced c 1600, runs roughly parallel to the sea from the south-east to the north-west, and in the centre of the city – at the Quattro Canti – bisects the Cassaro at 90 degrees.[85]

It was close to this central point that the Piazza Pretoria was laid out in 1574. Designed by Camillo Camilliani in 1574, the *piazza* barely accommodates the extravagantly decorated fountain designed by his father, Francesco Camilliani,

Photo 11.27   Porticoed street, Bologna, 16th century. One of many porticoes that characterise much of the red-brick city.

20 years earlier and relocated to the *piazza* in *c* 1574 from its original site in Florence. A semblance of unity is conferred upon the *piazza* by the development of imposing buildings on its south-western and north-western sides: the Palazzo delle Aquile, a 15th-century palace enlarged in the cinquecento and home to the city's senate until 1816, and the church and dome of S Caterina (begun 1566).

Other buildings incorporated into the overall scheme included two gateways, one at each end of the Cassaro and both commissioned by the viceroy Marc' Antonio Colonna in 1582–3. At the south-western end of the Cassaro is the triumphal gateway of the Porta Nuova built to celebrate the emperor Charles V's victory in Tunisia in 1535 (the gateway was reconstructed after damage by lightning in 1667); and at the north-eastern end the Porta Felicia is not an arch but an opening which on its seaward side is wedged between two monumental columns set on tall pedestals and mounted by massive entablatures. Probably designed by Giovan Battista Collepietra (though there may have been others), the gateway provides a magnificent entrance to the city that allows 'the tall *vara* (or float) of S Rosalie to pass through it on her feast day'[86]– proof, if proof is needed, that Renaissance gateways were not built solely to control trade or, when closed, to repel enemies, but also with an eye to enhancing local ceremony.

A clean sheet: Palma Nova

Throughout the cinquecento, town planning had been applied to specific areas of existing cities and was evident in particular in the development of *piazze* and street patterns. Often development entailed demolition of existing buildings, while refurbishment of existing buildings was also frequently part of the architect or planner's brief. However, the concept of the 'ideal city' remained alive despite Filarete's Sforzinda (proposed in 1460–4; see Chapter 7) getting short-shrift from developers. It was not, therefore, altogether surprising that when the Venetian Republic wished to strengthen its north-eastern defences, it accepted Vincenzo Scamozzi's plan for a new city – Palma Nova – in 1593 to serve as an enormous fortress on the north-eastern fringe of the Venetian Republic (fig 11.6) – a precursor to many similar developments that occurred north of the Alps in the tumultuous 17th century.

Figure 11.6   Palma Nova: Scamozzi's nine-point star-shaped fortress (1593)

Conclusion

Driven by a desire to demonstrate their ecclesiastical or secular power, or to engender civic pride among their citizens, the princely courts and republics of Italy – as if to be *au fait* with the latest architectural fashions – eagerly commissioned more grandiose and less orthodox styles of classical architecture. The High Renaissance style that first took root in Rome was to a great extent replaced by Mannerism by the 1530s to 1540s, and in the second half of the cinquecento Palladianism was in vogue throughout the Veneto. Public patrons similarly funded large-scale planning schemes often involving the development of new *piazze* or major thoroughfares, or financed minor-scale development in the form of street arcading. For the first time since antiquity, whole areas of cities were being planned and developed in a spatially integrated manner.

Notes

1 W Lotz, *Architecture in Italy 1500–1600*, rev edn D Howard (New Haven and London: Yale University Press, 1995), p 15.
2 Ibid.
3 C Woodward, *Rome* (Manchester: Manchester University Press, 1995), p 71.
4 Ibid.
5 B Hintzen-Bohlen with J Sorges, *Rome and the Vatican City* (Cologne: Könemann, 2000), p 56.
6 Woodward, *Rome*, p 87.
7 D Howard, *The Architectural History of Venice* (New Haven and London: Yale University Press, 2002), p 152; G Zucconi, *Venice. An architectural guide* (Venice: Arsenale Editrice, 1995), p 64.
8 M Kaminski, *Venice* (Cologne: Könemann, 2000), p 51.
9 Zucconi, *Venice*, p 56.
10 Ibid.
11 Zucconi, *Venice*, p 65.
12 Ibid.
13 Zucconi, *Venice*, p 65; Kaminski, *Venice*, p 49.
14 Kaminski, *Venice*, p 177.
15 Howard, *Architectural History of Venice*, pp 170–1.
16 Zucconi, *Venice*, p 70.
17 Kaminski, *Venice*, p 180.
18 L Sutton, *Western Architecture* (London: Thames and Hudson, 1999), p 143; Lotz, *Architecture*, pp 83–5.
19 Howard, *Architectural History of Venice*, p 175.
20 Kaminski, *Venice*, p 48.

21 Zucconi, *Venice*, p 80.
22 Kaminski, *Venice*, p 178.
23 Zucconi, *Venice*, p 81; Kaminski, *Venice*, p 52.
24 Kaminski, *Venice*, p 344.
25 Ibid.
26 N De Mari, 'The City of the old walls: modern buildings', in *Genoa. Architectural Guide* (Turin: Umberto Allemandi, 1998), p 45.
27 Ibid, p 50.
28 Ibid, p 57.
29 Ibid, p 95.
30 S Della Torre, 'The city of the saint and the merchant', in *Milan. Architectural Guide* (Turin: Umberto Allemandi, 1999), p 95.
31 Ibid, p 96.
32 A Hopkins, *Italian Architecture from Michelangelo to Borromini* (London: Thames and Hudson, 2002), p 69.
33 Della Torre, 'City of the saint', p 98.
34 L Roncai, 'The Neoclassical city and residence', in *Milan. Architectural Guide* (Turin: Umberto Allemandi, 1999), p 109.
35 Hopkins, *Italian Architecture*, p 99.
36 Lotz, *Architecture*, pp 117–19.
37 Hopkins, *Italian Architecture*, p 105; Lotz, *Architecture*, p 142.
38 Lotz, *Architecture*, p 142.
39 Hopkins, *Italian Architecture*; Lotz, *Architecture*, pp 141–2.
40 Della Torre, 'City of the saint', p 102.
41 B Zucconi, *Florence. An architectural guide* (Venice: Arsenale Editrice, 1995), p 86.
42 Ibid, p 84; Hopkins, *Italian Architecture*, p 76.
43 Hopkins, *Italian Architecture*, p 76.
44 Zucconi, *Florence*, p 85.
45 Ibid, p 86.
46 Lotz, *Architecture*, pp 164–6.
47 Zucconi, *Florence*, p 88; Hopkins, *Italian Architecture*, pp 60–1.
48 Hopkins, *Italian Architecture*, p 60.
49 RC Wirtz, *Florence*, p 454; Zucconi, *Florence*, p 94.
50 Lotz, *Architecture*, pp 64–5.
51 Ibid.
52 Hopkins, *Italian Architecture*, p 76.
53 Lotz, *Architecture*, p 153.
54 Ibid.
55 Hopkins, *Italian Architecture*, pp 33–4.
56 Lotz, *Architecture*, p 67.
57 Ibid, p 116.
58 Hintzen-Bohlen with Sorges, *Rome*, p 51.
59 D Watkin, *A History of Western Architecture*, 3rd edn (London: Laurence King, 2005), p 235.
60 Hopkins, *Italian Architecture*, p 68; Watkin, *History*, p 235.

61 Hintzen-Bohlen with Sorges, *Rome*, p 51.

62 Watkin, *History*, p 235.

63 C Moughtin, *Urban Design. Street and Square*, 3rd edn (Oxford and Burlington MA: Oxford University Press, 2003), pp 109–11.

64 Lotz, *Architecture*, pp 120–1.

65 Ibid.

66 K Clarke, *Civilization* (London: BBC Books and John Murray, 1971), p 115.

67 Ibid.

68 Hopkins, *Italian Architecture*, p 66.

69 N De Mari, 'The city of the old walls: modern buildings', in *Genoa. Architectural Guide* (Turin: Umberto Allemandi, 1998), p 66.

70 Hopkins, *Italian Architecture*, p 116.

71 Lotz, *Architecture*, p 83.

72 De Mari, 'The city', p 66.

73 Hopkins, *Italian Architecture*, pp 55, 58.

74 Ibid.

75 Zucconi, *Florence*, p 88.

76 Wirtz, *Florence*, p 122.

77 Zucconi, *Florence*, p 88.

78 Moughtin, *Urban Design*, p 103.

79 Ibid.

80 Ibid.

81 Ibid, p 145; CF Black, *Early Modern Italy, A Social History* (London: Routledge, 2001), p 69.

82 Black, *Early Modern Italy*, p 69.

83 Hopkins, *Italian Architecture*, p 112.

84 Ibid, p 145.

85 E Grady, *Sicily* (London: A&C Black, 2003), p 76; Hopkins, *Italian Architecture*, p 145.

86 Grady, *Sicily*, p 94.

CHAPTER 12

ECONOMIC GROWTH AND URBAN DEVELOPMENT IN THE 16TH CENTURY

Introduction

Although the population of Italy in the cinquecento was still significantly less than in the years immediately preceding the Black Death of the mid-trecento, it increased by 20 per cent throughout the 16th century – notwithstanding a succession of plague epidemics – and was associated with the onset of an economic boom in mid-century. Resources thus became increasingly available for a spate of private development particularly, but not exclusively, within the secular sector.

The Long-lasting Legacy of the Black Death

The adverse effects of the Black Death on the urban population of Italy lingered on well into the 16th century. In northern Italy, where the plague had been particularly devastating, virtually all major cities had failed to make good population losses incurred over the previous 200 years (table 12.1). With urban populations decreasing by as much as 60 or 70 per cent between the 14th and 16th centuries, many cities would not regain their earlier levels of population until the 18th and 19th centuries. Even Milan, as the political and administrative heart of a large duchy, failed to recover more than a third of its population between 1300 and

1510, although it was a magnet for merchants, artisans, professionals, soldiers and functionaries, and attracted people and advantages away from neighbouring cities such as Cremona, Pavia and Piacenza.[1]

Table 12.1 Population of major northern Italian cities: 14th to 17th centuries

City	Date	Population	Date	Population	% change in population
Pisa	1293	38,000	1562	10,000	−74
Siena	1328	52,000	1520	21,000	−62
Florence	1338	95,000	1526	50,000	−47
Milan	1300	150,000	1510	>100,000	−33 or more
Padua	1320	38,000	1500	27,000	−29
Genoa	1290	60,000	1535	50,000	−17
Venice	1338	120,000	1509	102,000	−15
Modena	1306	18,000	1539	15,675	−13
Bologna	1320	54,000	1495	50,000	−7
Vicenza	1320	22,000	1548	21,000	−5
Lucca	1300	23,000	1540	18,000	−22
Verona	1325	38,000	1502	42,000	+11
Mantua	1320	28,000	1527	32,000	+14
Ferrara	1320	17,000	1520	41,000	+141

Source: L Martines, *Power and Imagination. City-States in Renaissance Italy* (London: Pimlico, 2002).

However, atypically, some cities in the north experienced notable growth. Ferrara enjoyed an increase in population of over 140 per cent between 1320 and 1520, almost certainly attributable to its role as a centre of brilliant court life under the O'Este. As a focus of conspicuous consumption the city attracted a wide range of immigrants drawn from the military and mercantile classes, as well as functionaries and prosperous visitors. Albeit at a much slower rate, Mantua grew for similar reasons, while the increase in population of Verona was attributable to the city's flourishing wine trade geared to the large Venetian market nearby, a locational advantage not shared, however, by Vicenza. Although the populations of Venice and Genoa were substantially lower in the early 16th century than in the late Middle Ages – 102,000 in 1509 and 50,000 in 1535 respectively – records show that there were marked gains in population during the later period.[2]

Despite the failure of individual Italian cities to recover from the Black Death by the early 16th century, the population of the peninsula as a whole increased steadily from around 10 million in 1500 to about 12 million in 1600 (table 12.2). While Italy's population was markedly lower than that of France in the 16th century, it was higher than that of Spain, and its greatest cities were larger or comparable in size to Paris and London. However, Italy was unique in Europe in comprising a large number of independent or semi-independent city-states, a factor which had helped render her impotent in the face of French and Spanish aggressive territorial aggrandisement during the earlier part of the century. Yet, there was little relationship between the size of a city and its ability to repel invasion. Rome and Milan succumbed, but Venice remained inviolate.

Population Increase and Urbanisation in 16th-century Italy

Population data presented in table 12.2 are tentative for 1500 and 1550 but fairly reliable in respect of certain urban areas and their dependent rural territories (the *contadi*) in 1600.[3] The table suggests that during the first half of the 16th century the population of Italy increased substantially, but that, to a lesser extent, the rate of growth slowed down between 1550 and 1600. Table 12.2 also reveals that throughout the century, the larger cities of Rome, Naples and Venice grew substantially, Mantua and Milan experienced only gradual growth, Florence stagnated, and Brescia and Perugia declined. Since death rates were significantly higher than birth rates in many cities – disease being more endemic in urban environments than in rural areas – the rate of urban growth (or decline) depended entirely on the level of migration from the *contado* or smaller cities. Death rates among children in their first year of 150–250 per 1,000 were quite normal but reached 450–500 per 1,000 at times of crises,[4] while birth rates were comparatively low – probably around 40–50 per 1,000 – since Italian adults married relatively late by historical standards (females in their mid-twenties and males in their early thirties).[5] Thus the growth of Rome or Naples in the 16th century was not dependent on a natural increase in population but, because of their political, cultural and economic attributes, on their ability to attract a substantial number of immigrants; in contrast, smaller cities such as Florence, Siena or Lucca were less successful in this respect.[6]

Urban growth was clearly associated with an increase in urbanisation. By 1550, the cities of Italy with populations in excess of 10,000 accommodated appreciably more than 8 per cent of the total population of the peninsula. Even when presenting data only on selected cities, table 12.2 shows that urbanisation increased from around 8 per cent in 1550 to nearly 8.4 per cent in 1600. According to one estimate, 'Italy was probably the most densely populated region

Table 12.2 Population of Italy and her principal cities, 16th century

	1500	1550	% increase 1500–50	1600	% increase 1550–1600	% increase 1500–1600
N Netherlands	900,000	n a	—	1,500,000	—	66
Spain	6,500,000	n a	—	8,500,000	—	31
France	15,000,000	n a	—	19,000,000	—	27
Italy	10,000,000	11,000,000	10	12,000,000	8	20
England and Wales	3,750,000	n a	—	4,250,000	—	13
London	40,000	n a	—	200,000	—	400
Amsterdam	14,000	n a	—	65,000	—	274
Paris	100,000	n a	—	220,000	—	120
Madrid	n a	n a	—	49,000	—	—
Rome	55,000	45,000	−18	99,312 (1602)	120	80
Parma	19,034	25,000	32	33,000	32	73
Naples	150,000	212,000	41	237,784 (1596)	12	59
Venice	100,000	163,627	64	142,804 (1624)	−13	43
Padua	27,000	35,852 (1557)	33	36,000	0	33
Bologna	55,000	70,661 (1581)	29	61,000 (1624)	14	11
Modena	18,000	16,000	−11	19,911 (1596)	25	11
Mantua	28,000	38,000	36	31,000	−18	11
Milan	100,000	n a	—	108,000	—	8
Genoa	60,000	65,500	10	62,396	−5	3
Florence	70,000	60,773 (1551)	16	70,000 (1622)	15	0
Perugia	25,000	19,876 (1551)	−20	19,722 (1618)	0	−20
Brescia	6,060 (1493)	42,660 (1586)	−13	36,000	−16	−36
Verona	n a	52,109 (1586)	—	n a	—	—
Turin	n a	14,000	—	24,000	71	—
Bergamo	n a	17,707 (1586)	—	27,000	50	—
Vicenza	n a	21,268 (1586)	—	37,000	76	—
Ferrara	n a	42,000	—	32,860 (1601)	−22	—
Lucca	n a	24,000	—	24,000	0	—
Siena	n a	13,679 (1560)	—	18,659 (1610)	36	—
Total	771,094	970,306		920,308	19	
% total population	7.71	8.09		8.36		

Source: CF Black, *Early Modern Italy: A Social History* (London: Routledge, 2001).

of Europe in 1600, with an average of forty-four people per square kilometre rising in such areas as Lombardy . . . to three or four times this level. The figure for France was thirty-four, and for Spain and Portugal only seventeen.'[7]

The Impact of Plague and Famine

Throughout the 16th century, population growth would have been substantially higher, and economic growth almost certainly much greater, had it not been for recurrent epidemics and plagues. Plagues, disease and wars sometimes came together. Pestilence was devastating in 1522–8 in nearly all of Italy, and associated with other diseases that affected both humans and livestock. Together with the impact of war, these afflictions resulted in mortality rates seven or eight times the norm in the worst affected areas, such as Tuscany. In 1575–7 the plague struck Venetia, Lombardy and Sicily with particular virulence and reduced the population of, for example, Venice by around 47,000. Other diseases intermittently had severe demographic effects, too. *Tifo* (which might have been typhoid or typhus) broke out in 1505, 1528 and 1590–1, resulting in death rates in Florence during these latter years up to four times the normal level. Less serious than the plague, *tifo* killed 'only' 20 to 40 per cent of those affected, compared with 70–80 per cent of those who contracted plague.[8]

Mortality crises were also the result of famine. Population growth took a dip as an outcome of food crises that occurred in Italy in the 1520s, 1549, 1555 and 1590s (as elsewhere in much of Europe). In consequence, infant mortality rates soared, and death rates for infants after the first year remained high because of malnutrition exacerbated by childhood disease and poor hygiene.[9]

But plagues and famine left a proportion of the population of many cities relatively unscathed. Clearly, '[i]f the general economic climate was favourable soon the population might rise and immigration into the cities be hastened'.[10] Venice, in particular, experienced this process after 1575–7. Thus, despite the impact of disease and food crises on population growth during certain periods of the 16th century, over the long term the population of Italy increased markedly and stimulated economic growth. The advent of peace after 1530 probably helped the process – since warfare had earlier amplified the scourge of disease and famine.

With a higher urban population, it was necessary to ensure that, in terms of their food supply, cities were sustainable. Land was thus brought under the plough on the mountainsides of Tuscany, while new land drainage initiatives – in part under the supervision of Leonardo da Vinci – were undertaken in Lombardy, particularly in respect of the waters of the Adda and Ticino.[11]

Although population growth might stimulate economic growth, the reverse is also true. There is clearly a symbiotic relationship between the two, and this was evident in Italy in the 16th century. In Rome, for example, economic growth and rising living standards attracted a large inflow of migrants, helping to drive up the population from 55,000 to about 99,000 between 1500 and 1602 – an 80 per cent increase; and over a comparable period, and for the same reason, the population of Naples grew from 150,000 to about 238,000 (a 59 per cent increase). In contrast, Milan grew from 100,000 to only 108,000, while the population of Florence failed to grow at all, in both cases with detrimental effects on economic growth.

Urban Population Growth: The Political Dimension

Political factors also played an important role in determining population levels in individual cities and their *contadi*. This was particularly evident in Rome. With the revived fortunes of the papacy after the sack of the Eternal City by the imperial army in 1527, successive popes attempted to show that Rome was fit to lead the Catholic world. In its ecclesiastical role Rome thus attracted more and more migrants such as pilgrims, artists and craftsmen – all of whom provided a market for locally produced goods and services and, to an extent, the labour employed on construction projects such as 'palaces for cardinals and their relatives or major new churches for the new religious Orders'.[12] Like many cities in transition, past and present, Rome also attracted migrants from the countryside pushed out by landowners who had adopted more profitable forms of agriculture – in this case, turning from arable to pastoral farming.[13]

Elsewhere in Italy, as an outcome of political machinations and variations in diplomatic and military power over several centuries, a small number of larger cities, notably Venice, Milan, Florence and Naples, had grown at the expense of the many middle-sized communities within their respective regions. In the 15th century, the political fragmentation of much of Italy, 'with many independent and quasi-independent cities run by communal oligarchies, dominant families or petty military *signori*',[14] provided the context for power struggles between competing communities.

Although the Peace of Lodi of 1454 brought a short period of fragile peace to Rome, Venice, Milan and Florence, fragmentation remained and it took a further hundred or more years of inter-state conflict before the major cities of Italy could enjoy another period of peace. By introducing the concept of a centrally organised absolutist state, the Treaty of Cateau-Cambrésis of 1559 strengthened the role of Rome, Milan, Florence and Naples as capital cities of states whose boundaries were unilaterally recognised. As a result, these cities 'attracted the most politically-active, those who wished to serve in a fuller bureaucracy, [and] those seeking a court environment. Servants and the service industries followed, especially in a changing cultural environment more disposed to conspicuous consumption.'[15] In contrast to the enhanced position of the major cities, the smaller political entities – such as Siena (consumed by the Tuscan state under the terms of the 1559 treaty), Pisa, Perugia, Rimini, Brescia and Bergamo – declined in political importance, while following the demise of the O'Este family Ferrara reverted to direct papal control and lost its political importance.[16]

It is difficult, however, to generalise on the relationship between the changing political importance of Italian cities and their population growth (if any). For example, it might be expected that as the capital of a large absolute state Florence would have increased its population like Rome and Naples, but regardless of an increase in its bureaucratic and court-centred population, the city was economically disadvantaged by its failure to retain its medieval role as a major textile producer. Unlike Florence, Genoa maintained its traditional role as a centre of banking and trading activity, but here the economy failed to generate a significant increase in population largely 'because of its location on the littoral with mountains behind restricting growth physically'.[17] Venice, on the other hand, overcame physical limitations on growth – although its expansion was restricted by its lagoons – because its population and economic activities encroached upon its islands with considerable success.[18] In the south and with its viceregal court dominating the politics and culture of a wide territory, Naples 'was the Mecca for the noble elite of the whole Viceroyalty and those who wished to serve them',[19] and for the peasants escaping the deprivations and abject poverty of feudalism in the remoter areas of the peninsula.

Economic Competition between States

In the early decades of the 16th century, as in the late 15th century, urban economic growth was in part an outcome of attempts to create and/or consolidate territorial states centred particularly on Rome, Venice, Genoa, Milan, Florence and Naples. Elsewhere 'petty princes, military *condiottieri* and lesser communes strove to avoid central domination'.[20] While inter-state struggles – manifested by armed conflicts and sieges – and civil unrest could seriously disrupt economic growth, in the larger cities in particular, power and economic leadership were often in the hands of a narrow elite that invariably indulged in conspicuous consumption, normally to the benefit of their own city but to the detriment of smaller cities or towns. The notion that 'the rich get richer and the poor get poorer' was not just confined to individuals but was also applicable to cities. Undoubtedly, Rome, Venice and Genoa grew richer throughout the 16th century, while among the losers were cities such as Brescia and Perugia that had once thrived as manufacturing centres.[21]

Notwithstanding these variations in power and economic dynamism – and within a demographic context which saw the population of Italy grow from 10 million to 12 million – from the mid-15th to late 16th centuries urban economic growth was attributable to the expanded role of the papacy (although, paradoxically, this also had adverse effects on the country's economies), further industrial development, the creation of a European world economy, the expansion of trade, a price revolution and the advance of banking, and the long-term effects of the Italian Wars. However, as with other lengthy boom periods, economic growth throughout most of the 16th century was followed by the beginnings of a Europe-wide slump in the 1590s leading to a major downturn in economic activity in 1619–22 and, in Italy specifically, to a period of recession that lasted throughout the remainder of the 17th century and beyond (see chapter 16).

The Resurgence of Rome and its Effects on Economic Development

In terms of both costs and benefits, the papacy had a major influence on urban economic development in Italy. The benefits included the multiplier effects on the Roman economy derived from papal expenditure on the construction of a large number of churches in Rome and on the completion of St Peter's basilica (see chapters 10, 11, 14, 15), but also from papal patronage of the Jubilee of 1600 that attracted over a million pilgrims and their collective spending power to the city. On the other hand, because of papal policy Italy experienced substantial costs. The Counter-Reformation that consolidated the power of the papacy throughout its temporal and spiritual domains in the second half of the cinquecento produced a reaction that encouraged the Protestant states of the north to reinforce their own economies and political structures and, in consequence, led to 'the transformation of northern Italy into a semi-peripheral arena of the world economy'.[22]

In addition to the substantial papal expenditure on the redevelopment of Rome's built environment (see chapter 10), a large volume of personal wealth was invested in the construction of both ecclesiastical and secular buildings in the Eternal City during the cinquecento, despite Rome having few manufacturing industries, a low volume of visible exports and an absence of indigenous banking services. From private resources, and out of reverence for the Church, King Ferdinand and Queen Isabella of Spain commissioned the construction of the Tempietto of S Pietro in Montorio (1502); the Siennese banker Agostino Chigi funded construction of the choir of S Maria del Popolo (1505); and Cardinal Alessandro Farnese II commissioned the church of Il Gesù (1568) as a bequest to the Society of Jesus. Private fortunes were also used to finance construction of magnificent secular buildings. Cardinal Alessandro Farnese, the Massimo family, Cardinal Capodiferro and Tommaso del Giglio all spent a substantial proportion of their wealth on, in turn, the Palazzo Farnese (1517), the Palazzo Massimo alle Colonne (1532), the Palazzo Spada (1548) and the Palazzo Giglio (1560) – the latter building being renamed the Palazzo Borghese after its purchase by Cardinal Camillo Borghese in 1596. Suburban villas such as the sumptuous Villa Farnesina (formerly Chigi) and Villa Medici were started respectively in 1508 and 1540, and funded by Agostino Chigi and Cardinal Ricci of Montepulciano. The Villa Medici was bought by Cardinal Fernando de'Medici in 1576 who subsequently oversaw the early stages of its completion (see chapter 13).

Elsewhere in Italy a complex amalgam of economic factors, both beneficial and detrimental, determined the extent to which the country's cities were destined to be developed and redeveloped in the cinquecento. We turn first to industry.

Manufacturing Industry in 16th-century Italy

In contrast to many of the industries of the 19th and 20th centuries, which saw factory workers use machinery to produce great quantities of standardised goods for the mass market, 16th-century Italian manufacturers utilised labour skills to produce a wide range of luxury goods for the wealthy across Europe. Production in Italy was unusual in that it was concentrated in a dense network of cities, where goods were manufactured in family-based workshops by craftsmen – and, to a lesser extent, craftswomen – by hand, supported by small numbers of apprentices and journeymen. The possession of technical secrets was crucial for the success of the enterprise or industry. Goods were noted for the rarity of their raw materials, their outstanding design and exquisite workmanship, 'all of which [were] reflected in the high cost of the article'.[23]

It must not be assumed, however, that production took place within a free unfettered market. Market forces were distorted both by the state and by guilds. In its attempt to protect the economy and increase the wealth of a city or nation, the state adopted a mercantilist approach in which competition was regarded as an inefficient way of utilising resources while balance of trade deficits (even temporary) were viewed as economically debilitating. To reduce the power of foreign competitors and to produce a healthy trade balance, the state adopted a wide range of measures to ensure that the value of exports exceeded the value of imports (with a corresponding inflow of gold or silver as a means of settling trading debt). To this end, industries in annexed territories were not permitted to compete with industries in the dominant city or nation – the *dominante*. Similarly, the industries of an independent city or nation abroad were rendered less competitive in home markets through the imposition of tariffs or quotas, and through restrictions on foreign shipping using home or dominion ports.

Competition at home was controlled by guilds that regulated production in order to keep standards high. In each city, guild functions were very wide ranging. According to research by Richard Hanlon, guilds 'inspected the level of expertise of the workers and monitored new admissions to the trade. They determined the entire manufacturing process: which products to make, the raw materials used, the procedures to follow, the duties of the masters and the journeymen, the duration of the working day. They fixed the wages of the workers, the price of the article, and often channelled its distribution too . . . Many ran their own benefit schemes for their members.'[24]

The attributes of industrial development in Italy in the late 16th century, and particularly in respect of the textile industries, were both negative and positive, with producers – when necessary – showing a willingness and an ability to adjust to changing market circumstances. However, as in Flanders, manufacturers in Italy were slowly pricing themselves out of European markets because of their comparatively higher production costs. Regarding the cities of central and northern Italy (and those in Flanders), Carlo Cipolla notes that in the late 16th and early 17th centuries, 'labour costs seem to have been too high in Italy in relation to the wage level in competing countries',[25] while Dominico Sella calls Venice 'a "rich city" [in which] the high cost of living was due to "burdensome rents and high wages". Comparative newcomers, such as Holland, England and to a lesser extent France benefited as a result.'[26] They enjoyed lower costs, secured larger markets and realised higher profits. The textile industry of northern Italy was further disadvantaged by having its capital invested in luxury goods production and being unable or unwilling to divert its products to 'new markets first made necessary by the monetary crisis of the fourteenth and fifteenth centuries [where prices had dramatically fallen] and then made profitable by the creation of a world-economy in the sixteenth century'.[27]

It is precisely in the 14th and 15th centuries, on the other hand, that in Italy there was 'a very marked development of a rural textile industry. The peasants engage[d] in it on behalf of entrepreneurs living in towns, or sometimes also on their own account.'[28] In Tuscany there was a gradual decline in the production of luxury goods in this period, and within the same state and across northern Italy a new type of textile production emerged in small towns and in the countryside, engaged in making poorer-quality, cheaper cloth within the reach of less well-to-do consumers.[29] In Prato, by the 16th century as many as one in four families owned a loom and used lower-grade local wool to produce affordable products for the mass market.[30]

Venice, Milan, Florence and Naples: The industrial hubs of Italy

As in Italy, a body of thought emerged across Europe in the 16th century that was concerned with the relationship between foreign trade and a nation's wealth. It was thought that if the value of exports exceeded the value of imports this would be conducive to an increase in national wealth, but if the value of imports was greater than the value of exports national wealth would be diminished. Thus, through various measures governments attempted to restrict imports and promote exports – a policy known as mercantilism. Because of the stage of economic development that western Europe had reached by the 16th century, an emphasis on manufactured exports often offered the best opportunity for realising a trading surplus and an increase in national wealth. What applied to nations also applied to the industrial hubs of Italy. Under mercantilism and with as many as 120 guilds, Venice was possibly the most industrial city in Europe, but in 1600 most of its industries were of fairly recent origin. The city's population of industrial workers was considerable: around 10,000 were employed in the woollen and silk textile industries (the latter benefiting from a new type of water-powered mill), while 4,000 worked in the Arsenale – the largest industrial complex in Italy by the end of the 16th century. The Arsenale, with its 'docks, storage sheds, workshops and yards for laying keels and building-up hulls... pioneered the line-production system, whereby teams of shipbuilders could assemble a galley hull in a single day [and where] workers... enjoyed lifetime jobs and benefits for their families... and invalid workers and widows benefited from pensions'.[31] The Venetian workforce also comprised 'stonemasons, canal dredgers, fullers of cloth, millworkers, the glassmakers of Murano, those employed in sugar refineries, leatherworkers, coppersmiths, blacksmiths and goldsmiths, and hundreds more in the new printing industry, of which Venice was Europe's largest centre'.[32] There was also employment in industries – unique to Venice – producing a range of luxury items, such as soap, lead crystal and plate glass for mirrors.

Industrial development in the *terraferma* was very much under the control of Venetian rectors, for example '[e]ntrepreneurs in subject cities such as Padua and Verona were [in response to mercantilist policy] forced by law to buy their raw materials in Venice, even though they could buy them more cheaply elsewhere... and [there was also] continual tension between the *dominante* and the subject cities over the production of wide and narrow woollen cloths, silks, cottons and linens'.[33] At the end of the 16th century, when Venice had secured a monopoly on damasks and magnificent silk brocades, mercantilist practice decreed that Vicenza and other subject cities were obliged to concentrate on lower-grade silks. However, the economy of the *terraferma* received a substantial boost between 1560 and 1600. When other parts of Europe – Spain, the Netherlands and England – were allocating more and more of their resources to maritime trade, Venice began to turn its back on the sea and diverted capital from seafaring to investment in real estate and industrial development on the mainland. Within the context of mercantilism, a large-scale textile industry emerged that was able to operate in near-monopolistic conditions created by their North Italian and Dutch competitors' involvement in European wars. The much expanded textile industry thus yielded – at least in the short term – rich rewards that enabled Venice to bask 'in an opulent splendour which made it seem as if the days of its former glory had miraculously returned'.[34]

Milan

As a region rather than a city, 'Milan and the cities surrounding it, such as Cremona, Pavia, Como and Lodi formed the hub of the most active manufacturing pole in Europe'.[35] Throughout Lombardy, cities manufactured fine woollen cloths, fustians (blends of cotton and wool), silk, soap and paper, high-quality leather goods and ceramics. Milan, according to Hanlon, also produced 'arms and armour of fine steel . . . [while] the endless wars of the king of Spain stimulated production of muskets, arquebuses, pistols and cannon. Nearby Brescia in Venetian territory produced firearms as well. At its height, the sector boasted 200 arms workshops, each employing several workers. Others toiled at the ovens, the forges and the water wheels; while others extracted ore from the mines, and transporters hauled it to smelters.'[36] In contrast to practice in Venice, mercantilism was seen as a hindrance rather than a benefit to economic activity throughout the region, where relatively small-scale production, diversity and competition (rather than monopoly), and warfare were principal drivers of manufacturing industry.

Florence

Like Lombardy, northern Tuscany also possessed a network of industrial towns and cities that manufactured a range of products. Florence, however, stood out as the industrial centre and mainly utilised higher quality wool, often imported. Its 'fine woollen industry produced a record 30,000 pieces in the 1570s [twice that of the 1520s] and perhaps more than half of the city's population of 60,000 drew income from it . . . Finished cloths were exported to France, Spain, the Levant, and later to Rome and southern Italy.'[37] As in Florence a century earlier and in the Venetian dominions in the 1500s, free market competition in Tuscany in the cinquecento was not much in evidence within the industrial sector of the economy. 'Guilds everywhere actively inhibited competition, and prevented master artisans from having more than one shop . . . Artisans rarely worked to full capacity, and depended upon a merchant who supplied them with thread . . . Not many weavers were still active after the age of 45, save a small percentage of those who became masters.'[38]

The state, by establishing mercantilist control over industrial development in its territory, was also instrumental in distorting market forces. Between 1537 and his death in 1574, and in accordance with the tenets of mercantilism, 'Cosimo I issued many regulations on the quality, prices and distribution of goods manufactured in Tuscany [and] Grand Duke Ferdinand I, who wished to compensate Pisa for its loss of independence, established silk-weaving there too, albeit of lower quality so as not to compete with Florentine workshops.'[39]

Naples

Somewhat akin to Venice, Naples accommodated a very diverse range of industries. 'Woollen spinning and dyeing expanded in the city [in the 16th century]... fed by fleece from Apulia. Calabrians raised silkworms, spun and sometimes wove silk into lower quality velvets... before sending them to Naples for finishing... Naples [also] produced a broad range of luxury goods [from laces and braids to fine linens] in addition to silk cloths sold across Europe'.[40] The city also produced leatherware – from shoes and boots to saddles and harnesses for domestic and military use – while the tendency among the nobility competitively to display their wealth created a demand for a wide range of luxury items such as fine furniture and musical instruments.

Smaller manufacturing cities

Aside from the four main industrial hubs of Italy and their satellites, other cities such as Mantua, Parma, Pienza, Bologna, Montepulciano, Palermo and Messina also accommodated industrial activity. On a small scale, they manufactured a wide range of products mainly for local consumption, but nevertheless they too enjoyed the benefits of economic growth, particularly in the latter half of the cinquecento.

The Creation of the European World Economy

Notwithstanding the importance of small-scale production and local markets from Lisbon to Warsaw, and Stockholm to Palermo, a European world-economy emerged in the 16th century based on the capitalist mode of production.[41] By the end of the century, the economies of the various states and nations of Europe had become subsumed under a wider economy which, in the view of Immanuel Wallerstein, comprised, 'not only northwest Europe and the Christian Mediterranean (including Iberia) but also central Europe and the Baltic region. It also included certain regions of the Americas: New Spain, the Antilles, Terraferma [Mexico and Central America], Peru, Chile, Brazil – or rather those parts of these regions which were under effective administration of the Spanish and Portuguese. Atlantic islands [such as the Canaries and Madeira] and perhaps a few enclaves on the African coast might also be included in it.'[42] This was now the maximum extent of Italy's trading hinterland and it was within major parts of this area that Italian states had to compete successfully with other European powers in order to thrive as economic entities.

However, to examine the principal attributes of the European world economy for our context it is necessary to define what is meant by the 16th century. Clearly, in terms of European economic development, it did not come into being in exactly 1500 nor end in 1599. Fernand Braudel suggests that the 16th century was divided into two, 'a first century beginning about 1450 and ending about 1550, a second one starting up at that point and lasting until 1620 or 1640',[43] but as far as an examination of Italian trade is concerned, it is more useful to accept Wallerstein's perspective when he argues that '[t]he starting points and ending points vary according to the national perspective from which one views the century'.[44] In considering the Italian economy we can thus focus on a shorter period fairly arbitrarily – determined by political considerations, ie from around 1495 at the beginning of the Italian Wars to the end of the Mantuan War in 1615.

A notable feature of the European world-system of the 16th century was that it was unclear in respect of trade exactly who was dominating whom. For example, if one confines one's attention to Italian states and their partners, '[d]id Genoese merchants and bankers use Spain or did Spanish imperialism absorb parts of Italy? Did Florence dominate Lyon, or France Lombardy, or both?'[45] Also, many cities attempted to be the centre of the European world economy. Genoa laid claim to such a role but so did Seville, Lisbon, Antwerp, Lyon and Hamburg. However, it was none of these but rather Amsterdam – a city of comparatively little importance in the 15th century – that attained preeminence at the end of the 16th.[46] Whereas the 'first' 16th century was characterised by dispersed nodes of industrial activity across Europe, when the 'industrial backbone of Europe ran . . . from Flanders to Tuscany',[47] in the 'second' 16th century – from about 1550 to 1620–40 – industrial activity was concentrated more and more in certain cities of northwestern Europe, particularly Amsterdam, to the detriment of areas elsewhere, notably Venice and the territories of Charles V's empire.[48]

Thus, as industry developed spectacularly in some areas and declined drastically in others, the European world economy divided itself into two parts: the north of Europe (the Dutch Republic, England, Denmark and Scotland) on the one hand, and northern Italy, France and Switzerland on the other. In the former 'there was an expansion in the heavy industries, and consequently of output, for which there had been no precedent, [and in the latter] there was a notable growth in the products of the artistic and the luxury industries, a fresh development of art and artisanry, but only a slight increase in the output of heavy industries, and consequently no remarkable change in the volume of output.'[49] In parallel with this divergence, levels of taxation were less oppressive in the north than in the south, and in the north technical organisation was more up-to-date and more economical – in each respect serving to reduce the competitive ability of the older centres of commerce (such as northern Italy) 'as early as the beginning of the "second" sixteenth century'.[50]

The Expansion of Trade

Although by the late 16th century northern Europe had become the centre of European trade with the rest of the world, the economy or economies of Italy continued vibrant and helped to ensure that the quality of life in many parts of the peninsula remained attractive and very much intact.

Across northern Italy and in Naples the manufacture and transhipment of precious goods to the rest of the world and the import of materials was the basis of prosperity. Clearly, 'long distance trade was a "balancing act" . . . What [merchants] lost on one deal, they recouped on another . . . [They] often banded together in companies . . . in which the profits and losses were borne equally'.[51] With this early form of insurance, risks were reduced so encouraging further trading activity. Through the medium of the *commenda* association (a Venetian invention) an early form of share capital was created whereby 'investors could finance other people's companies in exchange for a share of profits, without the responsibility of managing the money'.[52] In this way, a new source of capital facilitated industry and trade across much of Europe.

The great trading cities of Italy: Venice, Genoa and Florence

As a result of new Portuguese routes to the East and Turkish conquests of Venetian markets in Constantinople and Egypt, Venice experienced a slump in Mediterranean trade during the 'first' 16th century. In the 'second' 16th century, however, the competitive position of Venice improved and there was 'a great revival of trade, especially in the eastern Mediterranean. The revival had already begun [by] about 1540 and was due in part to Portuguese weakness in Europe as well as Spain's crisis in the Netherlands until Dutch independence in 1581'.[53]

By the mid-16th century, Venice again became a hub in the global network, although not the leading centre (a role now enjoyed by Amsterdam). Like all ports, it faced two ways: towards the open sea and towards its hinterland. Venice links the Adriatic to the Po Valley, the Alpine passes and Germany. From its historic trading colonies in Constantinople, Aleppo, Cairo, Alexandria and Tripoli, Venice 'purchased spices, cottons, silks, precious stones and other goods, and sold off woollen textiles, paper, metal products, glass, soap, sumptuous silk fabrics, and coarser English or Dutch cloth. Venice was also a conduit for silver specie towards the Middle East, for its commerce with the Levant was always in deficit.'[54] To correct this imbalance, and in accordance with the practice of mercantilism, Venice 'unilaterally declared a monopoly over trade in the Adriatic sea, and obliged ships trading there to bring their cargoes to the lagoon'.[55] Venice's Adriatic rivals complied since they 'needed the city's insurance brokers, cheap credit, abundant specie, and its transit facilities to markets beyond the lagoon. Venetian ships assuring this commerce then re-exported these products and others throughout the western Mediterranean and the North Sea.'[56] Through its adherence to the tenets of mercantilism, Venice was able to maintain a favourable balance of trade between the lagoon and northern Europe until the early 17th century.

Although Venice continued to be the major trading city of the peninsula throughout much of the cinquecento, Genoese trade was hardly less dynamic. Squeezed out of the Levant by Venice, Genoese merchants (employing vessels of more than 1,000 tons) consolidated trading links with Iberia, the Atlantic coast and the North Sea – exporting cargoes to Antwerp and London and importing woollen textiles from Flanders, France and England. 'They soon [also] controlled the market for American products like sugar, hides, drugs and cochineal.'[57]

Florentine merchants were equally familiar figures in Iberian and northern European cities such as Antwerp in the late 16th century, travelling as far as Poland selling their luxury fabrics in return for grain. They also helped establish the banking sector and stock exchange in Lyons as a means of improving trade with central France. Although the silting up of the Arno below Pisa temporarily deprived Florence of a natural port, the 'Medici developed Livorno just south of the Arno's mouth . . . [and subsequently] linked it to Florence via a barge canal to Pisa.'[58]

The Price Revolution and Italian Banking

In the 1470s, after nearly a century of equilibrium, prices began to rise and were destined to continue to do so until the end of the 16th century – the longest price revolution in modern history.[59] Prices then dipped in Italy, southern France and Spain, though they continued to rise in northern Europe until 1650.[60] With prices rising by an average of only 1 per cent per annum throughout the 16th century, the annual rate of inflation throughout this revolution was very moderate by modern standards. But 'the most remarkable feature of the Price Revolution was not the pace at which prices rose, but the fact that a rising trend was sustained for so long'.[61] Many historians cite population growth as the prime mover of the price revolution since the supply of material resources was subject to an increasing level of demand. 'The upward economic swing beginning circa 1450 created a buzzing prosperity first of all in the old centres of trade, in what has been called the dorsal spine of Europe – Flanders, Southern Germany, northern Italy – and, of course, as a result of the discoveries, Spain.'[62]

Rising prices had little effect on the standard of living of artisans and labourers. Until the mid-16th century, wages increased more or less at the same rate as the cost of food and shelter – sometimes producing a feeling of prosperity, but with the rising cost of public expenditure (especially on wars), governments throughout much of Europe incurred fiscal deficits. Regressive taxation and the unwillingness of governments to tax the rich compounded the effects of high public expenditure. In response, governments resorted to large-scale borrowing which, together with taxation, encouraged currency debasement that fuelled inflation further.

With rising prices during late 15th and early 16th centuries, and with heavy state spending, the demand for bullion in the Mediterranean soon exceeded supply. The Sudan, the region's main source of gold, reduced the flow of gold to Italy, southern France and Spain, possibly to redirect supply to the new Portuguese trading colonies on the west coast of Africa. Since the Genoese in Spain were not only Spain's bankers but also the purchasers of gold on Spain's behalf, the reduced availability of gold not only seriously impaired their financial activities, but reduced the outflow of banking profits to Italy. It was probably not feasible for the Genoese to have obtained gold from Portugal, since as the leading country in exploration Portugal would have charged a price for gold that would have left little or no room for profit for Genoese bankers selling it on to Spain.[63]

Notwithstanding the demise of Florence as the financial centre, confidence in banking did not diminish. In the 16th century, inflation – stoked by a substantial inflow of silver from the Potosi mines in Spanish Bolivia after 1560 – encouraged individuals 'to keep most of their assets active in order to avoid them losing value over time'.[64] Bankers thus borrowed coin and paid interest on it – a practice known as usury that was condemned but normally tolerated by the Catholic Church. People also needed credit on occasion and sometimes paid dearly for it in the form of very high interest rates, for example of up to 50 per cent per annum.

Unlike usurers, in accepting deposits public bankers funded the activities of the state. They lent money to governments (often at interest rates determined collectively among creditors) to meet the cost of their wars and buildings. 'Public banks multiplied after 1580, when the *Banco di San Giorgio* in Genoa resumed common banking functions. Between 1587 and 1593 others appeared in . . . Venice, Milan, Rome and Naples.'[65] Banks also purchased state assets auctioned off by the government for periods of up to nine years. The papal government similarly borrowed from public bankers by issuing bonds that yielded interest paid out of general tax revenues. Banks or syndicates of bankers also bought papal shares, or *luoghi di monte*. After being distributed retail, these provided their recipients with rising or falling values according to the laws of supply and demand. 'These developments constituted a revolution in the sixteenth-century money markets, as states learned to use credit on an unprecedented scale.'[66]

Clearly, both banking profits and smuggled coin were diffused throughout much of Italy. However, although this injection into the circular flow of money produced vast new wealth in much of the peninsula, the 'limits of the system lay in the strategic overreach of the Catholic king [Philip II], whose wars against numerous enemies required him to draw upon credit as never before.'[67] Despite Spanish bankruptcy in 1559 that substantially disrupted the activities of Italian banking houses, banking activity soon recovered. Extending credit to the king of Spain, the papacy and other states proved irresistible because of the comparatively high rates of interest they were willing to pay. By the late 16th century, because of inflated interest charges, manufacturing industry and trade were largely priced out of the credit market with serious long-term consequences for the economy of Italian states.

The Italian Wars and Economic Development

The long struggles between France and Spain between 1494 and 1559 to achieve dominance over much of Italy were motivated by desire to absorb the 'northern Italian city-states [that] had been in the late Middle Ages the centres of the most "advanced" economic activities, industrial and commercial, on the European continent'.[68] Although long-distance trade was no longer monopolised by these states, they had accumulated a substantial volume of capital and experience that predatory empire-builders sought to secure.[69] The city-states in question are situated in 'a narrow urban quadrilateral, Venice, Milan, Genoa, Florence, with their discordances, their multiple rivalries, each city having a somewhat different weight'.[70] The political problem for the majority of these states was that while they had emancipated themselves from feudal interference in the distant past, they needed to resist the threat of more centralised political control emanating from France.[71] It is possible that the Italian states welcomed absorption into the Holy Roman Empire under the Habsburgs since this not only rendered them immune from French territorial ambitions, but also integrated them yet further into the world economy. 'Within such a framework, the linkup of the city-states and the empire was [thus] primarily a "marriage of interests"'.[72]

Imperialism in 16th-century Italy involved not only military conquest but also 'compensation for the forfeiture of political independence by the Italian republics . . . a necessity, rendered especially urgent in the case of Genoa, whose citizens were eager to repair losses caused by the contraction of Levantine trade'.[73] Through her possessions in the New World and later in Flanders, Spain was amply resourced to provide compensation of this sort, facilitating a 'marriage of interests, the Spanish crown battening politically upon Italy, Italian businessmen battening economically upon Spain'.[74] Despite manufacturing industry, trade and banking contributing substantially to economic growth, arguably 'the main spur to the Italian economy [both within and outside the Empire] came from central government, whose powers and authority grew rapidly in most states from the mid-sixteenth century'.[75] Only the state could undertake vast schemes to develop the infrastructure, for example – within the Empire – the Grand Duke of Tuscany, Ferdinand I, facilitated the conversion of the small fishing village of Livorno after 1592 into a large port with a population in excess of 10,000, while – outside the Empire – the Venetian Senate funded the drainage of extensive areas of marshland around Padua.

Boom and Bust at the Century's End

The increased stability of the Italian states after 1530 was in large part attributable to growing prosperity, while with greater wealth-creation 'law replaced violence as the normal means of settling disputes between subjects, and revolts against the government were few'.[76] The latter part of the century was without doubt 'a period of economic expansion and optimism in Italy . . . The growth of maritime trade and the great voyages of discovery had given an impetus to the European economy as a whole, as had the price revolution.'[77]

Nevertheless, despite this prosperous and orderly facade, the well-being of the Italian economy – within a context of inflation – was structurally fragile. The price revolution that had commenced in the late 15th century was associated in the late 16th century with an increased flow of silver into Europe – imports of silver from the Americas rising 'from approximately 10,000 tons in 1550 to more than 23,000 tons in 1600'.[78] Although the import of silver (and gold) did not itself cause the price revolution (since prices had started to rise as early as 1480), it nevertheless supported an existing trend and intensified its effect.[79]

Undoubtedly, inflation stimulated economic growth, but since there was no shortage of labour in the late cinquecento wages lagged behind the rising cost of living, and real wages fell sharply. By 1570 real wages were less than half of what they had been before the price revolution.[80] Whereas landless labourers were the real victims of inflation, landlords and capitalists tended to do better. 'Returns to capital kept pace with commodity prices and even leapt ahead in some decades of the [late] sixteenth century . . . Returns to landlords also increased during the price revolution. A landlord who was secure in the possession of his property held many private remedies in his own hands [for example] he could raise the rent. During [the latter part of] the sixteenth century, rents and land prices rose even more rapidly than food and fuel.'[81] In a society that was already unequal, this was associated with widespread and largely uncontrolled property speculation and a building boom in cities such as Rome, Venice, Milan and Naples with their churches, palaces and villas.[82] These trends caused inequality to grow still further, increased the political power of the rich, and led to regressive taxation and a reduction in government revenues.

It was ironic that although '[l]eadership in economic matters passed slowly from the Mediterranean to the north . . . as the Italian cities declined [and those of the Netherlands rose] there was little in the way of business or industrial technique in use in the northern economies that would have been unfamiliar to a Venetian merchant or a Florentine clothier of the fifteenth century'.[83] However, during the final years of the 16th century, both Mediterranean and northern Europe faced a major downturn in their economic fortunes. The price revolution had 'entered a new stage during the 1590s – a prolonged and very painful period'[84] – that continued well into the 17th century. This eventually became 'the darkest era in European history after the catastrophe of the fourteenth century . . . Real wages and industrial prices were depressed, while the cost of food and fuel climbed higher ... The real wages of artisans and labourers fell farther behind the cost of living, while returns to land and capital continued to advance. Wealth became increasingly concentrated in a few hands.'[85]

The social and indirect economic consequences were profound. Although the rich grew richer and an increasing number of the poor grew poorer – to the point of starvation – there was simultaneously a major change in the economic activities of the bourgeoisie. Merchant entrepreneurs, the mainstay of the Italian economy for centuries, were now turning away from their traditional economic activities and adopting an aristocratic lifestyle. A new elite were transferring their money from trade and industry to land. 'The new Florentine elite lived on rent and patronage at the ducal court',[86] while in Venice former merchant entrepreneurs accelerated an existing trend by turning more and more to agriculture, and the development of real estate in the *terraferma*.

Although the reasons for the economic decline of Italy in the late 16th century are not clear – it has been suggested that the shift in the axis of world trade to the Atlantic, the historic power of the guilds and the controls that they set on pay and work practices, plus the narrowness of Italy's home market were all contributory factors – 'the extreme concentrations of wealth in the hands of an elite that preferred to invest in art and palaces rather than industry'[87] unquestionably played an important part. While it is probable that to an extent capital would have been invested in land efficiently (at least in direct terms), its indirect effects on the urban economy – at a time of population expansion – were far from positive.

Urban Development Outside Rome

To the north and south of the Eternal City, an amalgam of beneficial and detrimental economic factors determined the timing and magnitude of urban development (fluctuations in public policy also had a major impact; see chapter 8). Within an economic context, the construction of a large number of secular and ecclesiastical buildings in the 16th century was essentially an outcome of an increase in wealth attributed to industrial development and expanded trade, and the availability of credit – albeit at high rates of interest. However, building activity would, from time to time, have been constrained by war, and by economic recession in the final years of the century. Throughout much of the cinquecento, however, there was a tendency among secular patrons to indulge in conspicuous consumption. A substantial number of sumptuous *palazzi* and villas were constructed to meet this demand, exemplified by the Pallazo Vendramin-Calergi (1509) in Venice, the *palazzi* of the Strada Nuova (1558) in Genoa, the Palazzo Marino (1557) in Milan, and the Palazzo Giusso (1549) in Naples.

In addition, and as in previous centuries, economic growth and its corollary wealth-creation enabled both secular patrons and religious orders to commission new ecclesiastical buildings and their like, most notably in Venice (for example the church of S Giorgio Maggiore, 1579) and in Naples where a plethora of churches were funded by the religious orders.

Apart from dramatically altering the face of the major cities, increased wealth also had an impact on the development of prominent secular buildings in the many smaller cities of the peninsula such as Padua, Vicenza, Verona, Mantua, Bologna, Montepulciano and Palermo. Among the smaller cities, comparatively few ecclesiastical buildings were funded from private donations, though in Todi, Montepulciano and Lecce some influential and remarkable church architecture emerged.

Conclusion

Throughout Italy, economic and population growth in much of the cinquecento stimulated the construction of grandiose *palazzi* and magnificent churches, but during the latter years of the century a declining economy had an adverse effect on urban development throughout the peninsula. However, private investors often diverted their capital from trade and industry to land and buildings, particularly in the Venetian *terraferma* where there was a seemingly insatiable demand for villas and *palazzi*, particularly those designed by Andrea Palladio (table 12.3).

Table 12.3   Venetian *terraferma*: principal Palladian villas and *palazzi*

Villas	Location	*Palazzi*	Location
Godi, 1537–42	Lonedo		
Piovene, *c* 1539–40	Lonedo		
Forni-Cerato, *c* 1540–5	Montecchio		
Gazzotti-Marcello, early 1540s	Bertesini		
Pisani, after 1542	Bagnola	Thiene, after 1542	Vicenza
Thiene, mid-1540s	Quinto		
Saraceno, mid-1540s	Finale		

Table 12.3 Continued

Villas	Location	*Palazzi*	Location
Poiana, late 1540s	Poiana Maggiore	Iseppo Porto, late 1540s	Vicenza
Caldogno, 1548–9	Caldogno		
Cornaro, 1551–4	Piombino Dese	Chiericati, 1550	Vicenza
Pisani, *c* 1552–5	Montagnana		
Chiericati, mid-1550s	Vancimuglio		
Badoer, after 1556	Frata Polescine	Antonini, 1556	Udine
Barbaro, 1557–8	Maser		
Foscari, 1559–60	Malcontenta		
Valmarana, 1563–4	Lisiera		
Emo, *c* 1564	Fanzola	Valmarana, 1565–6	Vicenza
Zeno, before 1566	Cassalto	Schio-Angaran, before 1566	Vicenza
Rotonda, 1566–70	Vicenza		
Sarego, *c* 1568–9	S Sofia	Barbaran, 1570–1	Vicenza
		Porto-Breganze, 1570s	Vicenza

Source: JS Ackerman, *Palladio* (Harmondsworth: Penguin, 1966).

Clearly, the extensive development of villas was deemed a more prudent form of investment than financial support for the declining mercantile activities of Venice. Partly because of this diversion of funds, Venice never fully recovered its supreme role as the economic power-house of much of Italy and the Adriatic.

Chronology

1500	Population of Italy reaches 10 million (Naples has around 150,000 inhabitants, Milan and Venice both have around 100,000, Florence 70,000, Genoa 60,000 and Rome 55,000). Despite persistent pestilence and food crises, population growth throughout much of the 16th century conducive to long-term economic growth. Prices rise gradually throughout the century.
1502	**In Rome, King Ferdinand and Queen Isabella of Spain commission construction of Tempietto of S Pietro in Montorio. Beginning of High Renaissance.**
1505	**In Rome, Siennese banker Agostino Chigi funds construction of choir of S Maria del Popolo.**

	Tifo (typhoid or typhus) outbreaks strike numerous cities.
1508	Agostino Chigi commissions Villa Chigi (later known as Villa Farnesina).
1509	In Todi, work begins on church of S Maria della Consolazione.
	In Venice, work is completed on Palazzo Vendramin Calergi.
1515	In Venice, work begins on construction of Scuola Grande di S Rocco.
1517	In Rome, Cardinal Alessandro Farnese commissions Palazzo Farnese.
	In Florence, work begins on construction of Palazzo Panolfini.
1518	In Montepulciano, work commences on church of Madonna di S Biagio.
1520s	Food crisis drives up infant mortality.
1522–8	Pestilence devastates most of Italy.
1524	In Mantua, work starts on Loggia Cornaro and Odeon.
1525	In Padua, Palazzo Te commissioned by Federigo II Gonzaga.
	In Bologna, work begins on Palazzo Fantuzzi.
1527	Sack of Rome by imperial forces. Thereafter, papacy attempts to make Rome capital of Catholic world. Large-scale economic in-migration takes place and number of pilgrims escalates.
1528	In Naples, work starts on Palazzo Tappia.
	Tifo recurs.
1529	Advent of peace in wake of Treaty of Cambrai conducive to population increase (despite recurring food crises and pestilence), economic growth and construction activity.
1530	In Venice, Grimani family commissions church of S Francesco della Vigna.
	In Verona, work begins on Palazzo Bevilacqua.
	In Montepulciano, work starts on Palazzo Tarugi.
1532	In Rome, Massimo family commissions Palazzo Massimo alle Colonne.
	In Verona, work begins on Palazzo Canossa.
1535	In Venice, work commences on Scuola Grande della Misericordia.
1537–74	Cosimo I regulates quality, prices and distribution of Tuscan goods.
1538	In Venice, work starts on construction of Palazzo Dolfin-Manin.
1540	In Rome, Cardinal Ricci of Montepulciano commissions Villa Ricci (known as Villa Medici when acquired by Cardinal Fernando de'Medici in 1576).
1542–3	In Vicenza, work begins on Palazzo Thiene and Palazzo Porto.
1547	In Milan, work commences on reconstruction of Villa Simonetta.
1548	In Rome, Cardinal Capodiferro commissions Palazzo Spada.
	In Vicenza, work begins on Palazzo Iseppo.
1549	In Naples, work starts on Palazzo Giusso.
	In Lecce, Celestine nuns commission church of S Croce.

	Food crisis sparks increase in infant mortality.
1550	Population of Italy reaches 11 million.
1550–1620/40	Industrial activity in Europe increasingly concentrated in northwestern Europe, ultimately to the disadvantage of many Italian cities.
	In Italy, the second half of 16th century proves a period of economic expansion. Venice benefits from Portuguese weakness in Europe, and Spain's crisis in the Netherlands (until 1590).
1551–2	**In Palermo, work commences on Palazzo Castrone-S Ninfa.**
1551	Food crisis and soaring infant mortality.
	In Bologna, work begins on Palazzo Bentivoglio.
	In Vicenza, work commences on Palazzo Chiericati.
1555	**In Verona, work starts on Palazzo Pompei.**
1557	Genose banking begins long period of success under Doria, Grimaldi, Spinola and Pallavicino families.
	In Milan, work starts on construction of Palazzo Marino.
1558	**In Genoa, work begins on development of *palazzi* on Strada Nuova.**
1559	Treaty of Cateau-Cambrésis; role of Rome, Milan, Florence and Naples as capital cities strengthened benefiting their economies. Venice and Genoa also enhance their economic strength. Cities such as Siena, Pisa, Perugia, Rimini, Brescia and Bergamo decline in political and economic importance. Bankruptcy of the kingdom of Spain disrupts Italian banking system.
	In Naples, work begins on Palazzo Carafa di Montorio.
1560	Beginning of inflow of silver from Potosi mines of Bolivia stokes inflation throughout rest of century.
	In Rome, Tommaso del Giglio commissions Palazzo Giglio (renamed Palazzo Borghese in 1596).
1566	**In Vicenza, work commences on Palazzo Valmarana.**
1568	**In Rome, Cardinal Alessandro Farnese II commissions church of Il Gesù.**
1570s	Florence sees record output of woollen cloth. Half the city's population of 60,000 draws an income from it.
1575	**In Lecce, Jesuits commission the Gesù.**
1575–7	Venetia, Lombardy and Sicily stricken by plague.
1576	**In Lecce, Dominicans commission church of S Domenico.**
1579	**In Venice, Benedictines commission church of S Giorgio Maggiore.**
1580–93	In Genoa, Venice, Milan, Rome and Naples public banks established.
1582	**In Naples, work begins on Palazzo Maddaloni.**
1590s	Food crises drive up infant mortality.
	In Lecce, Theatines commission church of S Irene.
1590–1	*Tifo* outbreaks recur.
	Beginnings of Europe-wide economic slump. Italy unaffected until 1619–22.

1592	Development of Livorno as large port advantages Florentine trade. **In Venice, work starts on Scuola di S Fantin.**
1600	Population of Italy reaches 12 million (Naples has around 238,000 inhabitants; Venice, 143,000 inhabitants; Milan, 108,000; Rome, 99,000; and Florence, 79,000). Italy the most densely populated region of Europe with 44 people per square kilometre; Venice probably the most industrialised European city: 10,000 people are employed in its textile industry; Venetian Arsenale with 4,000 workers is largest industrial complex in Italy.

Notes

1 L Martines, *Power and Imagination. City-States in Renaissance Italy* (London: Pimlico, 2002), p 169.
2 Ibid.
3 CF Black, *Early Modern Italy, A Social History* (London: Routledge, 2001), p 21.
4 Ibid, pp 21–2.
5 Ibid, p 22.
6 Black, *Early Modern Italy*, p 21.
7 C Duggan, *A Concise History of Italy* (Cambridge: Cambridge University Press, 1984), p 66.
8 Black, *Early Modern Italy*, p 24.
9 Ibid.
10 Ibid, p 20.
11 Ibid, p 26.
12 Ibid.
13 Ibid.
14 Ibid.
15 Ibid.
16 Ibid.
17 Ibid.
18 Ibid.
19 Ibid.
20 Black, *Early Modern Italy*, p 32.
21 Ibid, p 34.
22 I Wallerstein, *The Modern World System, Capitalist Agriculture and the Origins of the European World-Economy in the Sixteenth Century* (New York and London: Academic Press, 1974), p 156.
23 G Hanlon, *Early Modern Italy, 1550–1800* (Basingstoke: Macmillan, 2000), p 81; C Cipolla, 'The decline of Italy. The case of a fully matured economy', *Economic History Review* (1952), pp 178–87.
24 Hanlon, *Early Modern Italy*, pp 81–3.
25 C Cipolla, 'The Economic Decline of Italy', in B Pullan (ed), *Crisis and Change in the Venetian Economy in the Sixteenth and Seventeenth Centuries* (London: Methuen, 1968), pp 139–40. See also Wallerstein, *Modern World System*, p 81.

26 Wallerstein, *Modern World System*, p 81. See also D Sella, 'Les mouvements longs de l'industrie lainière à Venise aux XVIe et XVIIe siècles', *Annales E.S.R.* 12 (1) (Jan–March 1957), pp 40–5.

27 Wallerstein, *Modern World System*, pp 123–4.

28 Ibid, p 123.

29 M Malowist, 'The Economic and Social Development of the Baltic Countries from the 15th to the 17th Centuries', *Economic History Review* 12 (2), 2nd series (1959), p 178.

30 Hanlon, *Early Modern Italy*, p 84.

31 Ibid, p 83.

32 Ibid, p 82.

33 Ibid, pp 82–3.

34 JH Elliott, *Europe Divided, 1559–1598* (New York: Harper, 1968), pp 58–9.

35 Hanlon, *Early Modern Italy*, p 83.

36 Ibid. See also F Braudel, *Civilization and Capitalism, 15th–18th Centuries*, Vol 1: *Structures of Everyday Life* (London: 1982), p 380.

37 Hanlon, *Early Modern Italy*, p 84.

38 Ibid, p 85.

39 Ibid.

40 Ibid, p 86.

41 Wallerstein, *Modern World System*, p 67.

42 Ibid, p 68.

43 F Braudel, 'Qu'est-ce que le XVIe siècle?', *Annales E.S.C.* 8 (1) (Jan–March 1953), p 73.

44 Wallerstein, *Modern World System*, p 68.

45 Ibid, p 129.

46 Ibid, p 165.

47 Sella, 'Les mouvements', p 64.

48 Wallerstein, *Modern World System*, pp 225–6.

49 JU Nef, *War and Human Progress* (New York: Norton, 1963), pp 6–7.

50 Wallerstein, *Modern World System*, pp 230–1.

51 Hanlon, *Early Modern Italy*, p 77.

52 Ibid.

53 Wallerstein, *Modern World* System, pp 215–16.

54 Hanlon, *Early Modern Italy*, p 78.

55 Ibid.

56 Ibid.

57 Ibid, p 80.

58 Ibid.

59 D Hackett Fischer, *The Great Wave. Price Revolutions and the Rhythm of History* (Oxford: Oxford University Press, 1996), p 70.

60 F Braudel, 'European Expansion and Capitalism, 1450–1650', in F Braudel (ed), *Chapters in Western Civilization*, 3rd edn (Columbia: Columbia University Press, 1961), p 263. See also Wallerstein, *Modern World System*, p 70.

61 Hackett Fischer, *The Great Wave*, p 70.

62 Wallerstein, *Modern World System*, p 165.
63 Ibid, p 169.
64 Hanlon, *Early Modern Italy*, p 87.
65 Ibid, p 88.
66 Ibid. See also L Pezzola, 'Elogia della rendita. Sul debito pubblico degli stati italiana nel Cinque e Seicento', *Revista di Storia Economica* 12 (1995), pp 283–328.
67 Hanlon, *Early Modern Italy*, p 90.
68 Wallerstein, *Modern World System*, pp 171–3. See also G Luzzatto, *Storia economica dell'età moderna e contemporanea*. Pt 1: *L'età moderna* (Padua: CEDAM, 1955), p 36; P Coles, 'The Crisis in Renaissance Society: Genoa 1448–1507', *Past and Present* (1957), p 41.
69 Wallerstein, *Modern World System*, pp 171–2.
70 Braudel, *La Méditerranée*, p 354.
71 H Pirenne, *Early Democracies in the Low Countries* (New York: Norton, 1971), p 183.
72 Wallerstein, *Modern World System*, pp 172–3
73 Coles, 'Crisis', p 41.
74 Ibid.
75 Duggan, *Concise History*, p 68.
76 Ibid.
77 V Lintner, *A Traveller's History of Italy*, 3rd edn (Gloucester: Windrush Press, 1989), p 123.
78 Hackett Fischer, *The Great Wave*, p 81.
79 Ibid, pp 82–3.
80 Ibid, pp 76–8.
81 Ibid, p 77.
82 Lintner, *Traveller's History*, pp 123–4.
83 CH Wilson, 'Trade, Society and the State', *Cambridge Economic History of Europe* 4 (1967), p 490.
84 Hackett Fischer, *The Great Wave*, p 91.
85 Ibid, pp 91–2.
86 Duggan, *Concise History*, p 69.
87 Ibid.

CHAPTER 13

PRIVATE PATRONAGE AND ARCHITECTURE: AFFLUENCE AND CONSPICUOUS CONSUMPTION

Introduction

Population growth, further industrial development, the emergence of a world economy, the expansion of trade, the advance of banking and the end of the Italian Wars all generated economic growth throughout most of the cinquecento. Much of the increase in income that resulted was distributed in favour of merchants, bankers and the nobility who invariably indulged in the conspicuous consumption of new or refurbished buildings. In Rome, where urban development was on an altogether larger scale than anywhere else in Italy, a number of prosperous families (some of whose members were destined to become popes) were the major patrons of new *palazzi*, villas and churches. It was within this economic context that architects across Italy responded to demand and attempted either to perfect Classicism or to introduce a substantially different variant of the genre – subsequently known as Mannerism.

The Cities of Central and Northern Italy

Rome

Soon after arriving in Rome, and having already produced some remarkable church architecture in Milan, in 1499 Donato Bramante was employed by Cardinal Oliviero to prepare plans for the construction of cloisters in the church of S Maria della Pace. In what became one of his finest commissions, he overcame the restriction of the cramped site and the configuration of the existing church by designing a square cloister with each side containing four two-storey modules. On the arcaded and vaulted ground floor, the modules are demarcated – as in the Coliseum – by sturdy Doric piers with Ionic pilaster attachments, while on the upper storey, and of lesser height than the arcade, a colonnade and architrave are supported by Composite pilasters and Corinthian columns that are respectively above the piers of the lower floor and the keystones of the arcade, in the latter case demonstrating that it was possible at the same time to break with the

Photo 13.1   Donato Bramante, cloisters of the church of S Maria della Pace, Rome, 1499. The architect's first commission in Rome provided the blueprint for the use of classical orders in countless cinquecento buildings.

convention that there should be 'void over void, and solid over solid', and to construct a minor masterpiece.

While working on the cloisters of S Maria della Pace, Bramante was commissioned by King Ferdinand of Aragon and his wife Isabella of Castille in 1502 to design a chapel on the alleged site of St Peter's crucifixion. Ferdinand and Isabella had earlier bought the church of S Pietro in Montorio for the Franciscans and it was in its courtyard that the chapel, the diminutive Tempietto, was constructed. Built on a platform, its circular plan – a concept widely employed north of Rome – was the first to be adopted in the Eternal City for over a millennium. A model of perfection, the domed Tempietto of S Pietro in Montorio consists of a cylindrical, two-storey core. On the ground floor, and surrounding the *cella*, a circular colonnade bearing a classical entablature is supported at equidistance by 16 unfluted granite columns of the Tuscan Doric order, while above, a balustrade surrounds a high drum containing windows that are interspersed with alternating rectangular and semicircular niches. Not only did the design of the Tempietto preordain the early stages in the reconstruction of St Peter's, but it also 'capitivated and strongly influenced subsequent generations of architects',[1] not least because the building was lauded as an extremely authentic recreation from antiquity.

Like the cloisters of S Maria della Pace, Bramante's work on the choir of S Maria del Popolo had no direct impact on the urban landscape of Rome, but indirectly one of its innovative features influenced the facades of many buildings in Italy in the cinquecento. Commissioned by Julius II in *c* 1508 to add an oblong bay and an apse to the church's square chancel, Bramante built into the extended chancel a pair of 'Palladian' windows, as they later became known, the first of their kind in use anywhere in Italy or elsewhere and a notable feature widely incorporated into buildings later in the century and beyond. Julius II again employed Bramante on ecclesiastical work in 1507 when he was commissioned to produce plans for the church of S Maria di Loreto. Inevitably based on his Tempietto, Bramante adhered to a central plan, but the final appearance of the church was quite unlike that of S Pietro in Montorio. Its ground floor was square with a triumphal arch motif set in each of its external walls, and on each wall six Corinthian pilasters encased a central pedimented portal and its two adjacent niches. Since Antonio da Sangallo the Younger succeeded Bramante as architect-in-chief on the latter's death in 1514, it is possible that much of the ground-floor design is attributable to Sangallo, as it was not completed until 1534. What is clear, however, is that the octagonal drum and the gigantic dome of the building were designed by Jacopo Del Duca, an assistant of Michelangelo, although these were not completed until 1576 after his return to Sicily.

Photo 13.2 Donato Bramante, Tempietto, S Pietro in Montorio, Rome, 1502. The diminutive but exquisite temple set the scene for much Italian High Renaissance architecture.

In part, the reason it took so long to complete S Maria di Loreto, a comparatively small church, was the long-lasting repercussions of the Sack of Rome on construction activity. Thus, from the time of the sack (1527) until mid-century very few sizeable buildings were erected, St Peter's basilica being an exception. The first of any note to be constructed when conditions had ameliorated was the church of S Andrea sulla Via Flaminia. Commissioned by Julius III in 1551 and located on the pontiff's family estate beyond the northern edge of the Aurelian Wall, the church was designed by Jacopo Barozzi Vignola in 1551. The building, based on an adapted central plan, had an oblong interior and an oval dome, and was the first of many of this type that would follow in the 17th and 18th centuries.

Vignola's approach to ecclesiastical architecture changed dramatically during his later years (he died in 1573). Five years before his death he received a commission from Cardinal Alessandro Farnese III to complete the construction of Il Gesù, whose foundation stone had originally been laid in *c* 1550 by the founder of the Jesuit Order, St Ignatius Loyola.

By this time classical architecture of the early cinquecento was being superseded by church-building in the emerging Baroque more in keeping with the

Photo 13.3 Giacomo Barozzi Vignola, church of S Andrea sulla Via Flaminia, Rome, 1551. The earliest Renaissance building to have an oval-shaped dome, a prelude to the Baroque of the seicento.

Counter-Reformation. New churches in this style were intended – through their increasing exuberance – to attract and retain believers in the Catholic faith and to dispel incipient Protestantism. They were designed in compliance with the new liturgical requirements of the Council of Trent (1545–63), and in particular to satisfy the needs of the Jesuits as a preaching order (such as the need to facilitate audibility, to ensure that the high altar was visible to all, and to house a larger congregation). It is within this context that Cardinal Alessandro Farnese funded the completion of Il Gesù on behalf of the Jesuits. The new church – to an extent reminiscent of Alberti's S Andrea in Mantua (see chapter 7) – is aisleless with side chapels, is devoid of a transept, has a relatively wide nave to enhance audibility, an enormous barrel-vaulted ceiling, and is large enough to accommodate a substantial congregation with an uninterrupted view of the high altar.

However, since it also has a dome over the crossing, the church is not without an element of Bramantian centralisation. Although he had produced plans for the

Photo 13.4 Giacomo Barozzi Vignola, facade of the church of Il Gesù, Rome, 1568–84. The first of many Jesuit churches that, with its sumptuous style inspired by the Counter-Reformation, set the scene for countless stylistic imitations worldwide.

facade, Vignola was sacked in 1571, one year before his death. He had proposed that the facade should consist of two storeys, the lower storey screening what would otherwise have been the aisles, the upper storey screening the nave, but his proposal was rejected in favour of one submitted by Giacomo della Porta who modified Vignola's plan. The attributes of the lower storey – from the outer edges to the centre – consequently comprise, in total, four outer pairs of pilasters, two side doors with triangular pediments and tabernacle niches above and, culminating in the centre, two further pilasters and engaged columns framing the main portal which is surmounted by a segmental pediment with a cartouche above displaying the Jesuits' symbol. Above an entablature and a large central triangular pediment, the upper storey is notable for its volutes that lead from the sides to the taller central section and in turn exhibit four sets of double pilasters interspersed by two pedimented niches and a large pedimented central rectangular window. The central section of this storey is crowned by a massive triangular pediment. Embracing elements of classical and Baroque architecture, the massive church of Il Gesù has provided a model for church building throughout much of southern Europe, but the building's facade was also replicated in the Americas and parts of Asia where Jesuit missionaries spread the gospel.

Taking a lead from papal and other ecclesiastical projects, the prominent display of classical attributes in the design of private palaces and villas was a further development of the physical fabric of Rome in the cinquecento.[2] The innovator in this respect was Bramante, as demonstrated by his design of *c* 1510 for a palace for the Caprini family. Later known as the 'House of Raphael' because it was acquired by the papal architect-in-chief in 1517, the facade of the two-storey Palazzo Caprini was noted for its five bays, rusticated arches and encapsulated portals and shops on the ground floor; a mezzanine floor above containing alternating square and round openings; and, above that, a *piano nobile* dominated by pairs of Doric half-columns separated by balustrades and rectangular windows capped by triangular pediments.[3] Although the building was demolished in the 17th century, a structure that strongly resembles it still exists in the form of the Palazzo Vidoni-Caffarelli – a palace once attributed to

Photo 13.5 Palazzo Vidoni-Caffarelli, Rome, 1524. Attributed to an unknown architect, the edifice is the first extant example of a High Renaissance palace in Italy. In an evolved form, it had a major impact on the architecture of palaces throughout the peninsula in the cinquecento.

Raphael, but whose authorship is now unclear. Commissioned in 1524 for the use of Cardinal Geronimo Caffarelli, this broadly similar two-storey building also had five bays, a rusticated ground floor containing shops and coupled columns on the *piano nobile* (albeit of the Tuscan rather than Doric order), but it differed from the earlier palace in having rectangular rather than square and circular openings on the mezzanine, and no pediments above the windows of the *piano nobile*.[4] At a later stage, the Palazzo Vidoni-Caffarelli was extended and a third storey added to the original structure. The Palazzo Maccarani is the second most notable private palace to derive from the Bramante model. Designed by Giulio Romano in 1549, the building shares some of the features of its two antecedents. It has five bays, a rusticated ground floor and a mezzanine above. However, it is a three- rather than a two-storey building; it has a large oblong central portico with a pediment and thus only four bays are available for shops; it has coupled pilasters on the *piano nobile* instead of half-columns, and alternating triangular and segmental pediments above the rectangular windows on the *piano nobile*.[5] Although the original structure has not been substantially altered, it is currently in a very poor condition.

Photo 13.6 Baldassare Peruzzi, Palazzo Massimo alle Colonne, Rome, 1532. The first palace built in Rome in the Mannerist style, its unusual curved facade concealing two court-yards within.

An altogether different approach to palace-building was adopted by Baldassare Peruzzi when, in 1532, he was commissioned by the three Massimo brothers to reconstruct their former palace which had been damaged during the Sack of Rome five years earlier. On the instruction of the brothers, Peruzzi duly designed three buildings: the main palace for the elder brother, and palaces to the left and rear of the main building for the younger brothers. Located on a convex curve of what is now the Corso Vittorio Emanuele II, the corresponding curvature of the main four-storey, smoothly rusticated building is in itself unique in cinquecento Roman architecture. Also unique are its ground-floor colonnaded loggia open to the street, its oddly positioned ground-floor Doric columns that broadly align with the windows above, its two bays to left and right of the columns that contain windows framed by pilasters, its central portico that leads to the edge rather than the centre of its internal courtyard, its lack of columns above its ground-floor architrave, its heavy balconies and hooded rather than pedimented windows on the *piano nobile* that coincide with the inter-columnar spaces below, and its picture-frame windows inserted on its two upper floors. The facade of the palace to the left of the main building is broadly similar, except that it lacks a loggia at ground-floor level and its portico leads to the centre of its courtyard. Thus, the unique attributes of the Palazzo Massimo alle Colonne – Peruzzi's last work – demonstrate that Classicism could be 'replaced by a different conception of architectural beauty [since] the effect of the facade does not come from its harmonious balance, but from its wealth of contrasts'.[6] At the very least it could be argued that '[t]he facade of the Palazzo . . . is the best example in Rome of Mannerist architecture',[7] if not one of the best in Italy.

Whereas Peruzzi's masterpiece owes its preeminence to its unique style, the Palazzo Farnese was notable for its sheer size. The completed palace measures 74 by 58 metres (242×190 ft) and, until the 19th century when it became the French embassy, it was the largest privately owned urban building in Italy. Only the Vatican Palace, the Palazzo Venezia and the Palazzo della Cancelleria were larger but these were not in private hands.[8] The Palazzo Farnese is partly built on a site previously occupied by the Palazzo Albergati-Ferriz, in an up-and-coming area favoured by the wealthy and powerful, and with its rear elevation adjacent to the newly constructed Via Giulia on the east bank of the Tiber. The Palazzo Albergati-Ferriz was bought by Cardinal Alessandro Farnese in 1493, and over the following decades he gradually acquired neighbouring properties to facilitate large-scale redevelopment. Eventually, in 1514–15, Antonio da Sangallo the Younger was commissioned to begin work on the new palace, but progress was slow due to the immense cost involved, the disruption caused by the Sack of Rome in 1527 and the effects of famine in 1530.

Photo 13.7 Antonio da Sangallo, Michelangelo Buonarroti and others, Palazzo Farnese, Rome, begun 1514. Occupying the whole of the western side of the Piazza Farnese, this enormous three-storey palace exhibits harmony and proportion.

Following Alessandro's election as pope in 1534, his accommodation require-ments increased and a new plan was produced by Sangallo in 1540 to double the size of the palace. The eventual outcome was a three-storey rectangular building on an island site with its front facade overlooking a *piazza*. Although its facades are mainly of brick, except for decorative stonework, the building boasts a range of classical features. At ground-floor level, it has a large rusticated central portal capped by voussoirs and leading to a central square courtyard, and six large rectangular windows either side of the entrance capped by hoods supported by half-columns. On the *piano nobile* there is a row of 13 rectangular windows, of which 12 are capped by alternating triangular and segmental pediments, while one – the central window – is inserted below an entablature and an enormous family crest. Each window is encased by half-columns except for the majestic central window that boasts two on each of its sides and two frontal three-quarter columns. A balustrade in front of the central window surmounts the central portal. On the upper storey, designed by Michelangelo after the death of Sangallo in 1546, a further row of 13 rectangular windows is capped by triangular pediments and encased by half-columns, and the whole building is crowned with a massive cornice. Although the ground floor of the Palazzo Farnese initially contained shops in the Roman manner, its eschews both the Roman order of columns and pilasters and the extensive use of Florentine rustication. Nevertheless, '[w]ith its uninterrupted mouldings and [its] long row of identical openings' it is more in the tradition of the Medici, Pitti or Strozzi *palazzi* than any other building in Rome.[9]

If the Palazzo Farnese cannot be said to be truly Roman, the Palazzo Spada is unlike any other extant 16th-century building in the whole of Italy. Based possibly on the long-demolished Palazzo Branconio of Raphael, the Palazzo Spada was commissioned by Cardinal Girolamo Capodiferro in 1548 and designed by Giulio Merisi da Caravaggio.[10] The building, free-standing on three sides and four storeys in height, had neither shops on its ground floor nor orders on its facade, and displays extraordinary stucco decoration on the *piano nobile* of the facade.[11] Acquired by Cardinal Bernardo Spada in 1632, and subsequently partly rebuilt by Francesco Borromini, the *palazzo* remains a remarkable example of Mannerism in Roman architecture.[12]

Although such palaces as the Massimo alle Colonne and the Spada broke away from the classical mode, antique design continued to stamp its mark on the development of private *palazzi* throughout the cinquecento and beyond. Such is the case of the Palazzo Borghese. Known originally as the Palazzo Giglio, since it was commissioned by Tommaso del Giglio in 1560, the original palace was designed by Giacomo Barozzi da Vignola and showed a marked similarity to the Palazzo Farnese. With three storeys, the first floor of the building has six rectangular unpedimented windows either side of a twin-columned and entablatured portico, the *piano nobile* boasts 13 rectangular windows of shorter height capped by triangular pediments, and the top floor has 13 small and unpedimented windows. The central window of the *piano nobile* is particularly notable since it overlooks a protruding balustrade and – set within a blind arch – is framed by flanking pilasters and a massive pediment. Unlike the Palazzo Farnese, small horizontal openings have been built into the facade above the windows on the first floor and *piano nobile* to provide extra light and ventilation but, like its predecessor, the Palazzo Borghese is crowned by an overhanging cornice. Following the death of Vignola in 1573, work on the palace was continued by Martino Longhi the Elder under the new owner, Count Pietro Dazza, and in 1596 the building became the personal property of Cardinal Camillo Borghese, who nine years later became Pope Paul V. Under his ownership, and under the direction first of the Milanese architect Flaminio Onzio and then of Carlo Maderno, the palace was extended

Photo 13.8 Giacomo Barozzi da Vignola and others, Palazzo Borghese, Rome, begun 1560. Taking on the shape of a harpsichord during the later stage of its construction, the facade of the palace is otherwise little different from others of the period.

westwards at an obtuse angle towards the Tiber where its river frontage, at 90 degrees to the principal facade, incorporates a ground-floor loggia and balconies above, the entire edifice reaching completion in 1614.

But palaces were not alone in symbolising the wealth of the new breed of patrons. Suburban villas also served this purpose and had a marked impact on the built environment of Rome. The first of many is the Villa Chigi, a two-storey edifice constructed on the western bank of the Tiber outside the city walls and situated on the Via Liguria that linked the Vatican with the Trastevere. Commissioned by the enormously wealthy Siennese banker Agostino Chigi in 1508 and designed by his compatriot Peruzzi, the building acted like all other *ville suburbane* and was both a symbol of affluence and a place where its owner could retire for a day's pleasure, in this case from the long-since demolished Palazzo Chigi east of the Tiber. The Villa Chigi is essentially a two-storey, free-standing building with the northern and eastern (or river) sides of its ground floor initially left open as loggias. It has a U-shaped plan with Doric pilasters, rectangular

Photo 13.9 Baldassare Peruzzi, Villa Farnesina, Rome, 1508. The first of several Renaissance suburban villas, the U shaped porticoed building – designed for the gratification of a prominent banker – later became a retreat for the Farnese family.

windows on both of its main floors (an innovation in Rome), pilastered attics above each wing, and – the finishing touch – its facade was decoratively painted rather than stuccoed or left bare. The villa, which arguably 'stands beside Bramante's works as the most important building of the first decade of the [16th] century',[13] became famous or, rather, infamous, for enabling Agostino to entertain his prosperous clients and influential friends lavishly in a countrified setting. After Chigi's death in 1520, the palace remained empty and fell into disrepair after being plundered during the Sack of Rome. It was eventually renovated and renamed the Villa Farnesina when the building was acquired by Cardinal Alessandro II Farnese in 1581. In the 17th century its appearance was modified, but not necessarily enhanced, by the removal of the loggia on the river side of the building.

Dating from many years after the construction of the Villa Farnesina, but before its restoration, the Villa Giulia is a further example of a *villa suburbana* built as a summer retreat for its patron. Commissioned by Giovanni del Monte on

Photo 13.10 Giacomo Barozzi da Vignola and others, Villa Giulia, Rome, 1550. The modest facade of the second of the great Roman surburban villas belies the very great beauty of the garden side of the development with its many interesting features from antiquity.

his election to the papacy as Julius III in 1550, the modest five-room villa was built on his family's estate on the edge of Rome, north of the Aurelian Walls. Designed mainly by Vignola under the artistic supervision of Michelangelo, and assisted by Bartolomeo Ammanati and Giorgio Vasari, the building is in the Mannerist style and consists of the villa itself, or Casino, and two interconnected walled gardens. With its two storeys, the Casino is notable for its austere rectangular facade, which is dominated at ground-floor level by a rusticated triumphal arch and two smaller side arches in its central bays – with flanking brick walls and rectangular rusticated windows at the sides (the *piano nobile* has fewer external attributes). The five bays of the facade are elegantly demarcated by pilasters, Doric at ground-floor level and Composite above. Through the triumphal arch, an entrance leads into an atrium and thence to the rear of the building whose facade, in marked contrast, is semi-circular with a colonnade at ground-floor level and smooth panelled surfaces and rectangular windows above, interrupted only by the repetition of the triumphal arch motif and side arches at the centre. In contrast to the front facade, Ionic columns are employed at ground-floor level while Composite pilasters are used on the *piano nobile*. Beyond the colonnade, the oblong site is subdivided into walled garden, a loggia and a nymphaeum with a further enclosed garden beyond.

Surpassing both the Villa Farnesina and Villa Giulia in architectural elegance, the twin-towered Villa Medici is the most majestic *villa suburbana* in Rome. In

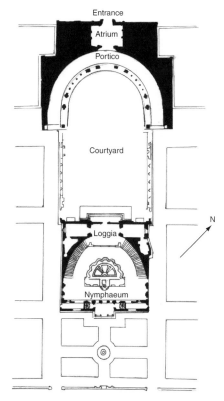

Figure 13.1 Villa Giulia, Rome

contrast to its rather plain facade that overlooks Rome from the Pincio above the Piazza di Spagna, its rear elevation with its two wings is highly ornamented and provides a stunning backdrop to its magnificent formal garden. Commissioned by Cardinal Ricci of Montepulciano and designed by Nanni di Baccio Bigio (Giovanni di Bartolomeo Lippi), his son Annibale Lippi and Bartolomeo Ammanati over the period 1540 to 1585, the property was eventually acquired by Cardinal Federico de'Medici who concentrated on developing the garden and collecting and displaying an extensive array of antique sculptures.

Venice

With peace in northern Italy secured by the Treaty of Cambrai in 1529, resources became available for construction activity throughout the region, and for the remainder of the cinquecento the late-medieval and Early Renaissance practice

Photo 13.11 Nanni di Baccio Bigio and others, Villa Medici, Rome, 1540–85. Although its enormous facade on the Viale Trinità del Monte is relatively austere, the garden front with its two wings is highly ornamented and noteworthy for its many classical sculptures.

of patrician families commissioning *palazzi* continued. Increased prosperity also brought a much greater use of sandstone in construction, rather than traditional Venetian brick.

Of the many palaces developed along the Grand Canal, the *palazzi* Vendramin Calergi, Dolfin-Manin, Corner Ca' Grande and Grimani are probably the most notable. The first is often singled out as a masterpiece, its attributes being truly classical. Designed by Mauro Codussi and the Lombardos according to the principles of Alberti, and built between 1481 and 1509, the palace is an enhanced version of Codussi's earlier Palazzo Corner-Spinelli. Its facade is particularly striking thanks to its round arches that enclose biforate windows topped by round oculi and separated by single and double half-columns, and for the typically Venetian practice of dividing the arched windows into groups – three in the middle and one at each end.

The second palace, the Palazzo Dolfin-Manin, was commissioned by Zuanne Dolfin in 1538 and designed by Jacopo Sansovino. It was constructed by remodelling the floor plan and facade of an older palace, and extending the upper floors over a public street adjacent to the canal bank. The facade at ground-floor level is a six-arched *sottoportego*, and at the centre of the *piano nobile* there is a set of quadrupled windows with double windows to the side, attributes repeated on the upper floor. A continuous balustrade adorns the *piano nobile*, and smaller discontinuous balustrades provide decoration on the upper floor. In deference to classical precedents, the facade displays Doric pilasters on the ground floor and Ionic half-columns on the *piano nobile* and upper floor, except where there are Ionic pilasters at the edges. To facilitate access from the canal, a water entrance was provided at the side of the building; the land entrance is at the rear.[14]

In contrast to his work on the Palazzo Dolfin-Manin, Sansovino reconstructed another Gothic palace, the Palazzo Corner della Ca' Grande, overtly inspired by High Renaissance Classicism. Commissioned by Jacopo Cornaro in 1545, Sansovino provided the immense new building with a rusticated ground floor pierced by three tall central arches and two rectangular and pedimented side windows, a *piano nobile* displaying eight pairs of Ionic columns and an upper floor with the same number of Corinthian columns. However, despite Sansovino's

Photo 13.12   Jacopo Sansovino, Palazzo Dolfin-Manin, Venice, 1538. With its fine ground-floor portico and balustraded upper storeys, the palace ranks among the best Renaissance buildings in Venice.

general adoption of a contemporary form of architecture common in Tuscany and Rome, the arrangement of the numerous windows (16 in total) on the *piano nobile* not only breaks up the facade but is reminiscent of an arcade and conforms very much to a Venetian tradition.[15]

Complying with a commission from Vettor Grimani in 1541, Michele Sanmicheli designed a monumental and ornate Late Renaissance *palazzo* for his paymaster which looks quite alien beside its Gothic neighbours.[16] Not only does the building display lavish stone carvings that only the wealthy could afford, but its substantial weight could only be supported by the construction of massive foundations. Built on a trapezoidal site at an angle to the Grand Canal and vertically divided into five bays, on its ground floor the Palazzo Grimani contains a tall triumphal arch as its waterside portal, smaller arched entrances to either side and diminutive rectangular windows towards the edges of the building.[17] The *piano nobile* exhibits a continuous balustrade with five alternating curved and flat-topped windows, an architectural device duplicated on the top floor except for the balustrade. The pilasters on the ground floor of the facade and the half-columns on the upper floors are of the Corinthian order. Following the death

Photo 13.13 Jacopo Sansovino, Palazzo Corner della Ca' Grande, Venice, 1545. A colossal and dignified edifice in true Renaissance style, and notable particularly for its rusticated ground floor and its three arched portals.

of Sanmicheli in 1559, Giangiacomo dei Grigi worked on the upper storey of the building and Antonio Risconi finally completed the palace in 1575.[18] Except for its internal layout at ground-floor level – which from the canal contains an atrium, *pòrtego* and entry court – the *palazzo* would almost be at home in Rome or Florence.

Apart from satisfying the demand among patricians for resplendent *palazzi*, the private sector of the Venetian economy – as during the quattrocento – also provided resources for the construction of *scuole*, but conditions had to be right. One successful development project was the the Scuola Grande di S Rocco. Funded by its commissioning confraternity in 1515, the building was designed in succession by Bartolomeo Bon, Sante Lombardo and Antonio Abbondi (better known as Scarpagnino).[19] Bon was responsible for the overall plan and the principal facade of the ground floor notable for its lavish decoration, use of Istrian stone and coloured marble,[20] Codussian biforate windows and imposing portals; Lombardo designed the facade on the Rio-side of the building; and the elevation overlooking the Campo was completed by Scarpagnino.[21] By the middle of the century, it seemed as though commissioned work on the building had finished, but

Photo 13.14   Michele Sanmicheli, Palazzo Grimani, Venice, 1541. A masterpiece of design more reminiscent of the architect's commissions in Verona than akin to other canal *palazzi*.

Photo 13.15 Bartolomeo Bon and others, Scuola Grande di S Rocco, Venice, 1515. Although Bon initiated the design of the building, the edifice is remarkable notably for its extravagant facade designed by Scarpagnino.

in order for the Scuola to compete favourably with the new Scuola Grande della Misericordia currently under construction, the S Rocco confraternity employed Giangiacomo dei Grigi to make the main facade of their building even more decorative and magnificent than hitherto.[22]

However, another project was an abject failure. Despite appearing to compete with the Scuola Grande di S Rocco and other *scuole* in terms of the magnificence of its design, construction of the Scuola Grande della Misericordia, commissioned in 1535, soon ran into difficulties. The plans of its architect, Sansovino, were rejected by the confraternity during the course of construction and, recognising that the cost of building work would be more than it could afford, the confraternity had little option but to leave the Scuola unfinished.[23] Although the building is decoratively finished inside, the exterior is unadorned and displays very few, if any, of the attributes of High Renaissance architecture.

As in previous centuries, the monastic orders were prominent patrons of new ecclesiastical buildings during the cinquecento. In Venice this is exemplified by two magnificent churches: S Francesco della Vigna and S Giorgio Maggiore. The former church was commissioned by an Observant branch of the Franciscan

Order supported by a host of wealthy nobles including the doge, Andrea Gritti, and designed in turn by Sansovino and Andrea Palladio.[24] High Renaissance in style, the harmonious interior of the church is dominated by its nave and an extended presbytery, while its side chapels compensate for the absence of aisles. Lacking a dome, the principal external attribute of the building is its impressive facade, the last part of the structure to be completed. With Sansovino reaching the age of 82 in 1568, work on this part of the building was transferred to Palladio who undertook the task with panache.[25] Completed in 1572, the facade is crowned by a large pediment supported on a common base by two pairs of Corinthian half-columns, while lower flanking half-pediments are supported by shorter half-columns of the same order.[26]

Despite its cramped site in a densely developed part of the *sestiere* of Castello where its full magnificence is not easy to appreciate, the church of S Francesco undoubtedly served as a model for further church development in terms of its

Photo 13.16 Andrea Palladio, church of S Giorgio Maggiore, Venice, 1565. With its white temple-like facade, four giant Corinthian columns, extensive use of brick and tall campanile, this church on the island of S Giorgio conspicuously faces the Piazzetta of S Marco.

composition and detail. In 1565 Palladio thus seized the opportunity to design his first complete church when commissioned by the Benedictine Order to build its new basilica, S Giorgio Maggiore, on the eponymous island at the east end of the Giudecca. The new building is a basilica with side aisles, a dome and crowning lantern over the crossing, and a long chancel, but its most notable attribute is its facade.[27] This consists of two pediments, 'a high one over a central portal (corresponding to the nave inside), flanked by the fragmentary ends of another broader, lower one (corresponding to the aisles)'.[28] Made of Istrian marble, the central pediment is supported by two pairs of three-quarter columns, while the largely illusory lower pediment of the same material is supported by pilasters.[29] The completion of the church of S Giorgio Maggiore post-dated the death of Palladio in 1580 and was finally achieved by Simone Sorella in 1610 very much according to the plans of its initial designer.[30] Situated 'offshore', the Palladian church provides a 'perfect counterpart to the buildings of the Piazza S Marco on the other side of the Basin'.[31]

Genoa

In contrast to cinquecento Rome, where the construction of private palaces preceded the development of *ville suburbane*, in Genoa the reverse was the case. The cramped conditions of the port and the slope of its terrain militated against financially viable new development, at least until the commune promoted the construction of the Strada Nuova in the heart of Genoa towards the end of the century. Of the several villas constructed on the edge of the city, foremost is the Villa Giustiniani (better known as the Villa Giustiniani-Cambiaso since 1797 when it was acquired by the Cambiaso family). Commissioned by Luca Giustiniani in 1548, designed by Galeazzo Alessi and possibly inspired by Peruzzi's Villa Farnesina in Rome, the facade of the three-storey villa comprises a three-bay loggia on its ground floor, rectangular pedimented windows above, and slightly projecting wings.[32] A total of 12 Doric half-columns on the ground floor and the same number of fluted Ionic pilasters on the *piano nobile* traverse the facade and are elegantly arranged in pairs on either side of each wing, while the main body of the building is surmounted by a large cornice in classical style with a balustrade above. The rear of the villa contains a first-floor loggia that affords a fine view over the Gulf of Liguria. The Villa Giustiniani-Cambiaso provided a model for the development of other *ville suburbane* on the outskirts

Photo 13.17 Giovanni and Domenico Ponzello, Palazzo Grimaldi Doria-Tursi, Genoa, 1564. The largest of Genoa's palaces, its facade is notable for its raised gardens and its interior for a magnificent arcaded courtyard.

of Genoa, for example the Villa Pallavicino (begun 1556), the Villa Grimaldi (1559) and the Villa Imperiale Scassi (1560).[33]

Of the many *palazzi* built as part of the Strada Nuova project set in train during the latter half of the cinquecento (see chapter 11), the Palazzo Grimaldi Doria-Tursi is perhaps the most magnificent. After acquiring a vast tract of land in the Strada in 1564 and further lots in 1568, Niccolò Grimaldi commissioned construction of a palace on the extended site based on the initial plans of Giovanni and Domenico Ponzello drawn up in 1564 but duly modified. The outcome was a building of considerable depth, rising up a slope from its facade on the Strada through its portal and an entrance hall, to a staircase and a courtyard, and thence up further staircases connecting each of its main floors behind lower and upper loggias. The width of the building was similarly unusual, its facade being extended laterally above street level by open loggias and flanking balustrades.[34]

If there are some doubts as to whether the 16th-century buildings of Genoa have more in common with their counterparts in Rome than with those of Venice, these can be dispelled when considering ecclesiastical edifices such as the church of S Maria Assunta in Carignano and SS Ambrogio e Andrea II or Il Gesù. The former church, begun in 1552 and completed in 1601, was designed by Galeazzo Alessi under the patronage of the Sauli family who owned the hill on which it stands. With its plan based on a Greek cross, the square building contains a central dome with a tall arcaded drum, four corner spaces with minor domes, and two campanili that rise up at both ends of its facade to match the height of the central dome.[35] The front facade is relatively featureless, its decoration confined to eight unfluted Corinthian pilasters, a small central portal and a large crowning pediment above that encloses a lunette. Being a centrally planned church it not only fails to conform to the design requirements of the Council of Trent but is also unlike any other ecclesiastical building in Genoa.[36] However, it is comparable to much of the the work of Antonio da Sangallo the Younger in Rome (for example, his church of S Maria di Loreto or his plans for St Peter's), and is broadly similar in concept to the church of the Madonna di S Biagio in Montepulciano or that of S Maria della Consolazione in Todi.[37] Somewhat in contrast, and although containing similar elements to Alessi's S Maria Assunta, Il Gesù is based on a Latin-cross plan and, in keeping with Counter-Reformation trends, comprises a longitudinal nave and lateral chapels rather than aisles. Located close to the centre of political power, the Palazzo Ducale, the church was not only funded by Father Marcello Pallavicino and his Jesuit brothers, but was probably designed by the Jesuit architect and artist Giuseppe Valeriani. Rather than demonstrating some similarity with contemporary churches in Rome, Il Gesù shows a strong resemblance to the Gesù Nuovo in Naples, also designed by Valeriani.[38] With Il Gesù begun in 1589 and finished in 1637, it is perhaps ironic that, after commissioning and designing the church, the Jesuit order discontinued its use in 1603 when it was 'reserved for the sole use of the new Casa Professa'.[39]

Milan

Comparable in grandeur to any villa in Rome or Genoa, the medieval Villa Simonetta on the edge of Milan was ceded in 1547 by its then owner Gian Pietro Cicogna to the newly appointed governor of Milan, Ferrante Gonzaga,[40] and its reconstruction predated the development of the city's major central residence, the Palazzo Marino, by at least a decade. Based on the design of the commissioned architect, Domenico Giunti, the original orientation of the villa was inverted so that the rear became the main facade of the building.[41] Modelled on the ancient Roman villa of Septizonium, its new three-storeyed portico consists of round-arched arcades on its ground floor supported by Bramantesque pillars and Doric half-columns, Tuscan columns and an architrave on its *piano nobile*, and Corinthian columns supporting a timber ceiling on its top floor.[42] The rear facade of the altered building contains a nine-arch arcade on Doric columns surmounted by a double architraved loggia, and side wings that extend outwards toward the countryside giving the villa a U-shaped plan into which an external courtyard is inserted.[43]

In contrast to the aristocratic patronage of the Villa Simonetta, the development of the Palazzo Marino was financed by a Genoese banker and tax-farmer, Tommaso Marino. After acquiring sites in the centre of Milan between 1553 and 1557, in 1558 Marino commissioned Galeazzo Alessi to design an enormous three-storey palace – one of the largest in Italy and comparable in floor space to

Photo 13.18   Galeazzo Alessi, Palazzo Marino, Milan, begun 1558. On the Piazza S Fedele, a lengthy and grandiose facade graces the palace which boasts a magnificent Mannerist courtyard within.

the Palazzo del Laterano in Rome.[44] Situated on the northern edge of the Piazza S Fedele, the long 15-bay front of the palace is soberly graced by Doric half-columns on the ground floor with twin columns of the same order encasing the main portal; Ionic pilasters on the *piano nobile*; and pilasters crowned by decorative blocks on the upper storey. The facade is further enhanced by aedicules on its upper floors, discontinuous balustrades on the *piano nobile* and a continuous balustrade on top of its immense cornice.[45] Although it was intended to flank the *palazzo* with further buildings of the same sort – akin to development in the Strada Nuova of Genoa – this was never undertaken. In 1568 work on the palace was interrupted because of the financial difficulties of its patron, and the building was consequently taken into public ownership by the city's Treasury that thenceforth funded its completion. As late as 1888–92, this involved constructing a facade at the rear of the palace on the Piazza della Scala intended to replicate the frontal facade on the Piazza S Fedele.[46]

Florence

During the Republic (1494–1512), new *palazzi* in Florence were often charmless, austere buildings eschewing all save the most basic classical attributes, but with the election of Giovanni de'Medici as Pope Leo X in 1512, changing taste brought a return to the humanist tradition, and new buildings were again designed broadly in accordance with Vitruvian principles. Of the many new private palaces that conformed to Classicism in the aftermath of Leo's coronation, the most prominent is the Palazzo Pandolfini, a building commissioned by its patron Bishop Giannozzo Pandolfino in 1515 and, based on a design by Raphael, built under the supervision of Giovanni Francesco and Aristotele da Sangallo.[47] Combining some elements of Florentine architectural style, as displayed in the palaces of the Medici and Strozzi, with the later Roman style typified by the Palazzo Caprini and Palazzo Vidoni-Caffarelli, the innovative new palace has a long asymmetrical facade, aediculed windows, a round-arched rusticated portico, and – unlike Roman *palazzi* of the period – an absence of shops on the ground floor; but most remarkably the palace has four bays that are two storeys in height and five bays of only one storey.[48]

While other palaces, such as the Palazzo Bartolini-Salimbeni (begun 1517) and the Palazzo Uguccioni (started *c* 1550), also exemplified the return of Classicism, it was the portico of the Confraternità dei Serviti that provided the most stunning demonstration of this style. Designed by Antonio da Sangallo the Elder and commissioned by the brotherhood in 1519, the portico was built on the western side of the *piazza* opposite Brunelleschi's Ospedale degli Innocenti on which it was modelled, and its construction – completed in 1534 – formed part of a long-term project to harmonise the architecture around the *piazza*.[49]

The design of new ecclesiastical buildings similarly incorporated classical features. On the death of Giuliano da Sangallo in 1516, Leo X commissioned Michelangelo to complete the Sagrestia Nuova on which Sangallo had been working, to provide a mausoleum for Lorenzo de'Medici and his heirs.[50] Influenced by Brunelleschi's Sagrestia Vecchia of 1419–22, Michelangelo's building was similarly based on a square ground plan and covered by a hemispherical cupola, but it was substantially taller, and exhibited many of the attributes of Mannerism that were becoming fashionable in Italy as the cinquecento progressed.

While working on the Sagrestia Vecchia, Michelangelo was also employed on another major Florentine project, the Biblioteca Laurenziana. The second Medicean pope, Clement VII, entrusted Michelangelo in 1519 with the design

Photo 13.19   Raffaello Sanzio and others, Palazzo Pandolfini, Florence, 1515. Built as a villa on the edge of cinquecento Florence, the edifice is the most important extant building designed by Raphael.

of a building to accommodate the family's exceptionally valuable collection of manuscripts.[51] Attached to the left transept of S Lorenzo, the resulting *biblioteca* – like the Sagrestia Vecchia – is an exercise in Mannerism. It has two separate parts: a small square vestibule, and a lengthy reading room and library 46 metres long.[52] The former space is, in effect, an enclosed courtyard with its walls featuring projecting aedicules and blind windows separated by recessed pairs of Doric columns, the latter space accommodating a series of chairs and reading desks along its length, illuminated by a row of 15 windows. Unfortunately, Michelangelo was unable to complete the *biblioteca* prior to his departure for Rome in 1534, where he spent the rest of his life. However, in accordance with his design – but in stone rather than wood – Bartolomeo Ammanati subsequently built a monumental triple staircase to connect the vestibule with the reading room and library.[53]

The Smaller Cities of Northern Italy

Vicenza

Having gained experience in designing his first palace in Vicenza, the Casa Civena, in 1540, Palladio seized the opportunity to complete the Palazzo Thiene after the death of its initiating architect, Giulio Romano, in 1542. Commissioned by Adriano Thiene, Palladio revised Romano's plans for the interior of the building, but these had been only partly implemented when work was abandoned in 1558.[54] The facade of the palace, however, was virtually finished. Intended to be of great length with a central portal, it was foreshortened and has the entrance on its extreme left-hand side. In Mannerist style, the building is rusticated both on the ground floor and on the *piano nobile*, and on the latter floor Corinthian pilasters separate modest balustrades, rectangular windows and alternating triangular and segmental pediments.

Designed only a little later than the Palazzo Thiene, the Palazzo Chiericati, on the edge of Piazza Matteotti, was more classical than Mannerist. Commissioned by Girolamo Chiericati in 1551, Palladio designed a building consisting of a continuous ground-floor colonnade open at its sides, Doric columns on the ground-floor facade, and Ionic columns on the *piano nobile*. Since the colonnade occupied public land and supported a *salone* and flanking loggias above, its development required the consent of the Commune.[55] Permission was granted

Photo 13.20 Andrea Palladio, Palazzo Thiene, Vicenza, 1550–8. Designed initially by Lorenzo da Bologna in 1489 and later modified by Giulio Romano, the palace was extended by Palladio by the addition of a porticoed courtyard, albeit unfinished.

and the building completed, the main facade of the Palazzo Chiericati becoming one of the most open in Italy outside of Venice and an integral feature of public space.

Returning to Mannerism, Palladio designed the three-storey Palazzo Valmarana in 1565, a development in the centre of the city. Its facade is notable for its central entrance with three bays either side, a row of windows on the *piano nobile* with triangular pediments at either end, discrete balustrades, one per window, but most remarkably for its giant Corinthian pilasters that rise from the ground floor to the cornice.

The use of the Giant order was also evident on the facade of the Palazzo Iseppo, commissioned in 1548. Built around a central court, the palace is, to an extent, reminiscent of Michelangelo's supreme examples of Mannerism, the Palazzo dei Conservatorio and Palazzo Nuovo in Rome.[56]

Padua

Like Palladio, Giovanni Maria Falconetto was an exponent of the classical school of architecture, albeit he was less prolific than his younger master. However, he was renowned for designing Padua's city gates (see chapter 11) and, in the same city, the Odeon and loggia in the courtyard of Alvise Cornaro's *palazzo*, now the Palazzo Giustiniani. Commissioned by Cornaro in 1524 to design these buildings to accommodate respectively musical and theatrical performances, Falconetto positioned the three-bay Odeon in the middle of the long side of the courtyard and the five-bay loggia across its width at its far end. Although the *al'antica* fresco decorations of the loggia and Odeon are among the finest in cinquecento Italy, '[the] relief of the pilasters and niches [in the Odeon] is strangely shallow [while] in the loggia the relationship between the engaged Doric columns facing the pillars of the arcades and the Ionic pilasters of the upper storey remains a little vague'.[57]

Photo 13.21 Andrea Palladio, Palazzo Chiericati, Vicenza, 1551. With porticoes on both floors, the palace is a majestic work overlooking the Piazza Matteotti.

Verona

While Andrea Palladio was stamping his architectural imprint on Vicenza, and Giovanni Maria Falconetto was leaving his mark on Padua, Michele Sanmicheli was monopolising the design of new private *palazzi* in Verona, which although similar to those in Vicenza in terms of height and fenestration, differed substantially in detail.

Photo 13.22 Andrea Palladio, Palazzo Valmarana, Vicenza, 1565. One of Palladio's less attractive buildings, but notable for its use of giant pilasters.

Inspired by Bramante's Palazzo Caprini and other flagship palaces of the High Renaissance in Rome, the Veronese-born architect Michele Sanmicheli – who early in life had lived and worked in the Eternal City – returned to his birthplace in 1527 and, over the course of the following three decades, did his best – among his diverse ventures – to replicate Roman *palazzi* but within a local context. His first commission in this field, secured in 1530, was the Palazzo Bevilacqua. Like the Palazzo Caprini, Sanmicheli's palace has a two-storey facade and a rusticated ground floor, but at this level its Doric pilasters are also rusticated, while the elaborately fluted Corinthian columns on the *piano nobile* separate high and low round-headed windows. It is on this floor that a balustrade stretches across the complete building, while above the upper floor a richly sculptured entablature surmounts the palace. If its design is lacking in any respect, it is because the seven bays of the facade – five to the right of the portal and one to the left – render the building asymmetrical, although some would argue that this is an attractive attribute.[58] It is unknown whether, in order to achieve symmetry, the portico was intended to be located in the central bay of the existing building or whether a further four bays were contemplated but, possibly for financial reasons, were not built.

Photo 13.23   Michele Sanmicheli, Palazzo Bevilacqua, Verona, 1530. A spectacular building integrating a rusticated ground storey, a balcony, tall windows on its upper storey, spiral columns and ornately carved cornice in a masterly way.

Built around the same time as the Palazzo Bevilacqua and also designed by Sanmicheli, the Palazzo Canossa similarly combines features typical of a Roman palace of the same period and attributes of contemporary architecture displayed in parts of the north. The smoothly rusticated ground-floor facade – devoid of orders – is surmounted by coupled pilasters on the *piano nobile* and stylistically is undoubtedly Roman having previously appeared on the *palazzi* Caprini and Vidoni-Caffarelli. However, the three central bays of the ground floor – open to the street – are reminiscent of the Palazzo Te in Mantua begun a few years earlier, while the narrow front and disproportionate depth of the Palazzo Canossa are traditionally Venetian.[59] Unlike the Palazzo Bevilacqua, Canossa's palace is largely undecorated except for a balustrade and statues above the cornice.

Photo 13.24 Michele Sanmicheli, Palazzo Canossa, Verona, 1532. The palace's elegant and relatively unadorned facade masks behind its three portals an attractive atrium and courtyard.

The Palazzo Pompei is Sanmicheli's third great palace in Verona. Commissioned in 1555, the *palazzo* has seven bays like his former *palazzi*, but unlike the Bevilacqua – though like the Canossa – the facade of the Palazzo Pompei is symmetrical since its main portal is positioned in the centre of the heavily rusticated ground floor. The *piano nobile* has engaged and fluted Doric columns separating a row of arched windows and interrupted balustrades and is surmounted by a modestly decorated entablature.[60]

Photo 13.25 Michele Sanmicheli, Palazzo Pompei, Verona, 1555. With its rusticated ground floor, balconies, and tall windows on its upper floor, this palace has more in common with the Palazzo Bevilacqua than with the Canossa.

Mantua

From his home in the Eternal City, Giulio Romano was summoned to Mantua by Federico Gonzaga in 1524 to discuss the development of a *villa suburbana* on an island south of the capital that for generations had been used by the Gonzaga for equestrian pursuits.[61] The intention was to erect a small building for the provision of refreshment and as a place of relaxation after riding but, because Romano's design called for a much larger structure, the outcome was a palace – the Palazzo Te – rather than a modest villa.[62] The palace is a square building comprising long single-storey blocks enclosing a large open and turfed courtyard. Access is through entrances situated in the centre of the western, northern and eastern blocks, but visitors coming from the city normally gained entry through the northern block where three arched portals lead into a courtyard and thence to a large loggia and garden.[63] Both the northern and western facades are rusticated and decorated with giant Doric pilasters but, because there are uneven gaps between the pilasters and the portals, the 'different systems collide at the corners'.[64]

Around the courtyard, columns, pilasters and blind-window surrounds are vigorously rusticated, while in the centre of each inter-columnal space, smooth architraves are interrupted by rusticated keystones, and one could be forgiven for thinking that on the western and eastern walls of the courtyard 'the triglyphs of the entablature look as though they were slipping down'.[65] In the corner of the courtyard, as on the exterior of the *palazzo*, different systems confront each other: on the north and south sides, the surfaces between the half-columns are of the same width, whereas on the west and east the narrower and wider wall sections alternate. Even more extraordinary, between the half-columns, 'rubbly rustication and fine ashlar stand side by side'.[66] The overall effect is that the facades seem unfinished, but this was the deliberate intention of Romano in experimenting with an early form of Mannerism.

However, the garden facade of the *palazzo* is much more classical in concept. It has a three-arch loggia situated centrally and the vaulting of each bay is supported by a group of four columns while, across the length of the facade, an entablature separates the round arches from the columns. Although Romano was architect, artist, contractor and clerk of works, his project was subject to many delays due to the complexities of his design and shortages of skilled labour, but the building was virtually finished by the end of 1534.[67] It is important to note, however, that although the design of Palazzo Te was unique, its Mannerist elements heralded a move away from the Classicism of the High Renaissance and led ultimately to the Baroque, a style widely adopted across the cities of Italy later in the cinquecento and beyond.

With Romano's acceptance of a further commission from Federico Gonzaga in 1538, this time to build a courtyard adjacent to his city residence, there was a further lurch to Mannerism. Attached to the south front of the Palazzo Ducale, a courtyard – subsequently called the *Estivale* or Cortile della Cavallerizza – was designed by Romano to create a venue for performances and tournaments. While its seven-bay facade is reminiscent of Bramante's Palazzo Caprini, the *piano nobile* is also rusticated and its projecting 'barley-sugar' columns – though standing on plinths – appear otherwise unsupported.[68] The window arches on the ground floor and *piano nobile*, being bent into a segmental shape, are also illusory, further demonstrating that many of the attributes of the courtyard are frozen in time and 'not of enduring harmony'.[69]

As a result of his services to Federico, the duchy presented Romano with a house in Mantua *c* 1540 which, during the following four years, he adapted to incorporate in a Mannerist style some of the attributes of the Palazzo Caprini.[70] Like its Roman counterpart, Romano's house has a rusticated ground floor, a row of square windows and a central portal within a depressed arch, but its *piano nobile* is unadorned by engaged columns and its large pedimented windows are recessed in blind arches with their keystones supporting the crowning cornice.[71] Probably the most striking Mannerist feature of the building is a gable over the portal which, together with a shallow niche above, replaces a first-floor window. The gable, however, is eminently compatible with the window pediments on the *piano nobile*, while the blind arches on this floor 'make the facade the most striking in the whole length of the street'.[72] His earlier buildings in Mantua were eccentrically innovative, but it was unfortunate that a design such as that adopted for his own house was no longer fashionable in Rome and, by

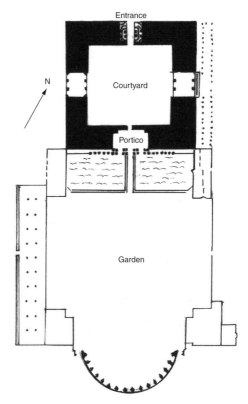

Figure 13.2 *Palazzo Te, Mantua*

comparison with the *palazzi* of Sanmicheli or Palladio in the Veneto, seemed to some to be rather provincial[73] – yet the same could be said of Mantua, since the city never regained its former glory as an Italian state after the death of Federico in 1540.

Parma

Coinciding approximately with the incorporation of Parma into the Papal States, the inhabitants of the city voluntarily funded construction of the pilgrimage church of the Madonna della Steccata. Designed by Gianfrancesco Zaccagni in 1521 to accommodate what was believed to be a miraculous image of the Madonna, the brick church was built according to a Greek-cross plan and has four projecting semi-circular apses (one of which contains the portal), a central

Photo 13.26 Giulio Romano, Palazzo Te, Mantua, 1524. A substantial achievement in the Mannerist style, the extraordinary villa is one of the most important and intriguing Italian buildings of the cinquecento.

hemispherical dome on an arcaded drum, and smaller hemispherical domes on each of its four equal arms. Unlike most other pilgrimage churches, which are for the most part located on the edge of towns, the Steccata occupies a cramped site in the urban core that obscures its many merits. It is of note that, within the new Papal State, where resources were allocated to a substantial amount of public development (see chapter 11), very little private development of any merit took place in the cinquecento.

Bologna

With its densely packed medieval urban fabric, Bologna is not an ideal location for the display of its many *palazzi* developed in the cinquecento, despite their often ingenious and attractively symmetrical design. However, two palaces

Photo 13.27 Giulio Romano, Cortile della Cavallerizza, Mantua, 1538. Mannerism carried to the extreme, this highly ornamented building provided an exuberant setting for the entertainment of the Gonzaga and their guests.

in particular clearly enhance the townscape: the two-storeyed Palazzo Fantuzzi and the three-storeyed Palazzo Bentivoglio. The former building, designed by Andrea da Formigine in 1525, has pairs of deeply rusticated orders along the 11 bays of both floors, an imposing central portal and heraldic stone elephants occupying niches in the end bays of the *piano nobile*.[74] By contrast, the latter building, the Palazzo Bentivoglio is devoid of rustication, spare in its use of orders and generally lacking in decoration, but it is very symmetrical. On its ground floor, its facade comprises a central portico encased by two Corinthian columns with five rectangular windows either side; its *piano nobile* has windows in each of its 11 bays with a balustrade above the portal; its upper floor similarly contains a row of 11 windows but unlike those below they are pedimented; and the building is crowned by a largely unadorned cornice.

Photo 13.28 Giulio Romano, Giulio Romano's House, Mantua, 1540. In the Mannerist style, an apt residence for the architect of Federico II Gonzaga's remarkable commissions.

Todi

In southern Umbria at the beginning of the cinquecento the ancient hill town of Todi became the location for the foundation of a new pilgrimage church, S Maria della Consolazione. Funded mainly by donations from the local population, construction of the church began in 1508 under the direction of its architect, Cola da Caprarola. Though it has often been regarded as a simplified version of Bramante's plan for St Peter's produced only two years earlier, the Consolazione is also broadly similar in concept to the church of S Maria delle Carceri in Prato, designed by Giuliano da Sangallo in 1484.

Probably the finest example of a centralised-plan Renaissance church, the Consolazione is based on a square plan with apses on each of its four sides.[75] Three of its apses are polygonal and contain a portal but the fourth – accommodating the miraculous image – is semi-circular and without an external entrance.[76] The circular facade of the building is adorned with flat pilasters above and below an interim entablature while a projecting entablature wraps its way around the building above its apses. Pedimented rectangular windows, with smaller square windows above, also encircle the building at an upper level. Rising above the

Photo 13.29 Andrea da Formigine, Palazzo Fantuzzi, Bologna, 1525. With its individualistic rustication, an interesting example of a Mannerist *palazzo*.

apses, the balustraded square core of the church is crowned by a tall drum decorated by alternating niches and coupled pilasters and surmounted by a pointed dome and lantern, the whole superstructure being supported by the arches of the crossing and their colossal piers. Because of the high cost of development and the many technical difficulties involved in construction, the church was not finally completed until 1606, ironically about the same time as St Peter's was finished. Located peripherally on a terrace outside the city walls, the Consolazione not only commands a fine view over the Umbrian countryside, but in dominating the scene provides a magnificent entry point into the built-up area of the city.[77]

Montepulciano

In the southern Tuscan city of Montepulciano, some 60 miles north-west of Todi, work began on the construction of the pilgrimage church of the Madonna di S Biagio in 1518. Designed by Antonio da Sangallo the Elder (brother of the architect of S Maria delle Carceri at Prato), like its counterparts the Madonna

Photo 13.30   Cola da Caprarola, church of S Maria della Consolazione, Todi, begun 1508. Inspired by the designs of Bramante, this domed church with its Greek-cross plan is a masterpiece of High Renaissance architecture.

di S Biagio was funded by voluntary donations and has many of the attributes of both S Maria dell Carceri and the Consolazione.[78] Like the latter church, it occupies a site on the edge of town and is to be seen against a rural backcloth, but like S Maria delle Carceri it is based on a Greek cross (rather than a square), and its portals, windows and pediments are reminiscent of those used at Prato. There is also an affinity with S Maria delle Calcinaio at Cortona. The resemblance with the Consolazione, however, is limited. Rather than being essentially circular, one side of the Madonna di S Biagio is clearly its front while the opposite arm of the cross is its chancel beyond which there is an oblong sacristy that looks from the outside to be a one-storey choir, a feature that Raphael had previously planned for St Peter's.[79]

However, like the structure of many Renaissance churches, the square of the crossing provides a base for the cylindrical drum and an hemispherical dome. Sangallo probably began the vaulting of the dome and the first of two planned campaniles that would grace the facade in the manner that Raphael had planned

Photo 13.31 Antonio da Sangallo the Elder, church of the Madonna di S Biagio, Montepulciano, begun 1518. Crowned by a dome and based on a Greek-cross plan, the partly unfinished church ranks among the finest religious edifices of the High Renaissance and was Sangallo's greatest commission.

for St Peter's, but after Sangallo's death in 1534, Baccio d'Agnolo built the lantern and his son Giuliano di Baccio completed one of the campanili in 1564. The second campanile never rose above its ground floor.[80]

Unlike Todi, Montepulciano was the location of notable secular as well as ecclesiastical development during the first half of the cinquecento. Of the many contemporary secular buildings constructed in the city, the finest is undoubtedly the massive Palazzo Tarugi (1530), sited in the Piazza Grande opposite the cathedral.[81] Designed initially by Antonio da Sangallo the Younger around 1500, but completed by Giacomo Barozzi da Vignola by mid-century, the three-storeyed palace – almost Baroque in its grandeur – boasts an imposing travertine five-bay facade that includes a triple-arched arcade on its ground floor and a double-arched opening in the two bays that face the cathedral. Along the length and width of the *piano nobile*, the bays accommodate rectangular pedimented windows and are separated by half-columns of the Ionic order; the latter rise above their

Photo 13.32 Antonio da Sangallo the Elder, Palazzo Tarugi, Montepulciano, 1530. With a triple-arched portico at one end on the ground floor and a similar open extension above it on the top floor (now bricked in), the palace is given a robust quality by the use of plinths, Ionic columns and pilasters on the rest of its facade.

high plinths to the decorative balustrades of the *piano nobile* where its bays are separated by pilasters that rise to the entablature that surmounts the building.[82]

The South

Naples

Since most of the prominent private *palazzi* built in the city of Naples during the cinquecento were key components of a major urban planning scheme and are considered in chapter 11, we refer in this chapter only to ecclesiastical buildings. However, this is not to imply that church-building in 16th-century Naples was solely the result of *ad hoc* development: it was in large part the outcome of viceregal legislation that, in the spirit of the Counter-Reformation, favoured the New Orders and 'inaugurated an innovative phase of religious building'.[83] Thus, among the many churches that were consequently built in Naples in the cinquecento, the Gesù Nuovo is arguably the most notable. Commissioned by Isabella Feltria della Rovere on behalf of the Jesuit Order in 1584, and designed by the Jesuit architect Giuseppe Valeriano, the Gesù Nuovo inherited the ashlar facade of the 15th-century Palazzo Sanseverino – the former building on the site – but otherwise its structure broadly conformed to that of its parent church, the Gesù in Rome. Thus although the Neapolitan church is based on a Greek-cross plan, its nave is extended by the addition of extra bays giving the church more of a basilican interior. The Jesuits also built the Gesù Vecchio (begun 1564) and the Gesù e Maria (started 1593), while the Theatines commissioned the churches of S Paolo Maggiore (1583), S Andrea delle Dame (1583) and S Maria degli Angeli a Pizzofalcone (1600), but these are only a fraction of the 400 or more churches built in Naples in the 16th century.

The Reformation, even in Catholic Naples, gave some encouragement to the development of religious buildings particularly if they were associated with ways to ameliorate the problems of poverty and usury. Commissioned by its religious confraternity and designed by Giovanni Battista Cavagna in 1599, the Monte di Pietà not only provided accommodation for worship but in effect performed the function of a pawnshop and offered low-interest loans.[84] With a chapel on the ground floor and a business hall above, the facade of the building is richly adorned by Ionic pilasters and a large pedimented portal on its ground floor, an imposing pedimented central window on its *piano nobile* and an ornate entablature supporting its roof.

Lecce

As in Naples, the New Orders were actively engaged in church-building throughout the rest of the south during much of the cinquecento and beyond. Lecce, in particular, witnessed a spate of such activity where at least three orders commissioned work of outstanding architectural merit. First, the Celestine nuns of S Croce entrusted a number of architects over a long period with the design of the church S Croce (see p 508–9). In what became a magnificent Baroque monument, Gabriele Riccardi produced the building's Latin-cross plan in 1549, Francesco Antonio Zimbalo (fl 1567–1615) was responsible for the projecting columns and triple portal on its ground floor together with the blind arcading and an elegant frieze immediately above, and Cesare Penna (in 1646) executed the upper portion of the facade with its decorative rose window flanked by sculpted columns and saints in niches.[85] Second, in 1575, the Jesuits employed a member of their own order, Giovanni De Rosis, to design the Gesù, a building also constructed on a Latin base plan and in accordance with their self-imposed needs.[86] Third, the Theatines commissioned one of their own members, the architect Francesco

Photo 13.33   Giuseppe Valeriano, church of Gesù Nuovo, Naples, 1584–1601. Dominating the Piazza del Gesù, the south front of the church is embossed with diamond-pointed lava stone.

Grimaldi, to design the church of S Irene. The finished building showed a greater resemblance to recent Roman models than to other new churches in the south that were being built in a more indigenous style.[87]

Palermo

As capital of Sicily, Palermo witnessed the development of a number of *palazzi* in the 16th century, though of very few churches of any note. The most prominent buildings of this period are the Palazzo Castrone-S Ninfa and the Collegio Massimo, begun in the 1550s and 1586 respectively, and both situated on the Cassaro, the city's main thoroughfare. The former building, commissioned by Giacomo Castrone, is a three-storeyed edifice with Giant order pilasters after the manner of Michelangelo across its facade and pedimented windows along its length and sides.[88] The latter building (now the Biblioteca Centrale della Regione Siciliana), was built by the Jesuits and with its lack of decorative features its facade 'exhibits a sober classicism appropriate for the members of a religious order'.[89]

Messina

In contrast to Palermo, Messina witnessed a proliferation of church-building in the cinquecento. The Jesuits led the way, the other orders soon following their lead.[90] The most prominent Jesuit foundation of the period is the church of S Giovanni di Malta. Commissioned in 1588 and designed by Giacomo del Duca, the facade of the church is endowed with a profusion of Giant order Doric pilasters that anticipate the widespread use of this motif across Sicily.[91] As in Palermo, the influence of Michelangelo is very evident. After all, Del Duca, a Sicilian from Cefalù, was an assistant to the master in Rome before returning to his roots on the island some time in the mid-1580s.

Conclusion

With increasing financial resources derived from economic growth in the cinquecento there seemed no limit to the extent to which private patrons would commission grandiose *palazzi* and magnificent churches in an attempt not only to satisfy their accommodation needs but to demonstrate their enormous wealth, social status and, occasionally, their piety. Throughout the century, architects, craftsmen and labourers attempted to satisfy this demand and, in partnership with their secular and ecclesiastical patrons, transmuted Classicism from near-perfection during the High Renaissance to Mannerism by the 1530s and Palladianism soon after. By the end of the cinquecento, the stage was set for the appearance of the Baroque.

Notes

1 C Woodward, *Rome* (Manchester: Manchester University Press, 1995), p 70.
2 M Hollingsworth, *Patronage in Renaissance Italy* (London: John Murray, 1994) pp 34–5.
3 W Lotz, *Architecture in Italy 1500–1600*, rev edn (New Haven and London: Yale University Press, 1995), p 27.
4 Ibid, p 28.
5 Ibid, p 76.
6 Ibid, p 51.
7 Woodward, *Rome*, p 77.
8 A Majanlahti, *The Families Who Made Rome. A History and Guide* (London: Chatto & Windus, 2005), p 140.
9 Lotz, *Architecture*, p 5.
10 B Hintzen-Bohlen with J Sorges, *Rome and the Vatican City* (Cologne: Könemann, 2001), p 162.
11 Woodward, *Rome*, p 81.
12 Hintzen-Bohlen with Sorges, *Rome*, p 162.
13 Lotz, *Architecture*, p 45.
14 G Zucconi, *Venice. An architectural guide* (Venice: Arsenale Editrice, 1995), p 71; D Howard, *The Architectural History of Venice* (New Haven and London: Yale University Press, 2002), p 80.
15 M Kaminski, *Venice* (Cologne: Könemann, 2000), p 74.
16 Ibid, p 54.
17 Zucconi, *Venice*, p 74; Howard, *Architectural History*, pp 183–4; Kaminski, *Venice*, p 54.
18 Kaminski, *Venice*, p 54.
19 Zucconi, *Venice*, p 67.
20 Ibid; Howard, *Architectural History*, p 157.
21 Zucconi, *Venice*, p 67.
22 Kaminski, *Venice*, p 252.
23 Zucconi, *Venice*, p 69.
24 Howard, *Architectural History*, p 186.

25 Zucconi, *Venice*, p 68.

26 Lotz, *Architecture*, p 150.

27 Kaminski, *Venice*, p 357.

28 I Sutton, *Western Architecture* (London: Thames and Hudson, 1999), p 147.

29 Kaminski, *Venice*, p 357.

30 Zucconi, *Venice*, p 77.

31 Kaminski, *Venice*, p 357.

32 C Bertelli, 'Albaro and the eastern suburbs', in *Genoa. Architectural Guide* (Turin: Allemandi, 1998), p 218; Lotz, *Architecture*, p 130.

33 E De Negri, 'The city of the new walls', in *Genoa. Architectural Guide* (Turin: Allemandi, 1998), p 140; P Cevini, 'Val Bisago', in Genoa. Architectural Guide (Turin: Allemandi, 1998), pp 215–16.

34 N De Mari, 'The city of the old walls: modern buildings', in *Genoa. Architectural Guide* (Turin: Allemandi, 1998), p 76.

35 Ibid, p 55.

36 Ibid.

37 Lotz, *Architecture*, p 130.

38 De Mari, 'The city', p 52.

39 Ibid.

40 B Adorni, 'The architecture of Milan from the fall of Ludovico Il Moro to Charles V', in *Milan. Architectural Guide* (Turin: Allemandi, 1999), p 92.

41 Lotz, *Architecture*, p 135–6.

42 Ibid.

43 Ibid.

44 Ibid, pp 133–4.

45 Ibid.

46 S Della Torre, 'The city of the saint and the merchant', in *Milan. Architectural Guide* (Turin: Allemandi, 1999), p 97.

47 Lotz, *Architecture*, p 43.

48 Ibid.

49 G Zucconi, *Florence. An architectural guide* (Venice: Arsenale Editrice, 1995), p 85.

50 Ibid, p 83.

51 RC Wirtz, *Florence* (Cologne: Könemann, 2000), pp 292–3.

52 Ibid.

53 Zucconi, *Florence*, p 84.

54 A Hopkins, *Italian Architecture from Michelangelo to Borromini* (London: Thames and Hudson, 2002), p 41.

55 Ibid, p 113.

56 JS Curl, *The Oxford Dictionary of Architecture* (Oxford: Oxford University Press, 2000), p 63.

57 Lotz, *Architecture*, p 63.

58 Ibid, pp 69–70.

59 Ibid, p 70.

60 Ibid, pp 70–1.

61 D Watkin, *A History of Western Architecture* (London: Laurence King, 2000), pp 230–1.
62 Lotz, *Architecture*, pp 77–9.
63 Ibid.
64 Ibid.
65 Ibid.
66 Ibid.
67 Ibid.
68 Hopkins, *Italian Architecture*, p 21; Lotz, *Architecture*, p 80.
69 Lotz, *Architecture*, p 80.
70 Curl, *Oxford Dictionary*, p 276.
71 Lotz, *Architecture*, pp 81–2.
72 Ibid.
73 Ibid.
74 Hopkins, *Italian Architecture*, p 111.
75 Lotz, *Architecture*, pp 39–41.
76 Ibid.
77 Ibid.
78 Ibid, pp 41–2.
79 Ibid.
80 Ibid.
81 AM Von der Haegen and R Strasser, *Tuscany* (Cologne: Könemann, 2001), p 407.
82 Ibid.
83 Hopkins, *Italian Architecture*, p 151.
84 Ibid, p 91.
85 P Blanchard, *Northern Italy from the Alps to Bologna* (London: A&C Black, 2001), p 485.
86 Hopkins, *Italian Architecture*, p 150.
87 Ibid, pp 150–1.
88 Ibid, p 145.
89 Ibid, p 146.
90 Ibid.
91 Ibid, pp 146 and 149.

PART 4

THE 17TH CENTURY

THE DEVELOPMENT OF GOVERNMENT IN ITALY IN THE EARLY 17TH CENTURY AND ITS EFFECTS ON THE BUILT ENVIRONMENT

Introduction

Established by the Treaty of Cateau-Cambrésis in 1559, the political boundaries of Italy were broadly intact at the beginning of the seicento and remained so until the succession wars of the 18th century. The principal territorial entities of Early Modern Italy – the Papal States, Venice, Milan, Tuscany and Naples – were even more firmly established than hitherto and represented a balance of power unimaginable in previous centuries. Despite this balance, however, Spain continued the dominant power in the peninsula and maintained hegemony throughout the 17th century by ensuring that representation in Milan, Naples, Sicily and Sardinia – and at all levels of government – was suitably rewarded by a range of privileges and rights. In both the *seggi* of Naples and the senate of Milan, representatives were appointed from among the powerful and wealthy nobility 'whether feudal (in the southern Italian states) or of urban patrician origin (in the State of Milan)'.[1] Within this context, public patrons throughout the peninsula recognised the merit of commissioning imposing and magnificent buildings as a means of engendering patriotism and civic pride among their citizenry. However, in contrast to the cinquecento, patrons were more inclined to adopt the Baroque style of architecture rather than adhere to Classicism or Mannerism, a preference that was compatible with the diminishing influence of humanism and the revival of religiosity driven in large part by the Jesuits.

The Counter-Reformation and its Effects on Government

Within the Papal State, Rome as a centre of temporal power retained the responsibilities it had exercised during the second half of the 16th century (see chapter 10). However, with regard to spiritual power, during the seicento the Counter-Reformation exerted a considerable influence not only on the Catholic Church within Rome's territorial possessions, but on Catholicism throughout the western world. Motivated by the desire to eliminate heresy, 'a succession of vigorous popes – from Pius V (1567–72) to Urban VIII (1623–44) – imposed, in highly centralized fashion, the application of the decrees of the Council of Trent'[2] manifested most dramatically by the Interdict of Venice in 1606.

It is remarkable that in states 'where humanism had flourished only a few decades earlier . . . the boundary between acceptable and unacceptable discussion was set unilaterally by the Church – as Galileo discovered to his humiliation in 1633'.[3] A reinforced Catholic culture was imposed on Italian society by the great reforming bishops of the later 16th century, diocesan bishops and parish priests 'trained through the Roman catechism to hear confessions . . . deliver socially appropriate sermons [and] guide and control the faithful from birth to death'.[4]

Without strong links to the Italian nobility, the strictures of the Council of Trent might never have been put fully into effect. The ecclesiastical hierarchy (especially the now predominantly Italian body of cardinals) was recruited from among its ranks, and its children were educated by the Jesuits. However, irrespective of the Church's close relationship with the nobility, it remained 'apart from and superior to lay society in the course of the seventeenth century. . . . From cardinals and bishops to religious and secular clergy, the figure of the priest was exalted and distinguished from laymen by cassock, speech and behaviour.'[5]

Using papal funds, work on a substantial number of Baroque buildings was undertaken in Rome during the first half of the 17th century, for example the nave and facade of St Peter's was completed in 1612, and work started on the Palazzo della Sapienza (1642), S Agnese in Agone (1652), and on the facade of S Maria della Pace (1656). Much attention was also paid to urban design, particularly in Rome where the Piazza Navona was redeveloped between the

1640s and '50s, the Piazza S Pietro completed by 1667 and the Piazza del Popolo by 1679 (see chapter 15).

The Formation of Regional States

Outside of Spanish Italy, independent regional states were firmly established in the peninsula by the mid-17th century. Dominant capitals such as Venice and Florence were appropriating many of the traditional responsibilities of subject-cities in respect of their *contadi*, and were gradually imposing direct authority over local communities. In this process, the centralisation of governmental functions had to be organised efficiently and with considerable care and, as far as the Republic of Venice was concerned, it was also deemed necessary to resist the extreme Catholicism of the Counter-Reformation, avoid adopting the Index of prohibited books proclaimed at the Council of Trent, and to expel the Jesuit Order from the city in reprisal for the papal interdict of 1605–6.[6] As an integral part of its policy aimed at safeguarding its political autonomy and privileges, the Republic of Venice not only funded the construction of the Procuratie Nuove (the New Procurators' Office) through to completion in 1616 to house the burgeoning state administration (see chapter 15), but also deemed it desirable to commission the most magnificent of Baroque churches in Italy, S Maria della Salute, in 1631 both to commemorate deliverance from the plague of 1628–30 and to demonstrate the republic's ecclesiastical independence from Rome (see chapter 15). However, in general the citizenry of regional capitals were loath to challenge the traditional powers of local nobles or patricians; for example, Venice never challenged the governmental role of Verona, and although the Tuscan civil service was very largely accommodated in the Ufizzi palace, Florence never questioned the monopoly powers of the *riseduti* of Siena. Regional states were thus the outcome of a delicate process of 'transition and opportunity, certainly not of the imposition of a superior centralized authority'.[7]

Although from time to time political opposition from subordinate cities, feudatories or parliaments prompted regional heads of state to impose direct rule and marginalise a city (Parma), fail to summon the legislature (Piedmont), or to build defensive fortresses (Fortezza da Basso in Florence), such instances of superimposed power were fairly rare, and over the long term compromises were reached by the different parties. Nevertheless, the power of regional states grew with the increase in administrative personnel, establishment of new magistracies and the centralisation of some judicial and fiscal activities – a situation reflected by the further development of their urban fabric.

Governance in the Spanish Dominions

Unlike political developments in France and Prussia, and because of the usefulness of the nobility to their imperial overlords, none of the Spanish possessions in Italy evolved into an absolute state. Both under Charles V and Philip II, it was considered expedient to delegate state control over extensive areas of their domain to local fiefs, while throughout the first half of the 17th century (during the rule of Philip III and then Philip IV) the rising tax burden necessary to finance the escalating cost of wars increased Spain's political dependence on the local nobility.

Taxation in the state of Milan increased substantially in the late 16th and early 17th centuries, with its burden being borne by citizens and patricians as well as peasants. However, its central administration (as in Naples) only coordinated the various tax obligations of each city, leaving it up to each civic authority to act as tax-collector on its behalf. But at a time of rising taxes this meant that a city such as Cremona had to raise its civic tax yield from 70,000 lire in 1565 to 1,359,000 lire in 1630,[8] while it became increasingly difficult for any 17th-century administration to exact vast sums of revenue from its population. With huge deficits in state finance, state governments raised loans from local families and foreign bankers, 'until the accumulated debts led to official bankruptcies'.[9] In the state of Milan, state revenue was bolstered by the sale of fiefs in the 1640s, while in Naples, 'Genoese and Tuscan financiers took advantage of the crisis in public finances until, following the bankruptcies, they were replaced by local speculators and wealthy nobles'.[10] In the cities of Naples and Palermo the rising burden of taxation ultimately sparked popular revolts against ministers, speculators and tax collectors in 1647, which soon spread to other provincial cities throughout the Kingdom of Naples so weakening the administrative structure and power of the state.[11]

Despite the problems associated with Spanish rule that were apparent even in the 16th century, there were certain advantages that compensated both Spain and Italy for their misfortunes. Milan served as the monarch's principal military base in the peninsula, halfway between Sicily and Naples on the one hand and Spanish Flanders on the other. 'At the same time, Sicily [and] Naples provided men, revenue and the strategic ports needed to control the central Mediterranean.'[12] The Spanish monarchy also assumed an informal but important role in helping to determine public policy not only in relatively minor states such as Ferrara, Mantua, Modena and Parma, but also in Florence, Genoa and the Papal States.[13] On a wider stage, the enormous strength of the Spanish Empire protected much of Italy from the threat of internal insurrection or external invasion and enabled its 'client states of Genoa, Florence and the Papal State, in particular, [to enjoy] an extended period of time free of prolonged and expensive wars'.[14] Yet all that applied mainly to the late 16th century. In the seicento, Spain began to lose its hold on its Italian dominions. It was embroiled in successive wars (most notably the Monferrato war of 1613–17 and the Thirty Years' War of 1618–48), was subjected to seemingly never-ending inflation, and through its delegated authorities imposed high levels of direct and indirect taxation on its Italian subjects mainly to cover the cost of military expenditure. By the time the Treaty of Westphalia put an end to 30 years of war, among the Italian states 'the disadvantages of political dependence or semi-dependence were not even balanced by the advantages of an effective protectorate'.[15] In the public sector, therefore, very few buildings of any distinction were commissioned by viceroys, governors and urban governments throughout most of the 17th century. The only major exception to this dearth of public patronage was when the viceregal government of Naples funded the development of the Palazzo Reale, but this mainly occurred in the late cinquecento, the palace being completed by 1602.

Conclusion

Both the Counter-Reformation and the establishment of regional states in the 17th century provided a favourable climate for the construction of magnificent churches and civic buildings as a means of stimulating awe and civic pride among the citizenry, and gaining the respect of outsiders. Within this context, public patrons throughout much of Italy chose the Baroque style of architecture in preference to Classicism or Mannerism both in celebration of their continued existence and with an eye to modernity. In contrast, the increasing weakness of the Spanish dominions meant that very few public buildings of any prominence were funded except for projects started in the previous century.

Chronology

1606	Papacy imposes Interdict on Venice.
	Venice expels Jesuit Order in reprisal.
1606	In Naples, Palazzo Reale commissioned by city's Spanish viceroy.
	Spain now at peak of its power in Italy.
1612	In Rome, nave and facade of St Peter's completed strengthening the city's role as capital of Catholic world.

1613–17	Spain embroiled in inter-Italian War of Monferrato.
1616	**In Venice, Procuratie Nuove completed reinforcing role of Venice as independent state.**
1618–48	Spain's hold on its northern Italian possession weakened by Thirty Years' War. Subsequently, very few buildings of any distinction commissioned in Italy by Spanish viceroys and governors.
1631	**Venetian Senate commissions church of S Maria della Salute as further sign of city's independence.**
1633	Galileo interrogated by Inquisition.
1640s–60s	Under a succession of strong popes, Rome reinforces its position as capital of Catholic world.
1640s–50s	**In Rome, Piazza Navona redeveloped.**
1642	**In Rome, work starts on Palazzo della Sapienza.**
1647	In Naples and Palermo popular revolts against rising taxation point to decline of Spanish power in southern Italy.
1650s–60s	Papacy continues to dominate Italian politics.
1652	**In Rome, work commences on church of S Agnese in Agone.**
1656	**In Rome, facade of S Maria della Pace reconstructed.**
1667	**In Rome, Piazza S Pietro completed.**
1679	**In Rome, development of Piazza del Popolo reaches its penultimate stage with the completion of S Maria dei Miracoli and S Maria in Monsanto.**

Notes

1 S Woolf, 'Italy 1600–1796', in G Holmes (ed), *The Oxford Illustrated History of Italy* (Oxford: Oxford University Press, 1997), p 118.
2 Ibid, p 121.
3 Ibid, p 123.
4 Ibid.
5 Ibid.
6 V Lintner, *A Traveller's History of Italy*, 3rd edn (Gloucester: Windrush Press, 1989), p 123.
7 Woolf, *Italy*, p 126.
8 Ibid, p 119.
9 Ibid.
10 Ibid.
11 CF Black, *Early Modern Italy, A Social History* (London: Routledge, 2001), p 13; C Duggan, *A Concise History of Italy* (Cambridge: Cambridge University Press, 1984), p 74.
12 TJ Dandelet, 'Politics and the state system after the Habsburg–Valois Wars', in JA Marino (ed), *Early Modern Italy* (Oxford: Oxford University Press, 2002), p 13.
13 Ibid.
14 Ibid, p 14.
15 G Procacci, *History of the Italian People* (Harmondsworth: Penguin, 1973), p 196.

CHAPTER 15

PUBLIC PATRONAGE: THE EMERGENCE OF BAROQUE ARCHITECTURE AND TOWN PLANNING

Introduction

Measured in terms of the volume of expenditure on public buildings, the 17th century was undoubtedly the age of papal supremacy. As a long-term legacy of the Council of Trent (1545–63), Rome was celebrating the failure of Protestantism to extend its influence beyond its northern European homelands and, despite the Thirty Years' War (1618–58), the papacy was completely confident that the Eternal City would remain the capital of Western Christendom, a belief increasingly reflected in the enhanced splendour of the built environment as the 17th century progressed. This is all the more remarkable because there were only four pontiffs from 1605 to 1667 yet each through their patronage had a substantial impact on the physical development of Rome. No other Italian city could boast such a surge of symbolic development, and only Venice could claim that it had a Baroque church to match or even surpass anything in Rome (St Peter's aside). While there were a small number of Baroque buildings in Milan and Florence commissioned by public patrons in the early seicento, there were few – if any – elsewhere in Italy.

Public Patronage in Rome: Exuberance and Extravagence

Commissioned by Sixtus V in the late cinquecento to embellish one of his processional routes, the Strada Pia, the reconstructed church of S Susanna is, however, essentially a 17th-century building. This is not only because it was completed in 1603 but, more importantly, because its architecture departed from the inconclusive and contradictory Mannerist style that was previously employed on the facade of Il Gesù, exhibiting instead an extension of Classicism that was to develop into the full-blown Baroque during the seicento. Designed by Carlo Maderno prior to his work on St Paul's,[1] the facade of S Susanna – despite its sumptuous adornments – is more compact than that of Il Gesù. It is essentially a vertical rectangle with low-slung volutes over the aisles, and its columns and pilasters are positioned to make the eye focus on the central door. In contrast, the facade of Il Gesù is more square, its volutes swing out at a higher level and its pattern of pilasters is more diffuse. In the view of Sir John Summerson, 'this comparison... is as handy a comparison as any to explain the difference between Mannerism and Baroque in architecture'.[2]

It took a further 50 years, however, before the papacy again became involved in commissioning work on ecclesiastical buildings. In 1644, in anticipation of the Year of Jubilee of 1650, Innocent X entrusted Francesco Borromini with the task of renovating the interior of S Giovanni in Laterano, the cathedral of Rome. Founded *c* 312, restored in 432–40 and expanded in 1220–36, the ancient building was in a deplorable condition; under papal patronage, Borromini was able to transform the venerable four-aisled basilica into an aisleless Baroque church without altering the original plan or the existing walls.

Innocent was less successful with his second major public project: the continuing development of the University of Rome. The university was founded by Boniface VIII early in the 14th century, but the Palazzo della Sapienza – as it became known – was still unfinished in 1632 when Innocent's predecessor Urban VIII commissioned Borromini to build the church of S Ivo alla Sapienza across the end of its large interior courtyard (built in the 1560s by Giacomo della Porta). But work dragged on and, despite being subsequently funded by Innocent X, the complex was only completed under his successor Alexander VII around 1660.[3] The plan of S Ivo alla Sapienza is based on two equilateral triangles to form a six-pointed star. The points of one of the triangles are chopped off to

Photo 15.1 Carlo Maderno, church of S Susanna, Rome, completed 1603. The facade of this much restored church is considered a masterpiece and provided a model for many Baroque churches that followed.

form concave curves, while the other three are moulded into convex semicircles.[4] The resulting concave facade is adorned with Corinthian pilasters and a prominent entablature, and an attic storey above is pierced with oval windows. With ornamental turrets at its corners, the facade is surmounted by a trifoliate drum which supports, in turn, a lantern, spire and cross which, according to Ian Sutton, constitute 'the most extraordinary steeple in Rome'.[5]

Prior to his association with the development of S Ivo, Alexander VII had been anxious to reconstruct the church of S Maria della Pace, a task on which he had set his sights since he was a young priest. The medieval church had been rebuilt by Sixtus IV (1480–4) to commemorate victory over the Turks, and in 1504 Cardinal Oliviero Carafa commissioned Donato Bramante to design the cloister (see p 384), but in Alexander's view the main body of the church needed to be repaired and updated. Since Bernini was fully employed on another commission, the development of the Piazza S Pietro, in 1656 Alexander entrusted Pietro da Cortona with the design of an edifice that was in keeping with the age. What emerged was a church that was manifestly Baroque. The lateral

Photo 15.2 Francesco Borromini, church of S Ivo alla Sapienza, Rome, 1642. With its courtyard designed by Giacomo della Porta and much embellished by its spiralling cupola and two small towers, the church is an outstanding example of Baroque architecture.

wings of the new building extend beyond the main body of the church to form a concave backcloth and, from the central part of this, a convex porch supported by Doric columns swells out into the Piazza della Pace. The almost equally protruding upper storey boasts rectangular vertical panels in its two outer bays and a large rectangular central window framed by Doric columns and surmounted by a large segmental pediment, while the facade as a whole is crowned by an even larger triangular pediment. During its construction, the new development required the demolition of nearby houses. Cortona thus took the opportunity to design the surrounding facades of the new five-sided Piazza della Pace to create harmony. In the view of Anthony Majanlahti, the outcome was undoubtedly 'one of the summit achievements of baroque urban planning'.[6]

By the late seicento, the Roman Renaissance was all but over, but a final example of public expenditure on the application of the Baroque to ecclesiastical buildings demonstrates that the papacy was, as yet, not quite ready to tone down the exuberance of this extravagant style. Thus, under Clement X (1670–6), Carlo

Photo 15.3   Pietro da Cortona, church of S Maria della Pace, Rome, 1656. Following a number of restorations over the years, the church assumed its present appearance when – at the behest of Pope Alexander VII – a beautiful semi-circular porch was added to its south front.

Rainaldi – an acknowledged exponent of Baroque architecture – was entrusted in 1673 with the rebuilding of the apse of the 4th-century basilica of S Maria Maggiore (previously rebuilt in the 13th century), and with construction of a magnificent flight of stairs that, like the apse, pointed north-westwards in the direction of Via delle Quattro Fontane.

Although publicly funded projects were mainly ecclesiastical in the Baroque age, papal patronage sometimes extended to public utility schemes. In an attempt to ensure that Rome continued to receive a flow of fresh water from springs north of its built-up area, in 1608 Paul V directed his engineers to repair Trajan's acqueduct from the sources of the water to the Eternal City, and in 1612 he commissioned Giovanni Fontana and Flaminio Ponzio to construct a new fountain, the Acqua Paola, in the Trastevere using stone from the Forum Transitoria. With its three triumphal arches flanked by columns taken from the porch of the Old St Peter's, its facade is further embellished by a delicately inscribed description of the building programme.[7]

Photo 15.4 Giovanni Fontana and Flaminio Ponzio, Acqua Paola, Rome, 1612. More like a temple facade than a fountain, the edifice is not only functional but prominently adorns the slopes of the Trastavere.

Public Patronage in Venice: Redemption, Independence and Glory

Over a period of 50 years (1631–81), and under the patronage of 10 successive doges from Niccolò Contarini (1630–1) to his descendant Alvise Contarini (1676–84), Baldassare Longhena spent most of his long career supervising construction of the church of S Maria della Salute that he so brilliantly designed. Located imposingly at the entrance to the Grand Canal and almost opposite the Piazzetta S Marco, it was commissioned in 1630 to give thanks to the Virgin Mary – protector of *salute* or health – for delivering Venice from its plague of 1629–30 in which 46,490 of its inhabitants died.[8]

In competition with 10 other proposals, Longhena's plans were chosen by the Senate since – in the face of the pressures of the Counter-Reformation – they symbolised Venetian religious independence, and because of this important political message the republic was willing to incur the enormous cost of constructing

Photo 15.5 Baldassare Longhena, church of S Maria della Salute, Venice, begun 1630. A distinctive landmark at the southern end of the Grand Canal, the enormous white edifice is notable for its two domes and concentric volutes.

the building.[9] However, by 1657, in the interests of Catholic solidarity in its struggle against the Ottoman Turks, 'the iconography of the Salute assumed a more orthodox Counter-Reformation stance';[10] for example, internally angels replaced Venetian saints, and externally the Virgin with a crown of 12 stars was erected on the huge dome.[11]

The most prominent feature of the church when viewed from any angle, near or far, is its huge dome. It stands on an octagonal drum whose sides are supported by 16 scroll buttresses. Adjacent to it, on the seaward side of the church, there is a smaller dome flanked by two bell towers that do not quite reach the height of the lower *cupola*. Among the attributes of the central facade are four huge columns mounted on high bases and framed niches containing statues. Either side of the facade three protruding chapels partly encircle the church and, like the central facade, they are crowned with large triangular pediments. In this magnificent structure, 'Longhena took advantage of the special visual qualities of Istrian stone. Whether sun-lit against the deep blue sky or plunging deeply into storm clouds, the Salute makes an unforgettable impression, casting its huge shadow right across the mouth of the Grand Canal.'[12]

Milan and Florence: the Rejection of Baroque

With the total failure of the Republic of Genoa, once Venice's chief maritime rival, to undertake any publicly funded development in the early 16th century, Baroque or otherwise, it was left to ecclesiastical and secular government in Milan and Florence to demonstrate that publicly funded urban development was not confined to Rome and Venice. In Milan, in 1602, Cardinal Federico Borromeo commissioned construction of a courtyard in the Seminary of the Archbishop founded nearly 40 years earlier by Carlo Borromeo in compliance with the dictats of the Council of Trent. Its design in the hands of Aurelio Trezzi and Fabio Mangone, the courtyard was framed by a 'double order of coupled columns – Doric on the ground floor and Ionic above – and surmounted by an architrave, frieze and cornice'.[13] The design was classical rather than Baroque, and in the seicento its solemn and severe aspect probably seemed appropriate for the purpose for which the building was constructed, an educational institution.

Classical architecture was also employed in the development of the Palazzo del Capitano di Giustizia. The rectangular building – which also served as a prison – was arranged around two turreted courtyards. Begun in 1578, the building was further developed in 1605 when the Spanish governor of Milan, the Count of Fuentes, commissioned the military engineer Piero Antonio Barca to modernise its structure. Within the courtyard (which has now been changed beyond recognition) Doric columns support an arcade and rustication emphasises the line of the arches that seem to anchor the structure to the ground.[14] As early as 1603, it was decided that the palace would be linked to the nearby Ducal Palace by the opening of a new road, the Via Alicanto, but this has now disappeared.[15]

The most novel civic building constructed in Milan in the early seicento is the Ambrosian Library, the first public library in Europe. Commissioned in 1603 with its design entrusted to Lelio Buzzi, the small building is entirely classical in concept. Its entrance is faced by four Doric pilasters that frame the central door and its flanking windows, and it is crowned by a full-width entablature and triangular pediment. Within, there is an arcaded courtyard accessed by means of a hallway and barrel-vaulted reading room.

It was not only in Venice that an architectural competition helped to determine the style of a public building. In Florence, the plans of Giulio and Alfonso Parigi were chosen by the Grand Duke Cosimo II de'Medici in 1619 to determine the future shape and appearance of his seat of government, the Palazzo Pitti. On the north side of the building, from 1620 three new arches were added to the urban facade in keeping with its classical image, and under Ferdinand II two lateral foreparts were added in 1640–50 to form a 'pincer' configuration.[16] By 1650 the facade had reached its full width of 674 feet (205 m).[17] From 1631 work started on the south side of the building integrating its courtyard with the Boboli Gardens.

Naples and Palermo: Baroque in the South

Public patronage that manifested itself in Naples in the cinquecento in the development of the Via Toledo continued into the early seicento when the

Photo 15.6   Domenico Fontana, Palazzo Reale, Naples, begun 1601. Occupying the whole of the eastern side of the Piazza del Plebiscito, and although retaining much of its original appearance, the enormous palace became more a monument to monarchy than a royal residence.

Spanish viceroy, Francisco de Castro (1601–3), commissioned construction of the immense Palazzo Reale on an enormous open site to the west of the medieval Castel Nuovo. With the design of the palace entrusted in 1601 to the Royal Architect, Domenico Fontana, construction took place under the direction of his son, Giulio Cesare.

The majestic Baroque facade of the palace incorporates a row of niches on its ground floor that over the years accommodated the statues of eight dynasties of Neapolitan rulers. Giulio Cesare Fontana succeeded his father as Royal Architect in 1607 and in 1611, while still engaged on the Palazzo Reale, was commissioned by the then viceroy, Pedro Fernandez de Castro (1610–16) to design the enormous Palazzo dei Regi Studi of the university. Initially, a stable block was converted into a two-storey academic complex built around two large courtyards separated by 21 continuous arcades but, after Fontana was succeeded by Bartolomeo Picchiatti as Royal Architect in 1627, the arcades were surmounted by two floors of public reception rooms.

In Sicily, the urban heart of Palermo was reconstructed in the late cinquecento when two thoroughfares (the Cassaro and the Via Maqueda) were built across the city at 90 degrees to each other to form a crossroads known as the Quattro Canti (see chapter 11). Under the patronage of the Spanish viceroy, the Duke of Vigliena, four lofty Baroque *palazzi* were constructed, one at each corner of Quattro Canti in *c* 1611, their four exuberant facades collectively adorned by fountains, statues of the four seasons, the four patron saints of Palermo and the four Spanish kings of Sicily.

Town Planning in Seicento Italy

In the cinquecento, town planning was practised in many cities throughout Italy from Venice to Palermo (see chapter 11), but in the seicento it was very largely confined to Rome where the papacy spared no expense in embellishing the Eternal City with *grands projets*. Three in particular are worthy of consideration. The first, the redevelopment of Piazza Navona, was undertaken during the pontificates of Innocent X (1644–55) and Alexander VII (1655–67). The *piazza* stood on the site of the Stadium of Domitian (from AD 86), but throughout the Middle Ages and beyond the crumbling remains of the stadium had been built over in an *ad hoc* manner so that by the 17th century the emergent *piazza* was in need of reconstruction. Innocent therefore undertook the development of his

Photo 15.7　Quattro Canti, Palermo, *c* 1611. Dividing old Palermo into a quadrant, the busy crossroads is adorned by Baroque buildings, statues and fountains.

Photo 15.8　Piazza Navona, Rome, 1644–67. Retaining the shape of Domitian's stadium, the long *piazza* is dominated by the church of S Agnese in Agone, the Palazzo Pamphilj and the Fontana dei Quattro Fiumi.

family's property on the western side of the square (see chapter 17). This began with the reconstruction of the Palazzo Pamphilj (1644–55), followed by the construction of the church of S Agnese (1652–66) and the Collegio Innocenziano (begun 1654).

However, Alexander also wished to decorate the *piazza* itself and thus commissioned Bernini to design and build an enormous fountain, the Fontana dei Quattro Fiumi (1647–51), close to its centre. With its obelisk and ornately sculpted base, the fountain symbolises a triumphant Catholic Church ruling the four known continents of the world as represented by the rivers Danube, Ganges, Nile and Plate, and surrounded by geographically related flora and fauna. To acknowledge his patron, Bernini incorporated the pontiff's coat of arms – a dove bearing an olive branch – on the rocky base of the sculpture on the top of the obelisk.[18] A further fountain, Bernini's relatively small Fontana del Moro (1652–4), graced the southern end of the *piazza* in line with his earlier and grander sculpture.

Photo 15.9 Gianlorenzo Bernini, Fontana dei Quattro Fiumi, Rome, 1647–51. A highly ornate Baroque sculpture and a masterpiece of Bernini, the fountain dominates the centre of the Piazza Navona.

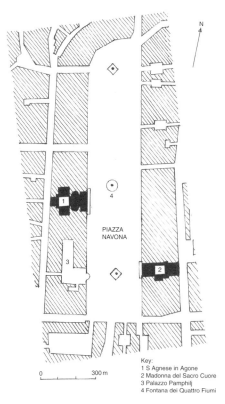

Figure 15.1 The Piazza Navona, Rome

Key:
1 S Agnese in Agone
2 Madonna del Sacro Cuore
3 Palazzo Pamphilj
4 Fontana dei Quattro Fiumi

0   300 m

Apart from its many fine artistic features, the *piazza* is also notable for its exceptional length (fig 15.1). Whereas Alberti had argued that the ideal square should have a length twice as long as its width,[19] and Vitruvius had suggested a ratio of 3:2,[20] the sides of the Piazza Navona are in the ratio of 5:1, 'reflected in the bold horizontal treatment of the facade of S. Agnese'[21] and the uncluttered positioning of the fountains on the lengthy longitudinal axis of the *piazza*.

The second project, the colonnade of the Piazza S Pietro, was on an altogther larger scale. Commissioned by Alexander VII in 1655 and designed by Bernini, the colonnade was an integral part of an enormous forecourt abutting the front of St Peter's and consisting of three connected open spaces: the *piazza retta* in front of the basilica's facade, the *piazza obliqua* edged by two encircling arms

Photo 15.10 Gianlorenzo Bernini, Piazza S Pietro, Rome, begun 1655. An architectural and town planning masterpiece, the *piazza* is adorned by two semi-circles of Ionic colonnades, each arranged in four rows.

198 metres (650 ft) apart, and the *piazza rusticucci* that was to serve as the entrance to the complex but was not completed until the 20th century (fig 15.2).[22] The *piazza obliqua*, in particular, provided a solution to the problem created by Carlo Maderno when he constructed the extraordinarily wide and lofty facade of St Peter's that overshadowed all in front of it. Bernini surrounded the open space of the *piazza obliqua* with two ovoid colonnades comprising a total of 280 free-standing columns, each is metres (50 ft) high, and then funnelled the space between the two angled lines of the *piazza retta* to make the basilica appear both closer and narrower.[23]

With the use of so many large columns standing four deep, in the enlightened view of Sir John Summerson the colonnade boasts the 'most imposing assembly of columns in the world'.[24] More specifically, since the columns are Doric and their bases Tuscan, and they carry an entablature that is neither Doric nor Tuscan but essentially Ionic, they display the blurred and confusing

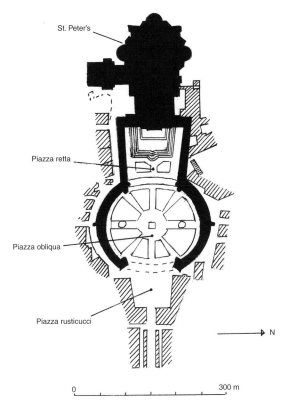

St. Peter's

Piazza retta

Piazza obliqua

Piazza rusticucci

N

0   300 m

Figure 15.2 The Piazza S Pietro, Rome

image of the Baroque rather than conformity to the rigid tenets of classical architecture.

The final planning project is the reconstruction and further development of the Piazza del Popolo (fig 15.3). On hearing that after her conversion to Catholicism, Queen Christina of Sweden intended to make a pilgrimage to Rome in 1655, Alexander VII commissioned Bernini to design a new facade for the inner face of the Porta del Popolo, a medieval gateway that served as the main entry point to Rome from the north. The reconstructed gateway took on the appearance of a classically inspired triumphal arch, with an entablature and attic storey above displaying a panel enclosing an inscription saluting the entry of Christina to Rome.[25] The gateway is crowned by a broken gable that encloses the pontiff's *monti* and star and a garland incorporating the wheatsheaf emblem

Photo 15.11 Carlo Rainaldi, Gianlorenzo Bernini and Carlo Fontana, Piazza del Popolo, Rome, 1662-79. Although the present form of the *piazza* did not take shape until the 18th and 19th centuries, since the late 17th century the square has been adorned in the south by the churches of S Maria in Monsanto (left) and S Maria dei Miracoli (right).

of the Swedish Vasa dynasty.[26] In 1878, two side passages were added to the gateway and, in the same year, two towers that flanked the edifice were demolished.[27]

The second major development in the *piazza* was the construction of the twin churches of S Maria dei Miracoli and S Maria in Monsanto on the southern side of the square. Like the Porta del Popolo, they were commissioned by Alexander VII, and construction began in 1662. With their design initially entrusted to Carlo Rainaldi, and later to Bernini and Carlo Fontana (1675–9), the churches with their pedimented porticoes separate the Via Babuini, Via del Corso and Via Ripetta that branch off dramatically towards central Rome, but the entrance to the Corso, in particular, 'is a stroke of pure genius in terms of urban design' (fig 15.3).[28]

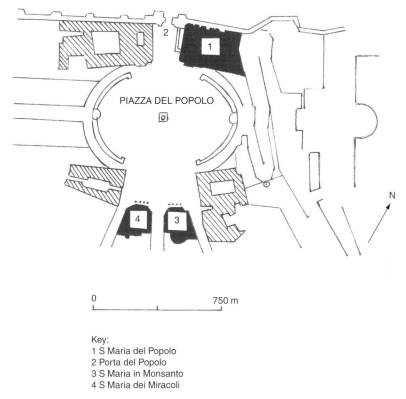

PIAZZA DEL POPOLO

0   750 m

Key:
1 S Maria del Popolo
2 Porta del Popolo
3 S Maria in Monsanto
4 S Maria dei Miracoli

Figure 15.3   The Piazza del Popolo, Rome

Conclusion

Public patronage in 17th-century Italy was very largely confined to Rome. As in the previous century, working partnerships developed between a succession of pontiffs and their architects but, in terms of expenditure, projects were often on an enormous scale – for example the final cost of constructing Innocent X's highly symbolic Fontana dei Quattro Fiumi was more than 29,000 *scudi* – expenditure that in involving the misappropriation of public funds created a public outcry at a time of extreme privation.[29] The cost of a further development, the colonnade of the Piazza S Pietro, was put at more than 1 million *scudi*, a highly unpopular item of expenditure at a time when Rome was losing much of its population, and a major cause of the widespread dislike of its initiator, Pope Alexander VIII.[30] Elsewhere in Italy, except for the construction of the Baroque church of S Maria della Salute in Venice, development in the public sphere was confined to a number of small projects, in Genoa, Milan and Florence for example, but these tended to be more classical than Baroque in style, a reflection of stylistic preference and the unwillingness to incur heavy public expenditure on exuberant architecture at a time of economic recession and population decline. The glory-days of public patronage in Renaissance Italy were now mostly over.

Notes

1   C Woodward, *Rome* (Manchester: Manchester University Press, 1995), p 93.
2   J Summerson, *The Classical Language of Architecture* (London: Thames and Hudson, 1980), p 67.
3   A Majanlahti, *The Families Who Made Rome* (London: Chatto & Windus, 2005), p 369.
4   I Sutton, *Western Architecture* (London: Thames and Hudson, 1999), p 176.
5   Ibid, pp 176–7.
6   Majanlahti, *The Families*, p 356.
7   Woodward, *Rome*, p 96.
8   D Howard, *The Architectural History of Venice* (New Haven and London: Yale University Press, 2002), p 213.
9   Ibid, p 214.
10 Ibid, p 215.
11 Ibid.
12 Ibid, pp 220–1.
13 L Roncai, 'The Neoclassical city and residence', in *Milan. Architectural Guide* (Turin: Allemandi, 1999), p 107.
14 Ibid, p 109.
15 Ibid.
16 G Zucconi, *Florence. An architectural guide* (Venice: Arsenale Editrice, 1995), p 101.
17 RC Wirtz, *Florence* (Cologne: Könemann, 2000), p 438.
18 B Hintzen-Bohlen with J Sorges, *Rome and the Vatican City* (Cologne: Könemann, 2001), p 178.
19 LB Alberti, *Ten Books on Architecture*, tr J Leoni (London: Tirani, 1955 edn), p 173.
20 Vitruvius, *Ten Books of Architecture* (New York: Dover, 1960 edn), p 132.
21 C Moughtin, *Urban Design. Street and Square*, 3rd edn (Oxford and Burlington, MA: Oxford University Press, 2003), p 107.
22 Ibid, p 93.
23 Sutton, *Western Architecture*, p 174.
24 Summerson, *Classical Language*, pp 88–9.
25 Majanlahti, *The Families*, p 248.
26 Ibid, p 348.
27 Hintzen-Bohlen with Sorges, *Rome*, p 229.
28 Moughtin, *Urban Design*, p 98.
29 Ibid, p 298.
30 Ibid.

CHAPTER 16

ECONOMIC STAGNATION AND URBAN DEVELOPMENT IN THE EARLY 17TH CENTURY

Introduction

Italy, then with more large cities than any other country in Europe, experienced a marked decrease in its total population during the first half of the 17th century, an outcome of intermittent periods of plague and famine. Simultaneously, the peninsula suffered from a prolonged recession, lowering the average standard of living well into the 18th century. However, what is remarkable about this sad period in Italian history is that population decline and economic stagnation had a perverse effect on the development of the built environment. Whereas in the later Middle Ages and in the 15th and 16th centuries there was a positive relationship between economic growth and increased construction activity on the one hand, and economic recession and a decline in construction on the other, in the seicento construction activity in the private sector continued to remain at a relatively high level in tandem with the long-term decline of the Italian economy. Private patrons – merchants, bankers and the nobility – eagerly sought to divert their investments from failing industrial and trading enterprises to land and buildings both in the cities and the countryside, a diversion of funds that had first become apparent in the late cinquecento.

Continuing Effects of Disease and Famine on the Urban Population

Mainly because of disease and famine, the population of Italy decreased markedly from 12 million in 1600 to 11 million in 1650, although it fell less dramatically than during the Black Death of the 14th century when it had plummeted by around 50 per cent. North of the Alps, the Thirty Years' War (1618–48) had a severely detrimental effect on population growth, but Italy was comparatively free of warfare and its effects on the rate of mortality.

Table 16.1   Population of Italy and selected cities, c 1600–1650

	1600	1650	% increase or decrease 1600–1650
France	19,000,000	n a	—
Italy	12,000,000	11,000,000	8
Spain	8,500,000	n a	—
England and Wales	4,250,000	n a	—
N Netherlands	1,500,000	n a	—
Paris	220,000	n a	—
London	200,000	n a	—
Amsterdam	65,000	n a	—
Madrid	49,000	n a	—
Naples	237,784 (1596)	300,000	29
Rome	99,312 (1602)	118,087 (1652)	19
Venice	142,804 (1624)	158,772 (1655)	11
Bari	15,000	15,000	—
Florence	70,000 (1622)	69,495	−1
Bologna	61,000 (1624)	58,000	−5
Milan	108,000	100,000	−7
Padua	36,000	32,714 (1648)	−8
Perugia	19,722 (1618)	17,385 (1656)	−15
Modena	19,911 (1596)	15,000	−25
Brescia	36,000	25,063	−31
Genoa	62,396	38,360 (1660)	−39
Parma	33,000	19,000	−42
Mantua	31,000	14,000	−55
% total population of Italy	8.1	8.4	

Source: CF Black, *Early Modern Italy, A Social History* (London: Routledge, 2001).

Despite its smaller size than France or Spain, the Italian population in the 17th century remained broadly the same as in the 15th century. Italy contained the largest number of major cities in Europe, most of which – as free-standing cities or state capitals – were independent or quasi-independent entities. Taking 10,000 people as a rather crude threshold, 'Italy had at least twenty-nine such cities in 1500, thirty-four in 1600 and forty-five in 1700'.[1] In France, the respective numbers were only 13, 12 and 8; in the Netherlands: 12, 15 and 11; and in England: 4, 5 and 3 cities.[2] Over the period Paris, Amsterdam and London grew into very large cities, but so did Naples and Rome.[3]

Table 16.1 shows that although some western European urban populations declined in the early 17th century, urbanisation increased from 8.1 per cent of the total population in 1600 to around 8.4 per cent in 1665. This could only have been attributable to migration from the countryside. If data were available for all towns with populations of (say) 10,000 or more, it might be shown that the level of urbanisation was considerably greater.

The decline in the urban population undoubtedly decreased the size of the total population of the peninsula – from 12 to 11 million (1600–50). Because of high densities and unsanitary water supplies, cities were particularly affected by disease. *Tifo* epidemics occurred in 1620–1, 1628–9 and 1648–9, and plague was endemic in 1629–31 in most of northern Italy except Friuli and Romagna. From July 1630 to October 1631, about half the population of Mantua, Milan, Padua and Verona, and one-third that of Bologna and Venice died from plague – in Venice alone the epidemic accounted for 46,490 fatalities.[4]

The Impact of Food Crises on Urban Population

Recovery from plague after 1631 was slower than it had been in the late 16th century because the economic climate of much of northern Italy – adversely affected by the Thirty Years' War north and south of the Alps – was less favourable. However, it was not the plague alone 'that was responsible for the overall fall in Italian population; for many towns barely touched by plague, like Macerata, experienced repeated mortality crises throughout the seventeenth century, coincidental with poor harvests and high wheat prices'.[5] Across Italy, there were food crises in 1602, 1637 and 1648 (a general European crisis year), all of which inflated death rates.

In Malthusian style, the pressure on agricultural resources in Italy prior to the Industrial Revolution in the 19th century was periodically relieved because earlier famine halted or slowed down the rate of increase in population. (Thomas Malthus in seting out his theory in his *Essay on the Principle of Population* (1789), positing that, without restraint, population growth is unsustainable and that living standards would fall.) By the beginning of the 17th century, after falling in the aftermath of the Black Death to 8 million in 1400, Italy's population had steadily risen to 12 million, well in excess of its medieval peak. However, food production failed to keep up. 'The traditional granaries of Sicily were no longer capable of making up the shortfall in northern Italy, as was demonstrated in the terrible famines of 1590–1.'[6] Plague in the first half of the 17th century then reduced the size of the Italian population to 11 million (in 1650) and diminished demographic pressure on food supply. However, whereas population increase in 16th-century Italy was associated with economic growth, a decreased population in the first half of the 17th century had severe effects on the economy of the peninsula.

The Long Recession

In addition to a declining population, early-17th-century Italy experienced a major downturn in economic activity. After a period of economic expansion throughout much of the cinquecento, the numerous Italian economies lurched into deep recession in the early years of the 17th century with a devastating effect on the overall standard of living of the peninsula for well over a hundred years. An assessment of economic performance over the two centuries shows that continuous inflation was superseded by recession; industrial development was followed by a serious decline in output; an expanding export trade was giving way to an inability to compete; and conditions favourable for economic growth were being eroded by an environment of war, plague and bankruptcy.

The onset of recession

During the final years of the 16th century Europe faced a major downturn in its economic fortunes. The price revolution had entered a new stage during the early 1590s – 'a prolonged and very painful period that historians call the "general crisis of the seventeenth century" .... This was the darkest era in European history after the catastrophe of the fourteenth century'.[7] While the cost of food and fuel escalated (in the case of the former because of a succession of failed harvests from 1594 to 1597), real wages and industrial prices were depressed. The real wages of artisans and labourers 'fell farther behind the cost of living, while returns to land and capital continued to advance [and] [w]ealth became increasingly concentrated in a few hands'.[8] In Italy, because of its own distinctive economic attributes, the downturn in the cycle occurred in the relatively early years of the seicento rather than at the end of the previous century, but its consequences – although different – were at least as severe.

Misplaced industrial optimism

Manufacturers in northern and central Italy – then one of the most developed industrial areas of Europe – felt they had good reason to be optimistic at the beginning of the 17th century since they had enjoyed an industrial boom over much of the cinquecento that it seemed, to many, would continue. Business enterprises located in Venice, Milan, Florence and a host of smaller cities were now concentrating on the production and export of mainly luxury goods such as textiles, cloth, ironware, firearms, crystal glass, ceramics, printed goods, quality soap and leatherware. Production rose to unprecedented levels: for example, 'Venice's production of fine woollen cloths rose from 1,310 pieces in 1503 to 28,729 in 1601; Milan had 3,000 silk looms in 1606; [and] Florence more than doubled its production of woollen cloths between 1553 and 1572, from 14,700 pieces to 33,312 pieces'.[9] Manufacturers in the north were also integrated with the major artisan centres of Naples and Salerno, from whence they imported commodities such as the wool of the vast sheep flocks on their seasonal passage through the *dogana* of Foggia and the crude silk of Calabria, while Venice imported cereals and olive oil directly from Apulia.[10]

The turning point in Italy's fortunes came with the slump of 1619–22 when industrial production and employment both declined dramatically. In Florence, the production of woollen cloth fell to only 6,000 pieces in 1650, and in Venice to as few as 3,820 by 1680,[11] while in Milan the number of silk looms fell from 3,000 in 1606 to a mere 600 in 1635 – resulting in the unemployment of as many as one-third of the city's 20,000 silk workers by 1620. The Piedmontese city of Saluzzo was even worse hit by recession, with around two-thirds of its population being destitute in the early 1620s.[12] Although warfare in the first half of the

17th century generally had a very disruptive effect on the economic condition of northern Italy, this was not everywhere the case there. Where cities were geared to the production of armaments and the construction of fortifications, their local economies remained buoyant until the cessation of hostilities in the mid-17th century.[13]

The decline of manufacturing in Italy in the seicento accelerated the shift in trade circuits to northern Europe, particularly to the Netherlands where 'Amsterdam and the ports around it now became the centres for exchange of information, technology, and investment throughout the world'.[14] Although Venice, Genoa and Florence were still blessed with entrepreneurial drive and vast stocks of capital, Italian states were now very much on the periphery of the Dutch world economy. To an extent, the Florentine silk industry was able to avoid this constraint by concentrating on the manufacture of luxury products, notably its black silks and satins that were unmatched anywhere for quality. Tuscan merchants in Livorno were thus able to exploit markets for these and other luxury products throughout Europe including new outlets in Amsterdam, Cadiz (for re-exporting to the Spanish colonies) and even Archangel in Russia. Italian silk textile output was on a sufficiently large scale to enable employment of more than a quarter of the economically active population of Florence, including women in the low-skilled preparation and spinning processes. Despite the rise in silk manufacture, the decline of wool – where output had diminished from 30,000 pieces in 1570 to only 6,000 in the 1640s – was of such a magnitude that it accounted for an overall reduction in textile production in the peninsula by about 35 per cent between 1560 and 1650.[15] Manufacturing output across northern Italy similarly declined: woollen textiles in Monza, Como and Venice; cotton in Cremona; and silk manufacture in Lucca and Genoa. Italian industrialists not only found it difficult to compete abroad, but even lost their domestic markets to lower-cost northern producers.

Although the Italian recession continued well into the 18th century, its longevity was attributable to a combination of factors that had been accumulating since the early part of the seicento. Italian products were overpriced in both foreign and home markets and had become outmoded; other countries, such as the Netherlands and England, were now more technologically advanced than Italy, while Northern European states learned to imitate Italian products and restricted their importation;[16] and restructuring of the Italian economy – in order to make it more competitive – was impeded by the guilds which, apart from opposing entrepreneurs straying from traditional techniques, 'demanded high wages for urban craftsmen and defended the strict specifications imposed on each item produced'.[17]

Inability to Compete in the World Economy and Deindustrialisation

The loss of Italian export markets, primarily because of competition from newer, lighter and lower-priced draperies produced in Northern Europe, was exacerbated by the inflexibility of the Italian guilds. They connived with the civil authorities to place a priority on traditional practices such as maintaining the quality of the product, engaging in monopolistic practices within the cities and underpinning high wage levels. In contrast, competitors across the Alps responded to the economic depression of the 17th century by relocating and restructuring their textile industry in rural areas, and the Dutch, English and French in particular soon took advantage of the Venetian–Ottoman wars to capture much of the Mediterranean textile trade.[18] However, although Venice declined as a trading port, Leghorn – as the free port established by the grand dukes of Tuscany in the 1590s – began to thrive as a base for foreign shipping, particularly English shipping 'that took over as transporters of goods in and out of Italy [joined by] Turks, Berbers, Ushoks and others in depredating Italian, especially Venetian, shipping'.[19] The merchant fleets of Genoa, like those of Venice, were also unable to compete with Northern European transporters, this time on routes to Spain and Naples, so lowering still further the investment horizons of Italian capitalists.[20]

By the middle of the 17th century, the manifestations of economic decline throughout the peninsula were becoming more and more apparent. Instead of being essentially a major exporter of manufactures such as textiles and metal products, Italy was now first and foremost a large importer of foreign manufactured goods and exporter of primary and semi-finished produce. Whereas, for example, 'northern Italy [was] once a major exporter of silk brocades and cloths, now [it] only managed to continue to export few and cheaper items, like ribbons, while expanding its production of crude silk as the main supplier to the Lyons silk industry'.[21] Italy's competitive ability in its traditional export markets was often weakened by commercial rivals trading in counterfeit Italian products, for example the English passed off 'cheap and shoddy cloths as Venetian by using false stamp marks in the Levant market [while] the French tried deceiving the world with imitation Venetian glass, when they could not bribe or cajole Venetian glass-blowers to emigrate'.[22]

Deindustrialisation led many small manufacturing cities such as Como, Cremona, Pavia and Lecce to pale into economic insignificance, while the major cities of Venice, Florence and Naples soon became more renowned for their administrative roles, their courts and their tourist attractions than for their economic strength.

The condition of the Italian economy during the first half of the 17th century, however, was not determined by endogenous economic factors alone. Weaknesses in the manufacturing and commercial sectors were subordinated to the seriously disruptive influences of war, famine and client-bankruptcy.

The Economic Effects of War, Plague and Bankruptcy

During the early 17th century, numerous armed conflicts wrought destruction across large swathes of northern Italy. From 1612, the dukes of Savoy attempted to seize Monferrato and later Mantua from Spain, a struggle that was joined by France in 1628; Venice took up arms against the Austrian Habsburgs in 1615 and from 1620 competed with France, Spain and Savoy to acquire control of the Alpine region of Valtellina; and in 1635 France, Savoy, Parma and Mantua allied against Spain.[23]

Notwithstanding the early impact of conflict in the north, and very real structural weaknesses in the Italian economy which rendered parts of the manufacturing industry increasingly uncompetitive in foreign markets, much of Italy enjoyed a period of economic prosperity well into the second decade of the seicento. Manufacturing and commercial activity were at their height – the peak of an upward trend that had begun in the late quattrocento. However, with the onset of the Thirty Years' War in Germany in 1618, the European world economy suddenly collapsed. Manufacturing plummeted between 1619 and 1622; and, for the duration of the war, major trading routes across the globe were disrupted by the contest between Spain and Holland. After 1635, full-blown hostilities strangled whatever commercial relations had existed between Spanish-controlled areas (such as Milan and Genoa) and France, while – on a vast scale – resources were squandered on 'unproductive' investments such as arms manufacture in Lombardy and Tuscany, and on the construction of fortifications across northern Italy, rather than on activities that would have broadened the economic base such as the production of non-military items.[24]

In addition to the loss of foreign markets, several Italian economies were also disadvantaged by the shortage of Spanish specie and by currency devaluation north of the Alps. This made it impossible for foreign companies to repay loans to Italian bankers, creating a banking crisis for much of the Thirty Years' War that not only disrupted overland trade across the German states but encouraged the Spanish government to increase taxation in its possessions to finance its war operations. Since to an extent Rome participated in the war, under the pontificate of Urban VIII the papacy incurred mounting debt (it doubled between 1623 and 1644). The population of the Papal States became liable for higher *gabelles* (indirect taxes) on a wide range of goods including basic commodities such as salt, oil, wine and cheese and services, but it was in the kingdom of Naples where *gabelles* (that trippled in the 1630s and 1640s) had the most debilitating effect on demand for consumer goods and services.[25]

Together with war activities associated with the struggle for the duchy of Mantua, a typhus epidemic of 1628 and plague pandemics of 1629–30 and 1657 cancelled out the gains of the periods 1580–1620 and 1631–55 and reduced the Italian population level to about 11 million by the mid-17th century.[26] In consequence, the population of cities such as Milan, Brescia, Genoa and Mantua plummeted catastrophically (table 16.1).[27]

However, the causal relationship between disease and the performance of the Italian economies was complex. At times of economic boom and full employment, incomes were sufficiently high in Italian cities to enable urban consumers to buy sufficient food – even if it was expensive – to maintain the demographic sustainability of their communities. But at times of recession, when unemployment spread widely through the labouring classes of Italian cities, consumers were particularly vulnerable to periodic harvest failures and soon became victims of lethal disease. This in turn exacerbated further economic recession, as occurred in 1629–30 (when French and imperial armies brought the bubonic plague into Piedmont and Lombardy).[28]

Although part of a European pandemic, the plague that hit northern Italy in the late 1620s/early 1630s was probably more severe than elsewhere in Europe because Italy was already debilitated by economic recession and harvest failures.[29] About 30 per cent of the population of Lombardy and the Veneto died as a result of the plague, in part because it was spread by refugees fleeing the worst-hit areas. The death rate was particularly high in Mantua, where two thirds of the population were struck down by the epidemic because a besieging imperial army blocked the way of anyone wishing to leave.

With population pressure being alleviated, demand for foodstuffs declined, suppliers suddenly had produce they could not sell and the price of food consequently fell. There was a further consequence: as with earlier plagues, such as the Black Death of the 14th century, the urban workforce was particularly decimated (possibly because of congested housing and places of employment), but survivors – particularly the highly skilled – were able to exploit their scarcity value after the epidemic to secure wages at a high level both in monetary and real terms.[30]

Bankruptcy, the third variable affecting the performance of the Italian urban economy, was centred on Spain. In the early 17th century, the Spanish crown was no longer able to meet the cost of war with the Dutch and declared itself bankrupt. Genoese financiers, comprising 20 or 30 banking families, had little alternative but to accept their losses, and their former role as bankers to the crown in Spain was, to an extent, taken over by Portuguese financiers based in Madrid.[31] In Naples and Sicily, however, Genoese bankers retained financial relations with the Spanish crown as they were contracted to fund the Spanish armies and fleets based in the Mediterranean. It was increasingly clear, however, that it was Amsterdam and not Genoa (or even London) that had become the foremost financial centre of Europe by the mid-17th century. The Genoese economy – to a significant extent reliant on the earnings of its financial sector – thus declined and, with it, its ability to sustain the level of the population it reached at the end of the cinquecento, although population decline was also associated with the decline of manufacturing industry and the effects of plague.

The Long-term Decline of the Italian Economy

Very early in the 17th century, the Italian economy entered a period of decline that lasted well over a century. The principal manifestation of this decline was deindustrialisation, particularly in the woollen textile sector, and a huge reduction in maritime trade. As was typical in a major recession, prices fell and – at best – population levels remained stagnant. The plight of the economy was exacerbated by plague, warfare and bankruptcy – each being part of a wider European problem. The plague was a continental-wide pandemic that showed no respect for international frontiers, while the Thirty Years' War – involving principally France, Holland, Sweden and different parts of the Habsburg Empire – impacted upon Italy as much of the peninsula was Habsburg territory and was thus liable to taxation that drained into the Spanish treasury to help defray the costs of war. For these reasons, Italy's economy and her traditionally strong trading position were so seriously damaged that her industries no longer dominated the markets of Northern Europe, and her trade routes – previously monopolies – were no longer under her control. With the Dutch, French and English on the ascendancy in both the industrial and shipping sectors of the European world economy, it was difficult for Italy to respond in an appropriate fashion to the loss of its traditional markets. Instead, the peninsula's wealthy 'reacted to the crisis in a classically defensive fashion, attempting to protect their own interests by sinking the available capital into real-estate, thereby starving the productive part of the economy of investment'.[32]

Economic Stagnation and the Further Development of the Built Environment

During the boom years of the cinquecento, the *nouveaux riches* of the burgeoning industrial and trading cities were soon absorbed by the urban elite, reinforcing inequalities in wealth. During the recession of the 17th century, in their determination to keep their capital intact the monied classes diverted their investments away from industry to urban buildings and rural property. Thus in the cities, as part of a property boom, Baroque residences – often named after their proud patrons – sprung up in abundance. In Rome, for example, work began on the Villa Borghese, the Palazzo Chigi-Odescalchi and the Palazzo Barberini between 1608 and 1622; in Venice, the Ca'Pesaro and Ca'Rezzonico were commissioned in 1652 and 1667 respectively; and in Florence development of the Palazzo Strozzi del Poeta and the Palazzo Corsini al Parione was started in 1619 and 1656. Private funding also facilitated work on a substantial number of Baroque churches in Rome and in the south during the first half of the 17th century (see chapter 17), but in Venice – while numerous churches were commissioned – there were very few buildings built for confraternities, such ventures wilting under the onslaught of recession. In contrast, in rural areas 'great villas were built in which the landowners could reside in splendour while all around them suffered the ravages of a disintegrating economy'.[33]

Although investment in property yielded some considerable architectural achievements, it might also have damaged the productive sectors by diverting funds away from industry and transport to the long-term detriment of the Italian economy and its per capita income. Possibly the situation could not have been otherwise. Referring to secular investors (although his argument could also apply to ecclesiastical patrons), EW Hobsbawm has suggested that while the Italian elite controlled huge agglomerations of capital, and in some respects misinvested funds in buildings and other immobile assets, they were acting quite sensibly: 'The experience of centuries had shown that the highest profits were not to be got in technical progress or even in production.... If [the elite] spent vast amounts of capital non-productively, it might simply have been because there was no more room to invest progressively on any scale within the limits of the capitalist sector.'[34] Had investment taken place in the productive sectors rather than in property, could Italy have followed the path of France and England? Probably not. For one thing, there was a lack of political unity in the peninsula. Could Italy, instead, have used the northern Netherlands as a role model? Almost certainly not, since 'there was probably not room for them both, and Holland was better suited to the task for a host of reasons than Venice, or Milan or Genoa'.[35] Northern Italy thus found itself in 'transition from core to semi-periphery [but it] never fell as far as some Mediterranean areas like southern Italy and Sicily, but this was small consolation in the centuries ahead'.[36]

Conclusion

After intermittent though lengthy periods of steady economic growth throughout the quattrocento and cinquecento, Italy entered a prolonged period of stagnation that lasted from the early 17th century until well into the 18th. In part, this was an outcome of population decline, but it was also due to the facts that the peninsula's location was no longer an economic asset and that her industries were becoming uncompetitive. Not only had the centre of gravity of European trade and industry shifted away from the Mediterranean to the Atlantic seaboard of Europe, but the Netherlands, England and France had now assumed the role of the continent's economic power-houses, a role forcibly relinquished by the relatively small and comparatively fragile states of Italy. Remarkably, none of this seemed to affect the development of the built environment of the country. Quite the reverse. Both secular and ecclesiastical patrons built up property portfolios mainly in the form of Baroque *palazzi* and villas. Also, encouraged by the revival of religiosity engendered by the Counter-Reformation, they donated large sums of money towards the construction of Baroque churches from Venice in the north to Palermo in the south.

Chronology

1591	**In Rome, work begins on construction of church of S Andrea della Valle.**
1600	Population of Italy is around 12 million.
	Italy has largest number of major cities in Europe.

	Industrial production reaches unprecedented levels.
1602	Food shortage affects Italy.
1604	**In Florence, the Theatine Order commissions church of SS Michele and Gaetano.**
1606–63	**In Florence, medieval hospital of S Maria Novella reconstructed.**
1608	**In Rome, Cardinal Scipione Borghese commissions Villa Borghese.**
1618	**In Genoa, Gio Agostino Balbi commissions Palazzo Balbi-Cattaneo.**
1619–22	Economic slump adversely affects industry. Economic recession continues until early 18th century.
	Italian manufactured goods overpriced in export markets.
1620–1	Northern Italy afflicted by *tifo* epidemic.
1622	**In Rome, work begins on construction of Palazzo Chigi-Odescalchi.**
1625	**In Rome, Maffeo Barberini commissions Palazzo Barberini.**
1628–9	*Tifo* endemic throughout much of northern Italy.
1629–31	Plague epidemic strikes northern Italy.
	Slow recovery of north Italian economy after plague.
1634	**In Rome, Trinitarian Order commissions church of S Carlo alle Quattro Fontane.**
	In Genoa, Stefano Balbi funds construction of Jesuits' college.
1637	Food crisis in Italy.
1642	**In Rome, Palazzo Madama receives new facade.**
1643	**In Genoa, Stefano Balbi commissions Palazzo Balbi (later Palazzo Reale).**
1644	**In Rome, Innocent X commissions Palazzo Pamphilj.**
1645	**In Milan, Bartolomeo Arese commissions Palazzo Litta.**
1648	Further food crisis hits Italy.
1648–9	*Tifo* epidemic again strikes northern Italy.
1650	Population of Italy falls to 11 million, 1 million less than in 1600.
1650	**In Rome, Innocent X funds development of Palazzo Montecitorio.**
1652	**In Rome, Innocent X commissions church of S Agnese in Agone.**
	In Venice, Pesaro family commissions Ca' Pesaro.
1658	**In Rome, Prince Camillo Pamphilj funds construction of church of S Andrea al Quirinale.**
1667	**In Venice, Bon family commissions Ca'Rezzonico.**
1700	Population of Italy, now 12 million, is no higher than in 1600.

Notes

1 CF Black, *Early Modern Italy, A Social History* (London: Routledge, 2001), p 63.
2 AF Cowan, *Urban Europe, 1500–1700* (Oxford: Oxford University Press, 1998), pp 4–12 with table 1.1.
3 Black, *Early Modern Italy*, p 63.
4 Ibid, p 23.

5   S Woolf, 'Italy 1600–1796', in G Holmes (ed), *The Oxford Illustrated History of Italy* (Oxford: Oxford University Press, 1997), p 117.

6   Ibid.

7   D Hackett Fischer, *The Great Wave. Price Revolutions and the Rhythm of History* (Oxford: Oxford University Press, 1996), p 91.

8   Ibid, p 92.

9   Woolf, 'Italy 1600–1796', pp 115–16.

10 Ibid.

11 Ibid, p 115.

12 G Hanlon, *Early Modern Italy, 1550–1800* (Basingstoke: Macmillan, 2000), pp 207–8; C Duggan, *A Concise History of Italy* (Cambridge: Cambridge University Press, 1994), p 71.

13 Woolf, 'Italy 1600–1796', p 115.

14 Hanlon, *Early Modern Italy*, p 210.

15 Ibid, pp 210–11.

16 Ibid, pp 212–13.

17 Ibid, p 211.

18 Woolf, 'Italy 1600–1796', p 116.

19 Black, *Early Modern Italy*, p 35.

20 Hanlon, *Early Modern Italy*, p 206.

21 Woolf, 'Italy 1600–1796', p 16.

22 Black, *Early Modern Italy*, p 35.

23 Duggan, *Concise History*, p 17.

24 Hanlon, *Early Modern Italy*, p 209.

25 Ibid.

26 C Cipolla, 'Four Centuries of Italian Democratic Development', in DV Glass and DEC Eversley (eds), *Population and History* (London: Edward Arnold, 1965), p 573.

27 Black, *Early Modern Italy*, table A2.

28 Hanlon, *Early Modern Italy*, p 208.

29 Ibid.

30 Ibid, p 210.

31 V Lintner, *A Traveller's History of Italy*, 3rd edn (Gloucester.: Windrush Press, 1989), pp 124–5.

32 Ibid, p 126.

33 EJ Hobsbawm, 'The Crisis of the Seventeenth Century', in T Aston (ed), *Crisis in Europe, 1560–1660* (London: Routledge & Kegan Paul, 1965), pp 18–19.

34 Ibid, p 221.

35 I Wallerstein, *The Modern World System, Capitalist Agriculture and the Origins of the European World-Economy in the Sixteenth Century* (New York and London: Academic Press, 1974), p 221.

36 Ibid.

CHAPTER 17

PRIVATE PATRONAGE AND BAROQUE ARCHITECTURE

Introduction

Private patronage in 17th-century Italy was at its most prolific in Rome, mirroring the scale and exuberance of public development in the Eternal City. With an economy based on the consumption rather than production of goods and services, and inhabited by a population directly or indirectly dependent upon the immense wealth of the Catholic Church, Rome was largely immune from the long recession of the Italian economy that set in around 1619 and lasted throughout and beyond the seicento. Private patrons, therefore, showed little caution, let alone reluctance, in using part of their accumulated wealth to commission construction of magnificent Baroque churches and sumptuous palaces intended respectively to reflect their religious faith and their economic status in society. Elsewhere in Italy the effects of economic stagnation were mixed. In the trading and industrial towns of the north, and particularly in Venice, there was a tendency to divert funds from the depressed industrial and trading cities of the region into real estate, while in Naples viceregal government and feudalism ensured that the economic recession of the capitalist north would not impinge on property development in the south as long as the wealth of patrons remained intact. However, whereas in northern Italy there was a comparatively modest amount of construction activity in the private sector, in Naples there was a substantial amount of Baroque development throughout the seicento, belying the belief that the south failed to experience the fruits of the Renaissance, albeit it did so late in the day.

Private Patronage of Ecclesiastical Buildings in Rome

The church of S Andrea della Valle is one of the most famous Baroque buildings in Rome. Funded initially by Cardinal Alfonso Gesualdo in 1591, and subsequently by Carlo Barberini and his brother Maffeo (the future Pope Urban VIII), Cardinal Alessandro Peretti Montalto and Pope Alexander VII, the church was built for the Theatine Order 'which had made the implementation of catholic reform its special concern'.[1] Locating their church only 450 metres (1,500 ft) west of Il Gesù, the Theatines hoped not just to emulate the Jesuit building but to surpass it in scale and magnificence. To this end, a succession of architects was commissioned over a 70-year period to design an enormous basilica and to supervise its construction. Starting in 1591, Giacomo della Porta revised Francesco Grimaldi's initial plans and designed the church's wide and spacious nave, its facade and its huge dome which was to become the second largest in Rome after St Peter's. Later, in 1604, Matteo Castelli designed the family chapels of the Barberini, and in 1622 Carlo Maderno supervised construction of the dome. Although in the previous year Maderno had encouraged his young protégé Francesco Borromini to add detail to Della Porta's plans for the facade, it was not until 1656–65 that the facade was completed by Carlo Rainaldo and according to his own plans.

Despite lacking many of the embellishments of later 17th-century architectural design, S Andrea della Valle is 'a robust demonstration of the emerging Baroque'.[2] Both of the two storeys of the facade are superimposed by four sets of monumental double columns, while single columns support its flanks; the five sections of the wall become progressively broader towards the centre; the central portal and window, as well as their adjacent niches, are surmounted by alternating triangular and segmental pediments; and the full width of the upper storey is crowned by a giant triangular pediment.[3]

If S Andrea della Valle was a Baroque edifice in the making, the later church of S Carlo alle Quattro Fontane exhibited the Baroque in all its exuberance. Commissioned by the Trinitarian Order in 1634 to honour its founder, S Carlo Borromeo, and situated on a site where four fountains mark the intersection of the Via del Quirinale and the Via delle Quattro Fontane, the small church was designed by Francesco Borromini intermittently over a period of 34 years. Its plan is based on two equilateral triangles joined to form a lozenge-shaped interior, and except for its central sections surviving as straight lines, its angles are curved to produce a wavy motion around the interior of the

Photo 17.1 Francesco Borromini, church of S Carlo alle Quattro Fontane, Rome, begun 1634. An early masterpiece by Borromini. Despite or perhaps because of its restricted site, the church displays all the Baroque ingenuity of his later works.

church. Since the plan assumed an ovoid shape, the main body of the church is surmounted by an oval dome in the manner of Vignola's S Andrea sulla via Flaminia (1551–4). Although Borromini was preoccupied with other commissions throughout his middle years, he resumed work on S Carlo in 1665 in later life and designed its facade. Reflecting the interior of the church, the facade 'undulates with a concave-convex rhythm',[4] a late-Baroque synthesis of architecture and sculpture that was extensively adopted throughout much of Europe.[5] The two-storey facade of S Carlo is supported by four equally spaced columns on each storey and, whereas its central section is convex, its flanking sections are concave. On the ground floor, niches with figures of saints embellish the facade, while the central section of the upper storey is adorned with a large medallion containing a sculptured portrait of S Carlo.[6]

At the time of Borromini's death in 1667, the facade was only partly finished, but under the direction of his nephew Bernardo it was completed in 1677.[7] Throughout its construction, the church – lacking rich sponsors – was underfunded. The poverty-stricken order appointed Borromini as their architect because, at the time of the church's foundation, he had been relatively unknown and thus cheap to employ. To economise further, the Trinitarians largely dispensed with stone and relied upon brick and stucco. It is therefore extraordinary that the outcome is one of the most beautiful Baroque churches in Rome that not only delights the eye but, internally, maintains an air of spiritual contemplation.

While S Carlo alle Quattro Fontane was under construction, Borromini was busy working – with a greater or lesser degree of success – on another private project, the church of S Agnese in Agone. Commissioned by Innocent X in 1652, the church was designed mainly by Girolamo Rainaldi and his son Carlo and was located in the Piazza Navona immediately to the north of the pontiff's palace, the Palazzo Pamphilj. As a centrally planned structure the church is based on a Greek cross with arms of equal length and deep niches. It is crowned by a centrally placed octagon from which the very large dome emerges. Since the site is squeezed between the *piazza* to the east and the Via dell'Anima to the west, it is very narrow and therefore its chapels extend sideways parallel to the axis of the building. However, its most novel feature is its Baroque facade. Its

Photo 17.2 Girolamo Rainaldi and others, church of S Agnese in Agone, Rome, begun 1652. Dominating the western side of the Piazza Navona, the church is notable for its concave facade which is not only attractive in its own right but also serves to emphasise the magnificence of the dome.

Photo 17.3 Giacomo Lorenzo Bernini, church of S Andrea al Quirinale, Rome, begun 1658. With its pink and grey marble facade of Composite orders, the church – in its simplicity – is one of Bernini's finest designs.

concavity adds emphasis to the dome by enabling it to be more visible from the ground than the great cupola at St Peter's which 'recedes behind the front of the basilica as the viewer approaches'.[8] The construction of the church, however, proceeded slowly and, in his frustration, Innocent dismissed the Rainaldis and commissioned Borromini to complete the facade. But Borromini's involvement was very limited. His proposals to alter Carlo Rainaldi's designs to make the facade more curved and to lower the flanking campanile were not implemented and, after the death of Innocent in 1655, the former pontiff's nephew and secular heir, Prince Camillo of S Martino, terminated Borromini's employment. After Camillo's demise in 1657, Borromini faced a further blow to his artistic standing when the princess of Rossano commissioned Bernini to complete the facade of the church, which involved positioning a simple triangular pediment above its main portal in preference to a more ornate version as envisaged by Borromoni.[9]

Before his fall from grace, however, Borromoni was entrusted by Innocent X with the design of the Collegio Innocenziano on the northern side of S Agnese. Begun in 1654, the building was intended as an educational institute for young men from the Pamphilj family lands who might wish to become priests and, together with the Palazzo Doria Pamphilj to the south, framed the church and gave much of the western side of the Piazza Navona a unified structure (see chapter 14).[10]

The last notable Baroque ecclesiastical building under consideration here is the Jesuit church of S Andrea al Quirinale. Although the Chigi pope Alexander VII endorsed its construction and encouraged his court to donate money, it was a prominent member of the Pamphilj family – Prince Camillo – who became the principal benefactor of the new building. Costing a staggering 60,000 *scudi* (twice as much as the Fontana dei Quattro Fiumi in the Piazza Navona), the church was the most expensive single project of its day. From its commissioning in 1658, its design was entrusted to Giacomo Lorenzo Bernini who was previously responsible for building the aforementioned fountain (1647–51). Even more than at Borromini's church of S Carlo, the oval plan of S Andrea (including its side chapels) not only formed a suitable base for its oval drum and dome but also determined the external shape of the church. The only substantial deviation from its ovoid plan are its large pedimented porch supported by giant pilasters and, within it, a smaller 'porchlet' supported by columns and capped by a semi-circular entablature, an arrangement that is more Mannerist than Baroque.

The Private Patronage of Secular Development in Rome and Venice

Begun in 1608, the Villa Borghese is the first of many secular buildings of any merit to be financed from private sources in the seicento. Commissioned by the nephew of Pope Paul V, Cardinal Scipione Borghese, and designed by Flaminio Ponzio and Jan van Santen, the villa was built in the extensive Borghese estate, just outside the Aurelian Wall. Required to house the family's sumptuous collection of paintings, antique sculpture and other historic artefacts, the building was based on the Villa Medici of the previous century (see chapter 13) where rooms were set aside to exhibit artwork, and where rich ornamentations – extracted from archaeological 'digs' – decorated the exterior walls. From the beginning, though privately funded the villa assumed the aspect of a civic building, where the display of paintings and sculpture was as much for the pleasure of the public as for the enlightened delectation of the Borghese clan.[11]

In contrast to the Villa Borghese, the Palazzo Chigi-Odescalchi – located in close proximity to the Piazza Venezia – is indisputably an urban palace and is the first of two palaces designed by Bernini (the other being the much later

Photo 17.4 Carlo Maderno and Giacomo Lorenzo Bernini, Villa Borghese, Rome, 1608. A suburban villa with its elegant western facade and imposing portico set within an extensive landscaped garden.

Palazzo di Montecitorio). Taking over from the building's first architect Carlo Maderno in 1622, Bernini created a pattern that was to serve as a basis for most future Baroque palaces throughout Europe. To the seven bays of the facade and its recessed three-bay flanks, Bernini innovatively added giant columns and pilasters, breaking the tradition of employing an astylar format as applied in the development of the Palazzo Farnese and similar buildings. But whereas in the cinquecento Michelangelo used Giant orders from ground level to the upper entablature (as in the case of the Capitoline *palazzi*), in the following century Bernini erected them on the facade of the Palazzo Chigi-Odescalchi above a rusticated ground floor and from there projected them upwards to the attic storey.[12] The palace was completed in the mid-18th century when a further seven bays were added to the facade by the new owners, the Odescalchi family.[13]

Built on a site recently acquired by Cardinal Francesco Barberini on the eastern side of the Quirinale Hill, the Palazzo Barberini was commissioned by Maffeo Barberini as his private residence soon after his election as Pope Urban VIII

Photo 17.5 Carlo Maderno and Giacomo Lorenzo Bernini, Palazzo Barberini, Rome, 1625–38. The U-shaped edifice, its two wings extending outwards from its west-facing facade, is one of the grandest palaces in Rome.

in 1625. Designed in turn by Carlo Maderno and Gian Lorenzo Bernini with the collaboration of Francesco Borromini, the palace was intended not only to accommodate the pontiff, but also to house other members of the Barberini family including Taddeo, prince of Palestrina, and the cardinal Francesco. The large building is a three-storey block which, on its western side, contains its present-day entrance and two lateral wings, while its eastern side incorporates the original entrance to the palace. While essentially classical in style, the three tiers of orders on its western facade (Doric, Ionic and Corinthian) are given Baroque treatment 'by means of richer ornamentation and a trick of perspective'[14] and, on all three floors, deep arcades extend across the seven bays of the facade. On the ground floor the arcade is open and its central bay contains a columned entrance surmounted by a balustrade, while the arcades above are glazed. Built as a family residence, the Palazzo Barberini is arguably the 'most magnificent of Roman noble houses [and] is an eloquent expression of the Baroque in secular architecture'.[15]

Very different from the Palazzo Barberini and dating from the late 15th century, the Palazzo Madama was constructed in the heart of Rome, a short distance from the Pantheon. It was restored for Giovanni de'Medici (later Pope Leo X) in 1503 and was subsequently owned by Margherita of Parma, from whom it derives its name. The massive facade of the palace, overlooking the Corso del Rinascimento, was constructed in 1642 and although devoid of columns and pilasters in the style of the Palazzo Farnese, is Baroque in its detail.[16] Largely because of its grandeur, the palace has been the seat of the Italian Senate since 1871.

Close to the Palazzo Madama is the Piazza Navona. By the 17th century, most of the western side of the *piazza* was owned by the Pamphilj family, and it was with regard to its redevelopment that Innocent X commissioned the reconstruction of his family's residence on the south-western edge of the square. The design of the new building, the Palazzo Pamphilj, was entrusted to Carlo Rainaldi and his father Girolamo, while its construction was supervised by Borromini (1644–55). Several buildings were combined with the original palace to form a single edifice, and it is noted particularly for its imposing gallery that stretches across the building from the *piazza* to the neighbouring street, the Via dell' Anima.

The last Roman palace to be commissioned in the first half of the seicento was the Palazzo di Montecitorio. Like the Palazzo Doria Pamphilj, it was funded by Innocent X, this time on behalf of the Ludovisi family, and was designed by Bernini, rather than Borromini or the Rainaldis. Begun in 1650, the huge, very long building has a convex facade and wings that are set back at a slight angle. Its 25 window bays are divided into five sections, its central storey is embellished with alternating triangular and segmental pediments, and at the centre of the facade there is a columned porch at street level while the attic storey is crowned by a clock tower. Under the later direction of Carlo Fontana, the palace was eventually completed in 1694 and, rather than assuming the role of a family palace, soon became the *curia innocenziana*, the papal law court, and after 1871 the Chamber of Deputies.

Venice: The Unpredictability of the Market

Whereas in 17th-century Rome both ecclesiastical and secular building projects attracted private funding, in Venice family palaces received by far the largest share of the financial resources directed at development. However, in contrast to Rome, the volume of construction activity in the private sector of the Venetian economy was on a small scale and subject to the vicissitudes of the market, as was demonstrated by the discontinuous development of the Ca'Pesaro and Ca'Rezzonico.[17]

After acquiring three adjacent *palazzi* on the Grand Canal (1558–1628), the Pesaro family demolished the buildings and entrusted Baldassare Longhena with construction of an enormous palace on the cleared site. What emerged was a three-storey building reminiscent of Sansovino's Palazzo Corner near San Maurizio (1532–61). It boasts a prominent rusticated base composed of ashlars cut to the shape of diamonds, two central portals, free-standing columns arranged in pairs on its *piano nobile* and is extensively embellished by animal masks, huge keystones and full-length balustrades. Because of the frequent financial difficulties of the Pesaro family and the long-term instability of the Venetian economy, the completion of the palace was severely delayed. When its first owner, Giovanni Pesaro, died in 1659 (a year after being elected doge), construction had barely started, and when Longhena himself died in 1682 only the ground floor of the palace had been completed.[18] It took a further 28 years for the building to be finished, much of the time under the direction of Antonio Gaspari. The palace

Photo 17.6 Baldassare Longhena, Ca'Pesaro, Venice, 1652–82. A bulky Baroque palace, the facade is particularly notable for its ground-floor diamond-pointed rustication – an unusual feature in Venice.

doesn't leave a happy legacy. From the time it was being built, it has been regarded as vulgar and ostentatious, and has been compared unfavourably with many other *palazzi* along the canal.[19] It is very likely that even Longhena had recognised that his style of architecture had reached its ultimate form and could be applied no further.[20]

Like the Ca'Pesaro, the Ca'Rezzonico (originally the Ca'Bon) was designed by Longhena and, because of economic instability, was similarly starved of financial resources. Commissioned by the Bon family in 1667, Longhena's plans led to the development of a building which, on its *piano nobile* and upper floor, is almost identical to the Ca'Pesaro, but on its ground floor is less rusticated and has three portals instead of two. Ca'Rezzonico was similarly affected by the death of Longhena in 1682: like the Ca'Pesaro, the building had only reached the first floor but it was not until the mid-18th century when the economy had recovered sufficiently that ownership of the building passed to the Rezzonico family who employed a new architect, Giorgio Massari, to complete the building according to Longhena's plans, 'warts and all'.

Genoa: Low-key Baroque

Lacking such flamboyant buildings as the enormous Ca'Pesaro and Ca'Rezzonico, the development of the Baroque in the private sector of the Genoese economy was relatively low-key in the seicento compared to that of Venice. However, throughout the century, a plethora of relatively small buildings was developed, both ecclesiastical and secular. The first of three churches of note, S Luca, was founded in the late 12th century, but it was put under the patronage of the Spinola and Grimaldi families by Innocent VII in 1485 and henceforth relied upon family funds for its further development. In 1626, the church was almost completely demolished to make way for a new Baroque-style building. Although its ornate interior is attributable to Bartolomeo Bianco, its facade – with its projecting central area and stuccoed decoration framed by paired pilasters – was designed by Carlo Muttone.[21] The second notable church of the period, S Carlo, was founded by the Discalced Carmelites in 1629, funded by a bequest from GB Spinola and, like the church of S Luca, was designed mainly by Bianco. Its Baroque interior, except for its lengthy choir, is based on a Greek cross with a dome surmounting the crossing, but its original frontage was replaced in the mid-18th century by a richly decorated Rococo facade opening to an arcaded portico on its lower storey.[22] The final ecclesiastical building of any merit is the church of SS Annunziata del Vastato. Under the patronage of the Minorites of St Francis, its construction commenced in 1520, but in 1537 the responsibility for funding further development was transferred to the Order of St Francis Observants.[23] Thereafter, in 1591, patronage passed to the Lomellini family who increased the size of its presbytery and financed provision of a dome over the crossing. In the early seicento, the facade was rusticated, an entrance bay added and many of the architectural features of the church faced with marble. However, the monumental gabled portico, with its six giant Ionic columns, was not superimposed on the facade until the mid-19th century.[24] It is remarkable that, while growing in piecemeal fashion over a 300-year period and under the direction of only minor architects, the hybrid church evolved into one of Genoa's most magnificent buildings.

Whereas the development of *palazzi* was heavily concentrated in the Strada Nuova in the late cinquecento, during the early seicento patrician patrons funded the construction of unpretentious residences along the Via Balbi on the north-western fringe of the city. The earliest of these buildings, the Palazzo Balbi-Cattaneo Adorno, was commissioned by Gio Agostino Balbi in 1618 and designed by Bartolomeo Bianco. The wide and otherwise austere frontage of the palace is accentuated by wings at either end of the ground floor that support balustraded side gardens on the *piano nobile*, and by loggias (also balustraded) at each end of the upper storey.[25] Commissioned at about the same time as the former palace, the Palazzo Balbi-Senarega was funded by Giacomo and Pantaleo Balbi, and its construction was again entrusted to Bianco. Completed *c* 1620, the palace consists of two separate three-storey blocks (one for each of the two brothers), separated by a projecting one-storey block surmounted by a balustraded garden. Although the seaward side of the palace is adorned by upper loggias, the facade parallel to the Via Balbi is austere and redeemed only by the asymmetrical arrangement of its windows which are closer together at the centre.[26]

A building with a different use was begun in 1634. With a commitment from Stefano Balbi to supply funds, the Order of Jesuits embarked on construction of their college on the Via Balbi in that year. Under the direction of Bianco, the building (now the Palazzo dell'Università) was erected on a site steeply sloping from the road at 90 degrees and, because of this, most of the rooms of the building (intended for the personal use of the Jesuits) had to rise vertically over the ground-floor courtyard and great hall. With building work interrupted by shortage of funds, it was not until 1650 that the facade was completed, not until 1672 that work resumed on the courtyard with its imposing staircase, and not until 1718 that the college was eventually completed.

The only prominent palace on the Via Balbi not designed by Bianco is the building opposite the university: the Palazzo Reale (formerly known as the Palazzo Balbi, Palazzo Centurione or Palazzo Durazzo). Funded by Stefano Balbi in 1643, the palace was constructed under the direction of F Cantoni and M Moncino, but was subsequently owned for a short period by the Centurione family before being acquired by E Durazzo in 1677, who developed it further through integrating it with other buildings. Only after Carlo Fontana unified the appearance of the whole complex in the early 18th century could the palace at last be said to be finished.[27]

Milan and Florence: Limited Patronage, Limited Development

In contrast to Rome, and even when compared to Venice or Genoa, there is a paucity of distinctive private buildings in Milan and Florence dating from the 17th century. In Milan, the few buildings of this period that do exist were commissioned largely by the nobility following their return to the city after the plague of the 1630s. In 1645, work started on two such buildings: the Palazzo Litta and Palazzo Durini. The former was funded by Bartolomeo Arese (a future president of the Senate) and was designed mainly by Francesco Maria Richini. Its rooms are arranged around three courtyards, of which one is colonnaded, but the original facade was replaced in 1743–60 by an elaborate Rococo structure designed by Bartolomeo Bolli.[28] The second palace was built under the patronage of Giovan Battista Durini, whose family originally derived their wealth from the silk trade, and its design was entrusted again to Richini. Completed as early as 1648, the Palazzi Durini is not dissimilar to the former palace, but it has two courtyards instead of three, and its partly rusticated facade is distinctly Baroque, with its 'balcony and closely spaced windows [highlighting] the entrance'.[29] A third family, the Arcimboldi, financed construction of a very different building. With a continuing bequest initiated by the Arcimboldi in 1608, by 1663 the Order of the Barnabites was able to commission construction of a college, the Scuola Arcimboldi, in an attempt to promulgate the edicts of the Council of Trent. Based on a design by Lorenzo Binago, the architects Francesco Castelli and Giuseppe Paggi respectively supervised erection of the facade and the creation of the arcaded courtyard backing onto the church of S Alessandro.[30]

Florence similarly experienced little private development in the seicento but, in contrast to Milan, what there was was spread over both ecclesiastical and secular sectors. Founded in the first half of the century, three ecclesiastical buildings deserve comment. The first, the church of SS Michele and Gaetano, was commissioned by the Theatine Order in 1604 and designed by Matteo Nigetti and Gherardo Silvani. As a reconstructed medieval building, the church was transformed by its architects, Nigetti giving it a Baroque facade in 1630, and Silvani providing it with an enlarged and redesigned nave in 1648. With its exuberant sculptural ornamentation and superimposed double pilasters the church is a remarkable hybrid displaying a harmonious relationship between classical and Baroque styles of architecture. In the view of Guido Zucconi, it 'is one of the most important pieces of architecture of seventeenth-century Florence'.[31] The second, the Capella dei Principi, was funded by the Medici family and designed by Nigetti, possibly in accordance with a plan drawn up by Don Giovanni de'Medici as amended by Buontalenti. Begun in 1604 and completed in 1650, the chapel was built as a pantheon for the Medici, and marked the last stage in the development of the church of S Lorenzo, to which it is attached. Octagonal in shape, the chapel is 59 metres (194 ft) in height and 29 metres (95 ft) in diameter and was covered by a great cupola in the mid-18th century. The third ecclesiastical building to be considered is the church of Ognissanti. Commissioned by the Franciscans (who took the original medieval church into their care in 1561), the construction of the 17th-century building was entrusted to Nigetti. Next to its medieval campanile the new building is graced by a magnificent Baroque facade (completed in 1637) and crowned by a lofty curved pediment.

The almost complete absence of the Baroque in secular buildings in 17th-century Florence is well acknowledged, and reference to three buildings of the period – taken at random – illustrates the reluctance of patrons to adopt the style, other than marginally. The first building, the hospital of S Maria Nuova, dating from 1288 and funded by private donations, was reconstructed between 1606 and 1663. Based on Buontalenti's plans, under the direction of Giulio Parigi arcades were built to unify the various parts of the hospital and were completed in the early 18th century by the erection of an upper storey. However, these additions to the medieval hospital were essentially classical rather than Baroque. With the development of private *palazzi* there was also a reluctance to adopt a more exuberant style of architecture. Designed by Gherardo Silvani, both the Palazzo Strozzi del Poeta (begun 1626) and the Palazzo Castelli-Marucelli (started 1634) have very bare facades and are only sparsely decorated in the Baroque manner, the former palace by 'little false balconies . . . statues on each side [and a] cornice with metopes and triglyphs',[32] and the latter building by 'odd corbels which hold up the balcony on the first floor'.[33]

The South: The Exuberance of the Baroque

In the 17th century, ecclesiastical buildings in Naples were commissioned almost exclusively by the new religious orders rather than by princes of the Catholic Church as was often the case in Rome and the north. Assisted by viceregal legislation in the wake of the Council of Trent, the Jesuits, Theatines and Oratorians transformed the built environment of parts of Naples by funding the development of a surprisingly large number of magnificent Baroque churches. In contrast to the relatively minor impact of Classicism on the architectural heritage of Naples in the quattrocento and cinquecento, the city was blessed with a remarkable flowering of the Baroque in the seicento which, to a significant extent, was attributable to architects from other parts of Italy, among them Antonio Dosio, Francesco Grimaldi and Cosimo Fanzago, each of whom may even have inspired the work of their contemporaries in Rome. In the 1590s, the Florentine Giovanni Antonio Dosio worked on the design of the Girolamini for the Oratorian Order;[34] in the early seicento, a Theatine monk from Calabria, Francesco Grimaldi, designed on

Photo 17.7   Francesco Antonio Zimbalo and Giuseppe Zimbalo, church of S Croce, Lecce, 1606–79. Built on top of a 16th-century classical facade, the upper storey of the church is sumptuously decorated in the Baroque style and demarcated from the lower edifice by a long balcony.

behalf of his order the churches of S Maria degli Angeli a Pizzofalcone (1600), S Paolo Maggiore and S Apostoli (1609) that were to epitomise Neapolitan Baroque at its best; and, much later in the century, Cosimo Fanzago, who had migrated from Bergamo to Naples, produced the votive spire of S Gennaro (1631–60), the exuberant facades of S Maria della Sapienza (1638–41) and S Giuseppe delle Scalze (*c* 1660), and the reconstructed 4th-century church of S Giorgio Maggiore after it had been destroyed by fire in 1640.

While a large number of Baroque churches were constructed in 17th-century Naples (of which the above are just a few examples), there was no lack of secular development in the city. Under the patronage of a large number of aristocratic families, numerous Baroque *palazzi* were constructed throughout the city and particularly along the Via Toledo (see chapter 7). With a population of well over 200,000 in the early 17th century, Naples was severely overcrowded and thus residential buildings of the period, such as Fanzago's Palazzo Zevallos (*c* 1630), tend to be higher than their counterparts elsewhere in the peninsula.[35] It is also common for the *piano nobile* of such palaces to be situated on the second rather than on the first floor while, below, a monumental doorway or *porte-cochère* – often two floors in height – normally leads to a large central courtyard from which a magnificent external staircase facilitates access to the different floors of the building.[36]

Aside from development in Naples, very few extant private buildings of any merit were constructed in southern Italy during the 17th century, but the completion of the church of S Croce in Lecce requires comment. Funded by the Celestine nuns, the development of the church proceeded slowly throughout the cinquecento under the direction of successive architects (see chapter 13), but it was not until after Francesco Antonio Zimbalo designed its lower facade *c* 1606 with its small portico and lateral doors alternating with composite half columns, and Giuseppe Zimbalo designed the upper facade in 1646 with its rose window and statued niches, that work on this amazingly decorated Baroque building reached completion.

Conclusion

The Baroque style of architecture in much of Italy reached its apogee in the second half of the seicento, but although its success as an architectural style – like any other architectural genre – can be attributed to the material predilections of patrons and the creative inspiration and energy of outstanding architects, it could be argued that once any architectural style becomes established it can only become more and more sensational,[37] and this was particularly true of the Baroque. Furthermore, whereas much urban development in the Middle Ages and in the Early and High Renaissance promoted a sense of civic pride, in the seicento the vast expenditure incurred on ecclesiastical buildings and town planning schemes – particularly in Rome – was often deeply resented by the urban citizenry at a time of economic recession, while, as asserted by Kenneth Clarke, 'the collosal palaces of papal families were simply expressions of private greed and vanity'[38] and, in his view, contributed little to civilisation. By 1700, the Italian Renaissance was all but over and within a few years a reversion to Classicism paved the way for the adoption of Neo-Classicism, a style that would eventually stamp its mark on the development of Italian cities during the Fascist era (1922–43).

Notes

1 B Hintzen-Bohlen with J Sorges, *Rome and the Vatican City* (Cologne: Könemann, 2000), pp 156–7.
2 C Woodward, *Rome* (Manchester: Manchester University Press, 1995), pp 91–2.
3 Ibid; Hintzen-Bohlen with Sorges, *Rome*, pp 156–7.
4 I Sutton, *Western Architecture* (London: Thames and Hudson, 1999), p 176.
5 Woodward, *Rome*, p 101.
6 Hintzen-Bohlen with Sorges, *Rome*, p 282.
7 A Hopkins, *Italian Architecture from Michelangelo to Borromini* (London: Thames and Hudson, 2002), p 209.
8 A Majanlahti, *The Families Who Made Rome* (London: Chatto & Windus, 2005), p 296.
9 Ibid, p 295.
10 Ibid.
11 Woodward, *Rome*, p 95; Hintzen-Bohlen with Sorges, *Rome*, pp 244–5.
12 Ibid, p 98.
13 Ibid.
14 G Bazin, *Baroque and Rococo* (London: Thames and Hudson, 1964), p 18.
15 Majanlahti, *The Families*, p 236.
16 Woodward, *Rome*, p 106.
17 D Howard, *The Architectural History of Venice* (New Haven and London: Yale University Press, 2002), pp 224–5.
18 M Kaminski, *Venice* (Cologne: Könemann, 2000), p 44.
19 Ibid.
20 Howard, *Architectural History*, pp 224–5.
21 N De Mari, 'The city of the old walls; modern buildings', in *Genoa. Architectural Guide* (Turin: Allemandi, 1998) p 84.
22 Ibid, p 93.
23 Ibid, p 83.

24 Ibid, p 88.
25 Ibid, p 90.
26 Ibid.
27 Ibid, p 91.
28 L Roncai, 'The Neoclassical city and residence', in *Milan. Architectural Guide* (Turin: Allemandi, 1999), p 112.
29 Ibid, p 113.
30 Ibid, p 114.
31 G Zucconi, *Florence. An architectural guide* (Venice: Arsenale Editrice, 1995), p 99.
32 Ibid, p 102.
33 Ibid.
34 Hopkins, *Italian Architecture*, p 99.
35 Ibid, p 112.
36 Ibid, p 111.
37 K Clarke, *Civilization* (London: BBC Books/John Murray, 1971), p 191.
38 Ibid, p 192.

APPENDIX

Principal Architects and Where They Mainly Practised

Arnolfo di Cambio	c 1245–c 1310	Florence
Giotto di Bondone	1267–1337	Florence
Talenti, Francesco	c 1300–69	Florence
Pisano, Andrea	d 1348/9	Florence
Brunelleschi, Filippo	1377–1446	Florence
Michelozzo di Bartolomeo	1396–1472	Florence
Averlino, Antonio (known as Filarete)	c 1400–69	Milan
Alberti, Leon Battista	1404–72	Rimini, Florence and Mantua
Bon or Buon, Bartolomeo	c 1405–c 1467	Venice
Rossellino, Bernardo di Matteo Gamberelli	1409–64	Florence and Pienza
Gambello, Antonio	d 1481	Venice
Laurana, Luciano	c 1420–79	Urbino
Giuliano da Maiano	1432–90	Florence and Naples
Lombardo, Pietro	c 1435–1515	Venice
Francesco di Giorgio Martini	1439–1501/2	Urbino and Cortona
Codussi, Mauro	c 1440–1504	Venice
Bramante, Donato	1443/4–1514	Milan and Rome
Sangallo, Giuliano da	1445–1516	Prato and Florence
Rossetti, Biagio	c 1447–1516	Ferrara
Leonardo da Vinci	1452–1519	Milan
Sangallo, Antonio da, the Elder	1455–1534	Montepulciano
Pollaiolo, Simone del (known as Il Cronaca)	1457–1508	Florence

Bon or Bono, Bartolomeo	*c* 1463–1529	Venice
Falconetto, Giovanni Maria	1468–1535	Padua
Abbondi, Antonio (known as Scarpagnino)	d 1549	Venice
Michelangelo Buonarroti	1475–1564	Florence and Rome
Peruzzi, Baldassare	1481–1537	Rome
Raphael (Raffaello Sanzio)	1484–1520	Florence and Rome
Sangallo, Antonio da, the Younger	1484–1546	Rome
Sansovino, Jacopo d'Antonio Tatti	1484–1570	Venice
Sanmicheli, Michele	*c* 1487–1559	Verona and Venice
Cola da Caprarola	fl 1499–1519	Todi
Vignola, Giacomo Barozzi da	1507–73	Rome
Palladio, Andrea	1508–80	Vicenza and Venice
Vasari, Giorgio	1511–74	Rome and Florence
Ammanati, Bartolomeo	1511–92	Rome and Florence
Alessi, Galeazzo	1512–72	Genoa and Milan
Pellegrini, Pellegrino (known as Tibaldi)	1527–96	Milan
Della Porta, Giacomo	1533–1602	Rome
Fontana, Domenico	1543–1607	Rome and Naples
Scamozzi, Vincenzo	1552–1616	Venice
Maderno, Carlo	*c* 1556–1629	Rome
Rainaldi, Girolamo	1570–1655	Rome
Bianco, Bartolommeo	1590–1657	Genoa
Fanzago, Cosimo	1591–1678	Naples
Longhena, Baldassare	1597–1682	Venice
Bernini, Gianlorenzo	1598–1680	Rome
Borromini, Francesco	1599–1667	Rome
Rainaldi, Carlo	1611–91	Rome
Fontana, Carlo	1638–1714	Rome

GLOSSARY

General Terms

arengario	Town hall
arengo	General assembly or parliament of adult non-clerical males with rights of citizenship
Arrabbiati	Most anti-Savonarola party in Republican Florence (1494–8), containing vehement Medici supporters
Arte	Guild
balia	Political committee established to recommend and implement constitutional changes in times of emergency
bottega	Shop
broletto	Town hall
capitano del popolo	Head of a government of the *popolo*, or head of a *popolo* faction
cittadini	Citizens, particularly of Venice
cinquecento	The 1500s or 16th century
Comune	Commune (in English). From *c* 1075–*c* 1140, the commune was composed of a group of local men of wealth and power who governed a city on the breakdown of imperial administration; from 1198 to 1250, middling landowners, shopkeepers, merchants and members of the craft guilds increased the size of the governing class;

	and from the mid-13th century communes began to fall under domination of a single individual (a *signore*) who was elected into office by a citizen assembly (an *arengo*) or legislative council
consorteria	Clan or extended family committed to mutual support particularly *vis-à-vis* the defence of property
contado	Surrounding countryside and settlements tied legally and fiscally to a city
castello	Fortified castle
fondaco	Warehouse and commercial base of foreign merchants
gonfalone	Military banner of an administrative district of a city
Gonfaloniere	Official responsible for a district to state government. In Florence, the title of Gonfaloniere was conferred on the chairman of the *signoria*
Maggior Consiglio	Great Council of Venice comprising all male patricians
Palazzo del Capitano	Palace of leading legal or administrative official
Palazzo Comunale	Town hall
Palazzo della Mercanzia	Court established by guilds to regulate trade
Palazzo della Ragione	Law court
Palazzo del Podestà	Palace of leading legal or administrative official
Palazzo della Prefettura	Palace of state prefect
Palazzo Pretoria	Magistrates' court
parlamento	see *arengo*
podestà	State official responsible for law and order. Either citizen of the town or city, or an outsider appointed on a short-term contract. Some became hereditary *signori*
popolo	Comprised of merchant and master-artisan interest groups
portego	Elongated hall
priore	Member of a *signoria*
rocca	Fortress
quattrocento	The 1400s or 15th century
scuola	Religious confraternity and its headquarters
seicento	The 1600s or 17th century

Serrata	Venetian legislation in 1297 that determined the nature of the hereditary patrician class, so defining the membership of the Great Council
Serenissima	Serene Republic of Venice
Signore	De facto political head of a city's government (a *signoria*). The nomenclature is discontinued if his heirs succeed to the post, or if he receives the title of count, marquis or duke when still in power
signoria	supreme political council in a republican government
terraferma	Venetian territory on mainland of Italy
trecento	The 1300s or 14th century

Architectural Terms

aedicule	Canopied niche framed by two columns, often containing a statue
all, antica	In the style of classical Rome or Greece
ambulatory	Polygonal or semi-circular aisle enclosing an apse
androne	Internal area of a Venetian palace for loading and unloading goods
apse	Polygonal or semi-circular extension to large rectangular space
arcade:	Series of free-standing arches supported by columns or piers
Serlian	Arches supported by series of coupled columns
arch:	Curved masonry structure spanning an opening
eliptical	Spans wide gaps in manner of parapet wall
ogee	Pointed arch characterised by compound curve of two parts, one concave and the other convex. Popular throughout the later Middle Ages and of Islamic origin
stilted	Raised on elongated straight piers
trilobed ogee	Pointed arch composed of three parts: concave, convex and concave
architrave	Lowest of three main parts of a classical entablature
ashlar:	Smooth blocks of masonry laid in horizontal courses
faceted	Sharp-edged blocks of masonry
atrium	In medieval architecture, open court in front of church; in Renaissance architecture, an entrance hall
attic	Storey above entablature of a building
baldachin	Canopy over altar or throne

balustrade	Series of short pillars supporting a rail
baptistery	Building or room for Christian baptismal rites
Baroque	Architecture of the 17th and 18th centuries characterised by exuberant decoration

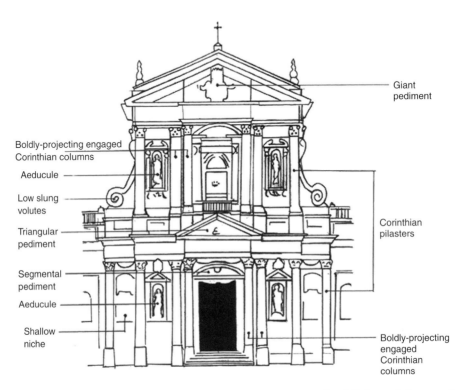

S Susanna, Rome, 1603. Derived from the late 16th-century style of Il Gesu, S Susanna is the first truly Baroque church in Italy, with many even more exuberant examples of the genre to follow.

bas-relief	Shallow sculpture on background
basilica	Oblong building with arcade (or colonnade), aisles and clerestory
bays	Vertical division of a building into single compartments marked by fenestration, columns, pilasters or buttresses
bell tower	High tower attached to or detached from building such as church and housing a belfry

bifore/biforate	*see* windows
blind arcading	Range of arches against a solid wall
buttress:	Mass of stone masonry or brickwork built against a wall to give it additional strength
curvilinear	Where clerestory is supported by series of curved buttresses
flying	Arch or half arch constructed from upper part of wall to outer support to counteract thrust of a roof or vault

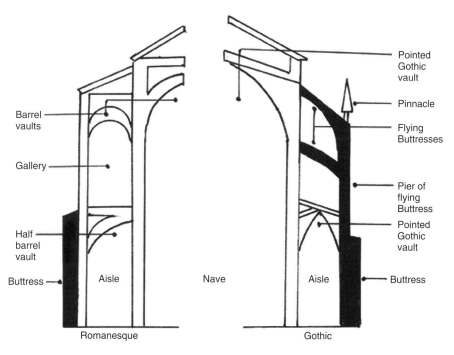

Romanesque and Northern Gothic buttressing. In Italy there is often little distinction between Romanesque and Gothic buttressing. With a few exceptions, most notably in Milan (where flying buttresses are employed), Italian Gothic churches are shorter than their counterparts north of the Alps and their naves are supported by pier buttresses only.

scroll	Ornamental design carved to imitate a scroll of parchment
Byzantine Roman	Style of architecture that originated in the Eastern Empire and was replicated for centuries, particularly in Venice

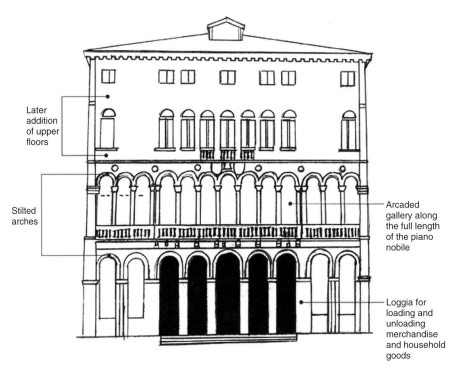

Later addition of upper floors

Stilted arches

Arcaded gallery along the full length of the piano nobile

Loggia for loading and unloading merchandise and household goods

Ca'Loredan, Venice, early 1200s. An example of a style of secular architecture derived from Byzantium but applied to Venetian site conditions. As a *casa fonduci* (or home/warehouse), the building is accessed mainly through a portal flanking the Grand Canal, and its facade – with design modifications – remained in vogue until the 18th century.

campanile	*see* bell tower
capital	Topmost part of column or pilaster
cella	Main enclosed room of a classical temple
chancel	Normally, easternmost end of church where main altar is placed. Reserved for clergy but the powerful were also accommodated there
chapel	Small chamber containing altar
choir	Part of church where divine service is sung
churches:	
centrally planned	Church whose plan is symmetrical in all four directions
mendicant	Church, normally Gothic in style, built for use of mendicant orders (the Dominicans, Franciscans, etc)

Classical   Style of architecture derived from ancient Greece or, more commonly, from ancient Rome, as promulgated by the treatises of Vitruvius and Alberti

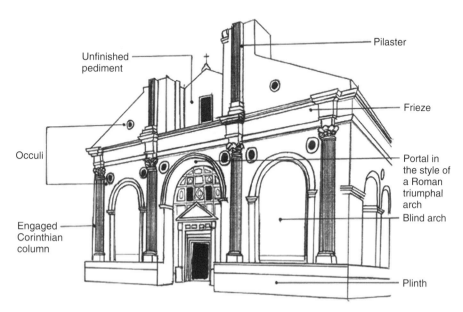

Pilaster

Unfinished pediment

Frieze

Occuli

Portal in the style of a Roman triumphal arch

Blind arch

Engaged Corinthian column

Plinth

Tempio Malatestiano, Rimini, 1450. Alberti's temple is the first ecclesiastical building of the Renaissance to demonstrate the application of classical motifs.

clerestory	Upper part of basilica, normally fenestrated wall above arcade
cloister	Courtyard surrounded by arcade
colonnade	Series of columns carrying an entablature
column:	Vertical cylindrical structure normally intended as a support; in classical architecture, consists of base, shaft and capital
coupled	Pairs of columns
engaged	Where column attached to wall
half-	Where only half width of column used as support
three-quarter	Where three-quarters of width of column used as support

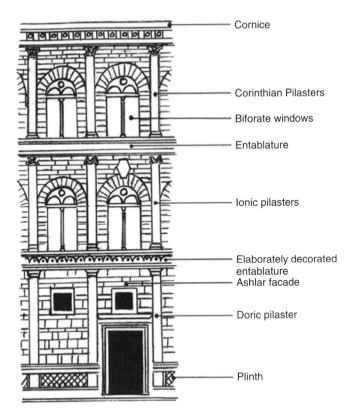

Cornice

Corinthian Pilasters

Biforate windows

Entablature

Ionic pilasters

Elaborately decorated entablature

Ashlar facade

Doric pilaster

Plinth

Palazzo Rucellai, Florence, 1452. The first *palazzo* of the Renaissance to demonstrate fully the application of the classical style of architecture to secular buildings. Another masterpiece of Alberti.

Composite	Late Roman combination of Ionic and Corinthian orders
Corinthian	Originating in Athens in 5th century BC, this order was later developed by the Romans. Its capital consists of acanthus leaves with cauls (stalks) sprouting volutes
cornice	Projecting uppermost section of classical entablature
cortile	Internal courtyard normally surrounded by arcades
crenellation	Parapet (battlement) with alternating indentations

crocket	Decorative spur-like projection of stone
cupola	Small dome on circular or polygonal base
dome	Vault of even curvature erected on a circular base or drum. Can be hemispherical or pointed
Doric	Classical order distinguished by plain moulded capital
drum	Circular, square or polygonal wall supporting drum or cupola
Early Christian	Church architecture extending from 5th to 7th centuries
entablature	In classical architecture, upper part of an order, comprising architrave, frieze and cornice
exedra	Large niche-like semi-circular extension to building
facade	Front or face of building
frieze	Middle section of classical entablature
gable	Triangular upper portion of wall closing end of pitched roof, but otherwise similar to classical pediment
gargoyle	Carved grotesque figure projecting from roof or parapet
Giant order	Any order of columns or pilasters that rise through two or more storeys
Gothic	Architectural style of medieval Europe, *c* 1150–1550 (in Italy, *c* 1200–*c* 1400)
Greek-cross plan	Centralised plan based on cross with four equal arms
Ionic	Characteristic of Byzantine and some Renaissance churches. Originating in Asia Minor in 6th century BC, the capital of this order has oblong top supported by two volutes
Islamic	Of the many features of Islamic architecture to have influenced the West, the most prominent has been the pointed arch and cusping (the meeting of leaf-shaped curves in tracery). The stilted ogee arch is also of Islamic origin
keep	Principal inner and strongest part of castle
keystone	Central wedged-shaped block at crown of arch

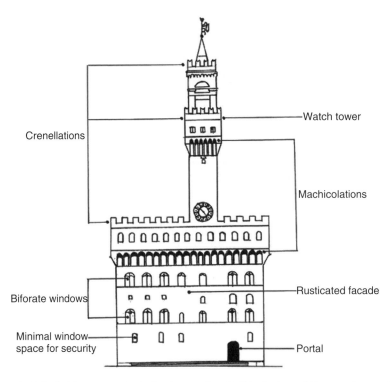

Crenellations

Watch tower

Machicolations

Biforate windows

Rusticated facade

Minimal window
space for security

Portal

Palazzo de Priori, Florence, 1299. An impressive Gothic fusion of the requirements of a fortress with those of a town hall.

lantern	Apex of dome having apertures in its sides by which interior of building is illuminated or ventilated
Latin-cross-plan	Plan based on cross with one arm longer than the other three; characteristic of Western medieval churches
latticework	Small light bars crossing each other at intervals that form regular square or diamond-shaped openings
lintel	Horizontal beam over door or window
loggia	Gallery or room with open arcade or colonnade on one or more sides

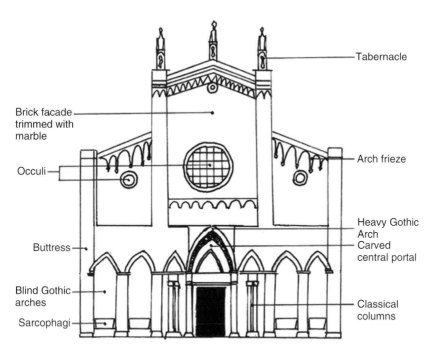

Brick facade trimmed with marble

Occuli

Buttress

Blind Gothic arches

Sarcophagi

Tabernacle

Arch frieze

Heavy Gothic Arch

Carved central portal

Classical columns

SS Giovanni e Paolo, Venice, 1333. With a massive but generally unadorned brick facade, and without flying buttresses, the edifice is typical of a north-Italian Gothic church of the 14th century.

longitudinal church	Church longer in one direction than another, as opposed to a centrally planned church
lucarne	Small window in attic or spire
lunette	Semi-circular opening or recess, usually over door or window
machicolation	Parapet projecting on corbels in front of castle wall, with openings in the floor to permit missiles and boiling liquid to be dropped
Mannerism	Architectural style in vogue in Italy from *c* 1520 to end of 16th century characterised by use of classical motifs in an unusual way
medallion	Decorative circular, eliptical, square or oval panel or tablet bearing a figure or inscription

Metope

Doric frieze

Architrave

Pediment protrudes into the architrave

Oversized keystone protrudes below top of the arch

Triglyph appears to have slipped below architrave

Irregular rustication

Blind arch

Palazzo Te, Mantua, 1524. One of the earliest Mannerist buildings, the *palazzo* exhibits many distortions of classical authenticity.

metope	Part of Doric frieze; square section (usually carved in relief) between two triglyphs
mezzanine	Subordinate storey inserted between two major ones
Moorish style	Characterised by interlacing foliate ornamentation
motif	Constituent feature or dominant idea
nave	Main body of longitudinally planned church, west of the crossing or chancel, where congregation assembles
niche	Shallow vertical recess in wall, usually arched and containing statue or other ornament
obelisk	Tall tapering four-sided shaft of stone
oculus	Circular opening or recess in wall
odium (or odeon)	Small roofed theatre for musical or theatrical performances
orders	Categories into which classical architecture has been divided, particularly in respect of its columns and capitals: Doric, Ionic, Corinthian and Composite
oratory	Small private chapel

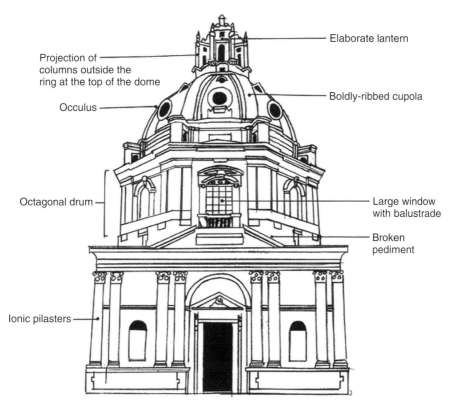

Elaborate lantern

Projection of columns outside the ring at the top of the dome

Occulus

Boldly-ribbed cupola

Octagonal drum

Large window with balustrade

Broken pediment

Ionic pilasters

S Maria di Loreto, Rome, 1551. One of several late-16th-century churches to dispense with the rigours of classical architecture and to adopt Mannerist motifs.

palazzo	Corresponding either to a town house, larger official residence or building of municipal or state government
pantheon	Building used as burial place for, or memorial to, the distinguished dead
parapet	Low wall at edge of building where there is a drop; where building is castle or town hall, the wall may be crenellated or machicolated
parlera	Central balcony
pediment	Triangular or segmental gable over portal or window
pedestals	Base supporting column or colonnade
peristyle	Row of columns surrounding building

piano nobile	Principal storey of Renaissance palace, containing reception rooms; normally higher than the other storeys
piazza	Open urban space, normally oblong and surrounded by buildings
pier	Detached mass of construction that acts as support usually for arch
pietra forte	Particularly strong building stone
pietra serena	Greenish-grey sandstone from Fiesole used prominently in Florentine Renaissance architecture
pilaster	Rectangular column set against a wall and conforming with one of the classical orders
pillar	Free-standing upright member, but unlike a column need not be cylindrical or conform with any of the orders
pinnacle	Small, steep ornamented cone or pyramid crowning spire, buttress and parapet angles
plinth	Projecting base of column or wall
porch	Covered and projecting entrance to building
portal	Monumental entrance doorway or gateway
portico	Covered entrance forming centre-piece of facade, with attached or detached columns and pediment
presbytery	Part of church east of choir and where high altar situated
Proto-Renaissance	Graceful Romanesque architectural style emerging in 11th-century Italy that utilised ancient Roman motifs
quadrifore	*see* window(s)
Rococo	Late-17th- and early-18th-century architectural style noted for lightness of colour and weight (last stage in development of Baroque)
Romanesque	Architectural style prevalent in central Middle Ages, *c* 1000–1200, noted for use of thick walls, sturdy piers and semi-circular arches and for using elements of Roman architecture
roundel	Small circular window, panel or niche
rustication	Massive blocks of masonry cut in a rough state, in contrast to dressed ashlar
salone	Italian term for large hall or reception room, often of double height

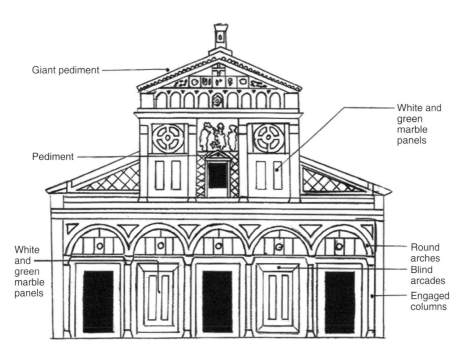

Giant pediment

White and green marble panels

Pediment

White and green marble panels

Round arches

Blind arcades

Engaged columns

S Miniato, Florence, 1018–1207. With several classical attributes, for example its round arches, columns and triangular pediment, the Byzantine and Romanesque church is an early precursor of a Renaissance building.

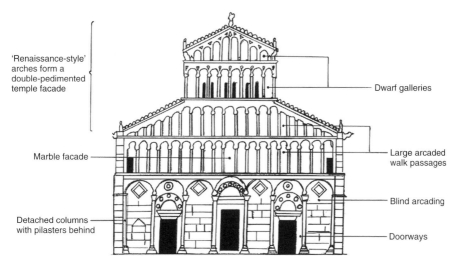

'Renaissance-style' arches form a double-pedimented temple facade

Marble facade

Detached columns with pilasters behind

Dwarf galleries

Large arcaded walk passages

Blind arcading

Doorways

Pisan Romanesque: Pisa Cathedral, 1063. While its lower facade is robust and character-istically Romanesque, its upper storeys exhibit an array of dwarf arches, a marble ensemble broadly replicated in Lucca and Pistoia.

scala aperta	Monumental external staircase
sottoportego	Where facade of building projects over public pathway to form arcade or colonnade
spandrel	Triangular space between side of arch framed by a horizontal line projected from the crown and a vertical line rising from the springing. In an arcade, also applied to space between two arches
spire	Tall conical, polygonal or pyramidal structure rising from a tower, turret or roof etc, and normally ending in slender point
string course	Continuous horizontal moulding set in or projecting from surface of an external wall
stucco	Slow-setting plaster made from gypsum, sand and lime. Known from antiquity, it facilitates modelling and ensures durability
tabernacle	Canopied niche containing image

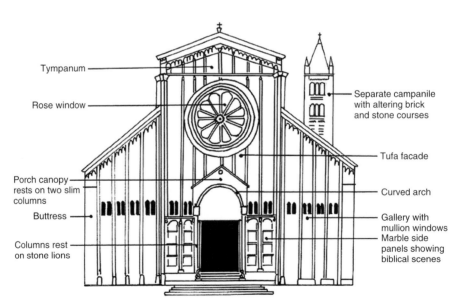

North-Italian Romanesque: S Zeno, 1120. Except for its magnificent rose window and ornamented portal, its mainly tufa facade is relatively austere.

terracotta	Hard clay-moulded and kiln-fired unglazed material from which tiles and architectural enrichments are made
tiburio	Artificial drum
tondo	Circular medallion often located in spandrel
transept	Transverse arm of cruciform church, normally between nave and chancel
travertine	Cream-coloured Italian limestone, with small irregular holes, quarried in the Tiber valley
tribune	Apse in basilican churche
triglyph	Stone block placed between metopes in a Doric frieze
triumphal arch	Free-standing monumental gateway or entrance of a type originating in ancient Rome, eg Arch of Titus (AD 82), Arch of Septimius Severus (AD 203) or Arch of Constantine (AD 315)
trompe l'oeil	Part of building designed (through the falsification of perspective) to give deceptive impression of greater space
tympanum	Area above doorway between lintel and arch
vault:	Arched masonry ceiling
barrel	Resembling elongated arch or half cylinder
dominical	Rises from square or polygonal base and is not a true dome or square
vestibule	Entrance hall or anteroom
villa:	Country house
villa suburbana	House on outer edge of a city
volute	Spiral scroll derived from characteristic feature of Ionic capital
voussoir	Wedge-shaped stone forming part of structure of arch
window(s):	
biforate	Two separate arched openings, divided vertically by a column
blind	With no openings or glazing
Gothic traceried	Complex tracery used to separate lights
mullion	Vertical post separating opening into two or more lights
multiforate	Series of arched openings divided by columns
ogee	Pointed opening characterised by compound curve of two parts, one concave and the other convex

Palladian	Three openings beneath an entablature, the central one arched and wider than the others
quadrifore	Four separate arched openings divided vertically by three columns
rose	Gothic circular opening with foils of patterned tracery radiating from centre
triforate	Three separate arched openings, divided vertically by two columns
wheel	*see* rose window
wing	Part of building projecting from and subordinate to central part

Biforate A style of window common in Gothic and Early Renaissance Italy that is divided by a column to form two separate arched openings.

Gothic tracerated With the spread of glazing in the Middle Ages, windows were divided into lights separated by mullions and surmounted by complex tracery.

Ogee A Gothic arch in the shape of curved lines made up of lower convex and upper concave parts. Widely employed to crown windows and portals in Venice.

Palladian A window with three openings, the central one arched and wider than the peripheral ones. Despite its name, its initial use during the Renaissance might be attributable to Donato Bramante rather than Andrea Palladio.

BIBLIOGRAPHY

Abulafia, D (ed), *Italy in the Central Middle Ages* (Oxford: Oxford University Press, 2004)

Ackerman, JS, *The Architecture of Michelangelo*, revd edn (Harmondsworth: Penguin, 1986)

Averlino, AP [Filarete], *Treatise on Architecture*, tr JR Spencer (New Haven and London: Yale University Press, 1965)

Battisti, E, *Brunelleschi, The Complete Work* (London: Thames and Hudson, 1981)

Benevolo, L, *The Architecture of the Renaissance* (London: Routledge; Boulder, Co: Westview Press, 1997)

Blunt, A, *Guide to Baroque Rome* (New York: Granada, 1962)

Brucker, G, *The Civic World of Early Renaissance Florence* (Princeton: Princeton University Press, 1977)

Burckhardt, J, *The Civilization of the Renaissance in Italy*, tr SGC Middlemore (Harmondsworth: Penguin, 1990)

Burr Litchfield, R, 'The social world: cohesion, conflict and the city', in JA Marino (ed), *Early Modern Italy* (Oxford: Oxford University Press, 2002)

Coldstream, N, *Medieval Architecture* (Oxford: Oxford University Press, 2002)

Dean, T, 'The rise of the *signori*' in D Abulafia, *Italy in the Central Middle Ages* (Oxford: Oxford University Press, 2004)

Frankl, P, *Gothic Architecture* (Harmondsworth: Penguin, 1962)

Hale, JR (ed), *Renaissance Venice* (London: Faber, 1973)

Hibbert, C, *The House of the Medici. Its Rise and Fall* (Harmondsworth: Penguin, 1982)

Hibbert, C, *Rome. The Biography of a City* (Harmondsworth: Penguin, 1985)

Holmes, G, *Florence, Rome and the Origins of the Renaissance* (Oxford: Clarendon Press, 1986)

Holmes, G, *The Florentine Enlightenment, 1400–1500* (London: Weidenfeld & Nicolson, 1986)

Howard, D, *Jacopo Sansovino: Architecture and Patronage in Renaissance Venice* (New Haven and London: Yale University Press, 1987)

Howard, D, *Venice and the East: The Impact of the Islamic World on Venetian Architecture, 1100–1500* (New Haven and London: Yale University Press, 2000)

Jones, PJ, *Italian City-State: From Commune to Signoria* (Oxford: Oxford University Press, 1997)

King, ML, *The Renaissance in Europe* (London: Laurence King, 2003)

Luzzato, G, *An Economic History of Italy. From the Fall of the Roman Empire to the Beginning of the Sixteenth Century*, tr P Jones (London: Routledge & Kegan Paul, 1961)

Macchiavelli, N, *The Discourses*, ed B Crick (Harmondsworth: Penguin, 1970 edn)

Macchiavelli, N, *The Prince*, tr G Bull (London: Penguin, 1988 edn)

Mack, C, *The Creation of a Renaissance City* (Ithaca, NY: Cornell University Press, 1987)

Marino, JA, 'Economic structures and transformations', in JA Marino (ed), *Early Modern Italy* (Oxford: Oxford University Press, 2002)

Marino, JA (ed), *Early Modern Italy* (Oxford: Oxford University Press, 2002)

Muir, E, 'Representations of power', in JM Nagemy (ed), *Italy in the Age of the Renaissance* (Oxford: Oxford University Press, 2004)

Mumford, L, *The City in History* (London and New York: Penguin, 1990)

Murray, P, *The Architecture of the Italian Renaissance*, 3rd edn (London: Thames and Hudson, 1986)

Nagemy, JM (ed), *Italy in the Age of the Renaissance* (Oxford: Oxford University Press, 2004)

Norwich, JJ, *A History of Venice* (London: Penguin, 1983)

Palladio, A, *The Four Books of Architecture* (New York: Dover Publications, 1965)

Parks, T, *Medici Money – Banking, Metaphysics and Art in Fifteenth-Century Florence* (London: Profile Books, 2005)

Pevsner, N, *An Outline of European Architecture* (New York and London: Penguin, 1990)

Pullan, B, *A History of Early Renaissance Italy. From the Mid-Thirteenth to the Mid-Fifteenth Century* (London: Allen Lane, 1973)

Quill, S, *Ruskin's Venice. The Stones Revisited* (London: Lund Humphries, 2003)

Robertson, C, *Il Gran Cardinale: Alessandro Farnese. Patron of the Arts* (New Haven and London: Yale University Press, 1992)

Skinner, P, 'Material life', in D Abulafia, *Italy in the Central Middle Ages* (Oxford: Oxford University Press, 2004)

Strathern, P, *The Medici. Godfathers of the Renaissance* (London: Pimlico, 2005)

Tabacco, G, *The Struggle for Power in Medieval Italy. Structures of Political Power*, tr RB Jensen (Cambridge: Cambridge University Press, 1989)

Tangheroni, M, 'Trade and navigation', in D Abulafia (ed), *Italy in the Central Middle Ages* (Oxford: Oxford University Press, 2004)

Vasari, G, *Lives of the Artists*, tr J C Bondanella and P Bondanella (Oxford: Oxford University Press, 1991)

Wittkower, R, *Art and Architecture in Italy*, rev edn, J Connors and J Montage (New Haven and London: Yale University Press, 1965)

Wittkower, R, *Architectural Principles in the Age of Humanism* (London: Academy Editions, 1988)

INDEX

Photo credits

The author and the publisher gratefully acknowledge the people who gave their permission to reproduce material in the book. While every effort has been made to contact copyright holders for their permission to reprint material the publishers would be grateful to hear from any copyright holder who is not acknowledged here and will undertake to rectify any errors or omissions in future editions.

Cover image:
Copy of the map known as the Carta della Catena: Florence around 1470 – detail (Santissima Annunziata amd San Marco). Florence, Museo di Firenze com'era. © 1990, photo Scala, Florence.

All photos taken by Paul Balchin unless stated below:
p 56 Photo 3.5, The Duomo, Milan, Italy. London, Spectrum © 2005. Photo, Spectrum/HIP/Scala, Florence; p 79 Photo 3.23, View of the Piazza del Popolo. Todi © 2003 Photo Scala, Florence; p 172 Photo 7.12, Facade. Mantua, Church of Sant'Andrea © 2005, Photo Scala, Florence; p 176 Photo 7.16, photo courtesy of C.G. Davies; p 221 Photo 9.12, Angled view of the façade. Venice, San Zaccaria. 1990. Photo Scala, Florence; p 443 Photo 17.7, Zimbalo, Giuseppe (1617–1710): Facade. Lecce, Church of Santa Croce. © 1990 photo Scala, Florence.